UTAH
HIKING

UTAH
HIKING

The Complete Guide to More Than 300 Hikes

Second Edition

Buck Tilton

**AVALON
TRAVEL**

FOGHORN OUTDOORS UTAH HIKING
The Complete Guide to More Than 300 Hikes

Second Edition

Buck Tilton

Printing History
1st edition—1999
2nd edition—June 2005
5 4 3 2 1

Avalon Travel Publishing
An Imprint of
Avalon Publishing Group, Inc.

AVALON
publishing group incorporated

ISBN: 1-56691-892-8
ISSN: 1523-8849

Editors: Erin Raber, Kay Elliott
Series Manager: Ellie Behrstock
Acquisitions Editor: Rebecca K. Browning
Copy Editor: Chris Hayhurst
Graphics Coordinator: Deborah Dutcher
Production Coordinator: Darren Alessi
Cover and Interior Designer: Darren Alessi
Map Editor: Kevin Anglin
Cartographers: Ben Pease, Mike Morgenfeld, Kat Kalamaras

Front cover photo: Navajo Loop, © George H.H. Huey

Printed in the United States of America by Malloy Inc.

About the Author

Born in South Carolina, Buck went west with all the young men, stepped out of a vehicle on the verge of a limitless expanse of slickrock, and became a committed believer in love at first sight. His initial extended hike, a month along the Escalante River, was extended even further by taking a turn up the wrong canyon. To borrow a memory from Daniel Boone, he wasn't lost, but was a bit unsure as to where he was for a few days.

For more than 22 years he's been traveling around Utah via foot and paddle, covering too many thousands of miles to ever remember it all—but cherishing the multitude of trails that he can. In Utah, more than any other place, the heart of the earth seemed laid bare, and traveling there touched his heart. In the wilderness he felt at home in body and soul. He wrote about his experiences, and the process of writing rooted the journeys deep within his spirit.

For Buck, writing is an act of reliving the experience on a profound level. But the words gathered dust on many an editorial desk, so he took to teaching. Focused on education, and writing on the side, his tales started finding space in magazines, and now more than 1,000 articles of his have found ink—not to mention two dozen books.

If he could do it all again, he would.

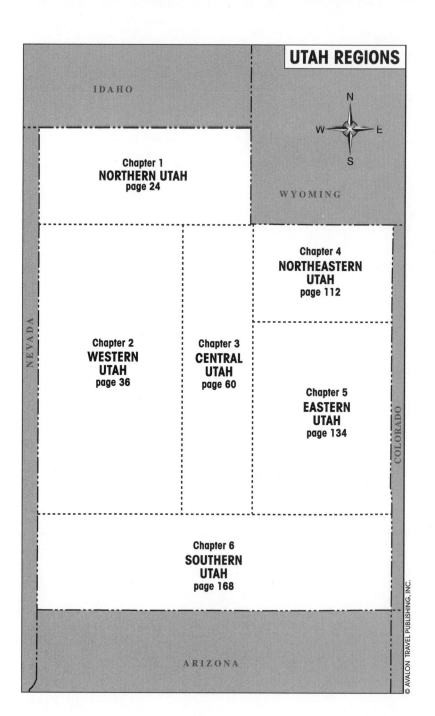

UTAH REGIONS

IDAHO

N
W E
S

WYOMING

Chapter 1
NORTHERN UTAH
page 24

Chapter 4
NORTHEASTERN UTAH
page 112

NEVADA

Chapter 2
WESTERN UTAH
page 36

Chapter 3
CENTRAL UTAH
page 60

Chapter 5
EASTERN UTAH
page 134

COLORADO

Chapter 6
SOUTHERN UTAH
page 168

ARIZONA

© AVALON TRAVEL PUBLISHING, INC.

COURTESY OF UTAH STATE PARKS AND RECREATION

Contents

SPECIAL TOPIC

The Great Western Trail 20

Including:
- Antelope Island
- Bear River Range
- Great Salt Lake
- Mount Naomi Wilderness
- Raft River Mountains
- Sawtooth National Forest
- Wellsville Mountain
  Wilderness

Including:
- Basin and Range Province
- Deep Creek Mountains
- Deseret Peak Wilderness
- Fishlake National Forest
- House Range
- Silver Island Mountains
- Stansbury Mountains
- Tushar Mountains
- Wah Wah Mountains

Including:
- Big Cottonwood Canyon
- Capitol Reef National Park
- Little Cottonwood Canyon
- Lone Peak Wilderness
- Mount Nebo Wilderness
- Mount Olympus Wilderness
- Mount Timpanogos Wilderness
- Timpanogos Cave
  National Monument
- Twin Peaks Wilderness
- Uinta National Forest
- Wasatch–Cache
  National Forest

Including:
- Ashley National Forest
- Dinosaur National Monument
- Flaming Gorge National
  Recreation Area
- Rocky Mountain Province
- Uinta Basin
- Uinta Mountains
- Uintah and Ouray
  Indian Reservation
- Wasatch-Cache
  National Forest

How to Use this Book

Foghorn Outdoors Utah Hiking is divided into six chapters based on major regional areas in the state. Each chapter begins with a map of the area, which is further broken down into detail maps. These detail maps show the location of all the hikes in that chapter.

This guide can be navigated easily in two ways:

1. If you know the name of the specific trail you want to hike, or the name of the surrounding geographical area or nearby feature (town, national or state park, forest, mountain, lake, river, etc.), look it up in the index and turn to the corresponding page.

2. If you know the general area you want to visit, turn to the map at the beginning of the chapter that covers the area. Each chapter map is broken down into detail maps, which show by number all the hikes in that chapter. You can then determine which trails are in or near your destination by their corresponding numbers. Hikes are listed sequentially in each chapter so you can turn to the page with the corresponding map number for the hike you're interested in.

COURTESY OF THE NATIONAL PARK SERVICE

inside Dinosaur National Monument

About the Trail Profiles

Each hike in this book is listed in a consistent, easy-to-read format to help you choose the ideal hike. From a general overview of the setting to detailed driving directions, the profile will provide all the information you need. Here is an example:

Map number and hike number

Round-trip mileage (unless otherwise noted) and the approximate amount of time needed to complete the hike (actual times can vary widely, especially on longer hikes)

Map on which the trailhead can be found and page number on which the map can be found

Symbol indicating that the hike is listed among the author's top picks

The difficulty rating (boot—rated 1–5) is based on the steepness of the trail and how difficult it is to traverse; the quality rating (mountain—rated 1–10) is based largely on scenic beauty, but it also takes into account how crowded the trail is and whether noise of nearby civilization is audible

General location of the trail, named by its proximity to the nearest major town or landmark

1 SOMEWHERE USA HIKE
9.0 mi/5.0 hrs
At the mouth of the Somewhere River on Lake Someplace
Map 1.2, page 24

Each hike in this book begins with a brief overview of its setting. The description typically covers what kind of terrain to expect, what might be seen, and any conditions that may make the hike difficult to navigate. Side trips, such as to waterfalls or panoramic vistas, in addition to ways to combine the trail with others nearby for a longer outing, are also noted here. In many cases, mile-by-mile trail directions are included.

User Groups: This section notes the types of uses that are permitted on the trail, including hikers, mountain bikers, horseback riders, and dogs. Wheelchair access is also noted here.

Permits: This section notes whether a permit is required for hiking, or, if the hike spans more than one day, whether one is required for camping. Any fees, such as for parking, day use, or entrance, are also noted here. Frequently required passes are covered in the Hiking tips section.

Maps: This section provides information on how to obtain detailed trail maps of the hike and its environs. Whenever applicable, names of U.S. Geologic Survey (USGS) topographic maps and national forest maps are also included; contact information for these and other map sources are noted in the Resources section at the back of this book.

Directions: This section provides mile-by-mile driving directions to the trailhead from the nearest major town.

Contact: This section provides an address and phone number for each hike. The contact is usually the agency maintaining the trail but may also be a trail club or other organization.

About the Maps

This book is divided into chapters based on regions; an overview map of these regions precedes the table of contents and is printed on the inside of the back cover. At the start of each chapter, you'll find a map of the entire region, enhanced by a grid that divides the region into smaller sections. These sections are then enlarged into individual detail maps. Trailheads are noted on the detail maps by number.

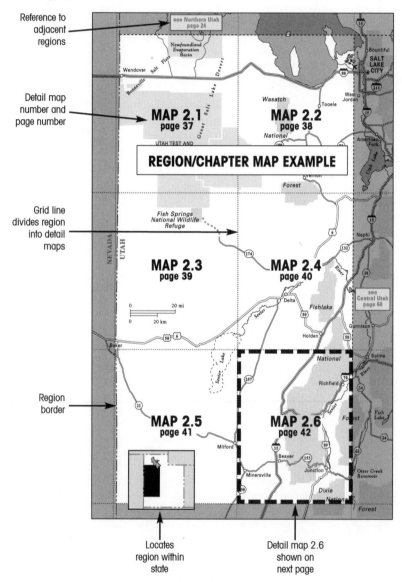

Reference to adjacent regions

Detail map number and page number

Grid line divides region into detail maps

Region border

Locates region within state

Detail map 2.6 shown on next page

REGION/CHAPTER MAP EXAMPLE

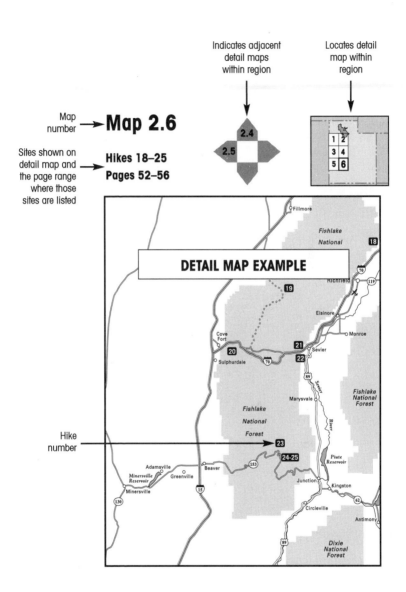

Map number → **Map 2.6**

Sites shown on detail map and the page range where those sites are listed → **Hikes 18–25**
Pages 52–56

Indicates adjacent detail maps within region

Locates detail map within region

DETAIL MAP EXAMPLE

Fillmore

Fishlake National

Richfield

Elsinore

Cove Fort

Sulphurdale

Sevier

Monroe

Marysvale

Fishlake National Forest

Fishlake National Forest

Hike number

Adamsville

Minersville Reservoir

Greenville

Beaver

Piute Reservoir

Minersville

Junction

Kingston

Circleville

Antimony

Dixie National Forest

Our Commitment

We are committed to making *Foghorn Outdoors Utah Hiking* the most accurate, thorough, and enjoyable hiking guide to the state. With this second edition you can rest assured that every hiking trail in this book has been carefully reviewed and is accompanied by the most up-to-date information. Be aware that with the passing of time some of the fees listed herein may have changed, and trails may have closed unexpectedly. If you have a specific need or concern, it's best to call the location ahead of time.

If you would like to comment on the book, whether it's to suggest a trail we overlooked, or to let us know about any noteworthy experience—good or bad—that occurred while using *Foghorn Outdoors Utah Hiking* as your guide, we would appreciate hearing from you. Please address correspondence to:

Foghorn Outdoors Utah Hiking, second edition
Avalon Travel Publishing
1400 65th Street, Suite 250
Emeryville, CA 94608

email: atpfeedback@avalonpub.com
If you send us an email, please put "Utah Hiking" in the subject line.

Introduction

Barefoot, stripped down to cotton shorts, I walk in shadow and in sand that retains the warmth of the midday sun. A mile, perhaps more, from camp, the rock maze twists like a hollow serpent far into several million years of sandstone. Around every bend is another bend. Pink and tan, the water-polished stone stretches above me until the sky is reduced to a narrow band of pale blue. Wind brushes the insides of the serpent and my skin, soothing after a day of high heat. Stepping in pools of old seepage, mud gushes up between my toes. More walking, and I wear sandals of red mud and white sand that harden protectively. It must have been so for the Anasazi a thousand years ago. Always extravagant, the sandstone faces defy description, carved in sweeping lines, majestic beyond wildest dreams. There are simply no words to equal the wonder of this canyon tributary of the San Juan River in southeastern Utah.

But Moonlight Water Gulch represents only a tiny pocket of splendor. If you can imagine it, you can probably find it somewhere in this state of bountiful diversity and indescribably beautiful extremes. The diversity of landforms may be divided, somewhat loosely, into three provinces: the Rocky Mountains, Basin and Range, and the Colorado Plateau. This book describes a large sampling of that diversity in more than 300 specific routes and more than 400 places your feet can carry you.

Sample the highest country in the Uinta Mountains and the Wasatch Range. In the northeast section of Utah, the High Uintas run about 150 miles east-west and 30 miles or so north-south. They rise to sublime alpine expanses with 24 peaks higher than 13,000 feet, including the highest point in the state, Kings Peak at 13,528 feet. Many small lakes, an estimated 1,400, lie snuggled in these towering mountains, and a large number may be reached by well-maintained trails. But the Uintas are only one of four ranges that include the La Sals, Deep Creeks, and Tushars (all in other geographic provinces), with summits soaring more than 12,000 feet skyward. West of the Uinta Mountains and less wide, the Wasatch Range runs north-south for approximately 200 miles, from Idaho to the central region of the state. These peaks shoot abruptly toward the clouds on their western front, catching and holding deep snow on their steep and rugged flanks, creating some of the best skiing and winter mountaineering in the world. Here, too, trails lead to magnificent mountain scenery.

Or walk on the western half of Utah, most of which, excluding the immensity of the Great Salt Lake, stretches out barren, flat, and featureless. A part of the Great Basin, this region was once at the bottom of prehistoric and vast Lake Bonneville, a body of water that once submerged the area between the Wasatch Range and Mono Lake in California. Elevations, between 4,000 and 5,000 feet, typically vary little on this seemingly endless open land. With no outlet to the sea, the Great Salt Lake lies ultra-salty, a graveyard for streams and rivers that spill out of the Rocky Mountains and die in the shallow waters. Here in western Utah, however, you'll find, standing above the searing salt flats, numerous secret desert mountain ranges rising mysteriously to striking heights. In the Stansbury and Deep Creek Mountains these heights reach to more than 11,000 feet. It is an area filled with hidden valleys, extensive alluvial fans, scenic treasures, and splendid solitude. Be prepared to walk with map and compass, without trail or even evidence of a world peopled, somewhere in the distance, by humans.

Or choose Beaver Dam Wash in the southwest corner, claiming the state's lowest elevation: 2,340 feet. Between the Beaver Dam Mountains Wilderness and Dinosaur National Monument in the northeast, and in all of southern and southeastern Utah (nearly half the state) you'll be hiking on, or deep within, the Colorado Plateau. Here is one of the most interesting landforms on this planet—millions of acres of colorful slickrock carved by epochs of erosion into an unbelievably intricate network of deep canyons, massive walls, buttes, mesas, arches, bridges, cracks, fissures, fins, pinnacles, spires, slots, hoodoos, ravines, and washes. This is "slickrock country," a name given the terrain for which Utah is most famous. In south-central Utah, the Grand Staircase–Escalante National Monument encompasses approximately 1.9 million acres of supremely majestic and ultimately irreplaceable sandstone, always and never the same. The national parks of this region—Zion, Bryce, Capitol Reef, Canyonlands—are sought out, and deservedly so, by visitors from around the world. And here, in the southeast section of the state, you'll find Lake Powell, manmade, more than 185 miles long and with more than 2,000 miles of stony, often windswept, and outrageously lovely shoreline. Elevations on the Colorado Plateau usually range between 3,000 and 6,000 feet, but ancient, rounded mountains—the Navajos, Abajos, and Henrys, to name three—rise sometimes to more than twice that height. Trails, where they exist, are often subtle, marked with cairns instead of beaten into the earth. Canyon walls may be your guides, and whims your itinerary.

Yet Utah offers far more than geography. Hiking often carries you deep into history—to the Mormons and other early settlers, yes, but most intriguingly to the history of the prehistoric peoples who left their pictographs and petroglyphs, their isolated homes and small towns, their granaries and towers of precisely stacked stones, their ultimate mysteries scattered in a hundred thousand places.

Utah's approximately 85,000 square miles makes it the 11th largest of the United States. About 63 percent of this land is owned and operated by the federal government: 12 national parks and monuments, 15 designated wilderness areas, huge expanses of Bureau of Land Management redrock. A great mass of land, but Utah claims less protected wilderness in relation to size than any other Intermountain state. For more than 20 years conservationists have fought for America's Redrock Wilderness Act, a law that, once passed, will protect millions of acres of land singled out as unique and infinitely worthy of designation as "wilderness." Walk here, enjoy it, appreciate it, love it, leave no trace of your passing. And add your voice to the multitude that must continue to cry for preservation of the national treasure that is Utah.

Hiking Tips

The wild outdoors: It's a world of wonder, drama, anticipation, and keen satisfaction. It's also a world capable of creating discomfort, irritation, and, in the worst-case scenario, problems that threaten your safety . . .if you walk unprepared. If you're planning an extended wilderness trip, you've undoubtedly created a list of all the things you'll need: sleeping bag, sleeping pad, tent or tarp, stove and fuel, pots and pans, food and water, clothing, and other gear you don't want to leave home without. Unless you're hiking a paved nature trail at a state park, however, and even if your plan calls only for a few miles from the car and back, you still can, and should, be ready for anything.

The Ten Essentials

The basic essentials are well defined. In fact, wise old men and women of the wild once generated a list called The Ten Essentials, and the half century separating the original list and today's list has seen little change in what all savvy hikers need to pack along. Plan to carry something for:

Insulation

Between you and the wind, cold, wet, and heat lies your clothing. Dress for success, and carry extra clothing for the unexpected changes in temperature, wind speed, and precipitation . . .and the unexpected night on the trail.

A cotton shirt and shorts can work great on a hot Utah day, but you need to be able to cover your arms and legs with long sleeves and pants. Those additional layers of clothing should not be cotton. Synthetic materials will wick sweat away from your body, keeping you drier and thus safer. Synthetics wet with sweat or rain also retain most of their ability to hold in your body heat, and cotton most definitely does not. When the sun dips behind a canyon rim or mountain ridge, you'll want a fleece vest or sweater. If the wind rises, you'll want something to stop it from blowing away your body heat. A windproof jacket or parka, preferably with a hood, is highly recommended. Make it a windproof/waterproof (or at least water resistant) parka, and you're prepared. And don't forget a cap or hat.

Hydration

You are more water than anything else, and you need to keep replenishing the water inside you on a relatively regular schedule to remain healthy. You'll need two to three quarts per person per day, and more if the heat is extreme.

When streams, rivers, or lakes promise a source of water, you can save weight by carrying a means to disinfect what you drink. With a lightweight stove you can, of course, boil water. Once it reaches the boiling point, water is safe to drink. The lightest option for disinfection of water comes in the form of iodine tablets, such as Potable Aqua, that dissolve and kill most of the germs that cause disease. For emergencies, pack a small bottle of these at all times. Why not? An unpleasant taste left by chemicals can be eliminated by tossing in a powdered drink mix after the disinfection process is complete. Lightweight water filters are a second option. Despite the extra weight, many filters give you safe water with a few minutes of pumping. No waiting for chemicals to work, and no bad taste. But filters are not all created equal: Read the label to make sure you're filtering out all the nasty life forms that may inhabit wilder-

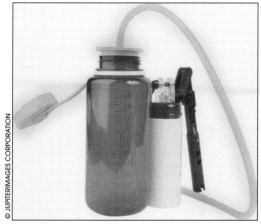
water filter
© JUPITERIMAGES CORPORATION

ness water. Some of these filters are available within a water bottle. As you squeeze water from the bottle, it passes through a filter on the way to your mouth.

Nutrition

If you're drinking enough water, you can live for weeks without food . . .but why bother? Pack a few snack items at all times: granola bars, energy bars, candy bars, cheese and crackers, trail mix, whatever pleases your palate. Better to have it and not need it than need it and not have it. Full day hikes ask for a thoughtful lunch. Be ready to sit down in a comfortable and scenic spot and set a "table" fit for a mountain king . . . or a desert queen.

Solar Protection

There could be no life without the sun, but there can be also be death from the sun: the death of skin, the death later (from cancer) of the individual, and, more immediately important, the death of fun. Carry sunglasses and sunscreen at all times. Your sunglasses should protect your eyes from 100 percent of ultraviolet light. Your sunscreen should protect you from ultraviolet A and ultraviolet B radiation, and it should have a sun protection factor (SPF) of 15 to 30. Screens work optimally if applied 30 minutes prior to exposure. If you're going to apply an insect repellent to your skin as well, put it on after the 30 minutes so the sunscreen has a chance to bind to your skin first. Remember: Children are more susceptible to the damaging rays of sunlight than adults, even though evidence of the damage may not show up for years. Lips do not tan, so a lip balm with an adequate SPF is highly recommended. Utah's sun also demands a brimmed head covering to shade your face.

Heat

Environmentally speaking, fires are often unacceptable. But to the lost, lonely, and cold, fires can serve as a signal, offer psychological support, and provide life-sustaining warmth. Know how to build a fire, and pack matches or a lighter. Also pack some form of fire starter such as a small candle.

Illumination

When darkness descends sooner than expected, you'll want a flashlight. It should be small and lightweight. Test it before you leave home, and always carry a spare set of batteries.

Navigation

The first rule is simple: Never trust the trail alone to get you where you want to go, especially in vast areas of trailless Utah. The second rule is likewise simple: Carry an accurate map and a

compass

compass you know how to use. Get your bearings with map and compass before stepping away from your vehicle. Set the map on the ground, set the compass on top of it, and orient them both to north. Keep the map handy and refer to it often. Remember, your map will not help you locate your position if you don't know fairly accurately where you are on the map.

If you're more into technology, you may choose to carry a Global Positioning System (GPS). Models such as Brunton's Atlas are easy to use and terrifically accurate.

Shelter

If the rain pours down, the cold deepens, the night surrounds you, you'll do better, sometimes much better, with some form of shelter. It need be nothing more than an emergency blanket and 20 feet of lightweight cord. With these two items you have all the material you need to construct an emergency shelter.

Cutting Tools

The first use of a cutting edge dramatically separated humans from other animals. A knife remains the single most useful tool for the outdoor enthusiast. But why limit yourself to an edge? Carry a multi-purpose tool—one with knife, pliers, and screwdriver, perhaps with tweezers and scissors—and you'll be able to remove cactus spines and splinters, repair equipment, and who knows what else.

Emergency Preparedness

The most important first-aid kit is inside your head: a brain filled with knowledge and skills. Take a first-aid course or, much more useful, a wilderness-medicine course. You will learn how to pack and use a first-aid kit, an item you'll most assuredly be carrying. See the Trail Hazards section later in this chapter for more specific information.

Footwear and Foot Care

You'll see hikers in Utah, especially in the high-desert region, wearing athletic shoes or even sandals. They all have one thing in common: tough, strong feet. Much more often you'll want footwear made for hiking: lightweight, midweight, or heavyweight boots.

Lightweight "boots" look, and perform, more like athletic shoes. The uppers are usually a fabric, and the soles flexible, and these are worthy considerations for short trips over easy to moderate terrain with a light load on your shoulders. Midweight boots, although similar to lightweights, have a heavier overall construction with a sole decidedly thicker and stronger. They're supportive enough for longer trips over moderate terrain under heavier loads. Heavyweight boots are manufactured with strong and rigid uppers and soles. The uppers may be plastic or, more often, full-grain leather that uses the entire thickness of animal hide. Split-grain leather, as the name implies, utilizes less than the full thickness of the hide. Within the sole you'll often find a piece of slightly flexible or inflexible material, called a shank, that runs two-thirds to the full length of the boot, providing security on difficult terrain. Generally not as comfortable as lighter boots, heavyweights provide you with safety and support for your feet and ankles on tricky ground. Most people prefer leather heavyweight boots over plastic.

Shopping for Shoes and Socks

Nothing ranks higher than fit when shopping for footwear. Put on the socks you intend to hike in, slip into the boots, and lace them up. The second and third lacing fixtures down from the top of the boot are the ones that hold the heel in place. Snug up the laces there. With an ideal fit, your heel won't move from side to side and will move only slightly up and down. You should feel contact with the sides of the boot, a supportive pressure on the sides of your feet at the ball of your foot. There should be gentle contact across the arch. Your toes should wiggle freely, even when you press the toe of the boot firmly against a wall.

The time required for your personal flex patterns to develop in new boots (the break-in time) is of critical importance. For the first week wear the boots around the house, or on short walks, gradually increasing the length of time you're in them. By the end of the first week, you should be able to wear the boots all day, but keep wearing them around town for a second week before hitting the trail under a pack.

For most people, two pairs of socks are better than one. Wool or synthetic lightweight liner socks, the inner socks, provide a small amount of insulation but, more importantly, create a "lubricating" layer that transfers friction away from your feet to help prevent blisters. They also transfer moisture from your feet into outer socks to help keep your feet dry. Wool or synthetic heavyweight outer socks provide insulation and comfort. Remember: Try on the socks, too, to make sure they fit.

Trail Hazards

As mentioned earlier, the best prepared hikers have undergone wilderness medical training. If you've already completed such a course, then what follows should remind you of important considerations concerning the recognition, treatment, and prevention of emergencies.

Altitude Illness

At elevations of approximately 8,000 feet and higher, high-altitude illnesses may occur, though they are rarely serious below 10,000 feet. Minor symptoms usually include a headache, and may include unusual fatigue, nausea, loss of appetite, and insomnia. Do not continue going up until these symptoms begin to subside. Serious signs and symptoms, indications of fluid collecting in the lungs or brain, include shortness of breath while at rest, chest pain and/or tightness, coughing, a raging headache, loss of coordination, and a sudden and bewildering change in level of consciousness. Immediate descent is imperative for anyone suffering serious altitude problems.

Supplemental oxygen will greatly benefit the patient. To avoid altitude illnesses, gain altitude gradually, sleeping no more than 1,000 to 1,500 feet higher than the night before once you've ascended above 10,000 feet. As always, adequate nutrition and hydration are important.

There are drugs appropriate for the treatment and, in some cases, the prevention of altitude illness. A physician's advice and prescription are necessary before these can be taken.

Dehydration

Inadequate internal water reduces energy, carries potential danger via heat exhaustion and heat stroke, and often catches the hiker by surprise. Sweating, breathing, urinating, defecating, episodes of diarrhea, and vomiting all contribute to dehydration. Thirst is an indication that dehydration has already started to deplete you. To avoid dehydration, start each day with a half quart of water and keep drinking regularly throughout the day. Drink a quart per hour during periods of extreme exercise. The best field test for ample hydration is urine that runs clear. Any color to urine, other than a very light yellow, indicates a need for more water.

Heat Illnesses

The signs and symptoms of heat exhaustion may include, in addition to feeling hot and tired, headache, nausea, pallid skin, and fainting. Treat heat exhaustion by resting in shade and drinking at least one quart of water. Salty snacks may add benefit to treatment. When you feel okay again, you probably are.

Heat stroke is potentially fatal. Signs and symptoms usually include hot, red skin and an altered, typically bizarre, level of consciousness. Treat heat stroke immediately by removing any clothing that may retain heat, soaking the body with water, fanning, and massaging the limbs. Cold packs, if available, may be applied to the head, neck, armpits, and groin. Evacuate as soon as possible. Even when someone appears to have recovered from heat stroke, serious problems may linger. Prevent heat illnesses with adequate hydration, slower paces in hot weather, and by limiting exercise to the cooler periods of the day in extremes of hot weather.

And yes, you can drink too much water. Hyponatremia, potentially life-threatening, occurs when you drink lots but fail to snack. The sodium in your body is washed out, and you need sodium to live. Eating regularly, and supplementing with an occasional lightly salted snack, will prevent the problem.

Hypothermia

Hypothermia, a loss of heat from the body's core, is signaled early by the "umbles": stumbling, fumbling, mumbling, and grumbling. Your body may try to warm itself now and then by causing shivers, an involuntary form of exercise. This mild form of hypothermia should be treated immediately to prevent the body's core temperature from continuing its descent. Stop, put on dry clothes and additional insulation, drink water, and eat a snack rich in simple sugars. Ideally you should rest before continuing. Convulsive shivering, continuous and violent, indicates an immediate need for rest and treatment. This moderate form of hypothermia brings an increasingly rapid loss of core body heat. You need dry clothes, additional insulation, shelter from wind and cold ground, warm liquids, food (especially simple sugars), and supplemental heat sources such as fires and huddling with non-hypothermic hikers. Exercise should not be restarted until the cold person is completely warm again. Severe hypothermia is indicated by a stop in shivering followed by loss of consciousness and a body growing more and more rigid as heartbeat and breathing rate slow down. A person severely cold seldom returns to a normal core temperature without hospital treatment. In the meantime that person needs gentle handling. Wet clothing should be removed, preferably by cutting it away, and the person should be completely sheltered from the environment with layers of insulation and a final covering of a tarp or emergency blanket that prevents any moisture or wind from passing through. And help should be sought. Prevent hypothermia by staying dry and well hydrated, pacing yourself to prevent overexertion, eating regularly, and keeping an eye peeled for the early signs and symptoms.

Hantavirus

Rodents carrying hantavirus don't get sick, but they spread the germs in their saliva, urine, and feces. After drying, microscopic viral particles may rise into the air when dust is disturbed, and humans can inhale them, the source of an extremely dangerous respiratory syndrome. So far, approximately half of the people diagnosed with hantavirus have died. Infected humans appear to have the flu (fever, ache-ridden muscles, headache, cough) then, suddenly, lungs fill with fluid and patients suffer respiratory failure, usually within two to six days. It's scary, and it's in Utah, but the risk to hikers is extremely small, especially if you: 1) avoid contact with all rodents and their burrows, 2) stay out of old, enclosed shelters (such as prehistoric ruins and caves), 3) do not pitch tents or place sleeping bags near rodent burrows, 4) use tents with floors or sleep on ground tarps that extend two to three feet beyond sleeping bags, 5) store food away from possible rodent contact and appropriately dispose of all trash and garbage.

Wild Animal Attacks

While attacks from bears, mountain lions, and other large mammals pose a minor threat to Utah hikers, animal encounters can be dangerous. Reduce the threat from wild animals to a minimum by keeping camps clean, storing all food and aromatic materials well away from camp, making noise while traveling, never traveling alone, and never feeding, harassing, or approaching wild animals. If confronted by a bear or lion, back away slowly, avoiding threatening movement and direct eye contact. Running away, though instinctively appealing, is not a good idea. They can run much faster, and they may be excited by the sight of something possibly edible trying to escape. If attacked by a bear or lion in Utah, fight back aggressively. This is something they don't expect, and they are often repelled by a counter attack.

Large Reptile Bites

There are rattlesnakes in Utah, and the most common encounters with them occur in the desert regions. They rarely bite unless disturbed by the unwary stepping on them or the unwise attempting to capture one. When they do strike, the attack comes with great speed, and the bite is delivered by one or both of two retractable fangs. Localized pain is immediate, and swelling begins within approximately 15 minutes. Blister formation and discoloration usually occur, and may lead to local skin destruction. Victims often report lip-tingling and a funny taste in their mouth within an hour or so. Muscle twitching may result. Death is rare. The amount of damage done to the victim depends on several variables, the largest being the amount of venom injected by the snake. One rattlesnake bite in four carries no venom. The other three out of four may inject mild, moderate, or severe amounts of venom. In all cases, however, the management of the victim is the same: (1) Get away from the snake; (2) Remain as physically and emotionally calm as possible; (3) Remove anything, including rings and watches, that might restrict circulation when swelling occurs; (4) Gently wash the bite site; (5) Splint the bitten arm or leg, and keep the bite site on a level with the victim's heart; (6) Transport the victim to a doctor; (7) Do not use cold packs, tourniquets, cutting-and-sucking, or electrical shocks.

There are also Gila monsters in Utah, but only in the extreme southwestern corner of the state. As with most reptiles, these lizards rarely bite unless disturbed. They have powerful jaws to compensate for primitive teeth and no means to inject their poison. They lock on while the venom drools into the wound the bite creates. You may be required to heat the underside of their jaws with matches or a lighter to break the grip, or pry the mouth open with something rigid. There may be a great deal of local swelling and pain, but deaths in humans are rare. Perform first aid simply by removing the attached lizard, cleaning the wound, and evacuating the victim to a doctor for definitive assessment.

Most reptile bites can be prevented by (1) never touching one, either accidentally or on purpose; (2) checking places you intend to put your hands and feet, especially at night, before exposing your body part to a bite; and (3) keeping your tent zipped up in reptile country.

Small Bites and Stings

The little biters (especially mosquitoes) are the most bothersome but the least serious of Utah's creatures. Bites can be prevented by wearing: (1) Clothing they can't bite through. Lighter colors also appear to offer some repellent qualities; (2) Insect repellents on skin. Products containing DEET or lemon eucalyptus have both been proven effective. Follow the directions on the label carefully with all products; (3) Permethrin products on clothing. You can buy clothing impregnated with permethrin or do the impregnating yourself. In both cases insects and ticks are not only repelled but killed if they spend too much time on your garments. A wipe with a sting relief pad can ease the itching of a bite. Antihistamines, especially diphenhydramine (often sold as Benadryl), can reduce itching and swelling of more severe reactions.

Bees and their relatives (such as wasps) invade camps now and then. Their stings are almost always painful but harmless. The stinger left by honeybees should be removed as soon as possible. Despite popular beliefs to the contrary, any means to get the stinger out, such as scraping or grabbing and pulling, is acceptable. Ice or cold packs on the sting sites will relieve pain and reduce swelling. Diphenhydramine may be given for itching and swelling. Those people who have serious allergic reactions to bees and their relatives should carry a bee-sting kit at all times. Bees are undeterred by insect repellents, but you can make your camp less attractive by keeping food covered when you're not eating.

Spider bites are seldom serious in Utah, but the possibility does exist. Shiny with an hourglass shape almost always on the abdomen, black widow spiders have a bite that often goes unnoticed at first. Local pain and redness will show up at the bite site within an hour, however. Pain from muscle cramping usually develops in the area bitten, as well as in the abdomen and back. The pain may be incredibly severe. Fever, chills, sweating, and nausea may develop. Ice or cold packs applied to the bite site usually provide some relief. Painkilling drugs may be used, if available. Although most patients recover within 24 hours, evacuation to a doctor is strongly recommended, especially for children and the elderly. Recluse (fiddleback) spiders have a violin shape on their back and a bite that usually produces local pain and blister formation within a few hours. A "bulls-eye" of discoloration often surrounds the blister. The blister eventually ruptures, leaving a growing ulcer of skin destruction. Ice or cold packs can relieve local pain. Painkilling drugs may also be useful. When the blister ruptures, treat the open wound will a dressing and a bandage. The patient should be seen by a physician for consideration of drug treatment to minimize damage. Most spider bites can be prevented by watching where you stick your hands and where you step with bare feet.

Scorpion encounters are common in southern Utah, and scorpion stings produce immediate pain and swelling. Sometimes you'll develop numbness around the sting site. Ice or cold packs will reduce pain. Diphenhydramine can be given for swelling and itching. The patient will soon recover, except, perhaps, if they've been stung by the species known as *Centruroides,* a scorpion that may produce a systemic reaction characterized by unusual anxiety, sweating, salivation, gastrointestinal distress, and, most importantly, respiratory distress. No specific first aid is useful for Centruroides stings, and immediate evacuation is required.

Utah ticks may pass diseases to people. Insect repellents repel ticks, and ticks crawling around on your skin do not transmit disease until they dig in and feed for hours to days. Careful "tick checks" should be performed at least twice a day in tick-infested country, since early removal of imbedded ticks prevents the transmission of many diseases. They should be removed gently with tweezers, without excess squeezing, by taking hold of the tick as near the skin as possible and pulling straight out. Any other removal method increases the risk of germ transmission. If a little of the patient's "skin" comes off with the tick, you have done well. If possible, save the tick for evaluation in case of illness in the patient. Wash the wound. A swipe with an antiseptic may be useful. Watch the patient carefully for signs and symptoms of illness, such as a rash or fever. If either occurs, see a doctor as soon as possible.

Poison Oak

Utah's poison oak typically grows as a shrub with leaves in groups of three. And it usually grows near water even though it can appear in surprisingly dry places. Not technically a poisonous plant, despite the name, the oil in poison oak soaks into skin. In more than 85 percent of those who contact enough of the oil it causes a delayed and outrageously angry, itchy allergic reaction. The oil can remain active on clothing, gear, pets, and just about anything it touches for years. The oil remains equally devastating throughout the year, so beware of both the brown stems and roots of winter and the red leaves of fall if they're still attached to the stems.

Nothing cures the rash, but there are several ways to relieve the itch. Nonsteroidal anti-inflammatory drugs (such as ibuprofen) have no effect, but an oral antihistamine, such as diphenhydramine, might relieve some of the itching. Topical lotions, creams, or sprays that contain antihistamines or anesthetics (words that usually end in "-caine") should be avoided since the additives have a tendency to make things worse. Topical corticosteroids sold over-the-counter are too weak to work well. Your physician may be able to prescribe a strong topical steroid that will work, if you start using it before the reaction has turned to blisters. Topical application of calamine lotion dries the area and usually reduces the itch. Many home remedies and folk medications also abound. If you've tried one, and it works for you, use it.

Avoiding Poison Oak: Remember the old Boy Scout saying: "Leaves of three, let them be."

In addition to recognition and avoidance of the plant, several actions may prevent the reaction. Of prime importance is washing as soon as possible after contact. Copious cold water inactivates the oil, so plunging into a nearby stream or lake, depending on

© BOB RACE

your ability to swim, is a reasonable act. If you have plenty of cold water available, especially within the first three minutes of contact, soap, say the experts, is not necessary. Avoid hot water that may just spread the oil around more and open the pores to let it soak in faster. Repeated washings with soap, however, is still recommended by many dermatologists after the three-minute period ends.

Lightning

Lightning storms, especially when you're on high ridges or peaks, pose a serious threat. Keep an eye on the weather, and move away from high or open ground immediately when storms are approaching. Don't wait for the flash and boom; a distant roll of thunder should be all it takes to send you looking for the safest spot. Avoid isolated trees, low places that collect water, shallow caves, and long conductors such as fences. Move away from metal objects. Seek shelter in low rolling hills or thick stands of trees of approximately uniform height. Crouch on packs or sleeping pads with feet close together. Camp in low-risk areas. If someone is struck by lightning, check the victim's breathing and pulse immediately. If you can perform CPR, you might be the victim's only means of survival.

Flash Floods

The slickrock and loose soil that covers much of Utah does little or nothing to retain falling precipitation. Rain landing on huge tracts of land for miles and miles around may end up funneled ferociously down the canyon or wash in which you're hiking. The force of these flash floods can carry away you, your gear, trees, and even your vehicle. Those who don't drown may be beaten to death against rock walls or by debris carried by the flood. Deep in canyons, especially slot canyons, it's often impossible to watch the weather, so it's always a good idea to know the forecast. If hikes through areas susceptible to flash floods are in your immediate future, land managers can usually evaluate the risk for you. When hiking in canyons and deep washes, keep an eye open for escape routes where you can get off the bottom and uphill. Gaining 60 feet of elevation will put you higher than almost any flash flood has ever risen. For those who get a chance to view a flash flood from a safe position, the spectacle is awesome and unforgettable. Floods are typically brief, but if there's any doubt whether it's over, stay put. A cramped, uncomfortable camp is far more appealing that being washed away.

Hiking with Dogs

Most hikers stand firmly either for or against dogs, with few straddling the canine fence. Wherever you stand, here are a few facts worthy of consideration: (1) Dogs are not immune to trail hardships, including sore feet, heat, cold, insects, and dehydration. To take a dog and not attend to its health is irresponsible at best and inhumane at worst; (2) Dogs are not permitted on many trails, and this book lets you know when they aren't; (3) Dogs chase wildlife, reducing your experiential opportunities and possibly inflicting irreparable harm; (4) Dogs do not follow the guidelines of Leave No Trace so you have to do it for them. Read more about LNT later in this chapter; (5) Dogs are often subject to specific rules and regulations, such as leash requirements; (6) Dogs tend to become a source of friction between you and other hikers by being overly friendly or overly aggressive.

Leave No Trace

A large part of the wonder and joy of an outdoor experience, at least a wilderness experience, lies in finding the natural world not only wild but also unaffected ("untrammeled," according to the Wilderness Act of 1964) by other humans. If you want to find it that way, you should leave it that way.

Wild land can be extremely fragile, and Utah's wilderness is as fragile as any. Pollution of water sources, erosion of soils, trampling of vegetation, and graffiti on sandstone walls are just some of the more obvious impacts linked directly to recreational activities. Even the simple fact that you are there has an influence. Considerable damage can be prevented if wilderness users are better informed, especially about how to leave no trace. But true preservation results not just from knowing how to act, but from actually acting appropriately.

At the core of Leave No Trace are not only ethical beliefs but also seven principles for reducing the damage caused by outdoor activities, particularly nonmotorized recreation. Leave No Trace principles and practices extend common courtesy and hospitality to nature and to other wilderness visitors. They are based on respect for nature and the science behind leaving no trace. For more about the Leave No Trace organization, visit their website at www.lnt.com.

Planning

Consider your goals and expectations, and plan ahead, taking pre-trip steps to preserve the wild places. Prepare by gathering information and skills. Plan, for instance, to reduce the amount of garbage you carry by repackaging food, getting rid of trash you might accidentally leave behind. Prepare by learning specific minimum-impact techniques for the area you are visiting. A desert needs respect in ways that differ from subalpine meadows. It is your responsibility.

Hiking and Camping

Candy wrappers and food scraps are ugly but easily picked up. Vegetation trampled into mush and eroded trails might last for years . . . or a lifetime. Set your feet and your tent on surfaces that endure: rock, sand, gravel, dry grasses, sedges, or snow. In high-use areas, concentrate your use where it is obvious other visitors have already left an impact. Stay on trails, avoid shortcuts, use established campsites and fire rings. Good campsites, says the old maxim, are found, not made. Leave your campsite as clean and natural looking as possible. In pristine areas without noticeable impact, disperse your use. When you travel off-trail, walk on durable surfaces and avoid creating obvious campsites. Groups should not walk in single file, as this just tramples the earth into a visible pathway. Spend no more than one night at a pristine site.

Waste Disposal

"Pack it in, pack it out" is a part of proper waste disposal. Inspect your campsites and your rest-break spots, and leave nothing behind. Carry garbage bags and pack out leftover food as well as your trash. Lend a hand to those less careful and to those who will follow you by packing out the refuse discarded by others.

Dispose of your human waste thoughtfully and appropriately. If there's an outhouse, use it. Otherwise dig a cat hole 6–8 inches deep at least 200 feet (about 70 adult steps) from water, drainages, trails, and campsites. If you use toilet paper, pack it out. Urinate on rocks or bare ground rather than on vegetation, and well away from camps and trails. Where water is plentiful, dilute the urine by rinsing the site.

When it's time to clean up after meals, carry water and your dirty cookware 200 feet away from streams or lakes. Strain dirty dishwater with a fine mesh strainer (an old nylon stocking will do) before scattering the dirty water. Pack out the material left in the strainer. Soap, even biodegradable soap, can affect the water quality of lakes and streams, so minimize its use. Always wash yourself well away from shorelines (200 feet), and rinse with water carried in a pot. Consider using a hand sanitizer that allows you to wash your hands without worrying about wastewater disposal.

Souvenirs

Sometimes what you hope to see but don't creates the most disturbing impact of a wilderness trip. Archeological and historical artifacts are reminders of the rich human history of Utah, and they belong to all people for all time. Structures, dwellings, and artifacts on public lands are protected by the Archaeological Resources Protection Act and the National Historic Preservation Act, and should not be disturbed. Do not pick the flowers, collect the rocks, gather potsherds, or take deer antlers home to decorate your office wall. If you want a souvenir, take a photo, draw a picture, or write a description in your journal.

Campfires

Open fires, even the best tended, will almost always leave lasting scars that can be avoided by using lightweight stoves. If fires are acceptable, build a low-impact fire: use an existing fire ring, a mound fire, or a fire pan. Use only dead and downed wood—nothing bigger around than your wrist. Keep the fire small, burn all the wood down to ash, saturate the ash with water, and scatter the ash broadly. Get rid of all evidence of your fire.

Wildlife

Some wild animals adapt to having humans nearby, but others flee, sometimes abandoning their young and their preferred habitat. Observe quietly from a distance. Avoid quick movements and direct eye contact, actions that may be interpreted as aggression. And do not, intentionally or unintentionally by leaving trash or insecurely stored food, feed the animals.

Other Visitors

You'll most often be hiking on public land, and that means you and millions of other people own it. And you all deserve respect. The little things are often the most important. Simple courtesies such as offering a friendly greeting on the trail, wearing earth-toned clothing to blend in with the environment, stepping aside to let someone pass, waiting patiently for a turn, or preserving the quiet, all make a difference. Trail etiquette also asks that hikers should move to the downhill side and talk quietly to horseback riders as they pass. Before passing others, politely announce your presence and proceed with caution. Lend a hand, if appropriate, to help those ahead. Take breaks a short distance (but out of sight when possible) from the trail on durable surfaces. If possible, camp out of sight and sound of trails and other visitors. Treat others, says the wisest of sayings, as you wish to be treated.

Best Hikes in Utah

⚑ Top 10 Canyon Hikes

Bell Canyon–Little Wild Horse Canyon Loop, Eastern Utah, page 144. More than 1.5 miles of slot canyon, and more than half of it less than two yards wide.

Buckskin Gulch, Southern Utah, page 202. Twelve miles of constant narrows, the longest and one of the most beautiful slot canyons on earth.

Death Hollow, Southern Utah, page 190. One of the most exciting and challenging canyon hikes in the world.

Little Death Hollow, Southern Utah, page 197. There are 1.5 miles of extreme slots in this 7.5-mile-long narrow and beautiful canyon.

Lower Paria River Gorge, Southern Utah, page 202. Partly in Arizona, the Paria River has carved out one of the most strikingly beautiful canyons on earth.

Lower White Canyon–The Black Hole, Southern Utah, page 206. Long stretches requiring wading and swimming, and truly narrow narrows, make this one of the greatest canyoneering challenges you will ever find.

Maidenwater Creek–Trail Canyon Loop, Southern Utah, page 203. A hidden jewel, the hike down Maidenwater Creek will challenge you and leave you greatly satisfied.

The Narrows, Southern Utah, page 186. Seventeen miles of thin and deep canyon, this is Zion National Park's most famous hike.

Peek-a-boo and Spooky Gulches, Southern Utah, page 200. Two awfully narrow and awesomely beautiful slot canyons, with the possibility of adding on a third.

Woodenshoe–Dark Canyon–Peavine Loop, Southern Utah, page 209. A splendid backpacking trip through the Dark Canyon Wilderness.

⚑ Top 10 Hikes to Geological Wonders

Chocolate Drops Trail, Eastern Utah, page 160. Impressive rectangular towers in the Land of Standing Rocks in Canyonlands National Park.

Devils Garden Trail, Eastern Utah, page 150. If you want to see arches, no trail in Arches National Park provides more.

Fairyland Loop Trail, Southern Utah, page 184. Some of the most fascinating geological formations in Bryce Canyon National Park can be seen from this trail.

Fiery Furnace, Eastern Utah, page 151. A wandering walk takes you through a beautiful and utterly complex maze of red sandstone fins in Arches National Park.

Fisher Towers Trail, Eastern Utah, page 152. Contour around a mesa to view these raw, red, delightfully sculpted towers of sandstone.

Frying Pan Trail–Cassidy Arch Trail, Central Utah, page 102. Take a walk through some of Capitol Reef National Park's sandstone wonders to one of the world's best pothole arches.

Kolob Arch Trail, Southern Utah, page 175. Hike the scenic trail to one of the world's largest and most spectacular natural arches.

Natural Bridges Loop, Southern Utah, page 206. Nowhere on earth are natural bridges found in such close proximity.

Trail to Rainbow Bridge, Southern Utah, page 208. A beautifully desolate trail to the world's largest natural bridge.

Upper Muley Twist Canyon Semi-Loop, Southern Utah, page 194. Hike past five arches, deep in a narrow canyon, and along a canyon rim with extravagant views.

⑮ Top 10 Extended Backpacking Trips

Dirty Devil River, Eastern Utah, page 147. A deep and lovely gorge whittled from the Colorado Plateau by the persistence of the river.

Grand Gulch, Southern Utah, page 210. More than 50 miles of splendid canyon hiking past some of the best-preserved of all Anasazi ruins.

Highline Trail, Northeastern Utah, page 126. Follow the ridgeline of the Uintas, and be treated to the best of high-mountain Utah.

High Uintas Wilderness Loop, Northeastern Utah, page 121. This is the best high-mountain loop hike in Utah.

Little Cottonwood Canyon to Spanish Fork Canyon, Central Utah, page 71. At 65 miles in length, this is one of the most scenic sections of the Great Western Trail.

Lower Escalante River, Southern Utah, page 196. With dozens of side canyons beckoning, this is arguably the best long canyon hike in Utah.

Lower Paria River Gorge, Southern Utah, page 202. Partly in Arizona, the Paria River has carved out one of the most beautiful canyons on earth.

Robbers Roost Canyon, Eastern Utah, page 147. Easy walking through a beautiful canyon system with deep alcoves, vast overhangs, and sweet water.

Summit Trail, Southern Utah, page 175. Challenge yourself with this strenuous trek along the crest of the Pine Valley Mountain Wilderness.

Woodenshoe–Dark Canyon–Peavine Loop, Southern Utah, page 209. A splendid backpacking trip through the Dark Canyon Wilderness.

⑮ Top 10 Hikes to Ruins and Rock Art

Arch Canyon, Southern Utah, page 211. Numerous ruins secreted in a main canyon and in side canyons, accessible to those willing to walk.

Bullet Canyon to Grand Gulch, Southern Utah, page 213. Seven miles of canyon leading to Grand Gulch with numerous beautifully preserved ruins.

Fish Creek–Owl Creek Canyons Loop, Southern Utah, page 212. Exemplary ruins, some inaccessibly high on canyon walls, lie in two relatively rugged canyons.

Grand Gulch, Southern Utah, page 210. More than 50 miles of splendid canyon hiking past some of the best-preserved of all Anasazi ruins.

Horseshoe Canyon Trail, Eastern Utah, page 146. Unparalleled ancient rock art are in a subunit of Canyonlands National Park.

The Maze Loop from Chimney Rock, Eastern Utah, page 159. The best introductory hike in The Maze includes one of the greatest ancient pictograph panels in the world.

Mule Canyon, Southern Utah, page 210. See numerous well-preserved ruins in this easily accessible and beautiful canyon.

Road Canyon, Southern Utah, page 213. Excellent ruins and not a lot of human traffic.

Slickhorn Canyon Loop, Southern Utah, page 213. Many ruins, some hard to find, along a wonderful loop with several side canyons.

Square Tower Trail, Southern Utah, page 214. The outstanding ruins of several Anasazi villages are preserved in Hovenweep National Monument.

ⓕ Top 10 Gut-Busting Hikes

Birch Canyon Trail to Mount Jardine, Northern Utah, page 28. It starts deceptively easy, but soon gains more than 4,000 feet to a summit with magnificent views.

Cottonwood Canyon, Eastern Utah, page 153. A narrow meandering canyon with a rough bottom and several precipitous drops.

Death Hollow, Southern Utah, page 190. One of the most exciting and challenging canyon hikes in the world.

Deep Canyon–Coldwater Canyon, Northern Utah, page 25. A steep hike leads into the rugged heart of the Wellsville Mountain Wilderness.

Dry Creek to Lone Peak, Central Utah, page 73. Climb almost 6,000 feet to the top of the Lone Peak Wilderness.

Rattlesnake Trail to Box Elder Peak, Northern Utah, page 29. A steep climb to the top of the Wellsville Mountains.

Summit Trail, Southern Utah, page 175. A strenuous trek along the crest of the Pine Valley Mountain Wilderness.

Upper Black Box of San Rafael River, Eastern Utah, page 140. With a lot of swimming in dark pools in a narrow canyon, this may be the scariest, most adventurous hike in Utah.

West Fork of Whiterocks Trail, Northeastern Utah, page 122. A rugged ascent through absolutely stunning mountain scenery in the Uintas.

Whipple Valley Trail, Southern Utah, page 176. A steep climb into the heart of the Pine Valley Mountain Wilderness.

ⓕ Top 10 Hikes with Kids

Alpine Pond Loop Trail, Southern Utah, page 183. A relatively gentle trail around a lovely pond to an outstanding overlook of Cedar Breaks National Monument.

Bell Canyon–Little Wild Horse Canyon Loop, Eastern Utah, page 144. More than 1.5 miles of slot canyon, and more than half of it less than two yards wide.

Black Dragon Canyon, Eastern Utah, page 142. Easy walking in a deep canyon decorated with many pictographs.

inside a cave on the Timpanogos Cave Trail

Crystal Lake Loop, Northeastern Utah, page 117. A short, easy hike past several attractive mountain lakes.

Goblin Valley, Eastern Utah, page 145. Too numerous to count, the "goblins," big and small, are towers capped with mushroom-like tops.

Lower Calf Creek Falls Trail, Southern Utah, page 195. An interpretive hike to a desert oasis: a waterfall plunging into a delightful pool.

Mesa Arch Loop Trail, Eastern Utah, page 158. A short, interpretive hike to a small arch and an excellent view.

Pinhole Point Loop, Eastern Utah, page 161. A short, interpretive hike with great views and no dangerous drops into surrounding canyons.

Timpanogos Cave Trail, Central Utah, page 74. A paved walk up to and into a deep cave illuminated for your viewing pleasure.

Wild Horse Canyon, Eastern Utah, page 144. An easy hike through a lovely canyon with many petroglyphs and pictographs.

Ⓕ Top 10 Hikes to Fishing Spots

China Meadows to Red Castle, Northeastern Utah, page 113. The stream along the way and the lakes at the end of this hike are typically full of hungry fish.

Dry Fork Creek Trail, Central Utah, page 66. A great, though somewhat rugged, hike to several richly stocked lakes.

Fish Creek Lake to Blind Lake Semi-Loop, Central Utah, page 103. In a series of small lakes on Boulder Top Plateau you'll find some of the best fishing in Utah.

High Uintas Wilderness Loop, Northeastern Utah, page 121. The best high-mountain loop in Utah with stops at numerous stocked lakes.

Island Lake via Spirit Lake, Northeastern Utah, page 122. Two to three days of backpacking in the Uinta Mountains past a host of fish-rich lakes.

Jones Hole Trail, Northeastern Utah, page 127. The trail follows lovely Jones Hole Creek below a fish hatchery and into Dinosaur National Monument.

Little Hole National Scenic Trail, Northeastern Utah, page 125. A gentle trail along the Green River with pools of hungry trout.

Take the North Fork of the Provo River Lakes Semi-Loop for great fishing.

Left Fork of Huntington National Recreation Trail, Central Utah, page 85. Follow the north side of a waterway famous for brown, cutthroat, and rainbow trout fishing.

North Fork of the Provo River Lakes Semi-Loop, Northeastern Utah, page 116. Several lakes set in splendid surroundings offer opportunities for some very fine fishing.

Red Lake Trail, Northeastern Utah, page 124. Lakes along the way to Red Lake offer excellent trout fishing.

✈ Top 10 Hikes to Lakes

Amethyst Basin, Northeastern Utah, page 115. This stunning mountain basin with a beautiful lake is a popular destination.

China Meadows to Red Castle, Northeastern Utah, page 113. A lovely, but popular, trail leads to several beautiful lakes.

Hell Hole Lake, Northeastern Utah, page 115. Due to the popularity of nearby lakes, this little jewel sees relatively little human visitation.

Highline Trail to Four Lakes Basin, Northeastern Utah, page 118. It's mighty popular, but it's about as pretty as a lake-filled mountain basin gets.

Island Lake via Spirit Lake, Northeastern Utah, page 122. You'll pass several lovely lakes on the way to your destination lake in the High Uintas.

Kabell Lake Trail, Northeastern Utah, page 114. A well-maintained trail passing beautiful lakes on the way to Kabell Lake in the High Uintas Wilderness.

North Fork of the Provo River Lakes Semi-Loop, Northeastern Utah, page 116. Several lakes set in splendid surroundings offer opportunities for some very fine fishing.

Notch Mountain Lakes Loop, Northeastern Utah, page 116. Simply a stunning array of mountain lakes, almost all above 10,000 feet.

Swift Creek Trail to Timothy Lakes, Northeastern Utah, page 120. A high-mountain trail to many, many lakes.

White Pine Lake Trail, Northern Utah, page 27. A hike for the whole family to great campsites in a lovely setting.

✈ Top 10 Hikes for Solitude

Bullfrog Canyon, Southern Utah, page 205. A lovely, little-used route cut by Bullfrog Creek from the Henry Mountains to Lake Powell.

Dirty Devil River, Southern Utah, page 147. A seldom-walked gorge whittled out by a silty river with several lovely side canyons.

Hackberry Canyon, Southern Utah, page 199. With so much more popular splendor nearby, this little-used but excellent trail takes you past a small lake and a spectacular arch.

Lower Beaver Creek, Eastern Utah, page 155. A year-round creek will lead you beneath tall, seldom-seen slickrock walls to the Dolores River.

The Needle, Western Utah, page 51. The high country of the Mountain Home Range, with great views that few ever see.

Sand Creek, Southern Utah, page 191. A challenging route through a slim canyon that seldom feels the tread of human feet.

Silver Island–Graham Peak, Western Utah, page 43. Climb to the summit of a desert mountain range that rarely sees a human.

Swett Canyon, Southern Utah, page 204. A narrow, steep-walled, sandstone canyon that runs from a paved road to Lake Powell.

Tule Valley, Western Utah, page 47. A flat hike past surprising wetlands in the western desert country.

Upper Paria River Gorge, Southern Utah, page 186. Not as splendid as the Lower Paria, but that's why you may find yourself alone . . . and it's still wonderful.

 ## Top 10 Hikes to Great Views

Canyon Rim Trail, Northeastern Utah, page 125. Look down sheer cliffs to Flaming Gorge Reservoir from the most easily accessed viewpoint in the state.

Dead Horse Point, Eastern Utah, page 156. One of the best overlooks in the world, down more than 2,000 feet into Canyonlands National Park.

Goosenecks Trail, Central Utah, page 98. A very short hike to a fascinating view of Capitol Reef National Park.

Grand View Trail, Eastern Utah, page 159. An easy walk to the best overlooks into Canyonlands National Park.

Highline Trail, Northeastern Utah, page 126. Walk the crest of the Uinta Mountains for 60 miles and endless views.

Mount Nebo, Central Utah, page 82. It's the highest summit in the Wasatch Range, and the views are correspondingly grand.

Mount Tukuhnikivatz Trail, Eastern Utah, page 156. From the summit of this mountain at an elevation of 12,000 feet, see eastern Utah spread out at your feet.

Naomi Peak Trail, Northern Utah, page 27. Hike to the highest point in northern Utah for an outstanding view of the Bear River Range.

Notch Peak, Western Utah, page 48. The best-kept secret in western Utah, this hike takes you through stunningly beautiful terrain to a seemingly endless view.

Swasey Peak Loop, Western Utah, page 48. Hike through amazing geological formations for an outstanding view of western Utah and its mysterious desert peaks.

 ## The Great Western Trail

Dreamers and planners of the Great Western Trail (GWT) envision a continuous corridor from Canada to Mexico through some of the most spectacular and fascinating geological and cultural regions of Montana, Idaho, Wyoming, Utah, New Mexico, and Arizona. Actually more than a trail, the corridor will be a combination of trails, roads, and passageways, most of which already exist, with opportunities for hikers, mountain bikers, horsepackers, cross-country skiers, boaters, snowmobilers, and all-terrain-vehicle (ATV) riders. In order to provide the highest-quality experience for all users, the trail sometimes splits into separate routes: one for motorized traffic, one for nonmotorized traffic. This book does not pretend to be a complete guide to the GWT in Utah. But it does provide information about some sections of the GWT that have proven to be especially inviting to hikers. In this book those hikes are indicated as part of the GWT.

For more information on the Utah portion of the GWT, on the entire GWT, and on how to join the Great Western Trail Association, contact Great Western Trail Association, P.O. Box 1428, Provo, UT 84602.

Chapter 1

COURTESY OF THE SALT LAKE CONVENTION & VISITORS BUREAU/ERIC SCHRAMM

Northern Utah

Think of Utah. You may imagine deep sandstone canyons with walls streaked artistically in desert varnish, gravity-defying arches framing endless miles of rolling slickrock, or maybe thousand-year-old Anasazi ruins perched inaccessibly on narrow ledges. And it is all there, in abundance. But you won't find it in northern Utah.

If, on the other hand, your mental snapshot is of salt flats as far as the eye can see, welcome to the northern region of the Beehive State. Once the bed of a prehistoric sea, this land gives new meaning to the word "flat." Here you can see for miles on the salt flats without gaining a single step of elevation. And here in the north you'll find most of the Great Salt Lake. At 1,700 square miles, the Great Salt Lake is the fourth-largest terminal (no outlet) lake in the world. Its shallow waters reach a maximum depth of no more than 35 feet, and are, on average, three to five times saltier than the waters of the Atlantic or Pacific. The lake's worth a visit, and there is one fine trail around its largest island, but for you, the hiker, the mountains of Utah's northern region are the main attraction.

Northeast of the Great Salt Lake, mountains cloaked in evergreens explode from the earth. Douglas firs dominate the forest, reigning over smaller firs, pines, spruce, and aspen. What may be the oldest juniper on the planet, a sprout 3,000 years ago, grows at the end of one trail. The forest inhabitants include squirrels, chipmunks, rabbits, and skunks. The deer family is well represented here, and you'll see mule deer and an occasional moose or elk. You may see canines, the foxes and coyotes, as well as black bears and mountain lions. Bears and lions are rarely a problem for hikers. Remember to hang your food bag, and keep aromatic items out of your tent. You might also see a few beaver, but famous mountain men—Bridger, Ogden, Ashley, Provo, and Weber—the first nonnatives to explore this region, came looking for pelts in the 1820s but moved on after discovering these mountains were not prime trapping country.

East of Logan, between the city and the northeast state line, stands the Bear River Range, its basins and valleys carved by the relentless glaciers of the great ice ages that ended approximately 10,000 years ago. Trails ascend steeply up the western slopes, but the interior of these mountains is more easily accessed from the eastern side, and several trails provide can't-miss hiking opportunities. If you don't have a lot of time to do the north, consider the Mount Naomi Wilderness. Here is some of the most splendid alpine scenery in Utah, challenged only by the Uinta Mountains of the northeast region. A hike to the top of Naomi will take you to almost 10,000 feet in elevation. And if you're looking for a forest-service campground, you can easily access nine of them along the road that runs through Logan Canyon.

West of Logan the Wellsville Mountain Wilderness, rugged and picturesque, includes terrain that gains and loses elevation very quickly. The U.S. Forest Service calls the Wellsvilles "the steepest range in the United States." Once devastated by overgrazing, this semi-vertical world is well on its way to recovery. Rigorous trails climb up into the Wellsville Mountains, and along the range's crest you can hike with views west across the Great Salt Lake and salt flats and east to the Bear River Range. It's a great place to find solitude, as the steep terrain keeps all but the most avid hikers out.

Moving west, all the way to the northwest corner of Utah, you come to the virtually undiscovered—at least by hikers—Raft River Mountains. Most of this small range is trailless, a chance to wander aimlessly and contentedly on gently rising slopes and into hidden basins. Standing just tall enough to give excellent views of desert flats and more robust mountains in the distance, its best trails are accessible from the lovely Clear Creek Campground.

The sandstone, slickrock, arches, and ruins can wait. You'll miss too much if you don't spend some of your hiking days in northern Utah.

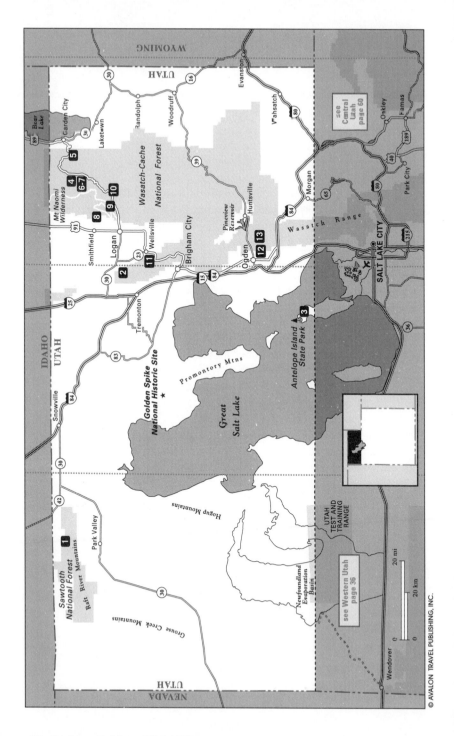

1 BULL FLAT TRAIL TO BULL MOUNTAIN
9.0 mi/8.0 hrs

in the northwest corner of Utah in the Sawtooth National Forest

Map 1, page 24

Ask a Utah-born and -raised backpacker about the Raft River Mountains, and you'll almost always hear a befuddled "Huh?" Rising with unassuming slowness from the farmlands of the northwestern corner of the state, this east-west range attracts few humans other than ranchers who run cattle here and hunters chasing deer. That, however, is a poor reason to avoid the Bull Flat Trail, which enters the mountains from the north. The trail starts at Clear Creek Campground. The campground charges no fees, sites are open on a first-come, first-served basis, and water is available. From the west end of the campground, the trail wanders through a lovely forest of aspens and alders, and up Bull Canyon. After 1.0 mile, a side trail leads off to Bull Flat. Stay on the main trail (now the Lake Fork Trail) through fir and pine up to Bull Lake, settled in a surprisingly pretty cirque beneath sheer cliffs. To the west of the lake a faint path leads along a rocky slope to the summit of Bull Mountain, at 9,931 feet the highest point in the Raft River Mountains. You'll have gained 3,530 feet in elevation in the 4.5-mile hike from the campground. A long summit ridge of rolling grassland provides panoramic views across barren desert to the Great Salt Lake. Peaks of Utah, Nevada, and Idaho rise in the distance.

User groups: Hikers, dogs, horses, and mountain bikes. No wheelchair access.

Permits: No permits are required. Parking and access are free.

Maps: For USGS topographic maps, ask for Rosevere Point and Standrod.

Directions: From Snowville, take State Route 30 west 18.0 miles. Bear north at a junction onto State Route 42 for 8.5 miles. Turn west onto the gravel Strevell Road 3600 South and drive for 3.2 miles. Turn south at the Clear Creek Campground turnoff, and follow this road for 6.0 miles to the campground.

Contact: Sawtooth National Forest, Minidoka Ranger District, 3650 South Overland Avenue, Burley, ID 83318, 208/678-0430.

2 DEEP CANYON- COLDWATER CANYON
8.0 mi/9.0 hrs

west of Mendon in the Wellsville Mountain Wilderness

Map 1, page 24

From the trailhead, the Deep Canyon Trail ascends rapidly and steadily for 3.0 miles to the divide of the Wellsville Mountains at approximately 8,100 feet, an elevation gain nearing 3,000 feet. This, in other words, is steep country. Once on the ridge, keep an eye peeled for hawks. This range reportedly has more raptors winging by during the fall migratory season than any other in America. Also be sure to enjoy the view, including that of the Bear River as it meanders through cultivated land to the west. The trail follows the crest of the divide south to Stewart Pass, contouring around Mendon and Scout Peaks along the way. If you're interested, you can follow the ridgeline 2.0 miles more to Box Elder Peak, the highest point in the Wellsvilles, and on down to the Rattlesnake Trail. Otherwise, from Stewart Pass, the Coldwater Lake Trail descends a knee-poundingly steep 1.5 miles to tiny Coldwater Lake. From there, it's less than a mile to the mouth of Coldwater Canyon, but a long hike back to the Deep Canyon Trailhead. It's much better if you leave a vehicle at both ends. Beware: Not only is this hike virtually devoid of surface water, but high winds on the ridge sometimes make things terribly cold. Be prepared.

User groups: Hikers, dogs, and horses. No wheelchair access.

Permits: No permits are required. Parking and access are free.

Maps: For a USGS topographic map, ask for Wellsville.

Directions: From Mendon, on State Route 23

north of Wellsville, turn west on Third North and travel 2.1 miles to the trailhead.

Contact: Wasatch-Cache National Forest, Logan Ranger District, 1500 East Highway 89, Logan, UT 84327, 435/755-3620.

3 WHITE ROCK BAY TRAIL
9.0 mi/4.0 hrs

just northwest of Salt Lake City
on Antelope Island

Map 1, page 24

Antelope Island is mostly grassland. It's also Utah's largest state park and the largest island in the Great Salt Lake. The park offers several trails, this one into the large and protected southern portion of the island. Relatively flat for most its length, the trail does involve a gentle rise with a corresponding view of the island's volcanic summit and north-south mountain spine. The main attractions, however, will probably be a herd of American bison numbering between 500 and 600 or, depending on the season, the plethora of birds that stop here during their migrations. Other island residents include mule deer, elk, and coyotes. Pleasant beaches open onto the super-salty water of the lake. The water's salt concentration is second only to that of the Dead Sea, allowing swimmers to float with remarkable buoyancy. But swimmers are rare—the water is simply too salty to enjoy. If time allows, Buffalo Point Trail involves a short climb to the top of Buffalo Point (4,785 feet) for an expansive view across the island and the lake.

User groups: Hikers and mountain bikes. No wheelchair access except to the restrooms.

Permits: An entry fee of $8 per vehicle is charged. Overnight camping is only allowed in a designated campground for a fee of $11 per site for the first night, $8 for each additional night. Reservations are strongly recommended and can be acquired for any Utah state park by calling 800/322-3770.

Maps: For USGS topographic maps, ask for Antelope Island, Antelope Island North, and

Buffalo Point. A park brochure, available at the visitors center, describes the trail.

Directions: From I-15, take Exit 335 near Layton, and go west across the causeway to the park entrance. The distance from the interstate is 15.0 miles.

Contact: Antelope Island State Park, 4528 West 1700 South, Syracuse, UT 84075, 801/773-2941.

4 STEAM MILL CANYON TRAIL
14.0 mi/9.0 hrs

northeast of Logan

Map 1, page 24

Here, on the eastern slopes of the Bear River Range and the Mount Naomi Wilderness, the elevation gain tends to be gradual and relatively smooth when compared to the rapid and rugged ascent of the western slopes. Head north from the trailhead for .4 mile and cross the Logan River on a bridge. From there the trail climbs briefly, then angles west across a meadow and into a forest of maple and aspen and, eventually, as the elevation increases, Douglas fir and then subalpine fir. After 2.0 miles, the trail reaches a ridge, turns north, and follows an old wagon road along the side of Steam Mill Canyon for about 3.5 miles of slow altitude gain. You'll reach Steam Mill Lake at 8,650 feet. Pleasant camping spots exist near the lake. With time, you can scramble due south to the saddle overlooking White Pine Creek, or continue up the steep trail from the lake to the divide of the Bear River Range and hike north to the summit of 9,873-foot Doubletop Mountain.

User groups: Hikers, dogs, mountain bikes, and cross-country skiers. No wheelchair access.

Permits: No permits are required. Parking and access are free.

Maps: For USGS topographic maps, ask for Naomi Peak and Tony Grove Creek.

Directions: From Logan on US 91, take US 89 east 23.3 miles up Logan Canyon. Park on the west side of the road at the Franklin Basin trailhead.

Contact: Wasatch-Cache National Forest, Logan

Ranger District, 1500 East Highway 89, Logan, UT 84327, 435/755-3620.

5 LIMBER PINE LOOP
1.25 mi/1.0 hr

northeast of Logan

Map 1, page 24

From the west side of a rest area, the Pine Loop Trail follows signposts into a forest of spruce and fir. Viewpoints along the way offer an expansive look at the blue-green waters of Bear Lake, once a famous rendezvous spot for the mountain men of the 1800s. You'll also see the forested mountains of northeastern Utah. After passing through a stand of limber pines, the trail descends gradually through forest and back to the rest area. With only about 800 feet of elevation gain, this trail is one of the few in Utah offering both splendid views and an easy hike. It's a trail for the whole family. And as a bonus you'll see a stand of limber pines that, at 500 years old and nearly 40 feet tall, are about as old and as tall as they get.

User groups: Hikers and dogs. No wheelchair access.

Permits: No permits are required. Parking and access are free.

Maps: For a USGS topographic map, ask for Garden City.

Directions: From Logan on US 91, take US 89 east 32.4 miles up Logan Canyon to the east side of Bear Lake Summit. Park in the rest area on the south side of the road.

Contact: Wasatch-Cache National Forest, Logan Ranger District, 1500 East Highway 89, Logan, UT 84327, 435/755-3620.

6 NAOMI PEAK TRAIL
6.4 mi/1 day

northeast of Logan in the Mount Naomi Wilderness

Map 1, page 24

Naomi Peak, at 9,980 feet, stands higher than everything else in the Bear River Range and the Mount Naomi Wilderness. For the first quarter mile, the trails to White Pine Lake and Naomi Peak travel together. Then, at a junction, the Naomi Peak Trail heads west. Entering a predominantly coniferous forest of pine, spruce, and fir, the trail gains altitude and eventually breaks out into open meadows. At 1.25 miles, the trail reaches a rocky ledge overlooking a subalpine basin. It then continues to a saddle and up a rocky ridge where, near the two-mile point, the summit of Naomi appears. Trees here are stunted by harsh living conditions. A mile later the trail tops out at the divide of the Bear River Range and a sign marks the boundary of the Mount Naomi Wilderness. The peak is not far to the north. Although from here the trail itself is not particularly clear, the route to the summit is plain to see. At the summit you'll have gained about 1,900 feet of elevation. As with, it seems, all "highest points," the rewards of being there are worth the effort.

User groups: Hikers and dogs. No wheelchair access.

Permits: No permits are required. Parking and access are free.

Maps: For a USGS topographic map, ask for Naomi Peak.

Directions: From Logan, on US 91, take US 89 east 21.6 miles up Logan Canyon to Tony Grove Road. Turn west up this road for 6.8 miles to a parking place at the trailhead to White Pine Lake.

Contact: Wasatch-Cache National Forest, Logan Ranger District, 1500 East Highway 89, Logan, UT 84327, 435/755-3620.

7 WHITE PINE LAKE TRAIL
8.0 mi/7.0 hrs

northeast of Logan

Map 1, page 24

Here is a hike for the whole family, with pleasant campsites in a lovely setting. For the first .25 mile, the trails to White Pine Lake and Naomi Peak are one. Then, at a junction of trails, a sign points north to the lake. The trail slowly and steadily gains elevation, (about 800 feet total) as it ascends an ancient glacier-carved basin. The path tops the first basin, eases by a couple more small bowls, and then ascends a slope to reach its highest point at about three miles. Passing through shady stands of aspen and fragrant fir, the trail switchbacks down, losing about 400 feet of elevation before reaching the creek that drains White Pine Lake. Cross the creek, turn west, and soon you'll see the waters of the lake tucked up against the limestone cliffs of a beautiful mountain wall, a wide basin stretching away to the east.

User groups: Hikers, dogs, and children. No wheelchair access.

Permits: No permits are required. Parking and access are free.

Maps: For a USGS topographic map, ask for Naomi Peak.

Directions: From Logan, UT, on US 91, take US 89 east 21.6 miles up Logan Canyon to Tony Grove Road. Turn west up this road for 6.8 miles to a parking place at the trailhead for White Pine Lake.

Contact: Wasatch-Cache National Forest, Logan Ranger District, 1500 East Highway 89, Logan, UT 84327, 435/755-3620.

8 BIRCH CANYON TRAIL TO MOUNT JARDINE
12.0 mi/8.0–10.0 hrs

east of Smithfield

Map 1, page 24

The trail begins as a four-wheel-drive road, and the first quarter mile crosses private land. Eventually you'll see a sign marking the border of the Wasatch-Cache National Forest. A half-mile later, the road narrows to a footpath that follows a creek up Birch Canyon. The creek must be crossed several times. The difficulty is low here, and the hiking pleasant among cottonwoods along a lovely waterway. As altitude is gained, trees change to aspen and fir, then the terrain opens into meadows with views east and south to the distant ridgeline. Growing steeper,

the trail still follows the creek, a rush of water now, and enters the subalpine zone awash in wildflower colors. For an overnighter, you can camp pleasantly high on the creek, but when you leave the water, you leave the good campsites behind. You'll hike through several high, beautiful bowls and, after about five miles and a lot of sweat, the trail reaches the saddle at the head of Birch Canyon. Check the compass, just to make sure, and head southeast along the ridge toward Mount Jardine. The route to the top is obvious. The summit of Jardine, at 9,566 feet, provides outstanding views: the forested Mount Naomi Wilderness stretching out to the north, wide open Cache Valley to the west, and Logan Peak to the south. You'll have gained about 4,100 feet.

The trip up Birch Canyon may be the start of several hiking options: take the ridge north to Mount Elmer (9,676 feet) and on along the ridge, after about six miles, to Naomi Peak (9,980 feet), drop down to Tony Grove Lake, descend Cottonwood Canyon.

User groups: Hikers and dogs. No wheelchair access.

Permits: No permits are required. Parking and access are free.

Maps: For USGS topographic maps, ask for Smithfield, Mount Elmer, and Naomi Peak.

Directions: From Smithfield on US 91, go east on 100 North. After two blocks, turn south and drive a half-block to Canyon Road. Go east on Canyon Road for 1.0 mile, and turn south onto Birch Canyon Road. Travel this winding road for 1.1 miles to a locked gate. The only parking available is off to the side of the road.

Contact: Wasatch-Cache National Forest, Logan Ranger District, 1500 East Highway 89, Logan, UT 84327, 435/755-3620.

9 WIND CAVE TRAIL
3.4 mi/3.0 hrs

east of Logan

Map 1, page 24

From the parking area, this popular day-hiking trail quickly gains altitude. At about a quarter mile, you'll reach a view across Logan Canyon to the China Wall, a picturesque cliff that extends approximately half the length of Logan Canyon on both sides of the Logan River. At the half-mile point, don't be led astray on a side trail. Instead, stay on the main trail as it heads northwest, rising in switchbacks and soon offering a peek at Wind Cave. After a total elevation gain of about 900 feet, the path reaches the top of the China Wall. Be careful here: You're not far from the edge and a long, deadly fall. Dig out a lunch and the water bottle and enjoy Wind Cave. Sit, relax, and soak up the view of Logan Canyon.

User groups: Hikers and dogs. No wheelchair access.

Permits: No permits are required. Parking and access are free.

Maps: For a USGS topographic map, ask for Mount Elmer.

Directions: From Logan on US 91, take US 89 east 7.1 miles up Logan Canyon. The trail is on the west side of the road.

Contact: Wasatch-Cache National Forest, Logan Ranger District, 1500 East Highway 89, Logan, UT 84327, 435/755-3620.

10 JARDINE JUNIPER TRAIL
9.0 mi/8.0 hrs

east of Logan

Map 1, page 24

Passing first through wide Wood Camp Hollow, the trail heads west and crosses below slopes known for winter avalanches. About a half mile in, the Jardine Juniper Trail forks right up a side canyon. A sign marks the junction. The trail rises, entering a series of steep switchbacks. A sign marks the boundary of the Mount Naomi Wilderness, and mountain bikes are prohibited beyond this point. Just as things seem to be easing up, the trail ascends a second series of switchbacks to a more open ridge and to another trail junction. Both trails wrap around the nameless peak that stands ahead. The north route passes through a stand of large aspen. The southern, more scenic route crosses open slopes with great views down into Logan Canyon and along the Wasatch Mountains. They both arrive at the Old Jardine Juniper, a tree that has survived, despite its decrepit condition and twisted limbs, for approximately 3,000 years. You won't find water on this hike, so carry plenty.

User groups: Hikers and dogs. Mountain bikes up to the wilderness boundary. No wheelchair access.

Permits: No permits are required. Parking and access are free.

Maps: For a USGS topographic map, ask for Mount Elmer.

Directions: From Logan on US 91, take US 89 east 12.4 miles up Logan Canyon. Park at the Wood Camp Campground turnoff.

Contact: Wasatch-Cache National Forest, Logan Ranger District, 1500 East Highway 89, Logan, UT 84327, 435/755-3620.

11 RATTLESNAKE TRAIL TO BOX ELDER PEAK
10.0 mi/1–2 days

southwest of Wellsville in the Wellsville Mountain Wilderness

Map 1, page 24

This trail runs north from a gate, crossing privately-owned, open grassland for about a half mile before bending east and entering the national forest. Little-used and overgrown with box elders and other vegetation, the trail can still be followed as it climbs steeply up Rattlesnake Canyon. At about 2.5 miles, in a stand of aspen, the trail attains a flat area and a possible camping spot. After another consistently steep mile or so through low bushes, the path reaches a saddle snuggled into the divide of the Wellsville Mountains. This is another good place to camp. From just below the east side of the saddle, the trail turns to the north and ascends the central ridge of the Wellsvilles toward Box Elder Peak (9,372 feet), the crown of this range. Passing through swathes of pine and fir, with overlooks on rocky points of Cache Valley to the east, the trail climbs with relative ease to the summit of Box Elder. The total elevation gain is about 3,700 feet. The entire Wellsville Range is long, narrow, high, and virtually dry. All water must be carried.

User groups: Hikers, dogs, and horses. No wheelchair access.

Permits: No permits are required. Parking and access are free.

Maps: For USGS topographic maps, ask for Wellsville, Honeyville, Brigham City, and Mount Pisgah.

Directions: From Wellsville, take US 91 south 3.0 miles from its intersection with State Route 23. Turn off on an unmarked dirt road on the north side of the highway, from near a large utility pole. No vehicles are allowed past the gate.

Contact: Wasatch-Cache National Forest, Logan Ranger District, 1500 East Highway 89, Logan, UT 84327, 435/755-3620.

12 MALANS PEAK LOOP
5.5 mi/7.0 hrs

east of Ogden

> Map 1, page 24

This surprisingly beautiful trail even more surprisingly leaves from the very edge of Ogden. Since you'll be crossing private land, you should contact the Ogden Ranger District prior to setting out to obtain permission from the owners. Just east of an apartment building, hike south on a dirt road, turning onto the first road heading east. If you get disoriented, remember you're headed for the obvious mouth of Waterfall Canyon a half mile to the south. Continuing up Waterfall Canyon, you'll find water flowing all year long. To the south of the falls, the route crawls up some ledges and a scree slope, contours around, and drops into the drainage again. In summer the shade of the canyon offers some relief from the heat. It's another half mile to Malans Basin, where pleasant campsites offer a good place to overnight. Don't plan on camping after you top out on the peak, as the down-

hill leg is dry. From the basin the trail is more obvious as it climbs to Malans Peak for a total elevation gain of about 3,300 feet. When you leave the basin, it's .75 mile to the peak. The summit offers completely satisfying views of the city and the Great Salt Lake. Hike across the peak, switchback down into Taylor Canyon, and turn west for the return to 27th Street, only two blocks from the start.

User groups: Hikers and dogs. No wheelchair access.

Permits: Parking and access are free, but the land is in private ownership and permission should be acquired by calling the Ogden Ranger District.

Maps: For a USGS topographic map, ask for Ogden.

Directions: In Ogden, drive to the east end of 29th Street. Park just east of the tall apartment building.

Contact: Wasatch-Cache National Forest, Ogden Ranger District, 507 25th Street, Ogden, UT 84403, 801/625-5112.

13 MOUNT OGDEN
10.0 mi/1–2 days

east of Ogden

> Map 1, page 24

This route, beginning right in the city of Ogden and continuing to the top of Mount Ogden, understandably attracts quite a few hikers. From the top, 4,700 feet above the city, you'll enjoy an excellent view of the surrounding area, including Snow Basin. The entire city is spread below your feet. The trail begins up Waterfall Canyon near Malans Peak and involves climbing around the canyon's waterfall, an endeavor you can avoid by ascending Taylor Canyon, described earlier in this chapter at the finish of the Malans Peak Loop. Either way the route ends up following the drainage of Waterfall Canyon toward the foot of Mount Ogden. The trail becomes an old jeep road from Snow Basin, a road you can drive if you want the view without the hike. As the trail climbs out of Waterfall Canyon, the going is extremely steep, and it doesn't let up. From the saddle at the head of the canyon you still have another quarter mile to the summit.

User groups: Hikers and dogs. No wheelchair access.

Permits: No permits are required. Parking and access are free.

Maps: For a USGS topographic map, ask for Ogden.

Directions: In Ogden, drive to the east end of 29th Street. Park just east of the tall apartment building.

Contact: Wasatch-Cache National Forest, Ogden Ranger District, 507 25th Street, Ogden, UT 84403, 801/625-5112.

COURTESY OF THE SALT LAKE CONVENTION & VISITORS BUREAU/ERIC SCHRAMM

Western Utah

From the window of your vehicle, speeding along one of western Utah's few highways, you see the Basin and Range Province: basin after basin separated by the upthrust of range after range of mountains. The land, both basin and range, tends generally toward a pale, soft brown color. It is serene country, silent and seemingly lifeless. The basin floors, once beneath an ancient sea, then beneath lakes, lie flat. This area was once all flat, but as the earth was stretched here by eons of shifting continental plates, great north-south-running cracks split the land apartand the mountains rose with infinite slowness as forces within the earth sought release upward. They rose steeply on their western fronts, at angles averaging 60 degrees, and today they are still rising.

The water that was once here is long gone. This is dry land, seeing very little rain and minimal snow. This is, in other words, a high desert. In summer it is territory typically devoid of shade and respite from high heat, and in winter it is often devoid of shelter from cold and wind. It is also pretty much devoid of humans. But resist the temptation to stay in your vehicle. If you know where to walk in western Utah, you'll find beyond the highways a region rich in geological wonder and biological diversity.

You can hike into the Deep Creek, Wah Wah, and Silver Island Mountains to find great vistas and very special places. There is the stark granite of Ibapah Peak in the Deep Creeks, and a wide, eye-stretching crest to walk in the Wah Wahs. The unique rock slabs of the Silver Islands, fallen into artistic disarray, are by themselves worth the effort of a visit. Here you'll stumble across caves that give mute reminders of a people who called these mountains home 10,000 years ago.

Western Utah is most remarkable, however, in the House Range with its high point, and an excellent view, at the top of Swasey Peak. The grandeur of the House Range is no more evident than around Notch Peak. From Notch Peak you could (but don't) drop a rock and watch it fall almost 3,000 feet down a sheer face before it hits the ground. At higher elevations ancient bristlecone pines stand silent and humble, as do pockets of fir, spruce, and aspen. On lower slopes woodlands of juniper and piñon pine rise above immense grasslands dotted with sage.

Hidden in the desert of western Utah are spring-fed marshlands where birds stop regularly on their annual migrations. Some species of plants not only thrive here but are also found nowhere else on earth. Antelope, bighorn sheep, and small herds of wild horses live here, finding nourishment from the plentiful springs. And a few unlikely streams offer trout fishing. Beyond the springs and streams, you'll find something precious: solitude.

Away from the desert, both flanks of the Stansbury Mountains are protected within the Deseret Peak Wilderness, and hikers walk in shady forest up to quiet lakes. Deseret Peak, with a trail to its summit, stands at over 11,000 feet and offers a magnificent view. Elsewhere, you may choose to hike in what is best described as a transition zone between the Basin and Range Province and the Colorado Plateau. Here you'll find treeless flats above, outstanding sandstone walls below. You'll also find trails into the relatively green abundance of the Fishlake National Forest, and into the truly high country of the Tushar Mountains. In the Tushars you can climb to over 12,000 feet on Delano Peak. You can also backpack along the Skyline National Recreation Trail, rarely dropping below 10,000 feet.

All things considered, you will do well to consider western Utah.

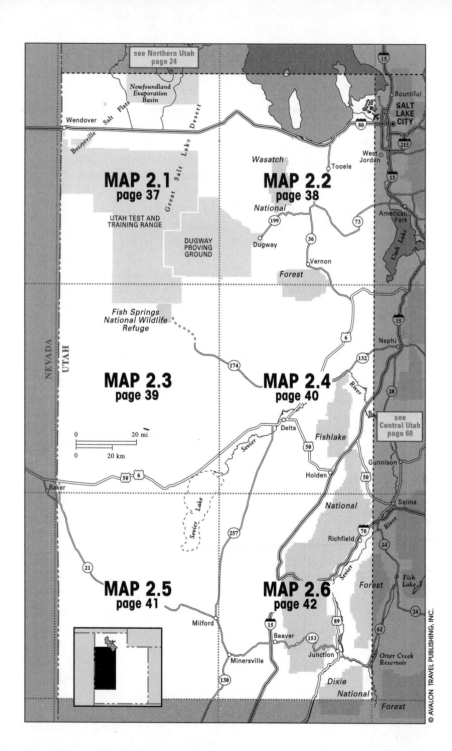

Map 2.1

Hike 1
Page 43

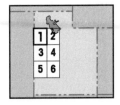

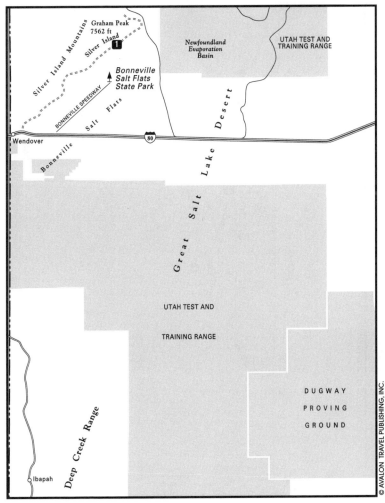

Map 2.2

Hikes 2–4
Pages 43–44

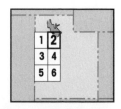

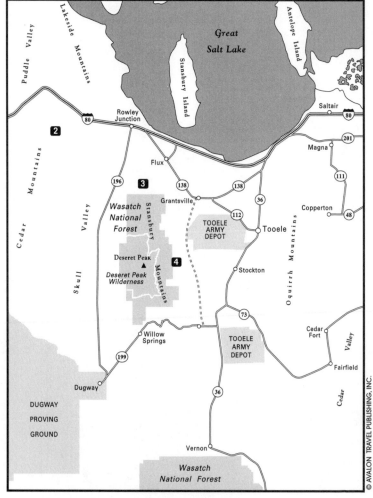

Map 2.3

Hikes 5–12
Pages 45–49

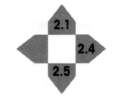

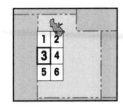

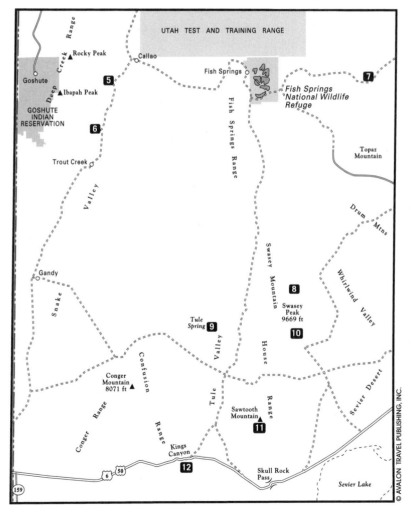

Map 2.4

Hikes 13–14
Page 50

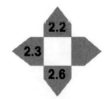

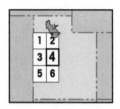

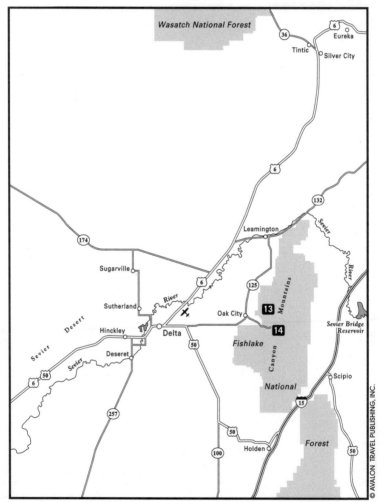

Map 2.5

Hikes 15–17
Pages 51–52

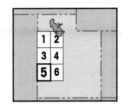

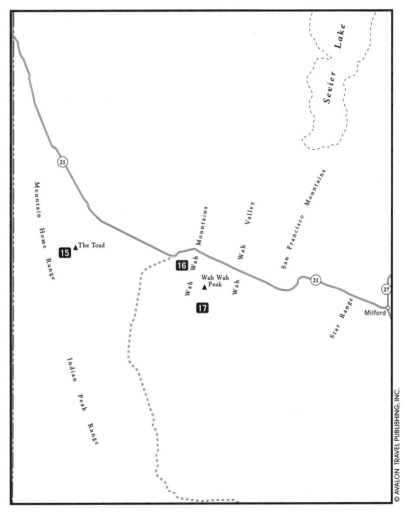

Map 2.6

Hikes 18–25
Pages 52–56

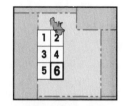

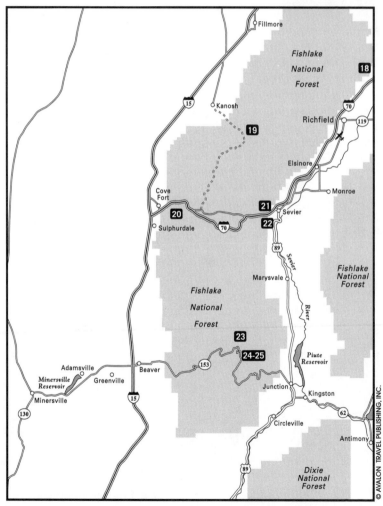

1 SILVER ISLAND– GRAHAM PEAK

2.0–10.0 mi/2.0–8.0 hrs

northeast of Wendover, not far from the Nevada border

Map 2.1, page 37

No trails exist in the Silver Island Mountains, a rough and tumble pile of rocks rising above Bonneville Salt Flats. Seldom visited, desert peace and quiet reign unchallenged, despite the fact that Bonneville Racetrack, scene of the world's fastest land speeds, lies below. The Silver Islands are surrounded by a dirt perimeter road with several old jeep tracks, most of them almost returned to invisibility, penetrating into the mountains. The core of the range stands never more than approximately two miles from the road. Little used, the road allows parking just about anywhere. One of the old jeep tracks ascends Cave Canyon, offering access to Graham Peak, which stands like a "silver island" (at 7,563 feet, the highest point in the mountains) on the northern end of the range. On the summit you'll have gained about 3,000 feet of elevation from the road. Numerous natural caves can be found in the area, some showing evidence of prehistoric use. Scrambling to the top of Graham is challenging but far from impossible, with rewarding views of miles of featureless desert, beyond which stand distant peaks. Since the area goes virtually without precipitation, there is no water in the Silver Island Mountains, and only sparse vegetation survives: lonely junipers lower down, rabbitbrush, sagebrush, shadscale higher up. An overnight hike requires, for safety, at least a gallon of water per person. Go in winter, avoiding the shadeless, pounding heat of summer.

User groups: Hikers, dogs, and horses. Mountain bikes on the perimeter road. No wheelchair access.

Permits: No permits are required. Parking and access are free.

Maps: For USGS topographic maps, ask for Graham Peak, Floating Island, and Bonneville Racetrack.

Directions: From Wendover, take I-80 east four miles. Take Exit 4, and go north. At a junction at 1.2 miles, go left and follow this road about one mile to another junction. Turn right at (as of this writing) a BLM sign for the Silver Island Mountains. Take this road north for 14 miles to where the mountains begin to slope down close to the road. Park here.

Contact: BLM Salt Lake Field Office, 2370 South 2300 West, Salt Lake City, UT 84119, 801/977-4300.

2 CEDAR MOUNTAINS CREST

12.0 mi/8.0 hrs

southwest of Salt Lake City in the Cedar Mountains

Map 2.2, page 38

From I-80 the arid Cedar Mountains, dotted with dry brush, rising to steep cliffs, barren and decidedly uninviting, roll away to the south. In the entire range there are no perennial streams, and only two springs that rise to the surface year-round: Redlam and Quincy. From Hastings Pass, an old jeep track heads south and joins a trail ascending a slope. After about a half mile and 800 feet of elevation gain, the trail reaches the juniper- and grass-covered ridgeline of the Cedars. The trail grows fainter and disappears as you follow the divide south, but this is not a concern since the ridgeline stays open and easy to hike. To the east, the much more rugged Stansbury Mountains rear up across the sand of Skull Valley. The Silver Island Mountains rise to the west, the Wah Wahs and Deep Creeks to the south. The ridgeline of the Cedars rises and falls like a gentle wave, with occasional cliffs falling off on the west. Watch for signs of wild horses. A herd of as many as 200 calls this empty space home. A vertical wall of broken limestone makes a picturesque resting place and is as good a spot as any to turn around and head back to the vehicle. Many more miles can be easily walked, but the lack of water, and the necessity of carrying it, would heavily burden long-distance hikers.

User groups: Hikers, dogs, and horses. No wheelchair access.

Permits: No permits are required. Parking and access are free.

Maps: For a USGS topographic map, ask for Hastings Pass.

Directions: From I-80, take the Delle exit (Exit 70) and drive south a short distance to the gravel frontage road. Turn west and drive the frontage road for two miles, then turn south on a dirt road and drive seven miles. There, turn west on a rough four-wheel-drive road and go 4.1 miles to Hastings Pass.

Contact: BLM Salt Lake Field Office, 2370 South 2300 West, Salt Lake City, UT 84119, 801/977-4300.

₃ MUSKRAT CANYON TRAIL
6.0 mi/6.0 hrs

southwest of Salt Lake City and south of Rowley Junction

Map 2.2, page 38

North of the Deseret Peak Wilderness, Muskrat Canyon lies on the west side of the Stansbury Mountains within an area being considered for wilderness designation. Although the east side of the range sees a relatively steady stream of visitors, the west side feels few human feet. From your vehicle, start hiking east up an old track. Wide-open Skull Valley appears to the west. Tromping past sagebrush, you won't realize you're in a canyon until you've gained quite a bit of elevation. Junipers have been left behind, exchanged for a few Douglas firs. The old track ends in a basin at 6,800 feet elevation (about 2,000 feet above your starting point). A stream should be flowing, and camping is possible here. A trail continues up Muskrat Canyon, leaving the water behind. Despite that fact, the upper Muskrat remains surprisingly green with mountain mahogany lower down, conifers higher up, and scattered stands of aspen. Persistent and durable hikers may continue on, climbing up the rocky slope to the ridgeline, with another 1,500 feet of elevation to be gained. A short distance

beyond the upper basin is a good place to turn around.

User groups: Hikers, dogs, and horses. No wheelchair access.

Permits: No permits are required. Parking and access are free.

Maps: For USGS topographic maps, ask for Timpie, Salt Mountain, and North Willow Canyon.

Directions: From I-80, take the Rowley/Dugway exit (Exit 77) and drive south approximately six miles. This road runs almost dead straight, making a slight westward bend at 5.5 miles. Near the six-mile point, turn east on a rough road. Four-wheel-drive vehicles are recommended. The road bears left at a power station, then right at a fork, before continuing up canyon for about 2.5 miles. Park where the road becomes too treacherous to drive. This road becomes the trail.

Contact: BLM Salt Lake Field Office, 2370 South 2300 West, Salt Lake City, UT 84119, 801/977-4300; Wasatch-Cache National Forest, Salt Lake Ranger District, 6944 South 3000 East, Salt Lake City, UT 84121, 801/733-2660.

₄ DESERET PEAK TRAIL
12.0 mi/8.0–10.0 hrs

southwest of Salt Lake City and south of Grantsville

Map 2.2, page 38

Straddling the Stansbury Mountains, the Deseret Peak Wilderness rises to its highest point of 11,031 feet on Deseret Peak. The trail climbs through a forest of aspen for three quarters of a mile before crossing a year-round stream and, shortly thereafter, reaching a fork. The left fork heads south toward the peak. The right fork leads to Willow Lakes. In the next mile and a half the trail climbs almost 2,000 feet, crossing several meadows below the sheer 1,500-foot southwest face of Deseret Peak. Climb the cirque at the head of the canyon to reach a saddle. Snow may linger at the tree line well into summer. Following the ridgeline, switchbacks sweep up the final ascent to the summit with spectacular views of the surrounding salt flats and distant mountains. You can retrace your steps to the starting point, or drop down a path to the north leading to Willow Lakes. From the lakes you can complete a loop of approximately 12 total miles back to the starting point. To take the loop, hike down Deseret Peak for two miles to where the trail forks, then take the south fork back instead of dropping down to the lakes.

User groups: Hikers and dogs. No wheelchair access.

Permits: No permits are required. Parking and access are free.

Maps: For a USGS topographic map, ask for Deseret Peak.

Directions: From Grantsville on State Route 138, take the South Willow Canyon Road south. After five miles, the road forks. Take the west fork and drive another seven miles to the trailhead.

Contact: Wasatch-Cache National Forest, Salt Lake Ranger District, 6944 South 3000 East, Salt Lake City, UT 84121, 801/733-2660.

5 THE BASIN LOOP
12.0 mi/8.0 hrs

southwest of Callao and not far from the Nevada state line

Map 2.3, page 39

Although about two-thirds of the Basin Loop—up Toms Canyon and up Middle Canyon—could be managed in a four-wheel-drive vehicle, the path invites hikers or horsepackers (and may someday, politics deciding, be accessible to only foot and hoof). From the trailhead, a steep double track leads up grass and sagebrush for approximately two miles to a pass above Toms Creek. From there it ascends to the rim of the basin, just over four miles from the trailhead. You'll pass two old log cabins on the way. Surrounded by ragged peaks, filled with rocky knobs and spires, treed with aspen and conifers, the basin spreads out like a dream come true. Drop into the lower basin and set camp near springs on the west side. If time al-

lows, camp a couple of nights and take a side trip north to the summit of Rocky Peak (10,748 feet). To continue the loop, travel east across the basin on the south side of Basin Creek, and find a well-defined trail leading up to a pass at the head of Middle Canyon. Look east, far below to the lava fields of Snake Valley. Another steep double track leads down Middle Canyon, curving, after a couple of miles, southeast along the sides of slopes to avoid the rugged canyon bottom. From the junction of Middle and Toms, a hike up to the parking spot rounds out the loop.

User groups: Hikers, dogs, horses, and cross-country skiers. No wheelchair access.

Permits: No permits are required. Parking and access are free.

Maps: For USGS topographical maps, ask for Goshute, Goshute Canyon, and Indian Farm Creek.

Directions: From the east side of Callao, turn south on the gravel Pony Express/Gold Hill Road. Drive past the landfill, then turn west after approximately two miles toward Toms Creek and Middle and Goshute Canyons. The road heads toward the mountains for another two miles before a junction is reached. Take the south (left) road at the junction and continue into the foothills on the rough road that heads toward a peak shaped like a triangle for another two miles to the meeting of Middle and Toms Canyon Roads. Turn south, drive a half mile up Toms Canyon, and park.

Contact: BLM Fillmore Field Office, 35 East 500 North, Fillmore, UT 84631, 435/743-3100.

6 GRANITE CREEK TRAIL TO IBAPAH PEAK
12.4 mi/1–2 days

southwest of Callao not far from the Nevada state line

Map 2.3, page 39

The white granite of Ibapah Peak, at 12,087 feet, rises higher than any other point in the Deep Creek Mountains. The first 1.2 miles of the Granite Creek Trail follows a rough four-wheel-drive track up the creek to a clearing. A faint path leads from the clearing straight toward the creek, and crosses the water to climb a sagebrush slope to where the path forks. Take the left fork. The trail crosses a ridge and ascends a valley. If the trail disappears, keep moving toward the top of the ridge at the head of the valley from where Ibapah Peak rises directly to the north. Demanding switchbacks lead up the final push to the summit. The view runs away, it seems, to infinity. The Deeps, standing above the Great Basin Desert, hide, among other treasures, green forests, marshy meadows, ragged rocky outcroppings, alpine tundra, and cirques carved by glaciers. Above typical desert shrub communities, the lower slopes support piñon and juniper, the higher slopes pine, fir, and spruce. Trout inhabit the clear-flowing streams of the Deeps. Watch for many species of birds, and, though not abundant, a rich variety of mammals. The availability of water makes multi-day wandering an option in these fabulous mountains.

User groups: Hikers, dogs, horses, and cross-country skiers. No wheelchair access.

Permits: No permits are required. Parking and access are free.

Maps: For USGS topographical maps, ask for Ibapah Peak and Indian Farm Creek.

Directions: From the east side of Callao, turn south on the gravel Pony Express/Gold Hill Road. Drive past the landfill, and make a turn west after approximately two miles toward Toms Creek and Middle and Goshute Canyons. The road heads toward the mountains, then turns south for eight miles to Granite Creek Road. Head west on Granite Creek Road. If you're in a four-wheel-drive vehicle, continue several miles along Granite Creek to a stream crossing, and park.

Contact: BLM Fillmore Field Office, 35 East 500 North, Fillmore, UT 84631, 435/743-3100.

7 PYRAMID PEAK
5.0 mi/6.0 hrs

southwest of Salt Lake City and west of Vernon

Map 2.3, page 39

No sign marks Dugway Pass. No sign marks the trailhead. In fact, there really is no trail. Other than a few sheepherders, humans rarely visit the Dugway Mountains. The standard was set in 1860 and 1861 when Pony Express riders streaked over the pass without slowing down. When most of Utah's mountains lie buried in snow, however, consider the Dugways, a dry range if ever there was one. From the pass, climb the hill north of the road to where Pyramid Peak becomes visible, just a little west of due north. The route continues up and down ridges, with no definite path for feet to follow. Continue up the hill, and see the panorama of the desert open to the west. With Pyramid Peak to the left, a triangular volcanic cone appears to the right. Now hidden valleys will surprise you, a reminder that from the desert floor, the apparent flatness of these mountains is a deception. The gentle slopes may be green with spring grass, highlighted with early summer wildflowers, dotted with juniper, but these arid hills support little wildlife or vegetation. There are a couple of options for reaching the summit. You can climb east or southeast ridges falling off the peak, but both ways involve losing and regaining altitude several times before the final cone is reached. The last portion of the ascent covers .1 mile and 500 feet of elevation gain over a rough surface with plenty of footholds and handholds. Avoid the sections of the summit cone that appear loose and uncertain. The small, flat top provides adequate room to relax and enjoy the view (dominated to the north by Castle Mountain, at 6,749 feet the highest peak in the Dugways). Carry all your water. There's no shade from the sun, no break if the wind blows.

User groups: Hikers and dogs. No wheelchair access.

Permits: No permits are required. Parking and access are free.

Maps: For a USGS topographical map, ask for Dugway Pass.

Directions: From Vernon on State Route 36, go west on the bumpy and unimproved Pony Express Road for 44 miles to Dugway Pass. Park on the pass.

Contact: BLM Salt Lake Field Office, 2370 South 2300 West, Salt Lake City, UT 84119, 801/977-4300.

8 ROBBERS ROOST CANYON– TATOW KNOB LOOP
14.0 mi/10.0 hrs

west of Delta in the House Range

Map 2.3, page 39

Wild and seldom seen, the House Range provides a first-rate wilderness experience. A double track heads up the first wash to the west from the parking spot. Follow it, up Robbers Roost Canyon, toward the unmistakable steep-walled mesa called Tatow Knob (8,416 feet), a landmark visible for many, many miles in every direction. Low juniper and sagebrush-covered ridges form boundaries for the first section of the canyon. After 2.5 miles, the double track fades in the sandy soil, and eyes should be peeled for sightings of wild horses, residents of this area. At about three miles the canyon narrows, then widens again at a junction. Stay left, in the main canyon, and follow it to Robbers Roost Spring. A cave (truly more of a large overhang) is easily accessible to the south of the spring. Is this the place where robbers once roosted? Climb the somewhat steep terrain southwest for a half mile to the crest of the House Range, a total of about four miles from the trailhead. The crest, a wide plateau, runs south for another four miles to Swasey Peak. To continue the loop, hike north toward Tatow Knob. Along the way, you'll find hidden valleys walled by awesome vertical cliffs. The going becomes more rugged as the route negotiates the east slope of Tatow Knob, traversing north to the broad ridge northwest of North Canyon Spring. Descend the steep terrain to the spring (at the head of North Canyon), and follow the double track down canyon to its mouth, then south a couple of miles to the parking spot.

User groups: Hikers, dogs, and horses. No wheelchair access.

Permits: No permits are required. Parking and access are free.

Maps: For a USGS topographic map, ask for Swasey Peak.

Directions: From Delta, take US 6 west. Five miles past Hinckley, turn west on the Antelope Spring Road, and take this road for 13 miles to a junction. Then turn northwest for 11 miles to another junction where, at this writing, a sign reads "Delta 35 miles." Continue north on the main road four miles to still another junction. From there keep going north on the main road for three miles more to yet another junction. Turn west here toward the blocky Tatow Knob. After three more miles on this road, go south at a fork in the road, and continue for 1.5 miles to where the road veers north across lower Robbers Roost Canyon. Park just north of the mouth of the canyon.

Contact: BLM Fillmore Field Office, 35 East 500 North, Fillmore, UT 84631, 435/743-3100.

9 TULE VALLEY
13.0 mi/1–2 days

west of Delta

Map 2.3, page 39

When snow smothers the more dramatic mountain hikes of Utah, consider the level and undeveloped Tule Valley, a remote piece of earth dotted with springs and dampened with wetlands. Tule Spring, at the trailhead (4,422 feet elevation), and Coyote Spring at trail's end (4,424 feet elevation), see very little precipitation. The "trail" is really an old road that travels north across a sagebrush flat. At 2.5 miles a wetland west of the road provides habitat for ducks, rails, and marsh hawks, as well as frogs, and leeches. At approximately three miles a bulge of land east of the track offers a pretty campsite. Along the way, the House Range lifts steeply to the east, the Deep Creek Mountains to the northwest, the low rise of the Confusion Range to the west. Distant peaks of Nevada are visible. At six miles, the old track intersects another track. Turn east for a half mile to Coyote Spring, an open body of water that sometimes attracts a bird or two. This is a good place to turn for the 6.5-mile walk back to the trailhead. Wind may blow enough to whip a hat off, but otherwise the silence and serenity tend to be outstanding. Water from the springs is not safe to drink without careful disinfection.

User groups: Hikers, dogs, horses, and mountain bikes. No wheelchair access.

Permits: No permits are required. Parking and access are free.

Maps: For USGS topographic maps, ask for Chalk Knolls, Coyote Knolls, and Swasey Peak NW.

Directions: From Delta, take US 6 west. Five miles past Hinckley, turn west on the Antelope Spring Road, and take this road for 24 miles before turning north to Antelope Spring. Continue on this road for approximately 22 miles, over Dome Canyon Pass to Tule Spring. Turn north and drive several hundred yards to a corral and a place to park.

Contact: BLM Fillmore Field Office, 35 East 500 North, Fillmore, UT 84631, 435/743-3100.

🔟 SWASEY PEAK LOOP
4.5 mi/6.0 hrs

west of Delta in the House Range

Map 2.3, page 39

Ⓕ Get ready to bushwhack in the truest sense of the word. From the northeast side of the road, climb to the top of the ridge, a distance of less than a mile and an elevation gain of only about 600 feet. You'll be struggling at times through dense tangles of mountain mahogany. Once on the ridge (and into easier hiking), ascend north toward the first of two summits. The second, true summit is that of Swasey Peak (9,669 feet), the crown of the House Range. The panorama here is stunning. You can see south to Sevier Dry Lake and the Tushar Range, west to the Confusion Range, northwest to the Deep Creek Mountains, and northeast to Mount Nebo. From the peak, the crest of the range runs north, a wide piñon- and juniper-covered plateau that provides access to the canyons of Sawmill Basin and Robbers Roost. You may see wild horses in either or both of these areas. To finish the loop, hike down the ridge to the northwest for .75 mile. Stay above the terrain falling steeply westward until you reach the Sinbad Spring Road. You'll be about a mile from your starting point. This journey offers no water other than Antelope Spring and what you carry. If you stop at the spring to fill your water bottles, don't miss the fossils of the Antelope Spring Trilobite Bed.

User groups: Hikers and dogs. No wheelchair access.

Permits: No permits are required. Parking and access are free.

Maps: For USGS topographic maps, ask for Swasey Peak and Marjum Pass.

Directions: From Delta, take US 6 west. Five miles past Hinckley, turn west on the Antelope Spring Road, and take this road for 24 miles before turning north to Antelope Spring. An additional nine miles must be traveled toward Antelope Spring before the road turns west and south toward Dome Canyon Pass. There the Sinbad Spring Road leaves to the north. After 3.2 miles on the Sinbad Spring Road, a large open area allows parking.

Contact: BLM Fillmore Field Office, 35 East 500 North, Fillmore, UT 84631, 435/743-3100.

🔟🔟 NOTCH PEAK
9.0 mi/8.0 hrs

southwest of Delta in the House Range

Map 2.3, page 39

Ⓕ After a mile of easy hiking west from a cabin, the track enters the dramatic Sawtooth Canyon with walls rising steeply on the south side. Indeed, no other region of the House Range nears the spectacular display of the Notch Peak area, a place you have to see to believe. A Wilderness Study Area, Notch Peak may soon be fully designated as protected wildland. The terrain eventually opens up and divides into two drainages. Be sure to bear left. The hiking remains easy in the open drainage. About three miles from the trailhead the canyon narrows, steepens, meanders more, and requires a bit of scrambling over several ledges. After four miles, the drainage disappears on slopes covered with sagebrush and mountain mahogany. Ascend the slopes northwest toward an obvious saddle just east of Notch Peak. The saddle provides an excellent opportunity to relax and stare at the impressively huge drop off the west side of Notch Peak into the Tule Valley. At 4,450 feet, this limestone cliff is one of the tallest in America, comparable in size to the granite walls of Yosemite. A tough quarter-mile climb separates the saddle from the summit of Notch Peak, but the reward for the effort is the view: the Sevier Desert to the east, Sevier Dry Lake to the southeast, the Wah Wah Mountains to the southwest, the Confusion Range to the west, and the Deep Creek Mountains to the northwest. You'll have gained about 3,000 feet in elevation. No water can be found on this hike unless it rains. In of the event of heavy rain, the narrows of the canyon may be dangerous, and should be avoided.

User groups: Hikers and dogs. No wheelchair access.

Permits: No permits are required. Parking and access are free.

Maps: For USGS topographic maps, ask for Miller Cove and Notch Peak.

Directions: From Delta, take US 6 west approximately 38 miles to an unmarked dirt road that heads north. After 4.7 miles along this road, turn left on another road for 1.3 miles, then right onto the Miller Canyon Road. After 5.5 miles veer left into Miller Cove. Three miles later you'll find a stone cabin on the north side of the road. The cabin is privately owned, but there's a place to park just beyond it.

Contact: BLM Fillmore Field Office, 35 East 500 North, Fillmore, UT 84631, 435/743-3100.

12 CAT CANYON TO LITTLE HORSE HEAVEN
12.0 mi/1–2 days

southwest of Delta

Map 2.3, page 39

King Top Wilderness Study Area is certainly one of the best kept secrets of the western Utah desert. Surprisingly, King Top is reached by the easiest road access in the desert. Unlike other desert ranges where jagged peaks dominate, this area, from the road, appears to be a vast and relatively flat plateau protected on all sides by intimidating walls. And that is exactly what it is. This place is for hikers who enjoy a challenging walk. But once beyond the barriers, King Top hides a splendid and gentler interior. From the pullout on the road, hike south into Cat Canyon, through its mouth of dark rock. You hike beneath canyon walls decorated by nature with towers and arches, broken here and there by wide grassy slopes. Watch for signs of the mountain lions who gave this canyon its name, and signs of the wild horses who call this place home. As the canyon meanders, it narrows at times to no more than 10 feet in width. Then, at approximately two miles, the canyon suddenly opens into a valley. About halfway across the valley, just before limestone cliffs rise abruptly to the sky, a slope ascends the east side of the cliffs to the top of the ridge. Continue south along the ridge to its high point at 7,480 feet. From here Notch Peak's tremendous west wall stands to the northeast, Nevada's mountains to the west. Descend southeast into a saddle, climb to the crest of the next knoll, cross from there to another ridgeline, and descend the wooded slope to a clearing where you can look across Little Horse Heaven. Named for the wild horses often seen by a quiet observer, it's 800 acres of grass and sage surrounded by a forest of piñon, juniper, and fir. The Utah desert offers few, if any, greater surprises. Carry water, as there is none in the area.

User groups: Hikers, dogs, and horses. No wheelchair access.

Permits: No permits are required. Parking and access are free.

Maps: For a USGS topographic map (recommended), ask for Bullgrass Knoll.

Directions: From Delta, take US 6 west 62.5 miles. About halfway between mile markers 26 and 27, where Kings Canyon narrows, a pullout on the south side of the road allows parking.

Contact: BLM Fillmore Field Office, 35 East 500 North, Fillmore, UT 84631, 435/743-3100.

13 NORTH WALKER CANYON TO FOOL CREEK PEAK
4.0 mi/6.0 hrs

east of Oak City in Fishlake National Forest

Map 2.4, page 40

One thing that makes the summit of Fool Creek Peak special is the fact that it stands relatively near the geographic center of the state. The trail up North Walker Canyon is an old jeep track for about a mile, at which point it thins down to a footpath. Toward the head of the canyon, the trail becomes noticeably steeper as it leads to a pass with Buck Peak to the west and Fool Creek Peak to the east. Vegetation covers the ground below the pass. Oak, pine, and fir stand above everything else except the peaks and the sky. At the pass, turn east and follow the ridgeline for a steep mile to the summit of Fool Creek Peak at 9,717 feet. You'll have gained about 2,700 feet in elevation. The peaks of the Manti–La Sal National Forest stretch out to the east, the Tushars to the south, the Wasatch Range to the north, the ranges of the Great Basin to the west.

User groups: Hikers and dogs. No wheelchair access.

Permits: No permits are required. Parking and access are free.

Maps: For USGS topographic maps, ask for Fool Creek Peak and Williams Peak.

Directions: From Oak City on State Route 125, drive east on Center Street. This road turns southeast and becomes Forest Service Road 089. At 4.5 miles, the road reaches Oak Creek Campground. Then, at 6.5 miles, it reaches the North Walker Canyon turnoff, which heads north. A determined four-wheel-driver could continue up the rough track for about a mile, but parking is available near the road.

Contact: Fishlake National Forest, Fillmore Ranger District, 390 South Main Street, Fillmore, UT 84631, 435/743-5721.

14 LYMAN CANYON TRAIL
7.0 mi/6.0 hrs

east of Oak City in Fishlake National Forest

Map 2.4, page 40

Hike south along a creek, keeping an eye open for trail-marking rock cairns and blazes on trees. The path ambles gently and pleasantly through maple, oak, and conifers for about a mile. Then the route says good-bye to the stream to ascend a knoll with the first of numerous views to come. Travel grows more arduous now on the trail, climbing and passing, intermittently, through open meadows and trees, and eventually reaching a pass at about 9,000 feet. You'll gain almost 2,000 feet of elevation. From the pass, a couple of low peaks, not much more than one or two hundred feet higher than the pass, offer excellent views of the surrounding forest and distant peaks. The trail continues downhill for about a mile to Forest Service Road 416, but most hikers go home satisfied after reaching one of the peaks.

User groups: Hikers and dogs. No wheelchair access.

Permits: No permits are required. Parking and access are free.

Maps: For a USGS topographic map, ask for Williams Peak.

Directions: From Oak City on State Route 125, drive east on Center Street. This road turns southeast and becomes Forest Service Road 089. At 4.5 miles the road reaches Oak Creek Campground and, at 7.5 miles, the Lyman Canyon Trailhead.

Contact: Fishlake National Forest, Fillmore Ranger District, 390 South Main Street, Fillmore, UT 84631, 435/743-5721.

15 THE NEEDLE
9.0 mi/8.0 hrs

west of Milford and near the Nevada border

Map 2.5, page 41

As with other ranges in the western Utah desert, the Mountain Home Range feels the tread of few feet other than small numbers of deer, elk, and wild horses. Isolation and general lack of water are two primary reasons that most people stay away. On the other hand, here lies an opportunity to travel terrain with virtually no indication of human interference once you leave the road. Head north from a cabin, across the bed of a spring's flow, ascending the gentle slope and hiking northwest up the drainage. Stay to the north side of the drainage as the going gets tougher. The hiking is easier on the slope of the ridge. Keep gaining altitude, traveling toward the top of the ridge. At a high point on the ridge the route drops into a saddle and then continues up the slope to the west. You'll reach the crest of the range. Hardy vegetation, the kind that likes to tear at skin (mountain mahogany, Mormon tea, shad scale), grows thicker, slowing your progress. Look for game trails that ease the frustration a bit. Finally the route emerges at the base of a limestone wall that marks the southern end of the main crest. From this end of the crest, there remains approximately 1.5 miles of hiking and scrambling. You'll eventually reach The Needle (the highest point in the Mountain Home Range at 9,480 feet, about 2,000 feet above the trailhead. Fir and pine, sturdy trees able to withstand the hard winds and arid climate, grow on the summit plateaus. The view is as-

tounding: mountains beyond mountains as far as the eye can see.

User groups: Hikers and dogs. No wheelchair access.

Permits: No permits are required. Parking and access are free.

Maps: For a USGS topographic map, ask for Lopers Spring. Contact the BLM for Wah Wah Mountains South, a 1:100,000 map very useful in finding the trailhead.

Directions: From Milford, take State Route 21 west 35 miles to the unmarked Pine Valley Road at Lime Point (approximately four miles past Wah Wah Summit). Turn south on Pine Valley Road. Drive south, following the road toward Hamlin Valley. After passing Sawtooth, turn north on the road to Lopers Spring. Beyond Lopers Spring four-wheel-drive vehicles are recommended. Go past Spike Hollow (see sign), and continue 1.25 miles to the turn to Lopers Cabin. Turn west here and continue for a quarter mile to the cabin.

Contact: BLM Cedar City Field Office, 176 East D. L. Sargent Drive, Cedar City, UT 84720, 435/586-2401.

16 WAH WAH POINT
5.0 mi/6.0 hrs

west of Milford in the Wah Wah Mountains

Map 2.5, page 41

As with so much of Utah's wilderness, especially in the western desert, there are no maintained trails in the Wah Wah Mountains. A compass, topo map, and water are necessities. The Wah Wah Mountains rank high among the least-seen, most-remote regions of western Utah. Numerous alkaline seeps, *wah wahs* to the Paiute Indians, lie in the surrounding desert. Lower slopes support grasses and sagebrush, while stands of piñon and juniper reside higher up. Groves of aspen, pine, and fir huddle on north-facing slopes where what little moisture that falls is held the longest. The hike up Corral Canyon to Wah Wah Point passes through these zones, and provides the quickest peek into these mountains. From the parking area, ascend the slope dotted with piñon and juniper on the north side of the canyon. Keep climbing. The route leads to a rocky point near the northern end of the main ridge. Once on the ridge, hike south 1.5 miles to where the crest of the Wah Wahs reaches the tree-clad summit of Wah Wah Point at 8,695 feet. If you have the time, extend the hike by traveling south along the crest of these mountains.

User groups: Hikers and dogs. No wheelchair access.

Permits: No permits are required. Parking and access are free.

Maps: For a USGS topographic map, ask for Sewing Machine Pass.

Directions: From Milford, take State Route 21 west 31.5 miles, about 1.5 miles past Wah Wah Summit. Turn south on the first dirt road that leads south after crossing the summit. Follow this road for two miles—until just before you cross Corral Canyon a second time—and park.

Contact: BLM Cedar City Field Office, 176 East D. L. Sargent Drive, Cedar City, UT 84720, 435/586-2401.

17 CENTRAL WAH WAH CREST
4.5 mi/4.0 hrs

west of Milford in the Wah Wah Mountains

Map 2.5, page 41

The ragged core of the central Wah Wahs offers great scenery and spectacular solitude. From the high point of the road, hike northeast through the trees to a rounded summit a half mile away. Don't look for a trail—you won't find any. From near the rounded summit, follow a north-south-running fence line north for another half mile to the next little summit. Between these summits an old fire burned away the vegetation, and the new growth sometimes shelters deer and a variety of birds. Continue to ascend the ridgeline, a relatively easy walk in a forest, toward the northwest and to an unnamed peak. This unassuming peak, at 9,393 feet, stands higher than any other point in the

Wah Wah Mountains. Your elevation gain: about 1,200 feet. Wah Peak rises to a point 10 feet lower about a quarter mile to the north. Check out the bristlecone pines rooted on a ridge that falls off to the east of Wah Peak. Some of these trees were likely growing when Socrates was spouting wisdom in ancient Greece.

User groups: Hikers and dogs. No wheelchair access.

Permits: No permits are required. Parking and access are free.

Maps: For USGS topographic maps, ask for Lamerdorf Peak and Sewing Machine Pass.

Directions: From Milford, take State Route 21 west for 24 miles, and turn south on a gravel road not far from mile marker 51. At 2.5 miles the road forks; take the west route. Travel approximately 13 miles to the high point of the road on the crest of the Wah Wah Mountains. Park here.

Contact: BLM Cedar City Field Office, 176 East D. L. Sargent Drive, Cedar City, UT 84720, 435/586-2401.

18 SOUTH CEDAR RIDGE TRAIL
20.0 mi/2–3 days

north of Richfield in Fishlake National Forest

Map 2.6, page 42

The name "Ridge" is misleading since the trail follows the bottom of this lovely red and white canyon along a year-round stream. The water pools in some places, drops over low waterfalls in others. You may get wet feet from the numerous stream crossings. Piñon, juniper, and large boulders accent the floor of the canyon, and the walls rise higher as you hike west. Twists and turns, narrows and overhangs all combine to keep your interest high. Many side canyons open enticingly, but quite a few are blocked by tall pour-offs. You will find ample places to set a camp at canyon mouths. The trail ends at Forest Service Road 096, after gaining about 2,100 feet in elevation, and you can turn around here for the 10 miles back to your vehicle. But you could also hike north and into Mill Canyon, dropping down Mill into South Cedar Ridge Canyon for a longer and even more interesting semi-loop. This entire area is under consideration for wilderness designation.

User groups: Hikers, dogs, and horses. No wheelchair access.

Permits: No permits are required. Parking and access are free.

Maps: For USGS topographic maps, ask for Richfield and White Pine Peak.

Directions: From I-70 between Richfield and Salina, take Exit 46 and drive one mile south. Turn west on North Bastian Lane, drive past the Vermilion Cemetery, and turn west on a dirt road that passes beneath I-70. Bear left under the power lines, then right at a fork to the end of the road at the mouth of South Cedar Ridge Canyon.

Contact: Fishlake National Forest, Fillmore Ranger District, 390 South Main Street, Fillmore, UT 84631, 435/743-5721.

19 LEAVITTS CANYON– CRAZY HOLLOW–CORN CREEK LOOP

18.0 mi/2–3 days

west of Richfield in Fishlake National Forest

Map 2.6, page 42

This is a beautiful backpacking loop in the Pahvant Mountains with lots to see and do, and plenty of water near lovely campsites. It does, however, involve about 3,500 feet of elevation gain. Three miles up the North Fork of Corn Creek, Leavitts Canyon opens to the west. Horse traffic has made the trail very easy to follow. Leavitts Spring provides a great campsite about halfway up the canyon. Climbing past the upper end of the canyon and Leavitts Peak, the trail grows much more obscure. Beyond the peak, watch for an old road, closed to vehicles, that leads to Forest Service Road 500. Follow 500 north for less than two miles to an overlook of the Devil's Armchair in Hell Hole Canyon. From here the trail continues

south down Crazy Hollow. You can take a side trip down into Hell Hole Canyon, which is filled with old mine shafts, but you won't find a trail. The walking in Crazy Hollow is pleasant, but the trail again grows obscure. When you meet Corn Creek, you may see the wreckage of a small plane. From the creek, head west through a colorful red canyon, eventually returning to the starting point. An accurate topographic map will add much to your adventure and your peace of mind.

User groups: Hikers, dogs, and horses. No wheelchair access.

Permits: No permits are required. Parking and access are free.

Maps: For USGS topographic maps, ask for Sunset Peak and Joseph Peak.

Directions: From Kanosh on State Route 133, turn east on 300 South. The drive continues on Forest Service Road 106 about five miles to just before Adelaide Campground. Turn north on a four-wheel-drive track up the North Fork of Corn Creek for .25 mile, and park.

Contact: Fishlake National Forest, Fillmore Ranger District, 390 South Main Street, Fillmore, UT 84631, 435/743-5721.

20 COVE CREEK TRAIL

14.5 mi one-way/1–2 days

near the junction of I-70 and I-15

Map 2.6, page 42

This relatively high-elevation backpacking trip takes you past the fascinating rock formations of "Little Bryce" in Trail Canyon, and offers pleasant campsites almost all the way. After a start down an old jeep road, the trail leads south into shady forests and open parks, where it remains for most of the journey. After about four miles, the trail splits to cross Butterfly Flat. The east fork is the more direct route. Near the midpoint of the hike, a high point of about 10,000 feet is reached with wonderful views of the Tushar Mountains and westward across the Wah Wah Mountains, Pine Valley Mountains, and the desert lands of Utah. At 13 miles, you'll reach Trail Canyon, so plan on taking some time to explore "Little Bryce." The trail ends at Indian Creek and Manderfield Reservoirs on Forest Service Road 119 about 11 miles off US 91. Leave a second vehicle here unless you want to make the hike back.

User groups: Hikers, dogs, and horses. No wheelchair access.

Permits: No permits are required. Parking and access are free.

Maps: For USGS topographic maps, ask for Cove Fort, Pole Canyon, and Mount Belknap.

Directions: From near the junction of I-70 and I-15, take the first exit off 70 and drive north on US 91 a short distance to Cove Fort. Turn east on the road across from the historical marker, and drive back under I-70. Four miles from Cove Fort, turn south on Forest Service Road 136 and continue a short distance to the first parking spot.

Contact: Fishlake National Forest, Beaver Ranger District, 575 South Main Street, Beaver, UT 84713, 435/438-2436.

21 FREMONT INDIAN STATE PARK LOOP
5.0 mi/4.0 hrs

southwest of Richfield

Map 2.6, page 42

When I-70 was laid down through lovely Clear Creek Canyon, builders discovered the largest Fremont Indian village ever known. To make room for the road, the village was moved and preserved as well as possible in the state park. After you tour the museum, follow the wheelchair-accessible Show Me Rock Art Trail for a look at some of the artistic endeavors of the Fremont people. From this loop trail, the Discovery Trail branches off north, gaining altitude via steps, to more rock art. This trail can be hiked back to the museum, completing a loop, or used as a connection to Forest Service Trail 365. Trail 365 leads north for about a mile to the rim of Clear Creek Canyon. Trail 365 also has a connecting trail (Trail 364) that

heads westward to Trail 363, which climbs four miles up to Big Bench. Big Bench is a pleasant, extensive, virtually treeless flat—a nice place to set up camp for a night. Trail 363 also can be followed down to the parking area, where it joins the Alma Christensen Trail (an interpretive trail), completing what may be called the Fremont Indian State Park Loop.

User groups: Hikers. Wheelchair-accessible for a short distance.

Permits: The park charges a day-use fee of $5 that includes the museum. The camping fee, if you camp in the park, is $11 per site. Reservations for all Utah state parks may be arranged by calling 800/322-3770.

Maps: For a USGS topographic map, ask for Marysvale Canyon. A park brochure, available at the visitors center, describes the trails.

Directions: From Richfield, take I-70 south 23 miles. Take Exit 17 for a short drive north to Fremont Indian State Park.

Contact: Fremont Indian State Park, 11550 West Clear Creek Canyon Road, Sevier, UT 84766, 435/527-4631. Fishlake National Forest, Fillmore Ranger District, 390 South Main Street, Fillmore, UT 84631, 435/743-5721.

22 JOE LOTT CREEK TRAIL
12.0 mi/1–2 days

southwest of Richfield

Map 2.6, page 42

This is a pleasant but uphill walk through a forested canyon with views of the geological formations of the Castle Rock area. With so many truly amazing natural rock sculptures in Utah, this hike ranks low if that's what you want to see. But it's an easily accessible escape into a quiet region. The route runs south from the Castle Rock Campground, which is administered by Fremont Indian State Park. At the start, you'll hike through piñon and juniper, past clumps of sagebrush, beneath a few cottonwoods, as you climb steadily uphill. The trail wanders back and forth across Joe Lott Creek. After three miles, three smaller creeks converge, and the trail follows the east fork, gaining altitude more quickly. Aspens and firs shade possible camping spots at several places. With an overall elevation gain nearing 3,000 feet, the terrain becomes more and more alpine as the trail continues. The trail ends at Forest Service Road 113, allowing a one-way hike with a vehicle at both ends.

User groups: Hikers and dogs. No wheelchair access.

Permits: No permits are required. Parking and access are free.

Maps: For USGS topographic maps, ask for Marysvale Canyon and Mount Brigham.

Directions: From Richfield, take I-70 south 23 miles. Take Exit 17 for a 1.5-mile drive south to Castle Rock Campground.

Contact: Fishlake National Forest, Beaver Ranger District, 575 South Main Street, Beaver, UT 84713, 435/438-2436.

23 DELANO PEAK
10.0 mi/1–2 days

east of Beaver in Fishlake National Forest

Map 2.6, page 42

For a peak surpassing 12,000 feet, Delano ranks among the easiest summits in Utah. The route starts on Trail 175 and heads north for 2.3 miles to where it meets the Skyline National Recreation Trail/Trail 225. Turn west on the Skyline Trail. After a half mile on this trail, a ridge rises to the northeast toward Mount Holly. This ridge can be followed to the summit of Mount Holly at 11,985 feet. The ridge connecting Mount Holly and Delano Peak, rough and somewhat steep in places, is approximately two miles long. Rocky cliffs fall away steeply on the northeast side of the saddle between Holly and Delano, and provide habitat for a herd of mountain goats. Delano Peak, at 12,173 feet, rises higher than anything within 100 miles, creating a mighty fine view of the ranges of the Great Basin to the west, the southern end of the Wasatch Mountains to the north (on a clear day), the Pine Valley

Mountains to the southwest, and the old volcanic peaks of the Tushar Mountains, of which Delano is one. Since much of the route to the top of Delano travels above timberline, you'll enjoy panoramic views for much of the hike. Winter dumps loads of snow on Delano, making a winter or early-spring ski ascent highly inviting. Skiers with moderate skills should be able to ski to within a few hundred yards of the summit.

User groups: Hikers, dogs, and cross-country skiers. No wheelchair access.

Permits: No permits are required. Parking and access are free.

Maps: For USGS topographic maps, ask for Delano Peak and Shelly Baldy Peak.

Directions: From Beaver on I-15, take State Route 153 about 18 miles east to the Elk Meadows Resort. Continue past the resort on 153 for one mile to the trailhead on the east side of the road. It is not well marked, so keep an eye open.

Contact: Fishlake National Forest, Beaver Ranger District, 575 South Main Street, Beaver, UT 84713, 435/438-2436.

24 SKYLINE NATIONAL RECREATION TRAIL
10.0 mi one-way/1–2 days

east of Beaver in Fishlake National Forest

Map 2.6, page 42

The Skyline National Recreation Trail/Trail 225 follows the crest of the Tushar Range, averaging well over 10,000 feet in altitude and providing views of forested mountains rolling away to the east and west. Put this on your list of overnight hikes—you'll be glad you did. The trail can be hiked from either end. From the southern end, at Big Flat, the route runs north, passing City Creek Peak, then bending west below Lake Peak for an elevation gain of about 1,000 feet. It terminates at Big John Flat on the northern end. Big John Flat lies northeast of Beaver, about five miles north of State Route 153 on Forest Service Road 123. Several trails provide "escape routes" from the Skyline Trail if you want to cut the hike short. From north of Big Flat you can, for instance, drop off the Skyline Trail via the City Creek Canyon Trail, and end up at City Creek Campground. Or follow Trail 175 where it leaves the Skyline Trail west of Lake Peak, taking it down to Elk Meadows. Check a map for details on these alternate routes.

User groups: Hikers, dogs, horses, and mountain bikes. No wheelchair access.

Permits: No permits are required. Parking and access are free.

Maps: For USGS topographic maps, ask for Delano Peak and Shelly Baldy Peak.

Directions: From Beaver, take State Route 153 east 23 miles, past Elk Meadows Ski Area and Puffer Lake to Big Flat. The trailhead lies a couple of hundred yards east of the start of Big Flat.

Contact: Fishlake National Forest, Beaver Ranger District, 575 South Main Street, Beaver, UT 84713, 435/438-2436.

25 CITY CREEK CANYON TRAIL
9.0 mi/6.0 hrs

east of Beaver in Fishlake National Forest

Map 2.6, page 42

The City Creek Canyon Trail gains altitude constantly along its 4.5 miles from City Creek Campground to the Skyline National Recreation Trail. The first two-thirds of the route follows the creek through a dense forest of fir, spruce, pine, cedar, and oak. Then a long series of switchbacks takes you steeply up the final leg to the Skyline Trail. The switchbacks ascend a slope that faces southeast with views across the Sevier Valley. As an access to the Skyline Trail, this works. But it works even better as a great escape route from the Skyline Trail if you want a day hike with excellent views of the surrounding mountains. Access via the Skyline Trail, however, adds approximately two miles to the 4.5-mile one-way distance, and you need a vehicle at both ends.

User groups: Hikers, dogs, horses, and mountain bikes. No wheelchair access.

Permits: No permits are required. Parking and access are free.

Maps: For a USGS topographic map, ask for Delano Peak.

Directions: From Beaver, take State Route 153 east 23 miles, past Elk Meadows Ski Area and Puffer Lake to Big Flat. The trailhead lies a couple of hundred yards east of the start of Big Flat.

Contact: Fishlake National Forest, Beaver Ranger District, 575 South Main Street, Beaver, UT 84713, 435/438-2436.

Chapter 3

COURTESY OF THE NATIONAL PARK SERVICE

Central Utah

With Salt Lake City on the north end and Capitol Reef National Park on the south, the central region of the state, more than any other region, typifies the great diversity of Utah. You can break camp beside a mountain lake rimmed in evergreens, hike to your vehicle, drive a few hours, hike in, and set camp deep within a treeless sandstone canyon. Not a bad way to spend a day . . . but why rush? Central Utah asks for a lot of your time.

The Wasatch Range serves as a backdrop to the east, and the Great Salt Lake lies to the northwest of Salt Lake City. The city began in 1847 as a settlement of early Mormons. Today it's Utah's largest city, attracting numerous tourists to its cultural and historical sites. They head most often for Temple Square, the heart of the Mormon Church. All roads, it seems, lead to Temple Square, and along them you'll find hotels ranging from inexpensive to elegant. You'll also find excellent restaurants that all share the requirement that you empty your first glass of beer before they'll serve you a second.

From the southeast edge of the metropolitan area of Salt Lake City, a trio of federally designated wilderness areas (Twin Peaks, Lone Peak, and Mount Olympus) contain some of the best of the Wasatch Range. Routes to the highest points and to lakes settled in granite basins are described in this chapter. Plan to spend some time, as well, further south at Timpanogos Cave National Monument, and in the Mount Timpanogos Wilderness and Mount Nebo Wilderness. You can drive the Nebo Scenic Loop Byway to view the mountain beauty from road level, then climb to Nebo's 12,000-foot summit, the highest point in the Wasatch Range. You'll find Nebo, and many other trails, waiting in the Uinta National Forest.

East and southeast of Nebo lies the Manti–La Sal National Forest, and south of that the Fishlake National Forest. You'll find hundreds of miles of maintained trails in the forests, tree-shaded trails that lead to awesome views from high peaks and peaceful campsites by sheltered lakes. You may see deer or elk, black bears or mountain lions, and you may catch fish in the lakes and streams. The left fork of Huntington National Recreation Trail in the Manti–La Sal, for instance, will take you past waterfalls and pools brimming with trout. In the Fishlake National Forest, Fish Lake itself can be a base for numerous hikes, including the Lakeshore National Recreation Trail, as well as a base for excellent mountain biking.

Continuing south you reach the northern section of the Dixie National Forest, given its name by Mormon pioneers who found that cotton, as in the real "Dixie," grew well in these parts. Here the land grows more arid, the trees often widely spaced and smaller. You're entering the transition zone between basin country and the Colorado Plateau. Talk about diversity! You can hike up to the Boulder Top Plateau, Utah's highest plateau, and discover small lakes rich in fish, or wander aimlessly along the Slickrock Trail in sandstone splendor.

And speaking of sandstone, before leaving central Utah you still have to see Capitol Reef National Park. Eons ago when an uplift created the San Rafael Swell of eastern Utah, another uplift squeezed out the Waterpocket Fold, named for its tendency to trap water in small pools in the slickrock. The Fold extends over a distance of approximately 100 miles from Thousand Lake Mountain in the north to Lake Powell in the south. Here you'll find massive, artfully colored cliffs, graceful spires, deep and convoluted canyons, and all manner of sandstone majesty. The best of it is preserved in the park. Early explorers found their way blocked by the Fold, comparing it to a reef blocking passage by sea. Rounded domes of the "reef" reminded them of the Capitol Dome in Washington, DC, and thus the park was named. Trails both short and long will lead you to the best of the best the park has to offer.

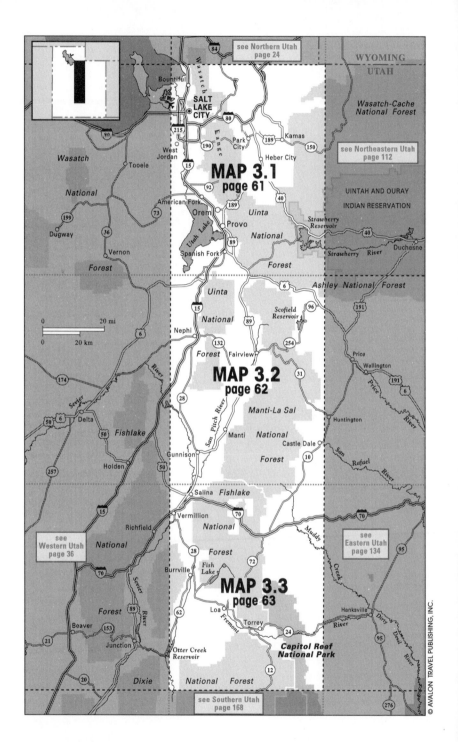

Map 3.1

Hikes 1–31
Pages 64–78

3.2

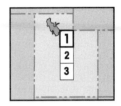

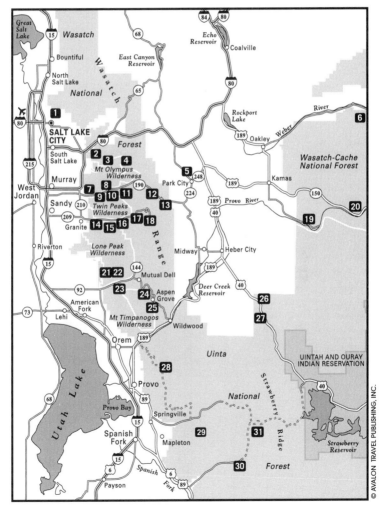

© AVALON TRAVEL PUBLISHING, INC.

Map 3.2

Hikes 32–53
Pages 78–87

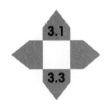

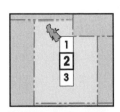

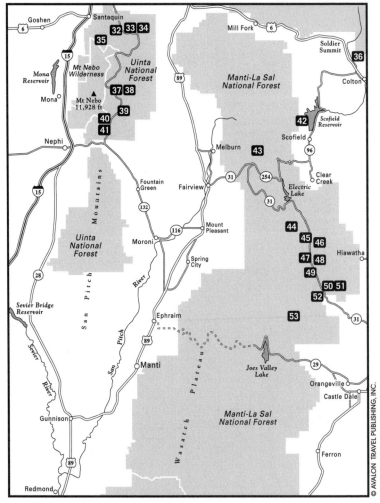

Map 3.3

Hikes 54–94
Pages 88–107

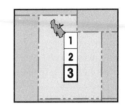

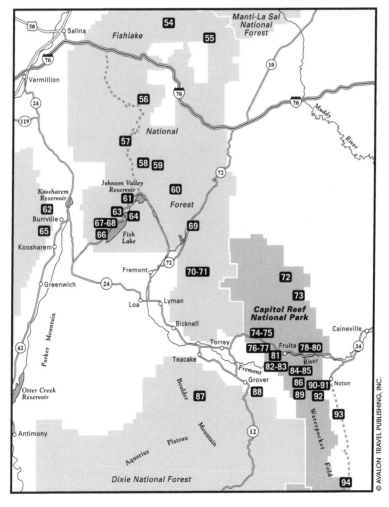

1 CITY CREEK CANYON TRAIL
12.0 mi/1.0–8.0 hrs

near the north end of Salt Lake City

Map 3.1, page 61

City Creek Canyon is owned and managed by Salt Lake City as a watershed until it enters national forest land on its upper end. If you're stuck in Salt Lake City and need a quick break on a trail, this is the one. You can turn back easily from any point whenever you choose. For the first half mile, the route is a paved road paralleling an old jeep track. You're following City Creek, with its occasional pools of water, through a shadowy forest, and there is very little elevation gain. About two miles up the trail you'll enter a small meadow, your last chance to fill up water bottles if you're going farther. At approximately three miles, the trail starts to climb, leaving the lush vegetation of the lower creek and ascending all the way to City Creek Meadows, an elevation gain of about 2,100 feet. The going is easy before the climbing starts, making the lower section of the trail a fine hike with kids. If you're headed for the meadows, you'll find the trail grows less distinct, and an accurate topographical map will come in mighty handy. The meadows lie below the crest of the Wasatch Range, and continuing up to the ridge above the meadows will give you a commanding view of this region. No overnight trips are allowed, but the meadow makes an excellent spot to have lunch before turning around for the 6-mile hike back.

User groups: Hikers. Dogs and horses are prohibited. Wheelchair accessible for the first half mile.

Permits: Permits are not required, and no fees are charged. Vehicles are sometimes allowed past the gate with a permit from the city if a reservation is made at least 24 hours in advance.

Maps: For USGS topographic maps, ask for Mountain Dell and Fort Douglas.

Directions: From Temple Square in the heart of Salt Lake City, take North Temple east to B Street and turn north. B Street turns into Bonneville Boulevard, which ends at Canyon Road. Canyon Road ends about 100 yards north at a gate.

Contact: Salt Lake City Department of Public Utilities, 801/535-7911, for permission to use the road; Wasatch-Cache National Forest, Salt Lake Ranger District, 6944 South 3000 East, Salt Lake City, UT 84121, 801/733-2660.

2 NEFFS CANYON TRAIL
7.0 mi/7.0 hrs

just east of Salt Lake City in the Mount Olympus Wilderness

Map 3.1, page 61

With homes so near, this little-used trail offers a surprisingly quick and quiet escape into a designated wilderness. The route immediately enters the wilderness, following an abandoned jeep road for about a third of the hike. You'll soon enter an area of tall Gambel oaks to cross a stream on the first of two footbridges. After

Neffs Canyon Trail

the bridges, the path grows more faint, passes through a meadow, and climbs up the wall at the head of Neffs Canyon. The trail ends after 3.5 miles at a notch in the ridge above the canyon. With accurate topographic maps, Neffs Canyon could be the start of several days of exploring the Mount Olympus Wilderness.

User groups: Hikers and dogs. No wheelchair access.

Permits: No permits are required unless a group has 10 or more members with plans to stay overnight. Parking and access are free.

Maps: For USGS topographic maps, ask for Sugar House and Mount Aire. Trails Illustrated's Wasatch Front/Strawberry Valley covers the area.

Directions: From Wasatch Boulevard in Salt Lake City, drive east on 3800 South. Turn south at the stop sign onto Parkview Drive. Take this street a short distance to Parkview Terrace and turn back east. The second street heading south leads quickly to White Park and the end of the road, and the trailhead.

Contact: Wasatch-Cache National Forest, Salt Lake Ranger District, 6944 South 3000 East, Salt Lake City, UT 84121, 801/733-2660.

🖸 DESOLATION TRAIL
17.0 mi/2–4 days

just east of Salt Lake City in the Mount Olympus Wilderness

Map 3.1, page 61

If you want to experience the full extent of the Mount Olympus Wilderness, pack up and head out on the Desolation Trail. A well-maintained path, the trail climbs out of Mill Canyon on a series of relatively easy switchbacks and, in less than two miles, reaches an overlook of the city. From there it meanders up a canyon to a small saddle. Rest here because a long series of switchbacks lies between the saddle and the next pass. From the pass, the trail runs up and down on its way to Dog Lake just outside the eastern boundary of the wilderness. Unlike most Utah mountain lakes, Dog Lake lies in the middle of a forested area instead of a cirque. From

Dog Lake it's fairly easy going to Desolation Lake. Desolation Lake sits in a picturesque mountain cirque and serves as a perfect terminus to a long hike after gaining about 3,600 feet of elevation. From Desolation, you can retrace your steps to your vehicle, or choose from a couple of shorter trails that lead south into Big Cottonwood Canyon. If you choose the latter option, it helps to have a second vehicle.

User groups: Hikers. No wheelchair access.

Permits: No permits are required unless a group has 10 or more members with plans to stay overnight. Parking and access are free.

Maps: For USGS topographic maps, ask for Sugar House, Mount Aire, and Park City West. Trails Illustrated's Wasatch Front/Strawberry Valley covers the area.

Directions: From Wasatch Boulevard in Salt Lake City, drive east on 3800 South into Mill Creek Canyon for a total of 3.5 miles to the trailhead on the south side of the road.

Contact: Wasatch-Cache National Forest, Salt Lake Ranger District, 6944 South 3000 East, Salt Lake City, UT 84121, 801/733-2660.

🖪 ALEXANDER BASIN TRAIL
3.0 mi/4.0 hrs
just east of Salt Lake City in a non-wilderness intrusion into the east side of the Mount Olympus Wilderness

Map 3.1, page 61

Alexander Basin is a lovely alpine basin with a trailhead just a few minutes from Salt Lake City. For those reasons it tends to draw a crowd. The trail is well-maintained, and the going rates as relatively easy for anyone experiencing a brief brush with fitness. From the trailhead, parallel the road northwest for a couple hundred feet, then turn southwest and begin to ascend. There are several switchbacks in the first mile, but they are laid out well, and not too demanding. After approximately one mile, at a junction of trails, you'll reach the edge of the basin, about 1,300 feet above the trailhead. Stay on the main trail for another half mile or so to reach the heart of Alexander Basin. You'll hike over several rocky places and around stands of spruce and fir. You'll also find many appealing campsites if an overnight stay is on your mind. By midsummer you're unlikely to find water, so plan accordingly.

User groups: Hikers and dogs. No wheelchair access.

Permits: No permits are required. Parking and access are free.

Maps: For a USGS topographic map, ask for Mount Aire. Trails Illustrated's Wasatch Front/Strawberry Valley covers the area.

Directions: From Wasatch Boulevard in Salt Lake City, drive east on 3800 South into Mill Creek Canyon for a total of 8.5 miles to the trailhead on the south side of the road.

Contact: Wasatch-Cache National Forest, Salt Lake Ranger District, 6944 South 3000 East, Salt Lake City, UT 84121, 801/733-2660.

5 RAIL TRAIL
25 mi one-way/1.0–10.0 hrs

starting in Park City

Map 3.1, page 61

Following the old Union Pacific railroad bed, the Rail Trail eases slowly downhill all the way from Park City to Echo Reservoir, along the foot of the eastern slopes of the Wasatch Range. This is an excellent route for bicycles. The highway runs nearby. Three additional trailheads along the way allow you to shorten the trip of you wish, but you can always turn back to Park City at any time. If you're hanging around Park City, it's a great way to get out and get some exercise.

User groups: Hikers, dogs on leashes only, and mountain bikes. No wheelchair access.

Permits: No permits are required. Parking and access are free.

Maps: For USGS topographic maps, ask for Park City East, Wanship, and Coalville.

Directions: From Kearns Boulevard in Park City, turn south on Bonanza and make a quick left onto Prospector. The trailhead lies on Prospector behind Brackman Brother's Bagel

Restaurant. Park near the trailhead at Sun Creek condos.

Contact: Mountain Trails Foundation, P.O. Box 754, Park City, UT 84060, 435/649-6839.

6 DRY FORK CREEK TRAIL
7.0 mi/6.0 hrs

east of Oakley in the Wasatch-Cache National Forest

Map 3.1, page 61

If you like mountain-lake fishing and subalpine scenery, you'll love this hike. If you have time, plan on spending a couple of days up here. About a quarter mile from the trailhead, you'll have to wade the creek, which may run high in midsummer, for the first time. Then you'll follow the creek for about a mile and a half to a meadow where the trail begins to ascend a slope to the southeast. Lots more climbing, and you'll eventually reach Round Lake, the first of three wet jewels. About a half mile southeast lies Sand Lake, and beyond that, Fish Lake. The best campsites are at Fish Lake, but the best fishing is usually in Round Lake, which is stocked with trout and grayling.

User groups: Hikers, dogs, and horses. No wheelchair access.

Permits: No permits are required. Parking and access are free.

Maps: For a USGS topographical map, ask for Whitney Reservoir. Trails Illustrated's High Uintas Wilderness covers the area.

Directions: From Oakley, take Canyon Road north. There may be a sign reading "Weber Canyon, Smith and Morehouse." Take this road for 19.0 miles, past the turnoff to Smith and Morehouse Reservoir. Bear right before crossing the Weber River, then bear left after passing Holiday Park. Cross Dry Fork Creek and park at the trailhead.

Contact: Wasatch-Cache National Forest, Kamas Ranger District, 50 East Center Street, P. O. Box 68, Kamas, UT 84036, 435/783-4338.

7 MOUNT OLYMPUS
6.0 mi/8.0 hrs

just southeast of Salt Lake City in the Mount Olympus Wilderness

Map 3.1, page 61

This popular trail climbs right out of Salt Lake into designated wilderness. If you want a bird's eye view of the city, take this hike. You'll also get a view of the Great Salt Lake, and up and down the Wasatch Front. But you're going to have to suck up some thinning air on the way. The total elevation gain is a bit more than 4,000 feet. From the trailhead, you'll climb switchbacks through a forest of oak and juniper into Tolcat Canyon with its year-round stream. Continuing east, the trail ascends more switchbacks with the bold west ridge of Mount Olympus to the north. Reaching a saddle after almost three miles, you'll find a few campsites shaded by Douglas firs. An overnighter here is a fine idea after all that climbing. The summit, reached via a rocky couloir, is about a quarter mile and 600 feet of elevation gain from the saddle. You'll need to use your hands in a few places, but the going is relatively easy. From the head of the couloir, the top of Mount Olympus (9,025 feet) stands about 200 feet away across a boulder field.

User groups: Hikers and dogs. No wheelchair access.

Permits: No permits are required unless a group has 10 or more members with plans to stay overnight. Parking and access are free.

Maps: For USGS topographic maps, ask for Sugar House and Mount Aire. Trails Illustrated's Wasatch Front/Strawberry Valley covers the area.

Directions: The trailhead stands just to the east of Wasatch Boulevard on the east side of Salt Lake City, near the intersection with 5700 South, about 2.5 miles north of the Big Cottonwood Canyon intersection.

Contact: Wasatch-Cache National Forest, Salt Lake Ranger District, 6944 South 3000 East, Salt Lake City, UT 84121, 801/733-2660.

8 MILL B NORTH FORK TRAIL TO MOUNT RAYMOND
8.0 mi/8.0 hrs

just southeast of Salt Lake City in the Mount Olympus Wilderness

Map 3.1, page 61

For someone semi-fit and ready to prove it, this relatively challenging day hike climbs steadily but unhurriedly to the summit of Mount Raymond for a splendid view of the steep western slopes of the Wasatch Front. The trail starts up a few switchbacks, but soon descends to Mill B North Fork Creek. It follows the creek for another quarter mile, passing through a stand of tall firs, then starts uphill near a pile of rocks. It then climbs the rest of the way, into a forest of fir, spruce, and aspen. You will have no difficulty staying on the obvious footpath, and several overlooks offer lunch stops and places to turn back if the going gets too tough. At 3.5 miles, the trail meets the Desolation Trail at a junction. Turn north on this trail. There is no maintained path to the summit. Mount Raymond is an obvious landmark, and when it stands due west of the trail, leave the trail and ascend the ridge on the northwest side of the summit. Then it's an easy ridge climb to the summit. At 10,241 feet, Mount Raymond offers a panoramic view: the Great Salt Lake to the west, the Uinta Mountains to the east, the Wasatch Range north and south.

User groups: Hikers. No wheelchair access.

Permits: No permits are required unless a group has 10 or more members with plans to stay overnight. Parking and access are free.

Maps: For a USGS topographic map, ask for Mount Aire. Trails Illustrated's Wasatch Front/Strawberry Valley covers the area.

Directions: From Wasatch Boulevard in Salt Lake City, drive east on 7200 South into Big Cottonwood Canyon for a total of 4.5 miles to the trailhead on the north side of the road. The trailhead stands at the end of an S curve in the road.

Contact: Wasatch-Cache National Forest, Salt Lake Ranger District, 6944 South 3000 East, Salt Lake City, UT 84121, 801/733-2660.

9 BROADS FORK TRAIL TO TWIN PEAKS

9.0 mi/10.0 hrs

southeast of Salt Lake City in the Twin Peaks Wilderness

Map 3.1, page 61

The almost identical Twin Peaks stand at the west end of the long, east-west Cottonwood Ridge, the ridge that separates Big and Little Cottonwood Canyons. These peaks also stand at the end of an arduous climb. Broads Fork Trail heads south, soon joining a creek to follow it up to the head of a canyon where the path disappears. The wall at the head of the canyon is steep and rocky, and much of that rock is loose. An unmaintained trail, sometimes visible, leads east from the end of the canyon, crosses the creek, and heads uphill, gaining about 1,000 feet to a little basin that makes a great place to camp. The awesome north face of Dromedary Peak rears up to the east. Continuing on to a saddle, you can choose your route for the last quarter mile to the 11,330-foot east summit of the Twins. If snow remains, which it often does, abandon the final ascent unless you're geared up for and comfortable climbing in such conditions.

User groups: Hikers. No wheelchair access.

Permits: No permits are required unless a group has 10 or more members with plans to stay overnight. Parking and access are free.

Maps: Trails Illustrated's Wasatch Front/Strawberry Valley covers the area. For USGS topographic maps, ask for Mount Aire and Dromedary Peak.

Directions: From Wasatch Boulevard in Salt Lake City, drive east on 7200 South into Big Cottonwood Canyon for a total of 4.5 miles to the trailhead on the south side of the road.

Contact: Wasatch-Cache National Forest, Salt Lake Ranger District, 6944 South 3000 East, Salt Lake City, UT 84121, 801/733-2660.

10 LAKE BLANCHE TRAIL

5.0 mi/4.0 hrs

southeast of Salt Lake City in the Twin Peaks Wilderness

Map 3.1, page 61

Although the climbing is steady at first and steep at the end, it is far from overpowering (about 2,400 feet in elevation gain), making this hike into a beautiful basin very popular. Surrounded by jagged spires and accented by waterfalls, the little lake is a can't-miss trip for enthusiasts in the area and a prized overnight destination. The trail follows the gurgling waters of Mill B South Fork, crosses a footbridge early on, and eventually begins to climb. You'll hike through rock outcroppings and shady stands of trees for 2.5 miles before arriving at the lake. Lake Blanche shares this basin with Lakes Lillian and Florence, all close together and all holding the promise of fish to catch. Stay on the north side of Blanche, the highest of the three, to easily reach the other two little bodies of water. Take care to leave no trace at the fragile campsites around the lakes.

User groups: Hikers. No wheelchair access.

Permits: No permits are required unless a group has 10 or more members with plans to stay overnight. Parking and access are free.

Maps: For USGS topographic maps, ask for Mount Aire and Dromedary Peak. Trails Illustrated's Wasatch Front/Strawberry Valley covers the area.

Directions: From Wasatch Boulevard in Salt Lake City, drive east on 7200 South into Big Cottonwood Canyon for a total of about 4.5 miles. At an S curve in the road, head south for .3 miles to the trailhead.

Contact: Wasatch-Cache National Forest, Salt Lake Ranger District, 6944 South 3000 East, Salt Lake City, UT 84121, 801/733-2660.

11 MINERAL FORK TRAIL

9.0 mi/7.0 hrs

southeast of Salt Lake City just east of the Twin Peaks Wilderness

Map 3.1, page 61

For the first three miles, from a big gate currently blocking all vehicular traffic, this route is an old road to the Wasatch Mine. It's not a great "trail," but it's easy to follow, and it makes for a good start if you're new to hiking. After several switchbacks, the road arrives at a commanding overlook of Big Cottonwood Canyon to the north. From the Wasatch Mine, if energy and interest remain high, a long series of switchbacks lead 1.5 miles to the Regulator Johnson Mine. A scramble to the pass about 200 feet above this mine will likely leave you breathless. But it will also give you a great view over your entire route.

User groups: Hikers, cross-country skiers, and mountain bikes. No wheelchair access.

Permits: No permits are required. Parking and access are free.

Maps: For USGS topographic maps, ask for Mount Aire and Dromedary Peak. Trails Illustrated's Wasatch Front/Strawberry Valley covers the area.

Directions: From Wasatch Boulevard in Salt Lake City, drive east on 7200 South into Big Cottonwood Canyon for a total of about six miles to the trailhead on the south side of the road.

Contact: Wasatch-Cache National Forest, Salt Lake Ranger District, 6944 South 3000 East, Salt Lake City, UT 84121, 801/733-2660.

12 DAYS FORK TRAIL TO FLAGSTAFF PEAK
7.5 mi/7.0 hrs

southeast of Salt Lake City just east of the Twin Peaks Wilderness

Map 3.1, page 61

Beginning as a jeep road from Spruces Campground, this route climbs briskly to a pretty basin with forested slopes all around. From this basin, the climbing starts again. The trail passes the remnants of several old mining operations to eventually flatten out into an alpine bowl with steep sides. This is a good place to rest up for the steep ascent to the crest of Cottonwood Ridge. From the ridge you might want to enjoy the sweeping view of the Wasatch Range, and turn around. But Flagstaff Peak, at 10,530

feet, beckons from the west. If the ground is bare, a faint footpath leads to the top, but snow often lingers, even into July. The route is not easy, and requires a bit of semi-technical scrambling over steep, rocky terrain. The summit is about 3,200 feet above the trailhead.

User groups: Hikers and cross-country skiers. No wheelchair access.

Permits: No permits are required. Parking and access are free.

Maps: For USGS topographic maps, ask for Mount Aire and Dromedary Peak. Trails Illustrated's Wasatch Front/Strawberry Valley covers the area.

Directions: From Wasatch Boulevard in Salt Lake City, drive east on 7200 South into Big Cottonwood Canyon 10 miles to the Spruces Campground.

Contact: Wasatch-Cache National Forest, Salt Lake Ranger District, 6944 South 3000 East, Salt Lake City, UT 84121, 801/733-2660.

13 BRIGHTON LAKES LOOP
3.0 mi/3.0 hrs

southeast of Salt Lake City at the end of Big Cottonwood Canyon

Map 3.1, page 61

If you want a walk into the depths of true wilderness, this probably won't satisfy you. But it's an easy hike in the woods to spectacular scenery including several beautiful mountain lakes. Nothing about this trail should intimidate a hiker. Starting from the parking lot at Mount Majestic Lodge, take the wide trail southwest a short distance to a road. Turn left, and take a few steps to a trailhead that directs you toward Brighton Lakes and Lake Mary. Climbing gently up a wooded slope, you'll soon get your first view, this one of the mountains around Brighton. Just past the overlook, a trail sign indicates the direction to Twin Lakes. On the ridge above Lake Mary's northeastern shore, the trail turns north, wandering through trees and boulders, to Twin Lakes (which, unfortunately, are no longer twins, as they were made into one with the building of a dam).

The lake is about two miles from the trailhead. From there, the trail drops down to picturesque Silver Lake, where a boardwalk leads to the road for the half-mile walk back to the starting point.

User groups: Hikers and cross-country skiers. No wheelchair access.

Permits: No permits are required. Parking and access are free.

Maps: For a USGS topographic map, ask for Brighton. Trails Illustrated's Wasatch Front/Strawberry Valley covers the area.

Directions: From Wasatch Boulevard in Salt Lake City, drive east on 7200 South into Big Cottonwood Canyon for a total of 15 miles to the Brighton Ski Area.

Contact: Wasatch-Cache National Forest, Salt Lake Ranger District, 6944 South 3000 East, Salt Lake City, UT 84121, 801/733-2660.

🔢14 RED PINE TRAIL
7.0 mi/6.0 hrs

southeast of Salt Lake City in the Lone Peak Wilderness

Map 3.1, page 61

Here is the best access to the northern end of the Lone Peak Wilderness, and a pleasant hike to a couple of beautiful and popular mountain lakes. Although it's a fine day hike, it's worthy of consideration as an overnighter. For the first mile, the trail is an old jeep road, a pathway shared with the hike up the White Pine Trail. Then, after crossing White Pine Fork Creek on a footbridge, Red Pine Trail traverses a ridge and enters Red Pine Canyon where it starts to climb. If you don't have adequate water at this point, you might start wishing you did. The trail doesn't meet the creek in Red Pine Canyon for another 1.5 miles. To compensate for lack of water, there are splendid views of the canyon you're ascending. At 2.5 miles in from the trailhead, the trail to Maybird Gulch leaves to the west, crossing the creek on another footbridge. You'll stay on the Red Pine Trail, and from here the last mile passes swiftly. Soon you're looking down at Lower

Red Pine Lake, nestled in a forest just below tree line. The trail circles the lake and numerous excellent campsites. Remember to camp at least 200 feet from the water. From the southeast corner of the lower lake, a fainter but easy-to-follow track leads up to Upper Red Pine Lake, tucked neatly into a small cirque above tree line. At this point you'll have gained about 2,000 feet in elevation overall. It is possible to scramble with some difficulty through a notch high in Red Canyon and over the ridge separating Red Pine from White Pine, and complete a perfectly satisfying loop.

User groups: Hikers. No wheelchair access.

Permits: No permits are required. Parking and access are free.

Maps: For a USGS topographic map, ask for Dromedary Peak. Trails Illustrated's Wasatch Front/Strawberry Valley covers the area.

Directions: In Salt Lake City, Wasatch Boulevard and 9400 South meet at a Y junction at the mouth of Little Cottonwood Canyon. From the Y, drive up Little Cottonwood Canyon 5.5 miles, one mile past Tanner Flat Campground, to the trailhead on the south side of the road.

Contact: Uinta National Forest, Pleasant Grove Ranger District, 390 North 100 East, Pleasant Grove, UT 84062, 801/342-5240.

🔢15 WHITE PINE TRAIL
9.0 mi/8.0 hrs

southeast of Salt Lake City and just east of the Lone Peak Wilderness

Map 3.1, page 61

White Pine Canyon exemplifies the beauty of a glacially carved valley bordered by deftly cut ridges. An abandoned road makes for easy hiking, despite the elevation gain of 2,500 feet, all the way to White Pine Lake. After the first mile, shared with the Red Pine Trail, the White Pine Trail switchbacks up to a meadow, crosses the meadow, and continues up gentle switchbacks to cross a ridge and drop into White Pine Lake. Set in a rocky cirque, walled off by cliffs on one side with a few spruce standing near, the setting is utterly lovely.

User groups: Hikers, cross-country skiers, and mountain bikes. No wheelchair access.

Permits: No permits are required. Parking and access are free.

Maps: For a USGS topographic maps, ask for Dromedary Peak. Trails Illustrated's Wasatch Front/Strawberry Valley covers the area.

Directions: In Salt Lake City, Wasatch Boulevard and 9400 South meet at a Y junction at the mouth of Little Cottonwood Canyon. From the Y, drive up Little Cottonwood Canyon 5.5 miles, one mile past Tanner Flat Campground, to the trailhead on the south side of the road.

Contact: Uinta National Forest, Pleasant Grove Ranger District, 390 North 100 East, Pleasant Grove, UT 84062, 801/342-5240.

16 SNOWBIRD BARRIER-FREE TRAIL

1.0 mi/1.0 hr

southeast of Salt Lake City at the end of Little Cottonwood Canyon

Map 3.1, page 61

Seeing little use, this short, wheelchair-accessible trail passes through forest, gains about 70 feet of elevation, exposes the traveler to alpine terrain, and ends at a raised picnic platform with truly pleasing views of the surrounding mountains.

User groups: Hikers, kids, and cross-country skiers. Wheelchair accessible.

Permits: No permits are required. Parking and access are free.

Maps: Trails Illustrated's Wasatch Front/Strawberry Valley covers the area. For a USGS topographic map, ask for Brighton.

Directions: In Salt Lake City, Wasatch Boulevard and 9400 South meet at a Y junction at the mouth of Little Cottonwood Canyon. From the Y, drive up Little Cottonwood Canyon about six miles to Snowbird Ski Area. Park at the Cliff Lodge.

Contact: Uinta National Forest, Pleasant Grove Ranger District, 390 North 100 East, Pleasant Grove, UT 84062, 801/342-5240.

17 LAKE MARY TRAIL

7.0 mi/6.0 hrs

southeast of Salt Lake City at the end of Little Cottonwood Canyon

Map 3.1, page 61

Looking for a way to connect the dead-end roads up Little Cottonwood Canyon and Big Cottonwood Canyon? This is it: Lake Mary Trail, rambling past rock-lined lakes, alpine cirques, wildflower-dotted meadows, and through silent forests. From Albion Basin Campground at the Little Cottonwood end, the trail climbs to Catherine Pass in about one mile. From the pass a spur trail leads south to Sunset Peak. Dropping to Lake Catherine, Lake Martha, and then Lake Mary, with a possible side trip to Dog Lake, the main trail eases down to the parking lot at Brighton.

User groups: Hikers and cross-country skiers. No wheelchair access.

Permits: No permits are required. Parking and access are free.

Maps: For a USGS topographic map, ask for Brighton. Trails Illustrated's Wasatch Front/Strawberry Valley covers the area.

Directions: In Salt Lake City, Wasatch Boulevard and 9400 South meet at a Y junction at the mouth of Little Cottonwood Canyon. From the Y, drive up Little Cottonwood Canyon 11.5 miles to the Albion Basin Campground.

Contact: Uinta National Forest, Pleasant Grove Ranger District, 390 North 100 East, Pleasant Grove, UT 84062, 801/342-5240.

18 LITTLE COTTONWOOD CANYON TO SPANISH FORK CANYON: GWT

65 mi one-way/1 week

southeast of Salt Lake City in the Uinta National Forest

Map 3.1, page 61

This section of the Great Western Trail, all in the Uinta National Forest, ranks right up there with the most scenic portions of the entire Canada-to-Mexico pathway. It begins on the Lake Mary Trail for about a mile until it meets the Alta Dry Fork Trail (Trail 032) and heads south. It then meets the Ridge Trail and follows it for about 15 miles, ending at the summit of the Alpine Loop Road. It follows the road down to Vivian Park, then up the South Fork of the Provo River to the Shingle Mill Trail. After leaving Shingle Mill, it follows a combination of roads and trails to reach the summit of Strawberry Peak at 9,714 feet. It then continues down Strawberry Ridge, overlooking what may be the most rugged piece of the Uinta National Forest. The route continues on the Center Trail and the Tie Fork Trail to Spanish Fork Canyon and US 6. Connecting trails provide almost endless possibilities for shorter or longer backpacking trips.

User groups: Hikers, dogs, horses, and mountain bikes. No wheelchair access.

Permits: No permits are required. Parking and access are free.

Maps: For USGS topographic maps, ask for Brighton, Charleston, Bridal Veil Falls, Wallsburg Ridge, Twin Peaks, Two Tom Hill, Strawberry Reservoir NW, and Strawberry Reservoir SW. Trails Illustrated's Wasatch Front/Strawberry Valley covers the area.

Directions: In Salt Lake City, Wasatch Boulevard and 9400 South meet at a Y junction at the mouth of Little Cottonwood Canyon. From the Y, drive up Little Cottonwood Canyon 11.5 miles to the Albion Basin Campground.

Contact: Uinta National Forest, Forest Supervisor, 88 West 100 North, Provo, UT 84601, 801/342-5100.

19 LOG HOLLOW–NOBLETTS CREEK LOOP
7.0 mi/6.0 hrs

northeast of Heber City

Map 3.1, page 61

If you like easy loops, especially loops with diversity down low and great views up high, try this one. The Log Hollow–Nobletts Creek Trail starts up the Nobletts Creek Trail. When the trail forks, hike north (left). You'll pass some

interesting rock formations, ascending somewhat steeply at first, but leveling out more as altitude is gained. From the top of the canyon, you'll ramble west along an open ridge with views stretching your eyes across neighboring valleys and up the slopes of more distant peaks. Then it's down Log Hollow through evergreens, oaks, and aspens, and back to the highway where you'll be about a mile from the start. From back at the fork in the trail, you may also consider hiking east (instead of north) up the 1.5 miles of the gentle bottom to the end of the South Fork of Nobletts Creek. The canyon geology is more attractive in here, but the creek, somewhat disappointingly, runs underground until near the end of the trail, where it suddenly bubbles up.

User groups: Hikers, dogs, horses, and mountain bikes. No wheelchair access.

Permits: No permits are required. Parking and access are free.

Maps: For a USGS topographic map, ask for Soapstone Basin. Trails Illustrated's Wasatch Front/Strawberry Reservoir covers the area.

Directions: From Heber City, take US 40 north for 3.4 miles. Turn east on State Route 32 for 10.4 miles to Francis. Continue southeast on State Route 35 for 10 miles to the trailhead on the north side of the road. You'll be about two miles past the boundary of the Uinta National Forest.

Contact: Uinta National Forest, Heber Ranger District, 125 East 100 North, Heber City, UT 84032, 435/342-5200.

20 SOAPSTONE BASIN LOOP
15.0 mi/10.0 hrs

east of Kamas

Map 3.1, page 61

This route follows U.S. Forest Service roads and has been laid out especially for mountain bikers, even though it can be hiked. It passes through rolling, open land, a mountain basin surrounded by distant peaks and overflowing with summer wildflowers. From Piuta Camp, take Road 037 south and uphill to Soapstone Pass, a distance of about 1.5 miles and an elevation gain of about 1,200 feet. At the pass, turn east on Road 089 and, when the road forks, take the north fork (Road 174). Signs will indicate Cold Springs. When you reach Road 304, turn west and follow it back to the start. **User groups:** Mountain bikes, hikers, and dogs. No wheelchair access. **Permits:** No permits are required. Parking and access are free. **Maps:** For USGS topographic maps, ask for Soapstone Basin and Iron Mine Mountain. **Directions:** From Kamas, take State Route 150 east 14.6 miles. Turn south on Forest Service Road 037 (Soapstone Road) for three miles to Piuta Camp, and park. **Contact:** Uinta National Forest, Heber Ranger District, 125 East 100 North, Heber City, UT 84032, 435/342-5200.

21 DRY CREEK TRAIL-DEER CREEK TRAIL
14.0 mi/1.0–2.0 days

southeast of Salt Lake City in the Lone Peak Wilderness

Map 3.1, page 61

The combination of Dry Creek Trail and Deer Creek Trail allows a hike or horseback ride across the full extent of the northern portion of the Lone Peak Wilderness. Despite its name, Dry Creek runs with water most of its way to a confluence with Deer Creek Trail. From the Dry Creek Trailhead, the path climbs a hill before entering the drainage of the creek. From there progress is steadily uphill to a grass-covered pass where it meets Deer Creek Trail at just over four miles. You'll have gained a tiring 4,000 feet of elevation. Descending Deer Creek Trail, you'll soon reach the water of Deer Creek, continuing down through sagebrush and mountain mahogany to finish in a series of switchbacks that end at Granite Flat Campground near State Route 92. A vehicle at both ends will, of course, allow a one-way hike. Not a bad way at all to spend a weekend.

User groups: Hikers, dogs, and horses. No wheelchair access. **Permits:** No permits are required. Parking and access are free. **Maps:** For USGS topographic maps, ask for Lehi, Dromedary Peak, and Timpanogos Cave. Trails Illustrated's Wasatch Front/Strawberry Valley covers the area. **Directions:** From I-15, take State Route 92 east for five miles. Turn north on State Route 74, which leads quickly to Alpine. Turn west on 2nd North, then turn north on Grove Drive. Grove Drive becomes a gravel road that ends about three miles from Alpine near the U.S. Forest Service boundary. Parking is available here. **Contact:** Uinta National Forest, Pleasant Grove Ranger District, 390 North 100 East, Pleasant Grove, UT 84062, 801/342-5240.

22 DRY CREEK TO LONE PEAK
14.0 mi/1.0–2.0 days

southeast of Salt Lake City in the Lone Peak Wilderness

Map 3.1, page 61

Lone Peak Wilderness was Utah's first federally designated wilderness area, and this route strikes deep into the very heart of these forested mountains, up to alpine meadows and bowls, and to the top of its namesake. This is a trip to be remembered and cherished. It is, however, a long and arduous route with a total elevation gain of about 6,000 feet. The trail begins by following an old jeep road for about a mile west from the trailhead. Then switchbacks lead to First Hamongog, a wide meadow from which you'll have a choice of a trail to Lake Hardy or a trail to Second Hamongog. Although they'll both get you there, the trail to Second Hamongog is recommended. It's steep, but not as steep. From Second Hamongog, another meadow, the trail climbs up and across the slopes of the main ridge of the wilderness to Lake Hardy, providing spectacular views across the southern half of the wilderness. Hardy lies hidden in an alpine bowl east of Lone Peak, and you'll find campsites nearby. It's about a mile west and northwest from the lake to the saddle of the ridge at the head of Bells Canyon. The views of stark and sharp Lone Peak on the approach are softened somewhat from the saddle, and a route to the top is possible by scrambling up from the southeast a half mile to the 11,253 foot summit. There you'll have a top-of-the-world experience: views to north and south along the Wasatch Range, east to the High Uintas, and west across the Great Basin.

User groups: Hikers and dogs. No wheelchair access.

Permits: No permits are required. Parking and access are free.

Maps: For USGS topographic maps, ask for Lehi, Dromedary Peak, Draper, and Timpanogos Cave. Trails Illustrated's Uinta National Forest covers the area.

Directions: From I-15, take State Route 92 east for five miles. Turn north on State Route 74, which leads quickly to Alpine. Turn west on 2nd North, then turn north on Grove Drive. Grove Drive becomes a gravel road that ends about three miles from Alpine near the U.S. Forest Service boundary. Parking is available here.

Contact: Uinta National Forest, Pleasant Grove Ranger District, 390 North 100 East, Pleasant Grove, UT 84062, 801/342-5240.

23 TIMPANOGOS CAVE TRAIL
3.0 mi/4.0 hrs

southeast of Salt Lake City in Timpanogos Cave National Monument

Map 3.1, page 61

Ⓕ The paved trail with its resting benches and interpretive signs makes this a hike that just about anybody can do. Kids will love it. Rocks have been blasted away to eliminate extremely steep grades as you gain about 1,100 feet in elevation. You can learn about the natural and human history of this area from the signs, the guides, and the visitors center. Inside the deep, dark cave, lights help show the way as a guide interprets the walk. Fascinating towering and spiraling forma-

tions glitter in the light. Accessibility and the wonder of caves makes this a very popular destination in Utah, but winter snow closes the monument.

User groups: Hikers. Although the trail is paved, wheeled devices are not allowed because it's too steep.

Permits: There is a fee of $3 per vehicle to enter the monument. After entering, the trail to the cave is free for the hiking, but cave tours are $6 per adult, $5 ages 6–15, $3 children ages 3–5, and free for children age two and under.

Maps: For a USGS topographic map, ask for Timpanogos Cave. Trails Illustrated's Uinta National Forest covers the area. A monument brochure, available at the visitor center, describes the trail.

Directions: From I-15 (Exit 287), take State Route 92 east nine miles to the monument entrance on the south side of the road.

Contact: Timpanogos Cave National Monument, RR3 Box 200, American Fork, UT 84003, 801/756-5239.

24 CASCADE SPRINGS INTERPRETIVE LOOP
0.6 mi/1.0 hr

southeast of Salt Lake City and just east of the Mount Timpanogos Wilderness

Map 3.1, page 61

The water from Cascade Springs falls into pools surrounded by ferns, giant hyssop, and other vegetation. The springs pour out an estimated seven million gallons per day. Two trails leave the parking lot; one is less steep and accessible to wheelchairs. A third trail loops through the area of the lower springs, traveling on boardwalks and pavement, with numerous interpretive signs. This is a place the whole family can enjoy.

User groups: Hikers. Wheelchair accessible for about half its length.

Permits: No permits are required. Parking and access are free.

Maps: For a USGS topographic map, ask for Aspen Grove. A map on a sign in the parking lot shows the trails. Trails Illustrated's Uinta National Forest covers the area.

Directions: From I-15 (Exit 287), take State Route 92 (Alpine Loop Road) east 15.1 miles to its intersection with Cascade Scenic Drive. Turn east for 6.5 miles to the parking lot.

Contact: Uinta National Forest, Pleasant Grove Ranger District, 390 North 100 East, Pleasant Grove, UT 84062, 801/342-5240.

25 TIMPANOGOS TRAIL
11.0 mi/1–2 days
southeast of Salt Lake City in the Mount Timpanogos Wilderness

Map 3.1, page 61

Second highest of the Wasatch peaks, and definitely the high summit most visited in Utah, Mount Timpanogos stands at 11,750 feet. The trail to the top heads west through a grove of aspen. After a relatively gentle hike of about .8 mile, the trail begins to climb, grinding up switchbacks for two miles more before entering a lovely hanging valley, a worthy destination for summer wildflower viewing. At about 3.5 miles a spectacular overlook awaits, with its view into Emerald Lake and the vast snowfield that descends into it. From the overlook, it's .75 mile to a saddle, and approximately .8 mile more to the summit. You'll hike along a narrow ledge with quite a bit of exposure on the way. From the summit, 5,000 feet above the trailhead, you can see north along the Wasatch Range, west across the Great Basin, and south across the wilderness to the Nebo Range. Retracing the path back to the trailhead is the most common means of returning to the start, but a more interesting trip is to drop down the northwest side across Timpanogos Basin on the Timpooneke Trail to the north end of the wilderness (accessible by road). Every year thousands of hikers climb Timpanogos, some of them very young children. Children tend to do better coming up the Timpooneke Trail, which is longer but more gradual. An overnight trip is recommended.

User groups: Hikers. No wheelchair access.

Permits: No permits are required. Parking and access are free.

Maps: For USGS topographic maps, ask for Aspen Grove and Timpanogos Cave. Trail Illustrated's Uinta National Forest covers the area.

Directions: From I-15 (Exit 287), take State Route 92 (Alpine Loop Road) east 19 miles to Aspen Grove. West of the homes, west of the Alpine Loop Road but near it, a paved parking lot sits at the trailhead.

Contact: Uinta National Forest, Pleasant Grove Ranger District, 390 North 100 East, Pleasant Grove, UT 84062, 801/342-5240.

26 DRY CANYON–CLEGG CANYON LOOP
11.5 mi/8.0 hrs

southeast of Heber City

Map 3.1, page 61

For a quick escape from Heber City, these two primitive and little-used trails, connected by a short piece of road, offer solitude and fine views. The Dry Canyon Trail, 3.25 miles long, climbs steeply up a narrow canyon most of the way, reaching an excellent viewpoint of the surrounding mountains dominated by Bald Knoll to the east. Elevation gain is about 500 feet. The trail ends on Forest Service Road 094. Hike about a mile east to Clegg Canyon, and down Clegg six miles to US 40. Clegg Canyon runs practically flat at both ends, but rises and falls substantially in the center, and passes through meadows and shady stands of conifers and aspens. You'll have to hike down a mile of US 40 to reach your vehicle at the Dry Canyon Trailhead. Pleasant campsites exist, but, despite the blue line on the maps, you'll rarely find water on either trail.

User groups: Hikers and dogs. No wheelchair access.

Permits: No permits are required. Parking and access are free.

Maps: For a USGS topographic map, ask for Center Creek. Trails Illustrated's Wasatch Front/Strawberry Reservoir covers the area.

Directions: From Heber City, take US 40 southeast approximately nine miles to the Dry Canyon Trailhead on the east side of the road. The trailhead is 1.5 miles past the boundary of the Uinta National Forest.

Contact: Uinta National Forest, Heber Ranger District, 125 East 100 North, Heber City, UT 84032, 435/342-5200.

27 FOREMAN HOLLOW LOOP
4.3 mi/4.0 hrs

southeast of Heber City

Map 3.1, page 61

Often overlooked, Lodgepole Campground lies in aspen and pine in lovely Daniels Canyon. Sites are $11 per night per site, and water and restrooms are available. The trail sees little use. It starts west, following an old abandoned road for .75 mile. The route follows Foreman Hollow, ascending through magnificent old aspen, to a viewpoint of Daniels Canyon. Then it bends north, crosses more open land, and descends steeply into Shingle Hollow to follow it down to another old road and back to the campground. Interpretive signs along the way make this hike a valuable learning experience the whole family can enjoy.

User groups: Hikers and cross-country skiers. No wheelchair access.

Permits: No permits are required. Parking and access are free.

Maps: Trails Illustrated's Wasatch Front/Strawberry Reservoir covers the area. For a USGS topographic map, ask for Twin Peaks.

Directions: From Heber City, take US 40 southeast about 14.0 miles to Lodgepole Campground on the west side of the road. Turn north up Loop B and drive about 200 yards to where an old road heading west is blocked off.

Contact: Uinta National Forest, Heber Ranger District, 125 East 100 North, Heber City, UT 84032, 435/342-5200.

28 DRY FORK TRAIL TO CASCADE MOUNTAIN
10.0 mi/1–2 days

northeast of Provo

Map 3.1, page 61

The lesser-known far-southern portion of the Wasatch Range can be explored via this arduous trail to the crest of the range and beyond to Cascade Mountain. From Rock Canyon Campground, the trail climbs without taking a break for two miles where it opens out into a meadow. If you're tired of gaining altitude, the meadow won't help much. It too is steep, and beyond the meadow the trail enters switchbacks that head up to the Wasatch crest at about 9,800 feet. Cascade Mountain looms to the northwest. Lone Peak and Mount Timpanogos stand in the distance in the same direction. At this point, many hikers are satisfied, and head back down. But just below the crest, the Dry Fork Trail meets the Big Hollow Trail and the Shingle Mill Canyon Trail. Big Hollow follows the crest for about a mile of easy hiking northwest before the going gets rugged and slower, climbing four more miles to the base of Cascade Mountain (10,908 feet). The mountain is a ragged piece of work, with cliffs on all sides. Routes to the summit may not qualify as highly technical, but the exposure is great, and climbers should give careful consideration to going further up. If you reach the summit, you'll have gained a total of almost 4,000 feet in elevation.

User groups: Hikers, dogs, and horses. No wheelchair access.

Permits: No permits are required. Parking and access are free.

Maps: For a USGS topographic map, ask for Bridal Veil Falls. Trails Illustrated's Wasatch Front/Strawberry Reservoir covers the area.

Directions: From Orem on I-15, take State Route 52 east about 3.5 miles to where it merges with US 189. Continue northeast on 189 for 2.1 miles, into Provo Canyon, and take the first paved road to the south. Take this road 11 miles to Rock Canyon Campground. In the campground, take the left loop. The trailhead, currently unmarked, starts at the top of the loop. **Contact:** Uinta National Forest, Pleasant Grove Ranger District, 390 North 100 East, Pleasant Grove, UT 84062, 801/342-5240.

29 MAPLE CANYON TRAIL TO SPANISH FORK PEAK
10.0 mi/1–2 days

east of Mapleton in the Uinta National Forest

Map 3.1, page 61

Panoramic views of Utah Valley and the mountains of the Uinta National Forest are only a few hours of hiking from this easily accessible trailhead. For .75 mile, the trail follows an old road, then continues south as the road veers east. Be ready for moderate to very steep grades on the trail as it passes through a forest of fir, aspen, and box elder. At higher elevations, the trail leads into open meadows near Maple Canyon Lake where you'll find campsites shaded by aspen and fir. The steep walls of Spanish Fork Peak now loom overhead. The trail circles the lake and climbs via switchbacks up the ridgeline toward the peak, and the views open out to the north and west across Utah Valley and east to Strawberry Ridge. Before descending into Sterling Hollow south of the peak, you can scramble to the summit, but loose rocks warrant a careful approach. On the top, you'll have gained about 3,500 feet of total elevation. You can retrace your steps to the starting point, or, with a vehicle at the other end, drop down Sterling Hollow Trail about the same distance to US 6 in Spanish Fork Canyon.

User groups: Hikers, dogs, horses, and mountain bikes. No wheelchair access.

Permits: No permits are required. Parking and access are free.

Maps: For USGS topographic maps, ask for Springville and Spanish Fork Peak. Trails Illustrated's Wasatch Front/Strawberry Reservoir covers the area.

Directions: From the east side of Mapleton, take Forest Service Road 025 east up Maple Canyon for 2.1 miles, about a half-mile past Whiting Campground, to the trailhead and parking on the south side of the road.

Contact: Uinta National Forest, Spanish Fork Ranger District, 44 West 400 North, Spanish Fork, UT 84660, 801/342-5260.

30 FIFTH WATER TRAIL
4.0 mi/3.0 hrs

east of Spanish Fork in the Uinta National Forest

Map 3.1, page 61

Crossing the water on a footbridge, this trail rambles pleasantly and easily along a shaded route for about one mile of Sixth Water Creek before continuing up Fifth Water Creek. It's a good one for the whole family. You'll reach an outrageous collection of natural pools and hot springs. After two miles a chilly waterfall tumbles into a large, warm pool, an understandably popular local destination. The trail, seldom traveled beyond the waterfall, continues on for about 7.5 miles to finally reach the top of Strawberry Ridge with a fine view east across Strawberry Reservoir. If you continue on and lose the trail, just stay near the bottom of the canyon and you'll hit an old jeep track for the last mile or so to the ridge. Fifth Water Trail can be connected via other trails north and south, such as the Center Trail, to create an extended backpacking trip that takes you back to where you started.

User groups: Hikers, dogs, horses, and mountain bikes. No wheelchair access.

Permits: No permits are required. Parking and access are free.

Maps: For a USGS topographic map, ask for Rays Valley. Trails Illustrated's Wasatch Front/Strawberry Reservoir covers the area.

Directions: From Spanish Fork, take US 6 southeast for about 11 miles. Turn north on Forest Service Road 029, a paved road, and drive 10 miles to Three Forks. Parking is available on the east side of the road at the trailhead.

Contact: Uinta National Forest, Spanish Fork Ranger District, 44 West 400 North, Spanish Fork, UT 84660, 435/342-5260.

31 CENTER TRAIL: GWT
15 mi one-way/1–2 days

east of Spanish Fork in the Uinta National Forest

Map 3.1, page 61

This little-used stretch of the Great Western Trail winds across large Diamond Fork Basin, traveling mostly in a forest thick with lush ground cover. It travels up and down rolling hills occasionally cut by trickling streams, gaining about 2,300 feet of elevation. On the path north to south, you cross Sixth Water Creek, the Fifth Water Trail, the Fourth Water Trail, and the Cottonwood Second Water Trail, allowing you to plan a pleasant backpacking trip that ends up where it started.

User groups: Hikers, dogs, horses, and mountain bikes. No wheelchair access.

Permits: No permits are required. Parking and access are free.

Maps: For USGS topographic maps, ask for Two Tom Hill and Rays Valley. Trails Illustrated's Wasatch Front/Strawberry Reservoir covers the area.

Directions: From Spanish Fork, take US 6 southeast for about 11 miles. Turn north on Forest Service Road 029, a paved road, and drive 16.1 miles to where the pavement ends. Take the dirt road to the east and drive seven miles to find the trailhead on the south side of the road near a gauging station.

Contact: Uinta National Forest, Spanish Fork Ranger District, 44 West 400 North, Spanish Fork, UT 84660, 435/342-5260.

32 JONES RANCH–BOX LAKE LOOP
2.5 mi/2.0 hrs

south of Payson in the Uinta National Forest

Map 3.2, page 62

A fairly short trail with a gentle elevation gain and loss of about 600 feet—a fine walk for the whole family—the route starts south along Jones Ranch Trail. It follows a closed road through stands of trembling aspen and narrow meadows aromatic with summer wildflowers for about a mile before reaching the junction with Box Lake Trail. Box Lake, one of the Payson Lakes, which nestle close together, lies less than a mile northeast, and there you'll pick up a short US Forest Service road back to the Nebo Loop Road. From there the starting point stands about a mile northwest.

User groups: Hikers, dogs, horses, and mountain bikes. No wheelchair access.

Permits: No permits are required. Parking and access are free.

Maps: For a USGS topographic maps, ask for Payson Lakes. Trails Illustrated's Uinta National Forest covers the area.

Directions: From Provo, take I-15 south 15 miles to the Payson Exit. From Payson take 600 East and drive south on Payson Canyon (Nebo Loop Road) for about 11.5 miles to the trailhead on the south side of the road.

Contact: Uinta National Forest, Spanish Fork Ranger District, 44 West 400 North, Spanish Fork, UT 84660, 801/342-5260.

33 LOAFER MOUNTAIN TRAIL TO SANTAQUIN PEAK
11.0 mi/1–2 days

south of Payson in the Uinta National Forest

Map 3.2, page 62

Not far from the hubbub of the Provo area, this well-defined trail climbs approximately four miles along forested drainages to a saddle. From there you'll see a cirque falling away to the east and the long ridge of Loafer Mountain to the north. To reach the top of Loafer Mountain (10,687 feet), leave the trail here and walk the ridge as it heads northwest then bends northeast to the summit, a distance of about a half mile. From Loafer Mountain, the vast Salt Lake Valley stretches out to the west and Santaquin Peak stands boldly to the north across a deep cut in the mountains. To summit Santaquin (10,685 feet), drop carefully off the end of Loafer Mountain's ridge and then climb another ridge to Santaquin. The going is steep but non-technical, the distance is about two miles round-trip, and the elevation lost and regained is about 450 feet one-way. Retrace the same steps to the trailhead, or descend to the saddle and follow the Deer Hollow Trail from there. Deer Hollow Trail ends on Forest Service Road 123. Follow the road for a half mile west to find the Bennie Creek Trail at the end of the road. The Bennie Creek Trail intersects the Loafer Mountain Trail one mile from where you started. Water sources on the Loafer Mountain Trail are undependable. Carry at least a gallon per person for this trip.

User groups: Hikers, dogs, and horses. Not recommended for mountain bikes. No wheelchair access.

Permits: No permits are required. Parking and access are free.

Maps: For USGS topographic maps, ask for Payson Lakes and Birdseye. Trails Illustrated's Uinta National Forest covers the area.

Directions: From Provo, take I-15 south 15 miles to the Payson Exit. From Payson, take 600 East south up Payson Canyon (Nebo Loop Road) for 12.5 miles to the Loafer Mountain Trailhead on the north side of the road. If you reach Payson Lakes Campground, backtrack .75 miles to the trailhead.

Contact: Uinta National Forest, Spanish Fork Ranger District, 44 West 400 North, Spanish Fork, UT 84660, 801/342-5260.

34 LOAFER MOUNTAIN–DEER HOLLOW LOOP
11.0 mi/1–2 days

south of Payson in the Uinta National Forest

Map 3.2, page 62

Not far from a populated area, this potential overnighter offers splendid peace and quiet. Well-defined, the Loafer Mountain Trail climbs approximately four miles to a saddle. There you'll see Loafer Mountain standing to the north, about a half mile away, and have exemplary views of the lower Salt Lake Valley. At this spot you'll have gained about 2,200 feet

in elevation. From the saddle the Deer Hollow Trail winds its way down about three miles southeast to end at Forest Service Road 123. Follow the road west .6 mile to the Bennie Creek Cutoff Trail, which continues northwest to intersect the Loafer Mountain Trail about one mile from the starting point. There should be water in Deer Hollow, especially in spring and early summer, and Bennie Creek runs year-round. But the hike up to Loafer Mountain can be dry, so carry plenty of water.

User groups: Hikers, dogs, and horses. Not recommended for mountain bikes. No wheelchair access.

Permits: No permits are required. Parking and access are free.

Maps: For USGS topographic maps, ask for Payson Lakes and Birdseye. Trails Illustrated's Uinta National Forest covers the area.

Directions: From Provo, take I-15 south one mile to the Payson Exit. From Payson take 600 East south up Payson Canyon (Nebo Loop Road) for 12.5 miles to the trailhead on the north side of the road.

Contact: Uinta National Forest, Spanish Fork Ranger District, 44 West 400 North, Spanish Fork, UT 84660, 801/342-5260.

35 SHEEPHERDER HILL TRAIL
8.0 mi/6.0 hrs

south of Payson in the Uinta National Forest

Map 3.2, page 62

A highly scenic pathway with almost all gentle grades, this trail begins as an old abandoned road. A well-constructed trail leaves the old road to drop into a series of meadows and a dense forest of conifers and aspen. Contouring a steep hillside, you'll eventually break onto a large ridge, cross through more forest, and come out on another abandoned road that leads northeast. From here you cross a stream and hike down relatively steep forested terrain through more meadows, and across a bridge just before the northern trailhead. Overall elevation gain and loss is about 900 feet. The northern trailhead may be accessed from the Nebo Loop Road by turning south on Forest Service Road 312 (Winward Reservoir Road) for a half mile. Check a topographic map to be sure of directions. Without a vehicle at both ends, you can retrace your steps and/or spend a night camped near the edge of one of the meadows.

User groups: Hikers, dogs, horses, and mountain bikes. No wheelchair access.

Permits: No permits are required. Parking and access are free.

Maps: For a USGS topographic map, ask for Payson Lakes. Trails Illustrated's Uinta National Forest covers the area.

Directions: From just south of Santaquin, take Forest Service Road 014 (Santaquin Canyon Road) south approximately eight miles to Santaquin Meadows. Take an unmarked, small dirt road north a short distance until it ends in a parking lot/turn-around area. The trail is a continuation of the road.

Contact: Uinta National Forest, Spanish Fork Ranger District, 44 West 400 North, Spanish Fork, UT 84660, 801/342-5260.

36 MIDDLE FORK OF WHITE RIVER TRAIL
12.0 mi one-way/8.0 hrs

south of Soldier Summit on US 6

Map 3.2, page 62

Although a scenic hike, this route would be better as a mountain bike ride since much of the trail is a double track used by four-wheel-drive vehicles. The elevation gain up the river is relatively gentle, but it gains more than 2,000 feet. At 12 miles, the Middle Fork Trail connects with the Right Fork of White River Trail, allowing a long loop hike/ride of more than 30 miles.

User groups: Hikers, dogs, horses, mountain bikes, and cross-country skiers. No wheelchair access.

Permits: No permits are required. Parking and access are free.

Maps: For USGS topographic maps, ask for Soldier Summit, Strawberry Reservoir SW, and Strawberry Reservoir SE.

Directions: From Soldier Summit, take US 6 south 1.5 miles. Turn east on the White River Road for 4.1 miles, bearing west when the road forks. Park at the trailhead.

Contact: Uinta National Forest, Spanish Fork Ranger District, 44 West 400 North, Spanish Fork, UT 84660, 801/798-3571.

37 NEBO BENCH TRAIL
12.0 mi/1–2 days

northeast of Nephi in the Mount Nebo Wilderness

Map 3.2, page 62

Although the Nebo Bench Trail has easy access from its south end, the north end offers an even easier hike with more elevation lost than gained. An exemplary highmountain-wilderness path, the trail drops mildly from the northern trailhead, passing through fir and aspen and across open meadows with excellent views to the east across the Uinta and Manti–La Sal National Forests. The first 2.5 miles or so make a pleasant and easy enough hike for kids. You'll hike in and out (with a few steep sections) of Hell Hole Basin, North Basin, Middle Basin, and South Basin, traversing the lower slopes of Mount Nebo to the west. In summer, these high meadows are blessed with wildflowers and fragrant grasses. Total elevation gain is about 2,850 feet. You'll find pleasant campsites in the basins. After South Basin, the trail descends steeply along Andrews Ridge into oak and maple to Salt Creek. This is a good place to leave a second car, but you can always hike back.

User groups: Hikers, dogs, and horses. No mountain bikes are allowed. No wheelchair access.

Permits: No permits are required. Parking and access are free.

Maps: For USGS topographic maps, ask for Nebo Basin and Mona. Trails Illustrated's Uinta National Forest covers the area.

Directions: From Nephi, take State Highway

132 east for approximately six miles. Turn north on the Nebo Loop Road for 12.2 miles to the parking lot and trailhead on the west side of the road.

Contact: Uinta National Forest, Spanish Fork Ranger District, 44 West 400 North, Spanish Fork, UT 84660, 801/342-5260.

38 BLACK CANYON TRAIL
5.0 mi/6.0 hrs

northeast of Nephi

Map 3.2, page 62

Here is the most beautiful canyon hike in the area. The trail descends the canyon, through thick stands of aspen and an occasional open meadow in the upper portion, along a stream in the lower portion. The stream cascades over moss-covered rocks to settle down time and time again in a myriad of small pools—nice places for summer splashes. The trail ends in a grassy meadow shaded by tall pines. You can return the way you came, but remember it's uphill now with an elevation gain of about 1,500 feet. Or you can connect with other drainages to return to the Nebo Loop Road. Topographic maps are a must if you do not retrace your steps.

User groups: Hikers, dogs, horses, and mountain bikes. No wheelchair access.

Permits: No permits are required. Parking and access are free.

Maps: For USGS topographic maps, ask for Nebo Basin and Spencer Canyon. Trails Illustrated's Uinta National Forest covers the area.

Directions: From Nephi, take State Highway 132 east for approximately six miles. Turn north on the Nebo Loop Road for 12.2 miles to the parking lot and trailhead on the east side of the road.

Contact: Uinta National Forest, Spanish Fork Ranger District, 44 West 400 North, Spanish Fork, UT 84660, 801/342-5260.

39 SUMMIT TRAIL
13.0 mi/8.0 hrs

northeast of Nephi

Map 3.2, page 62

As the trail name suggests, you can walk up high with increasingly spectacular views of the forested slopes and bold peaks of central Utah. After winding through an aspen grove, the trail reaches the crest of a long ridge that separates the Nebo Creek drainage to the north and the Pole Creek drainage to the south. You'll follow the ridge for most of your journey, passing through occasional stands of aspen and conifers, dropping down and back up several saddles in the ridge but generally maintaining a relatively level route. A fence cuts across the trail about 2.5 miles from the start. Be sure to close the gate behind you. Just past the fence the trail bends to the south and the view of Mount Nebo to the west becomes ever more awesome. You'll gain altitude steadily but not steeply, heading south three more miles before a turn to the west and a steep descent into Pole Canyon to the southern trailhead. Total elevation gain is about 1,000 feet before you start the descent. The southern trailhead may be accessed by taking Forest Service Road 016 (Pole Canyon Road) east from the Nebo Loop Road.

User groups: Hikers, dogs, horses, and mountain bikes. No wheelchair access.

Permits: No permits are required. Parking and access are free.

Maps: For USGS topographic maps, ask for Nebo Basin and Spencer Canyon. Trails Illustrated's Uinta National Forest covers the area.

Directions: From Nephi, take State Highway 132 east approximately six miles. Turn north on the Nebo Loop Road 7.5 miles to the trailhead on the east side of the road.

Contact: Uinta National Forest, Spanish Fork Ranger District, 44 West 400 North, Spanish Fork, UT 84660, 801/342-5260.

40 MOUNT NEBO
12.0 mi/1–2 days

northeast of Nephi in the Mount Nebo Wilderness

Map 3.2, page 62

The north summit of Nebo (11,928 feet) rises higher than any other point in the Wasatch Range, so standing on top is something lots of folks just have to do. You can ascend the Nebo Bench Trail (described in this chapter) for about four miles, climbing steadily and switchbacking at times up steep terrain. The first mile alone gains almost 1,500 feet before flattening a bit in a grassy meadow with excellent views. Then the Mount Nebo Trail leaves to the west, and climbs steeply up switchbacks for a half mile to Andrews Ridge. The trail splits and then rejoins itself after another half mile. The right trail is a bit easier going. Once the trails rejoin, be sure to keep going north, avoiding intersecting trails. You have about another mile to go, a mile of relatively rugged terrain that passes timberline on the ridge to the summit. The summit ridge, by the way, is not recommended for horses. Above the trees are excellent views: Nebo ridge nearby, the Wasatch Range to the north, forested mountains to the east and south, the great desert land to the west. The trail ends at the south summit (11,824 feet), but the middle and north summits can be reached by negotiating a long, somewhat dangerous knife-edged ridge for another mile.

User groups: Hikers, dogs, and horses. No mountain bikes. No wheelchair access.

Permits: No permits are required. Parking and access are free.

Maps: For USGS topographic maps, ask for Mona and Nebo Basin. Trails Illustrated's Uinta National Forest covers the area.

Directions: From Nephi, take State Highway 132 east for approximately 6.0 miles. Turn north on the Nebo Loop Road for 3.3 miles and bear west at the fork for another 1.5 miles to the trailhead on the west side of the road.

Contact: Uinta National Forest, Spanish Fork Ranger District, 44 West 400 North, Spanish Fork, UT 84660, 801/342-5260.

41 MAHOGANY HILL TRAIL
10.0 mi/1–2 days

northeast of Nephi

Map 3.2, page 62

On some maps you'll find this trail labeled the Rees Flat/McCune Canyon Trail. It's a pleasant summer overnight route. It crosses Salt Creek at the start, a wet undertaking in early summer, and then eases up a small drainage. Watch for a switchback that swings to the north and climbs up a reddish hillside into a stand of ponderosa pines. After a descent from there, you'll cross a meadow and follow the edge of a fenced pasture before entering another stand of pine. The forest changes to maple and oak with stands of aspen before a relatively steep climb takes you over a pass west of Mahogany Hill. From the pass you'll drop to the edge of Footes Canyon, then steeply into the canyon. A stream and the shade of cottonwood trees in Footes make this spot a delightful choice for camping. From Footes the trail climbs back up to a forest of oak and continues to Rees Flat. The trailhead at Rees Flat may be accessed by turning north on an unmarked dirt road from State Highway 132 about 1.5 miles from Nephi and taking the dirt road to its end.

User groups: Hikers, dogs, horses, and mountain bikes. No wheelchair access.

Permits: No permits are required. Parking and access are free.

Maps: For USGS topographic maps, ask for Nebo Basin, Mona, and Nephi. Trails Illustrated's Uinta National Forest covers the area.

Directions: From Nephi, take State Highway 132 east for approximately six miles. Turn north on the Nebo Loop Road for 3.3 miles and bear west at the fork for another .12 mile to the trailhead on the west side of the road.

Contact: Uinta National Forest, Spanish Fork Ranger District, 44 West 400 North, Spanish Fork, UT 84660, 801/342-5260.

42 FISH CREEK NATIONAL RECREATION TRAIL
10.0 mi one-way/6.0–7.0 hrs

north of Scofield

Map 3.2, page 62

This scenic and wet trail is especially attractive if you enjoy trout fishing or wildlife viewing. An active beaver population has created numerous ponds known for good fishing. Well-documented wildlife sightings include deer, elk, moose, bear, and mountain lion. Starting at the Fish Creek Campground, the trail runs along the bottom of the drainage of Fish Creek and requires multiple water crossings. Grass and willows grow along the creek, and aspen and conifers stand above sagebrush-covered hillsides as you gain elevation. For an overnight, should you be so inclined, the best campsites require hiking off trail into forested terrain. For an end-to-end hike, the trail comes out on Forest Service Road 150 (Skyline Drive) approximately 14 miles north of the junction of State Highways 31 and 264.

User groups: Hikers, dogs, horses, and cross-country skiers. No mountain bikes are allowed. No wheelchair access.

Permits: No permits are required. Parking and access are free.

Maps: For USGS topographic maps, ask for Scofield Reservoir and C Canyon. Contact the Price Ranger District for the Manti–La Sal Travel Map.

Directions: From Scofield, take the road to Scofield Reservoir north for six miles. You'll be on the west side of the reservoir. From there take Forest Service Road 123 for two miles to Fish Creek Campground.

Contact: Manti–La Sal National Forest, Price Ranger District, 599 West Price River Drive, Price, UT 84501, 435/637-2817.

43 SILVER CREEK TRAIL
8.0 mi one-way/6.0 hrs

northeast of Fairview

Map 3.2, page 62

Beaver ponds along the way typically offer fine trout fishing, and big wildlife species (deer, elk, and bear) seem to find this area especially appealing. For the first three miles, the trail follows willow-lined Gooseberry Creek before climbing a grassy hill to reach a rough dirt road. Although the road crosses private land, no-use restrictions are in force at this writing. Follow the road northeast for one mile until it ends above Silver Creek. Descending to the creek, you'll follow the north bank down four miles to the confluence of the Silver Creek and Fish Creek Trails. It's then two more miles down Fish Creek to Fish Creek Campground, where it helps to have a second vehicle waiting.

User groups: Hikers, dogs, horses, and cross-country skiers. Not recommended for mountain bikes. No wheelchair access.

Permits: No permits are required. Parking and access are free.

Maps: For USGS topographic maps, ask for Fairview Lakes, C Canyon, and Scofield Reservoir. Contact the Price Ranger District for the Manti–La Sal Travel Map.

Directions: From the junction of State Highways 31 and 264, northeast of Fairview, take the Gooseberry Reservoir Road north three miles to the trailhead at the northwest corner of the reservoir.

Contact: Manti–La Sal National Forest, Price Ranger District, 599 West Price River Drive, Price, UT 84501, 435/637-2817.

44 SCAD VALLEY TRAIL
6.0 mi/6.0 hrs

northwest of Huntington

Map 3.2, page 62

This is a quiet little trail—seldom used, easy to follow, and a great connecting trail for a backpacking loop. To access the trail, you'll have to wade Scad Valley Creek, a waterway that can run high and swift in spring. The trail follows Scad Valley Creek as Seeley Mountain rises more than 10,000 feet to the east. Much of the trail passes through grass and sagebrush near the edge of a conifer forest. You can turn back whenever you wish, but a beautiful loop can be completed by descending Horse Canyon and then ascending the Left Fork of Huntington Creek. The loop is 12 miles total, but requires approximately one mile of hiking along State Route 31.

User groups: Hikers, dogs, horses, mountain bikes, and cross-country skiers. No wheelchair access.

Permits: No permits are required. Parking and access are free.

Maps: For USGS topographic maps, ask for Candland Mountain and Rilda Canyon. Contact the Price Ranger District for the Manti–La Sal Travel Map.

Directions: From Huntington, take State Highway 31 north approximately 28 miles. Turn south on Forest Service Road 014 for four miles to Miller Flat Reservoir. The trailhead is near the south end of the dam.

Contact: Manti–La Sal National Forest, Price Ranger District, 599 West Price River Drive, Price, UT 84501, 435/637-2817.

45 MILL CANYON TRAIL
8.0 mi/7.0 hrs

northwest of Huntington

Map 3.2, page 62

Passing over rough terrain along the bottom and the north slope of Mill Canyon, this trail is not easy traveling. The ruggedness of the route, however, promises great solitude, and it is pretty country. With just 700 feet of elevation gain overall, the trail still requires you to ascend and descend three passes to cross Candland Mountain before reaching the western trailhead two miles from Miller Flat Reservoir. You'll have to wade Huntington Creek near the western end, a dicey undertaking during

spring high water. The rewards are scenic views of the surrounding forest and the Price River valley to the east. You can retrace your steps the four miles to Highway 31, or descend the lovely Left Fork of Huntington Creek Trail four miles to the highway, which leaves you about four more highway miles from your vehicle. Or continue on the Scad Valley and Horse Canyon Trails (described in this chapter), which leaves you about five highway miles from your starting point.

User groups: Hikers, dogs, horses, and mountain bikes. No wheelchair access.

Permits: No permits are required. Parking and access are free.

Maps: For a USGS topographic map, ask for Candland Mountain. Contact the Price Ranger District for the Manti–La Sal Travel Map.

Directions: From Huntington, take State Highway 31 north approximately 22 miles to the trailhead on the west side of the road.

Contact: Manti–La Sal National Forest, Price Ranger District, 599 West Price River Drive, Price, UT 84501, 435/637-2817.

46 POLE CANYON TRAIL
4.0 mi/4.0 hrs

northwest of Huntington

Map 3.2, page 62

For the first half of this rough and rugged trail, you'll be traveling in a forest of spruce and fir. The second half runs through sagebrush meadows dotted with aspen and mountain mahogany with excellent views of East Mountain to the southwest and Gentry Mountain to the east. The views come after you've gained about 1,600 feet of elevation. Intersecting cattle trails can make route finding difficult, so a map and compass are strongly recommended. From the eastern end you can return the two miles to the highway or travel down the Bull Pasture Trail five miles to the highway. At the highway end of the Bull Pasture Trail you'll be approximately four road miles from your starting point.

User groups: Hikers, dogs, horses, and mountain bikes. No wheelchair access.

Permits: No permits are required. Parking and access are free.

Maps: For USGS topographic maps, ask for Candland Mountain and Wattis. Contact the Price Ranger District for the Manti–La Sal Travel Map.

Directions: From Huntington, take State Highway 31 north approximately 20 miles to the trailhead on the east side of the highway.

Contact: Manti–La Sal National Forest, Price Ranger District, 599 West Price River Drive, Price, UT 84501, 435/637-2817.

47 LEFT FORK OF HUNTINGTON NATIONAL RECREATION TRAIL
16.0 mi/2 days

northwest of Huntington

Map 3.2, page 62

Certainly one of the most popular paths in the Price Ranger District, this relatively gentle trail follows the scenic left fork of Huntington Creek past numerous waterfalls and pools and through lovely stands of spruce and fir. The trail runs along the north side of the waterway, a creek famous for brown, cutthroat, and rainbow trout fishing. After about 4.5 miles toward Miller Flat Reservoir, the trail leaves the canyon and enters a wide valley of grass and sagebrush, and Scad Valley Creek enters from the south. If fishing is an interest, hike up Scad Valley, as the creek's water is running clear. After a rain, muddy water will keep the fish from biting. There's no maintained trail along Scad Valley Creek, but the going is not too bad. After three miles of Scad Valley Creek, you'll reach the Miller Flat Road (a good place to leave a second car). But it's far more fun to continue along the waterway as it crosses the wide valley and enters a narrow canyon, from which intermittent paths lead to Cleveland Reservoir. The reservoir also sits on State Route 31.

User groups: Hikers, dogs, and horses. No mountain bikes are allowed. No wheelchair access.

Permits: No permits are required. Parking and access are free.

Maps: For a USGS topographic map, ask for Candland Mountain. Contact the Price Ranger District for the Manti–La Sal Travel Map.

Directions: From Huntington, take State Highway 31 north for approximately 18 miles. Turn west on the Left Fork Road for .5 mile to the end of the campground.

Contact: Manti–La Sal National Forest, Price Ranger District, 599 West Price River Drive, Price, UT 84501, 435/637-2817.

48 HORSE CANYON TRAIL
8.0 mi/6.0 hrs

northwest of Huntington

Map 3.2, page 62

Deer are numerous enough in this canyon to attract the most use during hunting season, and that's probably the only time you might see a horse in here. Hunting season is, in fact, the only time you might see another human in here. From the highway, the trail ascends Horse Canyon, first along the bottom in a forest of conifers, then climbing onto the south-facing slope of the drainage through stands of aspen and across open meadows. It ends at Forest Service Road 014 (Scad Valley Road). Although it's in good condition, this trail is a very challenging mountain-bike ride with almost 2,000 feet of elevation gain. Near Scad Valley Road, you'll reach a junction with the East Mountain Trail, which connects with the Mill Fork Canyon Trail. Those trails are described in this chapter. You can return the four miles to Highway 31 or continue on the East Mountain Trail for a pleasant overnight trip.

User groups: Hikers, dogs, horses, and mountain bikes. No wheelchair access.

Permits: No permits are required. Parking and access are free.

Maps: For a USGS topographic map, ask for Rilda Canyon. Contact the Price Ranger District for the Manti–La Sal Travel Map.

Directions: From Huntington, take State Highway 31 north for approximately 18 miles to the trailhead on the west side of the road.

Contact: Manti–La Sal National Forest, Price Ranger District, 599 West Price River Drive, Price, UT 84501, 435/637-2817.

49 BULL PASTURE TRAIL
10.0 mi/1–2 days

northwest of Huntington

> **Map 3.2, page 62**

Considered one of the most strenuous trails on the Manti–La Sal National Forest, the Bull Pasture Trail crosses steep slopes composed of loose and rocky soil. Much of the path climbs through an open forest of juniper and piñon and grassy meadows dotted with sagebrush. Toward the upper end, where the elevation reaches almost 9,500 feet, you'll travel through scattered stands of conifers and aspen with fine views of Gentry Mountain and Gentry Hollow to the east, and East Mountain and Huntington Canyon to the west. You'll have gained a bit over 2,000 feet in elevation. You can retrace your steps the five miles to the starting point or descend Pole Canyon Trail to State Highway 31, which leaves you about four miles from the trailhead.

User groups: Hikers, dogs, and horses. Not recommended for mountain bikes. No wheelchair access.

Permits: No permits are required. Parking and access are free.

Maps: For USGS topographic maps, ask for Rilda Canyon, Candland Mountain, and Wattis. Contact the Price Ranger District for the Manti–La Sal Travel Map.

Directions: From Huntington, take State Highway 31 north approximately 16 miles to the trailhead on the east side of the road.

Contact: Manti–La Sal National Forest, Price Ranger District, 599 West Price River Drive, Price, UT 84501, 435/637-2817.

50 GENTRY HOLLOW TRAIL
10.0 mi/7.0 hrs

northwest of Huntington

> **Map 3.2, page 62**

Although it's open to ATV use, this trail is narrow and does not see heavy traffic by motorized vehicles. But you could be passed by a gas-burning machine. From the trailhead in Tie Fork Canyon, you'll generally hike upstream to Forest Service Road 251 on Gentry Mountain. Your elevation gain will be about 1,500 feet. The trail passes through a forest of spruce and fir before entering an environment of aspen and grassy meadows, and finishes, during the last mile or so, in open sagebrush country with fine views. Deer and elk are hunted here in the fall. You can descend the same five miles to the start, or complete a loop of 11 miles by descending Wild Cattle Hollow Trail. Two miles of travel west on Forest Service Road 251 and 250 are required to connect the two trails.

User groups: Hikers, dogs, horses, mountain bikes, and cross-country skiers. No wheelchair access.

Permits: No permits are required. Parking and access are free.

Maps: For USGS topographic maps, ask for Wattis and Hiawatha. Contact the Price Ranger District for the Manti–La Sal Travel Map.

Directions: From Huntington, take State Highway 31 north approximately 13 miles. Turn east on Forest Service Road 348 (Tie Fork Canyon Road) and continue for about two miles to the trailhead. Four-wheel-drive vehicles are recommended on Road 348.

Contact: Manti–La Sal National Forest, Price Ranger District, 599 West Price River Drive, Price, UT 84501, 435/637-2817.

51 WILD CATTLE HOLLOW TRAIL
8.0 mi/6.0 hrs

northwest of Huntington

> **Map 3.2, page 62**

While this trail is open to horses and mountain bikes, its lower section includes ledges that drop two to three feet—difficult going for hoof and fat tire. Along this section, there are great views of Wild Cattle Hollow. From a forest dominated by conifers, you'll move up into Douglas fir and aspen, and on into stands of aspen and open meadows. The last mile or so runs through open sagebrush country. Cattle trails connect with the main trail, making route finding difficult at times. An topographic map and compass are recommended. You can re-trace your steps the four miles to the start, or hike Forest Service Road 250 and 251 east for two miles and descend via Gentry Hollow Trail. If you do the loop, you'll hike 11 miles.

User groups: Hikers, dogs, horses, and mountain bikes. No wheelchair access.

Permits: No permits are required. Parking and access are free.

Maps: For USGS topographic maps, ask for Wattis and Hiawatha. Contact the Price Ranger District for the Manti–La Sal Travel Map.

Directions: From Huntington, take State Highway 31 north approximately 13 miles. Turn east on Forest Service Road 348 (Tie Fork Canyon Road) and drive about two miles to the trailhead. Four-wheel-drive vehicles are recommended on Road 348.

Contact: Manti–La Sal National Forest, Price Ranger District, 599 West Price River Drive, Price, UT 84501, 435/637-2817.

52 MILL FORK CANYON TRAIL
8.0 mi/1–2 days

northwest of Huntington

Map 3.2, page 62

Following a perennial stream with several low waterfalls for approximately three-fourths of its length, this trail starts in a diverse forest of pine, fir, cottonwood, juniper, and mahogany. Then the forest changes to primarily spruce and fir with aspen and open meadows along some upper trail sections. Switchbacks climb very steeply up the last mile to end at Forest Service Road 244, a section that might see

mountain bikers pushing instead of riding. The overall elevation gain is about 2,600 feet. From the upper trailhead, you can continue on the East Mountain Trail and descend the Horse Canyon Trail for an overnight trip of about 12 trail miles. A shuttle is required to connect the Horse Canyon Trailhead to the Mill Fork Canyon Trailhead.

User groups: Hikers, dogs, horses, and mountain bikes. No wheelchair access.

Permits: No permits are required. Parking and access are free.

Maps: For a USGS topographic map, ask for Rilda Canyon. Contact the Price Ranger District for the Manti–La Sal Travel Map.

Directions: From Huntington, take State Highway 31 north about 12 miles. Turn west on Forest Service Road 245 and drive 2.1 miles to the trailhead at road's end.

Contact: Manti–La Sal National Forest, Price Ranger District, 599 West Price River Drive, Price, UT 84501, 435/637-2817.

53 EAST MOUNTAIN TRAIL
8.0 mi/6.0 hrs

northwest of Orangeville

Map 3.2, page 62

Tracing the top of East Mountain, this trail connects the Horse Canyon Trail to the Mill Fork Canyon Trail (both trails are described in this chapter). East Mountain provides an opportunity for a pleasant overnight trip combining all three paths. You'll travel through grass and sagebrush with fine views of mountains and canyons while crossing East Mountain. From the southern trailhead on Road 244, the trail descends north to Horse Canyon. Deer and elk draw a few hunters here in the fall. Once you hit the Horse Canyon Trail, you can return the four miles to Road 244 or continue west in Horse Canyon to Scad Valley Road.

User groups: Hikers, dogs, horses, mountain bikes, and cross-country skiers. No wheelchair access.

Permits: No permits are required. Parking and access are free.

Maps: For a USGS topographic map, ask for Rilda Canyon. Contact the Price Ranger District for the Manti–La Sal Travel Map.

Directions: From Orangeville, take State Highway 29 west for approximately eight miles. Turn north on Forest Service Road 040 (which follows Cottonwood Creek) for 10 miles. Turn east on Forest Service Road 145 for another three miles, then north on Forest Service Road 244 for another three miles to the trailhead at the end of the road. For the last six miles, four-wheel-drive vehicles are recommended.

Contact: Manti–La Sal National Forest, Price Ranger District, 599 West Price River Drive, Price, UT 84501, 435/637-2817.

54 MUSINIA PEAK TRAIL
3.0 mi/4.0 hrs

east of Salina

Map 3.3, page 63

Also known as Mary's Nipple, Musinia Peak rises to 10,986 feet and is the most prominent landmark in the area and one of the remotest spots in the Fishlake National Forest. From your vehicle, head west toward the peak along the remains of an abandoned jeep track. The track passes through a stand of aspen and past a couple of springs before disappearing. Just past the last spring, a forested gulch heads steeply uphill. Old animal trails provide the only footpath up the gulch. Above the gulch and toward the summit, the terrain levels out, but you'll have to scramble through boulders for the final climb to the flat, barren top of the mountain. The view is outstanding, and you'll see large trailless tracts of land that beg to be explored. Retrace your steps 1.5 miles back to where you started.

User groups: Hikers and dogs. Not recommended for horses or mountain bikes. No wheelchair access.

Permits: No permits are required. Parking and access are free.

Maps: For a USGS topographic map, ask for Woods Lake.

Directions: From Salina, take I-70 east 17 miles to Exit 71. Continue east on Forest Service Road 010 for a half mile, then turn north on Forest Service Road 009 for 12.25 miles. Finally, turn east on Forest Service Road 001 and drive three miles to an open parking area on the right side of the road. A four-wheel-drive vehicle is recommended.

Contact: Fishlake National Forest, Richfield Ranger District, 115 East 900 North, Richfield, UT 84701, 435/896-9233.

55 WHITE MOUNTAIN TRAIL
12.0 mi one-way/1–2 days

east of Salina

Map 3.3, page 63

From Lizonbee Springs, the trail (an old jeep track closed to vehicles) heads north just past the spring, climbs a ridge, and descends to cross Skumpah Creek. From the creek, you'll ascend and contour around the long base of White Mountain. The mountain stands to the north and east. You can see it before you enter broad Salina Flats after gaining about 1,100 feet in elevation. Much of the trail lies on open ground with fine views of distant mountains. If you plan to spend the night, look for pleasant campsites in Salina Flats and north of the flats near Salina Creek. Near the northern end of the trail, Musinia Peak (Mary's Nipple) rises to almost 11,000 feet and is the most prominent landmark in the immediate area. You'll be hiking in shady stands of aspen by the time you reach the north-end trailhead. You can, of course, turn back at any time.

User groups: Hikers, horses, and dogs. Not recommended for mountain bikes. No wheelchair access.

Permits: No permits are required. Parking and access are free.

Maps: For USGS topographic maps, ask for Accord Lakes, Water Hollow Ridge, and Woods Lake.

Directions: From Salina, take I-70 east 17 miles to Exit 71. Continue east on Forest Service Road 010 for 9.1 miles. Turn north on Forest Service Road 007 for three miles and park at Lizonbee Springs.

Contact: Fishlake National Forest, Richfield Ranger District, 115 East 900 North, Richfield, UT 84701, 435/896-9233.

56 NIOTCHE CREEK TO HOGAN PASS: GWT

30.0 mi one-way/2–3 days

southeast of Salina

 Map 3.3, page 63

After following Forest Service Road 287 for about 200 yards, this section of the Great Western Trail leaves to the east, crosses Niotche Creek, and begins to climb. The trail is open to ATVs, which have created a well-worn path, up to UM Yogo Saddle. From the saddle, cross the UM Plateau (high point of 10,500 feet) and descend into the open, sagebrush-covered flats of Sheep Valley. From Niotche Creek to Sheep Valley is about nine miles. Sheep Valley can be accessed via Forest Service Road 015 north from State Route 25 and east of Johnson Valley Reservoir. From Sheep Valley the trail travels through aspen groves and up into a forest of spruce, across a ridge, and onto and across the middle of Willies Flat. You'll pass the south side of Willies Flat Reservoir, and descend gently to Forest Service Road 524. The trail here is Road 524 for more than a mile before it leaves to the south to pass through forest and then sagebrush enroute to hitting Hogan Pass. Your total elevation gain is about 1,300 feet. From Sheep Valley to Hogan Pass is approximately 21 miles. From Hogan Pass, State Route 72 runs 16 miles south to Loa.

User groups: Hikers, dogs, and horses. Portions are accessible to mountain bikes. No wheelchair access.

Permits: No permits are required. Parking and access are free.

Maps: For USGS topographic maps, ask for

Gooseberry Creek, Yogo Creek, Hilgard Mountain, Johns Peak, and Geyser Peak. Trails Illustrated's Fish Lake North & Central Capitol Reef covers the area.

Directions: From Salina, take I-70 east seven miles to Exit 61. Take Forest Service Road 640 (Gooseberry Road) south 14.5 miles, and turn east on Forest Service Road 287. Park a quarter mile in on Road 287.

Contact: Fishlake National Forest, Loa Ranger District, 138 South Main Street, Loa, UT 84747, 435/836-2811.

57 FISH LAKE HIGHTOP TRAIL

7.5 mi one-way/7.0 hrs

northwest of Loa

Map 3.3, page 63

From Daniels Pass, the trail gains most of its elevation (about 1,200 feet) in the first two miles of dense forest. Then it continues to the relatively flat Fish Lake Hightop Plateau with exceptional views in all directions of nearby mountains and distant misty peaks. A few spruce trees grow along the way in isolated stands. Near Tasha Spring huge boulders lie half buried in the ground like the backs of whales rolling at sea. You can turn back, or you can connect at Tasha Spring with either the Rock Canyon or Pelican Canyon Trails, or continue across Na-Gah Flat to the Doctor Creek Trail. These trails are described in this chapter. There are excellent mountain biking opportunities around nearby Lost Creek Reservoir.

User groups: Hikers, dogs, horses, and mountain bikes. No wheelchair access.

Permits: No permits are required. Parking and access are free.

Maps: For USGS topographic maps, ask for Mount Terrill and Fish Lake. Trails Illustrated's Fish Lake North & Central Capitol Reef covers the area. Contact the Loa Ranger District for a copy of *Mountain Bicycle Trails on the Fishlake National Forest.*

Directions: From Loa, take State Route 24 west 17 miles. Turn north on State Route 25 for 18 miles, then continue on Forest Service Road 640 for 7.5 miles. Just past the Mount Terrill Ranger Station, turn west on Forest Service Road 350, which leads past Lost Creek Reservoir approximately two miles to Daniels Pass and the trailhead.

Contact: Fishlake National Forest, Loa Ranger District, 138 South Main Street, Loa, UT 84747, 435/836-2811.

58 MOUNT TERRILL
5.0 mi/5.0 hrs

north of Loa

Map 3.3, page 63

Here's a fairly short climb to a really extraordinary view of the area, but since no trail to the summit of Terrill exists you'll be doing a bit of route finding. After following an old track into the forest from your vehicle, you'll find yourself on the south flank of Mount Terrill. Its wide, flat top is visible most of the way. From the old track you have to work your way up through the trees toward the summit. At the top (11,548 feet), after a gain of about 1,500 feet, you'll see Mount Marvine due south, Fish Lake Hightop Plateau to the southwest, Monroe Mountain to the west, Musinia Peak and White Mountain to the north, and Thousand Lake Mountain to the east. The UM Plateau to the near northeast invites off-trail exploration for those who want to keep hiking. You can retrace your steps 2.5 miles to your vehicle, or drop easily off the east flank and circle back. An map and compass are strongly recommended.

User groups: Hikers, dog, and horses. Not recommended for mountain bikes. No wheelchair access.

Permits: No permits are required. Parking and access are free.

Maps: For a USGS topographic map, ask for Mount Terrill. Trails Illustrated's Fish Lake North & Central Capitol Reef covers the area.

Directions: From Loa, take State Route 24 west 17 miles. Turn north on State Route 25 for 18 miles, then continue north on Forest

Service Road 640 at the north end of Johnson Valley Reservoir. After 3.75 miles on Road 640, turn east on Forest Service Road 042 and drive 1.4 miles. Look for an old track heading north, and park there. Four-wheel-drive vehicles are recommended for Road 042.

Contact: Fishlake National Forest, Loa Ranger District, 138 South Main Street, Loa, UT 84747, 435/836-2811.

59 MOUNT MARVINE
2.0 mi/3.0 hrs

north of Loa

Map 3.3, page 63

The view, the shape, and the challenge of Mount Marvine combine to make this arguably the most interesting peak in the Fishlake National Forest. No trail exists, but you'll see the 11,610-foot summit of Mount Marvine to the south from your vehicle. From the trailhead, you'll work your way through the forest, up the north face, and around to the east face. The long, ragged top runs north-south, rising on vertical walls above the lower flanks of the mountain. It's an obvious landmark from the east and west. From the north, as you approach, you'll see a sharp summit point. Many hikers are satisfied with the views from below the top. Several risky and relatively difficult routes may be found on the east wall of the summit if you wish to scramble to the very top, and gain a total of about 1,800 feet in elevation.

User groups: Hikers. Not recommended for dogs, horses, or mountain bikes. No wheelchair access.

Permits: No permits are required. Parking and access are free.

Maps: For a USGS topographic map, ask for Mount Terrill.

Directions: From Loa, take State Route west 17 miles. Turn north on State Route 25 for 18 miles, then continue north on Forest Service Road 640 at the north end of Johnson Valley Reservoir. After 3.75 miles on Road 640, turn east on Forest Service Road 042 for two miles

and park. Four-wheel-drive vehicles are recommended for Road 042.

Contact: Fishlake National Forest, Loa Ranger
District, 138 South Main Street, Loa, UT 84747,
435/836-2811.

60 HILGARD MOUNTAIN TRAIL
3.0 mi/3.0–4.0 hrs

northeast of Loa

Map 3.3, page 63

Hilgard Mountain (11,533 feet) provides the
best views in the Fishlake National Forest: mountain peaks to the west and north, barren sandstone beauty to the west. The trail runs due
south from a pass with blazes on the trees that
are sometimes difficult to spot. You'll ascend
steadily through a forest dominated by spruce
to an open ridge on Hilgard's northwest face.
From there the scramble to the summit, with a
total elevation gain of about 1,700 feet, is relatively easy. If you wish for a longer trip, descend
the south face to meet the Great Western Trail,
hike west and north to Forest Service Road 015,
and take the road two miles back to your vehicle. This loop totals about nine miles.

User groups: Hikers and dogs. Not recommended for horses or mountain bikes. No
wheelchair access.

Permits: No permits are required. Parking and
access are free.

Maps: For a USGS topographic map, ask for
Hilgard Mountain. Trails Illustrated's Fish
Lake North & Central Capitol Reef covers
the area.

Directions: From Loa, take State Route 24
west 17 miles. Turn north on State Route 25
for 20 miles, then continue north on Forest
Service Road 015 for eight miles. A four-wheel-
drive vehicle is recommended. The road switchbacks for about two more miles of climbing
to a pass with a fine view eastward. Park at
the pass.

Contact: Fishlake National Forest, Loa Ranger
District, 138 South Main Street, Loa, UT 84747,
435/836-2811.

61 ROCK CANYON– TASHA CREEK TRAIL
8.0 mi one-way/6.0 hrs

north of Loa

Map 3.3, page 63

Following Tasha Creek from its confluence
with Sevenmile Creek to its origin at Tasha
Spring, this trail climbs Rock Canyon through
a forest of evergreens and aspens. Occasionally little lakes and meadows open up the
canyon and serve as breeding grounds for
mosquitoes (pack repellent). About two miles
in from Sevenmile Creek, a short spur trail
leads north to Lake Louise, where the great
trout fishing draws many an angler. On the
main trail the views to the north and east im-
prove as the terrain rises. At Tasha Spring,
the trail meets the Fish Lake Hightop Trail
and Pelican Canyon Trail, both described in
this chapter. Your total elevation gain will be
about 2,200 feet. Rock Canyon is a popular
ride for horsepackers, as an equestrian trailhead stands on Route 25 about seven miles
north of the Fish Lake Lodge.

User groups: Hikers, dogs, and horses. Not
recommended for mountain bikes. No wheelchair access.

Permits: No permits are required. Parking and
access are free. Camping and fires are not permitted on this trail. Camping is restricted to
designated campgrounds on Fish Lake.

Maps: For USGS topographic maps, ask for
Mount Terrill and Fish Lake. Trails Illustrated's Fish Lake North & Central Capitol Reef
covers the area.

Directions: From Loa, take State Route 24
west one mile. Turn north on State Route 25
and drive 18 miles. Turn north on Forest Service Road 640 for a half mile to the trailhead
on the west side of the road.

Contact: Fishlake National Forest, Loa Ranger
District, 138 South Main Street, Loa, UT 84747,
435/836-2811.

62 MILL CREEK TRAIL
8.5 mi/1–2 days

north of Burrville

Map 3.3, page 63

This steep trail heads north across a slope dotted with mahogany and piñon for a quarter mile before crossing Mill Creek and turning west along the drainage of the creek. The trail follows Mill Creek for about two miles, then shifts into a southern tributary of the creek. Shady springs offer opportunities for pleasant breaks and a chance to set camp for an overnighter. The trail ends up in a forest of spruce and aspen, and exits on Forest Service Road 068 after gaining about 2,500 feet in elevation. The upper trailhead can be reached by taking Forest Service Road 068 west from Koosharem (a one-way hike of 4.25 miles), but you'll need to leave a vehicle there.

User groups: Hikers, horses, and dogs. No mountain bikes or wheelchair access.

Permits: No permits are required. Parking and access are free.

Maps: For a USGS topographic map, ask for Koosharem. Trails Illustrated's Fish Lake North & Central Capitol Reef covers the area.

Directions: From the only intersection in Burrville on State Route 62, take Forest Service Road 159 west for a half mile. The road then bears north along the power lines. It's about one mile more to the signed trailhead.

Contact: Fishlake National Forest, Richfield Ranger District, 115 East 900 North, Richfield, UT 84701, 435/896-9233.

63 CRATER LAKES LOOP TRAIL
6.0 mi/5.0 hrs

northwest of Loa

Map 3.3, page 63

Though barren of fish, lovely lakes await at the end of this hike. Follow the rutted route for about 200 yards east from the parking area, and cross Lake Creek. The path starts to climb almost immediately, then flattens in an aspen-

lined clearing after a quarter mile or so. You'll come to the junction of Trail 045 and Trail 116. Turn south on Trail 045. From here you'll climb up to and sweep around the south end of North Crater Lake, gaining a total of about 900 feet in elevation. The trail runs north from there to descend Porcupine Draw and return to the trail junction in the clearing. From North Crater Lake you can hike a half mile of trail to South Crater Lake, a worthwhile side trip. Both lakes sit in picturesque alpine surroundings with low forested mountains and bold rock formations overlooking the water.

User groups: Hikers, dogs, horses, and mountain bikes. No wheelchair access.

Permits: No permits are required. Parking and access are free. Camping and fires are restricted to designated campgrounds on Fish Lake.

Maps: For a USGS topographic map, ask for Fish Lake. Trails Illustrated's Fish Lake North & Central Capitol Reef covers the area.

Directions: From Loa, take State Route 24 west 17 miles. Turn north on State Route 25 for 15 miles to a parking area on the east side of the highway and north of Fish Lake.

Contact: Fishlake National Forest, Loa Ranger District, 138 South Main Street, Loa, UT 84747, 435/836-2811.

64 PELICAN CANYON TRAIL
5.0 mi one-way/6.0 hrs

northwest of Loa

Map 3.3, page 63

This is one of the most popular hikes near Fish Lake, with good reason: It's a lovely walk in the forest rising to great overlooks of the area. From the parking place, follow an old road south for an easy walk up to the Pelican Overlook and a fine view of the lake. About 100 yards west of the overlook, a sign marks the Pelican Canyon Trail, which begins by crossing a sagebrush-covered rise. You'll soon pass a spur trail that leaves to the south to end at a campground on the lake. Now the main trail climbs up Pelican Canyon and the going gets more strenuous. A stream flows downhill as you walk up, and a dense forest shadows the path. At approximately three miles, the left fork of Pelican Canyon Trail leaves to the west, climbs up to Na-Gah Flat, and connects, after crossing the Flat, with the Doctor Canyon Trail. If you take this trail you'll return to the lake after a total of about seven miles. Continuing on the Pelican Canyon Trail, you'll come the junction with the Rock Canyon and Fish Lake Hightop Trails. This is the turnaround point for this hike.

User groups: Hikers, dogs, and horses. Not recommended for mountain bikes except up to Pelican Overlook and back to the lake via a spur trail. No wheelchair access.

Permits: No permits are required. Parking and access are free. Camping and fires are not permitted on this trail. Camping is restricted to designated campgrounds on Fish Lake.

Maps: For a USGS topographic map, ask for Fish Lake. Trails Illustrated's Fish Lake North & Central Capitol Reef covers the area. Contact the Loa Ranger District for a copy of *Mountain Bicycle Trails on the Fishlake National Forest.*

Directions: From Loa, take State Route 24 west 17 miles. Turn north on State Route 25 for 14 miles to Widgeon Bay on the north end of Fish Lake. Turn west into the parking area.

Contact: Fishlake National Forest, Loa Ranger District, 138 South Main Street, Loa, UT 84747, 435/836-2811.

65 KOOSHAREM CANYON TRAIL
7.0 mi/6.0 hrs

northwest of Koosharem

Map 3.3, page 63

Following Koosharem Creek the entire distance, this trail climbs steadily from a forest of piñon and juniper to one of spruce, fir, and aspen. This shady trail—nice on a hot day—includes about 1,400 feet of elevation gain. Beaver activity in the creek has created numerous ponds with good trout fishing. The going is rugged at times. You'll finish after 3.5 miles of trail at the old Koosharem Guard Station, the southern trailhead for many more worthy hikes in the Fishlake National Forest.

User groups: Hikers, dogs, and horses. Not recommended for mountain bikes. No wheelchair access.

Permits: No permits are required. Parking and access are free.

Maps: For a USGS topographic map, ask for Koosharem. Trails Illustrated's Fish Lake North & Central Capitol Reef covers the area.

Directions: From near the post office/grocery store in Koosharem on State Route 62, take Forest Service Road 076 west for approximately two miles. Where the road forks, take the rutted path to the north and follow it as far as possible (about one mile). Pull off and park. The road becomes the trail.

Contact: Fishlake National Forest, Richfield Ranger District, 115 East 900 North, Richfield, UT 84701, 435/896-9233.

66 DOCTOR CREEK TRAIL
6.0 mi/3.5 hrs

northwest of Loa

Map 3.3, page 63

From near the shore of Fish Lake, just south of the Doctor Creek Campground, the trail heads west, easily passing through a stand of aspen before reaching the mouth of Doctor Creek Canyon. From there you'll climb a steep path along the creek and through a dense forest. At the upper end the land opens out onto sagebrush-covered Na-Gah Flat and ends at rough and rutted Forest Service Road 352 on the south end of the Fish Lake Hightop Plateau. From here you can turn around and drop down the three miles and 1,100 feet of elevation you just climbed. A more interesting option, if you have the time and inclination, is to cross the Flat and continue on either the Pelican Canyon Trail, Rock Canyon Trail, or Fish Lake Hightop Trail, all of which are described in this chapter.

User groups: Hikers, dogs, and horses. Not recommended for mountain bikes. No wheelchair access.

Permits: No permits are required. Parking and access are free. Camping and fires are not permitted on this trail. Camping is restricted to designated campgrounds on Fish Lake.

Maps: For USGS topographic maps, ask for Fish Lake and Burrville. Trails Illustrated's Fish Lake North & Central Capitol Reef covers the area.

Directions: From Loa, take State Route 24 west one mile. Turn north on State Route 25 for nine miles to the southern end of Fish Lake. A sign on the west side of the road indicates Doctor Creek Canyon.

Contact: Fishlake National Forest, Loa Ranger District, 138 South Main Street, Loa, UT 84747, 435/836-2811.

67 LAKESHORE NATIONAL RECREATION TRAIL
9.5 mi one-way/6.0 hrs

northwest of Loa

Map 3.3, page 63

Activity at Fish Lake, a popular vacation destination, centers around the Fish Lake Lodge. The Lakeshore Trail, and several other spots on State Route 25, are easily accessed from here. The trail can be divided into three general sections: 1) an easy middle section along the western shore about three miles long, 2) a moderate northern section about 2.5 miles long that climbs to Pelican Overlook and descends to Route 24 north of the lake, and 3) a more difficult southern section that wraps around the south end of Fish Lake and climbs steeply over about 1,000 feet to an overlook on Mytoge Mountain above the eastern shore. With a lunch on your back, the entire trail makes for a very pleasant summer day.

User groups: Hikers, dogs, horses, and mountain bikes. No wheelchair access.

Permits: No permits are required. Parking and access are free. Camping on Fish Lake is restricted to designated campgrounds.

Maps: For a USGS topographic map, ask for Fish Lake. Trails Illustrated's Fish Lake North & Central Capitol Reef covers the area. Contact the Loa Ranger District for a copy of *Mountain Bicycle Trails on the Fishlake National Forest.*

Directions: From Loa, take State Route 24 west 17 miles. Turn north on State Route 25 for 10 miles to Fish Lake Lodge. Parking is available at the lodge.

Contact: Fishlake National Forest, Loa Ranger District, 138 South Main Street, Loa, UT 84747, 435/836-2811.

68 MYTOGE MOUNTAIN LOOP
25.0 mi/1–2 days

northwest of Loa

Map 3.3, page 63

Although you could walk it, this route is an exemplary mountain bike ride and is the trail for the "Fishlake in the Fall" mountain bike rally. The loop can be started and finished anywhere. If you're parked at Fish Lake Lodge, however, descend Route 25 to Forest Service Road 046 south of the lake. Road 046 climbs to three lake overlooks. From a spring near the midpoint, leave road 046 and continue on 045 to weave between the picturesque Crater Lakes and descend Porcupine Draw, cross Lake Creek, and return to Route 25. The route gains about 1,200 feet in elevation.

User groups: Mountain bikes mostly. Hikers, dogs, and horses are allowed. No wheelchair access.

Permits: No permits are required. Parking and access are free. Camping and fires are not permitted except in designated campgrounds on Fish Lake.

Maps: For a USGS topographic map, ask for Fish Lake. Contact the Loa Ranger District for a copy of *Mountain Bicycle Trails on the Fishlake National Forest.*

Directions: From Loa, take State Route 24 west 17 miles. Turn north on State Route 25 for 10 miles to Fish Lake Lodge. Parking is available at the lodge.

Contact: Fishlake National Forest, Loa Ranger District, 138 South Main Street, Loa, UT 84747, 435/836-2811.

69 HOGAN PASS TO ELKHORN CAMPGROUND: GWT
12.5 mi one-way/1–2 days

northeast of Loa

Map 3.3, page 63

Although this section of the Great Western Trail offers extraordinary views, hikers who enjoy peace and quiet may be disappointed by the fact that ATVs use this segment regularly. From Hogan Pass the trail heads south around Willow Basin to become a dirt road. This road continues south, skirting the east side of Geyser Peak, to join Forest Service Road 206 about two miles from State Route 72 at Riley Spring. After a quarter mile trip on Road 206, the trail continues south, passing along the lower west flank of Hens Hole Peak before it reaches Elkhorn Campground. The elevation gain for the hike is about 1,200 feet. Horses are easily unloaded and loaded at both ends.

User groups: Hikers, dogs, horses, and mountain bikes. No wheelchair access.

Permits: No permits are required. Parking and access are free.

Maps: For USGS topographic maps, ask for Geyser Peak and Flat Top. Trails Illustrated's Fish Lake North & Central Capitol Reef covers the area.

Directions: From Loa, take State Route 72 north 16 miles to Hogan Pass and park in the turnout.

Contact: Fishlake National Forest, Loa Ranger District, 138 South Main Street, Loa, UT 84747, 435/836-2811.

70 ELKHORN CAMPGROUND TO TORREY: GWT
12.5 mi one-way/1–2 days

northeast of Loa

Map 3.3, page 63

From the east end of Elkhorn Campground,

the trail heads east for about a quarter, following a fence. Then it swings south through a series of aspen groves interspersed with views of the desert to the east and Thousand Lake Mountain to the west. At the south end of Thousand Lake Mountain, you'll reach Sand Creek Spring and then pass through Sulphur Basin where the trail becomes a sandy road. You'll descend into a canyon with towering walls of red and yellow sandstone. The terrain is increasingly desert-like until you reach a Fishlake National Forest map board, a mile or so west of Torrey. A four-wheel-drive vehicle can be driven about two miles north of the map board if you wish to shorten your trip. From north to south, most of this section of the Great Western Trail is downhill.

User groups: Hikers, dogs, and horses. Portions are accessible to mountain bikes. No wheelchair access.

Permits: No permits are required. Parking and access are free.

Maps: For USGS topographic maps, ask for Flat Top and Torrey. Trails Illustrated's Fish Lake North & Central Capitol Reef covers the area. Contact the Loa Ranger District for a copy of *Mountain Bicycle Trails on the Fishlake National Forest.*

Directions: From Loa, take State Route 72 north nine miles. Turn east on Forest Service Road 206 for seven miles to the Elkhorn Campground.

Contact: Fishlake National Forest, Loa Ranger District, 138 South Main Street, Loa, UT 84747, 435/836-2811.

71 THOUSAND LAKE MOUNTAIN
6.0 mi/4.0 hrs

northeast of Loa

Map 3.3, page 63

Thousand Lake Mountain, despite a paucity of lakes, offers splendid high-country hiking on numerous trails and across the vast plateau of its top to a summit of 11,305 feet. The summit plateau is truly broad: three miles north-south by 1.5 miles east-west. The access described here starts north of the Elkhorn Campground on the Neff Reservoir Trail, which ascends to Neff Reservoir over a distance of 2.5 miles. From north of the reservoir, the Flat Top Trail climbs briefly but steeply to Thousand Lake Flat Top, the summit plateau, after gaining about 1,000 feet in elevation. A lovely loop can be traveled by descending the Snow Lake Trail from the plateau to Snow Lake and following Forest Service Road 209 back to the Elkhorn Campground, a total distance of about eight miles.

User groups: Hikers, dogs, and horses. Local roads are excellent for mountain bikes. No wheelchair access.

Permits: No permits are required. Parking and access are free.

Maps: For a USGS topographic map, ask for Flat Top. Trails Illustrated's Fish Lake North & Central Capitol Reef covers the area. Contact the Loa Ranger District for a copy of *Mountain Bicycle Trails on the Fishlake National Forest.*

Directions: From Loa, UT, take State Route 72 north nine miles. Turn east on Forest Service Road 206 for seven miles to the Elkhorn Campground.

Contact: Fishlake National Forest, Loa Ranger District, 138 South Main Street, Loa, UT 84747, 435/836-2811.

72 LOWER CATHEDRAL VALLEY OVERLOOK TRAIL
1.5 mi/1.0 hrs
northeast of Torrey in Capitol Reef National Park

Map 3.3, page 63

Heading north from a rough road, this trail crosses the sandy bottom of Harnet Draw then climbs a short, steep path to the ridge overlooking Lower Cathedral Valley. As the climb is only about 150 feet, the whole family can enjoy this hike. What you'll see defies vivid description: the conspicuous pyramids of the Temple of the Sun and the Temple of the Moon, isolated and mysterious, jutting from the floor of the valley; the gray and red walls of the val-

ley; Black Mountain in the distant northeast; Thousand Lake Mountain dominating the west.

User groups: Hikers only. No dogs, horses, or mountain bikes are allowed. No wheelchair access.

Permits: No day-use permits are required. Parking and access are free.

Maps: For a USGS topographic map, ask for Fruita NW. An excellent source of information is the *Hiking Map & Guide to Capitol Reef National Park* from Earthwalk Press, available at the visitors center.

Directions: From Torrey, take State Route 24 east 22.5 miles. Watch for a small sign on the north side of 24 indicating the River Ford (Hartnet) Road. After a half mile the road forks and crosses Fremont River. The left fork is usually a bit easier. A high-clearance four-wheel-drive vehicle is a good idea for the crossing. Ask a ranger about fording conditions before taking the River Ford Road. Beyond the ford the two forks become one road again. After 17.5 miles look for a sign indicating the Lower Cathedral Valley Overlook and a wide spot in the road to park.

Contact: Capitol Reef National Park, HC 70, Box 15, Torrey, UT 84775, 435/425-3791.

73 LOWER SOUTH DESERT OVERLOOK TRAIL
3.0 mi/4.0 hrs
northeast of Torrey in Capitol Reef National Park

Map 3.3, page 63

Approximately .2 mile into this hike, you'll reach the overlook. Towers in strange shapes and oddly balanced rocks stretch across the weird landscape. To the west, Jailhouse Rock rises more than 500 feet from flat desert to a red pyramid peak. Far to the west the ragged sandstone crest of the Waterpocket Fold erupts from Thousand Lake Mountain. Following an abandoned road, the trail continues west through the evening shadow of Jailhouse Rock and toward the pointed top of Temple Rock. At about 1.5 miles the trail passes just north of Temple

Rock after gaining very little elevation. If you turn around, you'll have an easy 1.5 miles back to your vehicle. But if you have time, leave the trail to enter Deep Creek Wash and head west to the grassy expanse of Little Sand Flat. The flat, located just south of the wash, has abundant campsites and miles of slickrock to explore. The going gets rough, and the elevation gain is another 900 feet, but the solitude is splendid. Deep Creek rarely contains water, so carry plenty.

User groups: Hikers only. No dogs, horses, or mountain bikes are allowed. No wheelchair access.

Permits: No day-use permits are required. A free backcountry permit is required for overnight camping. Parking and access are free.

Maps: For USGS topographic maps, ask for Fruita NW and Cathedral Mountain. An excellent source of information is the *Hiking Map & Guide to Capitol Reef National Park* from Earthwalk Press, available at the visitors center. Trails Illustrated's Fish Lake North & Central Capitol Reef covers the area.

Directions: From Torrey, take State Route 24 east 22.5 miles. Watch for a small sign on the north side of 24 indicating the River Ford (Hartnet) Road. A half-mile in, the road forks to cross Fremont River. The left fork is usually a bit easier. A high-clearance four-wheel-drive vehicle is a good idea for the crossing. Ask a ranger about fording conditions before taking the River Ford Road. Beyond the ford the two forks become one road again. After 14 miles turn west onto the Lower South Desert Overlook spur road and drive to the end. Park here.

Contact: Capitol Reef National Park, HC 70, Box 15, Torrey, UT 84775, 435/425-3791.

74 CHIMNEY ROCK LOOP TRAIL
3.5 mi/2.0 hrs

east of Torrey in Capitol Reef National Park

Map 3.3, page 63

Winding through reddish-brown shale and sandstone hills of the Moenkopi Formation, this trail rises to the west of Chimney Rock. The rock is a 400-foot-tall pedestal with a hard cap of tan Shinarump sandstone that has prevented the tower beneath it from eroding away. You'll get a fine look at the barrier cliffs of Capitol Reef. After a series of switchbacks and 600 feet of climbing, you'll reach the rim of Meeks Mesa, where a tremendous panorama stretches south along the red cliffs and white domes of Capitol Reef to the distant Henry Mountains. The trail follows the rim, through stunted trees, before descending in a long loop back to rejoin itself on the canyon floor. No water is found here, so carry plenty.

User groups: Hikers only. No dogs, horses, or mountain bikes are allowed. No wheelchair access.

Permits: No day-use permits are required. A free backcountry permit is required for overnight camping. Parking and access are free.

Maps: For a USGS topographic map, ask for Twin Rock. An excellent source of information is the *Hiking Map & Guide to Capitol Reef National Park* from Earthwalk Press, available at the visitors center. Trails Illustrated's Fish Lake North & Central Capitol Reef covers the area.

Directions: From Torrey, take State Route 24 east 7.6 miles to the parking lot and trailhead on the north side of the road.

Contact: Capitol Reef National Park, HC 70, Box 15, Torrey, UT 84775, 435/425-3791.

75 CHIMNEY ROCK CANYON TRAIL
18.0 mi/2–3 days

east of Torrey in Capitol Reef National Park

Map 3.3, page 63

For the first 1.5 miles you'll follow the Chimney Rock Loop Trail in reverse. At the junction with the trail into the canyon, continue straight ahead instead of following the loop. You'll drop into the canyon where sandstone walls naturally decorated with black streaks of "desert varnish" rise several hundred feet into the sky. You'll soon reach an old livestock drift fence. From the fence you can hike upstream if you wish to explore the upper canyon. A spring flows approximately 1.5 miles upstream. Downstream the trail disappears, but the canyon narrows, and following it easy until you come to two dry waterfalls. Back up and you'll find a path marked with rock cairns leading along the bench on the north side. Numerous side canyons can be hiked here, and pleasant campsites abound. Approximately six miles below the dry falls Fremont River poses the last obstacle. You'll have to wade. Check with a ranger before your hike to determine the ease of the river crossing. Climb the river bank on the opposite side to State Route 24 where you'll be seven road miles from the trailhead. You can arrange a shuttle or hitchhike the road, or walk the nine trail miles back the way you came. Spring, the most popular hiking time for this trail, often brings quite a few visitors.

User groups: Hikers only. No dogs, horses, or mountain bikes are allowed. No wheelchair access.

Permits: No day-use permits are required. A free backcountry permit is required for overnight camping. Parking and access are free.

Maps: For USGS topographic maps, ask for Twin Rock and Fruita. An excellent source of information is the *Hiking Map & Guide to Capitol Reef National Park* from Earthwalk Press, available at the visitors center. Trails Illustrated's Fish Lake North & Central Capitol Reef covers the area.

Directions: From Torrey, take State Route 24 east 7.6 miles to a parking lot and trailhead on the north side of the road.

Contact: Capitol Reef National Park, HC 70, Box 15, Torrey, UT 84775, 435/425-3791.

76 GOOSENECKS TRAIL
0.2 mi/0.5 hr

east of Torrey in Capitol Reef National Park

Map 3.3, page 63

The whole family can enjoy this brief climb to the rim and a ramble through sandstone boulders to a fenced overlook. Prepare

for an excellent view. From 600 feet above, you'll look down on the meanders ("goosenecks") of Sulphur Creek. To the west lie the forested plateaus of Thousand Lake and Boulder Mountains. To the east and south you'll see the white and red of Capitol Reef and beyond to the Henry Mountains.

User groups: Hikers only. No dogs, horses, or mountain bikes are allowed. No wheelchair access.

Permits: No day-use permits are required. Parking and access are free.

Maps: For a USGS topographic map, ask for Twin Rock. An excellent source of information is the *Hiking Map & Guide to Capitol Reef National Park* from Earthwalk Press, available at the visitors center. Trails Illustrated's Fish Lake North & Central Capitol Reef covers the area.

Directions: From Torrey, take State Route 24 east 8.4 miles to the turnoff on the south side of the road.

Contact: Capitol Reef National Park, HC 70, Box 15, Torrey, UT 84775, 435/425-3791.

77 SUNSET TRAIL
0.6 mi/1.0 hr

east of Torrey in Capitol Reef National Park

Map 3.3, page 63

From the same starting point as the Goosenecks Trail, you'll hike east instead of west. After a brief stroll, and about 40 feet of elevation gain, the trail ends on the rim of Sulphur Creek Canyon with the Goosenecks below and the dramatic Fluted Wall of the Moenkopi Formation behind. It's an easy enough walk, even for kids. Come in the evening. The sunsets are often splendid.

User groups: Hikers only. No dogs, horses, or mountain bikes are allowed. No wheelchair access.

Permits: No day-use permits are required. Parking and access are free.

Maps: For a USGS topographic map, ask for Twin Rock. An excellent source of information is the *Hiking Map & Guide to Capitol Reef National Park* from Earthwalk Press, available at the visitors center. Trails Illustrated's Fish Lake North & Central Capitol Reef covers the area.

Directions: From Torrey, take State Route 24 east 8.4 miles to the turnoff on the south side of the road.

Contact: Capitol Reef National Park, HC 70, Box 15, Torrey, UT 84775, 435/425-3791.

78 HICKMAN BRIDGE TRAIL
2.0 mi/1.5 hrs

east of Torrey in Capitol Reef National Park

Map 3.3, page 63

All things considered, this trail offers perhaps the best quick look at the geological wonder of this national park. The trail follows the tree-clad banks of the Fremont River for a short distance, then climbs into the arid desert land typical of the park, crosses a small bench, and descends briefly into a sandy wash. You'll ascend the wash, past a tiny natural bridge and up and beneath splendid Hickman Bridge, one of the largest natural sandstone bridges in the park (height 125 feet, span 133 feet). Curving back toward the river, the trail continues to a fine overlook of the Fremont River before retracing the one mile back to the start.

User groups: Hikers only. No dogs, horses, or mountain bike are allowed. No wheelchair access.

Permits: No day-use permits are required. Parking and access are free.

Maps: For a USGS topographic map, ask for Fruita. An excellent source of information is the *Hiking Map & Guide to Capitol Reef National Park* from Earthwalk Press, available at the visitors center. Trails Illustrated's Fish Lake North & Central Capitol Reef covers the area.

Directions: From Torrey, take State Route 24 east 12.7 miles to the trailhead on the north side of the road.

Contact: Capitol Reef National Park, HC 70, Box 15, Torrey, UT 84775, 435/425-3791.

79 RIM OVERLOOK TRAIL
4.5 mi/3.0 hrs

east of Torrey in Capitol Reef National Park

Map 3.3, page 63

This hike follows the Hickman Bridge Trail for approximately .3 mile before turning north on the Rim Overlook Trail. Climbing into a dry wash, the trail ascends for a half mile to a great view of Hickman Bridge. Entering two more washes, the trail crosses a section of sand dunes and climbs in and out of another wash. Rock cairns then lead the way across an extended section of slickrock to the Rim Overlook with a beautiful view south along Waterpocket Fold. From here you can either return the 2.25 miles to the start or, with more time, continue to the Navajo Knobs (described in this chapter). From the Rim Overlook it's possible to hike north cross-country to the solitude of Longleaf Flat. The campsites here are pleasant, but dry, so bring water.

User groups: Hikers only. No dogs, horses, or mountain bikes are allowed. No wheelchair access.

Permits: No day-use permits are required. A free backcountry permit is required for overnight camping. Parking and access are free.

Maps: For a USGS topographic map, ask for Fruita. An excellent source of information is the *Hiking Map & Guide to Capitol Reef National Park* from Earthwalk Press, available at the visitors center. Trails Illustrated's Fish Lake North & Central Capitol Reef covers the area.

Directions: From Torrey, take State Route 24 east 12.7 miles to the trailhead on the north side of the road.

Contact: Capitol Reef National Park, HC 70, Box 15, Torrey, UT 84775, 435/425-3791.

80 NAVAJO KNOBS TRAIL
9.0 mi/7.0 hrs

east of Torrey in Capitol Reef National Park

Map 3.3, page 63

To reach Navajo Knobs, take the Hickman Bridge Trail and then the Rim Overlook Trail.

From the Rim Overlook, the Navajo Knobs Trail starts and climbs across slickrock east and north of a picturesque stone formation called The Castle. After hiking 2.25 miles from the Overlook, over uneven terrain with steady climbing, you'll end on a small table of rock with a 360-degree panorama of the park and the memorable domes of sandstone called the Navajo Knobs. It's a grunt of an elevation gain, about 1,700 feet, and it's now 4.5 miles back to the trailhead. Carry plenty of water.

User groups: Hikers only. No dogs, horses, or mountain bikes are allowed. No wheelchair access.

Permits: No day-use permits are required. A free backcountry permit is required for overnight camping. Parking and access are free.

Maps: For USGS topographic maps, ask for Fruita and Twin Rock. An excellent source of information is the *Hiking Map & Guide to Capitol Reef National Park* from Earthwalk Press, available at the visitors center. Trails Illustrated's Fish Lake North & Central Capitol Reef covers the area.

Directions: From Torrey, take State Route 24 east 12.7 miles to the trailhead on the north side of the road.

Contact: Capitol Reef National Park, HC 70, Box 15, Torrey, UT 84775, 435/425-3891.

81 FREMONT GORGE OVERLOOK TRAIL
4.5 mi/5.0 hrs

east of Torrey in Capitol Reef National Park

Map 3.3, page 63

After a rigorous uphill start, the trail eases as it crosses Johnson Mesa, which offers exceptional views in all directions of the sandstone majesty and distant gray peaks of central Utah. But then, just when you think you've got it made, the trail begins to climb again. Fortunately, the climb is worth the effort: an awesome view into the Fremont River Gorge, the bottom of which lies 1,000 feet below. You'll have to retrace your steps just over two miles

to the start. Carry plenty of water, as this trail offers none.

User groups: Hikers only. No dogs, horses, or mountain bikes are allowed. No wheelchair access.

Permits: No day-use permits are required. Parking and access are free.

Maps: For a USGS topographic map, ask for Twin Rock. An excellent source of information is the *Hiking Map & Guide to Capitol Reef National Park* from Earthwalk Press, available at the visitors center. Trails Illustrated's Fish Lake North & Central Capitol Reef covers the area.

Directions: From Torrey, take State Route 24 east 10 miles to the parking lot and trailhead at the Blacksmith Shop on the south side of the road.

Contact: Capitol Reef National Park, HC 70, Box 15, Torrey, UT 84775, 435/425-3791.

82 SULPHUR CREEK TRAIL
6.0 mi one-way/5.0 hrs

east of Torrey in Capitol Reef National Park

Map 3.3, page 63

From just west of the visitors center, this trail enters the depths of Sulphur Creek Canyon and follows it up between white and red sandstone walls. Approximately one mile into the hike, the first of several obstacles appears: a waterfall that drops about five feet. The narrow canyon here requires the use of hands and feet to climb around the falls. Eventually you'll reach the Goosenecks, more than a mile of deeply cut twists and turns through the canyon. Here, and for approximately 2.5 miles, there are no suitable campsites due to the canyon's narrow confines. Beyond the Goosenecks the trail leaves Sulphur Creek and continues about 1.5 miles up a low-walled side canyon to State Route 24 near the Chimney Rock Trailhead. From here it's three miles to the visitors center. The water of Sulphur Creek, as the name implies, is not potable. Carry plenty. Many hikers choose to start at Chimney Rock and descend Sulphur

Creek to the visitors center, but this requires some tricky down-climbing at the falls.

User groups: Hikers only. No dogs, horses, or mountain bikes are allowed. No wheelchair access.

Permits: No day-use permit is required. A free backcountry permit is required for overnight camping. Parking and access are free.

Maps: For a USGS topographic map, ask for Twin Rock. An excellent source of information is the *Hiking Map & Guide to Capitol Reef National Park* from Earthwalk Press, available at the visitors center. Trails Illustrated's Fish Lake North & Central Capitol Reef covers the area.

Directions: From Torrey, take State Route 24 east 10.7 miles to the visitors center.

Contact: Capitol Reef National Park, HC 70, Box 15, Torrey, UT 84775, 435/425-3791.

83 FREMONT RIVER TRAIL
2.5 mi/2.0 hrs

east of Torrey in Capitol Reef National Park

Map 3.3, page 63

This is the only wheelchair-accessible section of trail in the park, but wheelchairs can't make it to the overlook at the end. Kids can. From the west end of Campground Loop B, the trail, with a gravel surface for the first half mile, gently begins to follow the Fremont River past old apple, pear, and peach orchards. The orchards attract wildlife, especially mule deer, yellowbelly marmots, beavers, and human fruit-pickers with permits. After crossing a meadow and entering sagebrush country, the trail climbs steadily toward Fremont Overlook, gaining about 500 feet in elevation to a cairn marking trail's end. You'll find an exemplary eyeful at the overlook: the contrast of green river running through dry brown mesas, and tidy orchards beneath the upheaval of domes and ragged rock formations. The return hike follows the same trail. Carry plenty of water.

User groups: Hikers. No dog, horses, or mountain bikes are allowed. Wheelchair accessible for the first half mile.

Permits: No day-use permits are required. The "Scenic Drive" costs $5.

Maps: For USGS topographic maps, ask for Fruita and Twin Rock. An excellent source of information is the *Hiking Map & Guide to Capitol Reef National Park* from Earthwalk Press, available at the visitors center. Trails Illustrated's Fish Lake North & Central Capitol Reef covers the area.

wheelchair accessible section of the Fremont River Trail, Capitol Reef National Park

Directions: From Torrey, take State Route 24 east 10.7 miles to the visitors center. Turn south on the "Scenic Drive" and continue to the amphitheater parking area.

Contact: Capitol Reef National Park, HC 70, Box 15, Torrey, UT 84775, 435/425-3791.

84 COHAB CANYON TRAIL
3.5 mi/2.5–3.0 hrs

east of Torrey in Capitol Reef National Park

Map 3.3, page 63

For a relatively quick peek at what makes this sandstone area worthy of park status, this trail has no peer. From the campground, the opening to Cohab Canyon is a deceptively small notch. The first short stretch includes a relatively strenuous climb of about 400 feet, but the trail levels off after that and offers fabulous views across the park. The canyon becomes sparsely wooded with piñon and juniper growing below beautifully sculpted walls. After a mile, short spur trails leave to the north for outstanding views of the Fremont River. A few more steps and the Frying Pan Trail leaves toward the south, to Cassidy Arch and Grand Wash Trail. Cohab Canyon descends gently to reach State Route 24 near the Hickman Bridge Trailhead. Carry water.

User groups: Hikers only. No dogs, horses, or mountain bikes are allowed. No wheelchair access.

Permits: No day-use permits are required. A $5 fee is charged for the "Scenic Drive."

Maps: For a USGS topographic map, ask for Fruita. An excellent source of information is the *Hiking Map & Guide to Capitol Reef National Park* from Earthwalk Press, available at the visitors center. Trails Illustrated's Fish Lake North & Central Capitol Reef covers the area.

Directions: From Torrey, take State Route 24 east 10.7 miles to the visitors center. Turn south on the "Scenic Drive" to the campground. Continue to the parking area in Campground Loop C.

Contact: Capitol Reef National Park, HC 70, Box 15, Torrey, UT 84775, 435/425-3791.

85 FRYING PAN TRAIL– CASSIDY ARCH TRAIL
5.8 mi one-way/4.0 hrs

east of Torrey in Capitol Reef National Park

Map 3.3, page 63

This hike follows the first mile of the Cohab Canyon Trail to its junction with the Frying Pan Trail. The Frying Pan Trail turns south and climbs a series of switchbacks to the rim of Cohab Canyon, then over a low ridge and down via more switchbacks into a dry wash. Across the wash, you'll climb again for approximately 800 feet over the next mile to the ridgeline of the Capitol Reef escarpment. The escarpment offers truly extraordinary views, including one of Fern's Nipple, which dominates to the southeast. After following the ridge, the trail descends toward Grand Wash. Approximately 4.5 miles into the hike you'll reach the Cassidy Arch Trail, a short spur route from the Frying Pan Trail south to Cassidy Arch. Cassidy Arch is a magnificent example of a pothole arch, a bridge across a giant hole in the sandstone. Back on the main trail, descend on steep switchbacks with great views to the Grand Wash Trailhead and a road leading back to the campground. Carry plenty of water.

User groups: Hikers only. No dogs, horses, or mountain bikes are allowed. No wheelchair access.

Permits: No day-use permits are required. A free backcountry permit is required for overnight camping. A $5 fee is charged for the "Scenic Drive."

Maps: For a USGS topographic map, ask for Fruita. An excellent source of information is the *Hiking Map & Guide to Capitol Reef National Park* from Earthwalk Press, available at the visitors center. Trails Illustrated's Fish Lake North & Central Capitol Reef covers the area.

Directions: From Torrey, take State Route 24 east 10.7 miles to the visitors center. Turn south on the "Scenic Drive" to the campground. Continue to the parking area in Campground Loop C.

Contact: Capitol Reef National Park, HC 70, Box 15, Torrey, UT 84775, 435/425-3791.

86 GRAND WASH TRAIL
4.5 mi/6.0 hrs

east of Torrey in Capitol Reef National Park

Map 3.3, page 63

Immense pale-orange sandstone walls streak skyward as much as 800 feet above this trail, a route that follows the dry, hard, narrow bottom of Grand Wash. It's an easy walk in Grand Wash, one that kids can handle. Not long after starting out, just beyond the opening to Bear Canyon, you'll pass the southern end of the Frying Pan Trail. Several side canyons beg to be explored along Grand Wash, and you may wish to extend your time accordingly. You can, for example, hike up Bear Canyon to the south, a route that leads up and over slickrock for a lengthy, exhilarating cross-country trip to the Golden Throne Trail. After about a mile in Grand Wash you'll enter The Narrows, an extremely narrow canyon about a half mile long. The cliffs diminish in stature as the trail continues to State Route 24. Hiking west to east, as described, you'll lose 200 feet of elevation, but this wash can be hiked easily in either direction.

User groups: Hikers only. No dogs, horses, or mountain bikes are allowed. No wheelchair access.

Permits: No day-use permits are required. A free backcountry permit is required for overnight camping. A $5 fee is charged to take the "Scenic Drive."

Maps: For a USGS topographic map, ask for Fruita. An excellent resource is the *Hiking Map & Guide to Capitol Reef National Park* from Earthwalk Press, available at the visitors center. Trails Illustrated's Fish Lake North & Central Capitol Reef covers the area.

Directions: From Torrey, take State Route 24 east 10.7 miles to the visitors center. Turn south on the "Scenic Drive" for 3.5 miles. Turn east on Grand Wash Road, which leads to the trail-

head. Grand Wash Road can be treacherous in rainy weather.

Contact: Capitol Reef National Park, HC 70, Box 15, Torrey, UT 84775, 435/425-3791.

87 FISH CREEK LAKE TO BLIND LAKE SEMI-LOOP
5.0 mi/5.0 hrs

south of Torrey

Map 3.3, page 63

This route provides quick access to the edge of Boulder Top Plateau, the highest plateau in Utah. On the plateau you'll find about 50,000 acres of gently rolling terrain hiding numerous lovely little lakes with some of the best fishing in the state. The drive south from Torrey alone is worth the time. It's one of the most scenic roads in America. When you leave the highway, drive west on Forest Service Road 179, a part of the Great Western Trail. From a parking place, the hike goes south up Fish Creek along an old jeep track for about 2.5 miles. The jeep track turns into trail and passes just east of Fish Creek Lake. It then goes north to little Pear Lake, and then to Blind Lake, by far the largest of the three. The trail circles Blind Lake and rejoins the main trail for the hike back to the starting point. Short trails also leave Blind Lake, returning to Road 179 to the north. The fine fishing draws a large number of visitors, so don't be surprised if you're not alone.

User groups: Hikers, dogs, and horses. No wheelchair access.

Permits: No permits are required. Parking and access are free.

Maps: For a USGS topographic map, ask for Blind Lake. Trail Illustrated's Fish Lake North & Central Capitol Reef covers the area.

Directions: From Torrey, take State Route 12 (Boulder Mountain Highway) south approximately six miles. Turn south on Forest Service Road 179 for five miles. The trailhead is just past the junction of 179 and Forest Service Road 287 on the south side of the road.

Contact: Dixie National Forest, Teasdale Ranger District, P.O. Box 90, Teasdale, UT 84773, 435/425-9500.

88 SLICKROCK TRAIL
8.5 mi one-way/6.0 hrs

south of Torrey

Map 3.3, page 63

This Slickrock Trail, one of several in Utah, runs south, paralleling State Route 12. The road is on top of a long sandstone escarpment, while the trail is at the bottom. The trail follows part of the old wagon route from Grover to Boulder. The route, near the western boundary of Capitol Reef National Park, is cairned and the hiking is easy with a few rolling hills but very little elevation change overall. Water is almost always available along the route from Singletree and Chokecherry Creeks, Pleasant Creek, and Oak Creek, and these drainages make fine side trips. Campgrounds are easily accessible from the trail (on State Route 12) at Singletree, Pleasant Creek, and Oak Creek, and any of these could serve as places to end your hike or, for that matter, places from which to begin.

User groups: Hikers, dogs, horses, and mountain bikes. No wheelchair access.

Permits: No permits are required. Parking and access are free.

Maps: For USGS topographic maps, ask for Grover and Lower Bowns. Trail Illustrated's Fish Lake North & Central Capitol Reef covers the area.

Directions: From Torrey, take State Route 12 (Boulder Mountain Highway) south approximately 7.5 miles, or .5 mile past Grover. Turn east on Forest Service Road 182 and drive two miles to a junction. Turn southwest (right). The road quickly becomes very rough. Park here. The trail heads south from a point near the junction.

Contact: Dixie National Forest, Teasdale Ranger District, P.O. Box 90, Teasdale, UT 84773, 435/425-9500.

89 OLD WAGON SEMI-LOOP TRAIL
3.5 mi/5.0 hrs

southeast of Torrey in Capitol Reef National Park

Map 3.3, page 63

The vast summit of Miners Mountain was once approached along an old wagon road. You can follow the old road, now a trail, up the eastern flank of Miners Mountain to panoramic views of Windgate sandstone walls and Navajo sandstone domes, the best of this national park. Shortly after it begins, the trail climbs over uneven terrain to a high point, then begins a long loop back down. Carry plenty of water.

User groups: Hikers only. No dogs, horses, or mountain bikes are allowed. No wheelchair access.

Permits: No day-use permits are required. A free backcountry permit is required for overnight camping. A $5 fee is charged to take the "Scenic Drive."

Maps: For a USGS topographic map, ask for Golden Throne. An excellent resource is the *Hiking Map & Guide to Capitol Reef National Park* from Earthwalk Press, available at the visitors center. Trails Illustrated's Fish Lake North & Central Capitol Reef covers the area.

Directions: From Torrey, take State Route 24 east 10.7 miles to the visitors center. Turn south on the "Scenic Drive" and continue 6.5 miles to the trailhead on the west side of the road.

Contact: Capitol Reef National Park, HC 70, Box 15, Torrey, UT 84775, 435/425-3791.

90 THE TANKS TRAIL
2.0 mi/2.0 hrs

southeast of Torrey in Capitol Reef National Park

Map 3.3, page 63

From the trailhead in shadowy Capitol Gorge, you'll hike into Capitol Wash, with very little elevation gain, along the track of old State Route 24. Remnants of the old route appear in spots early in the hike. After .2 mile, fascinating petroglyphs of a crude human shape, credited to ancient Fremont Indians, appear on the walls of the wash. About a half-mile in you come to the Pioneer Register where travelers carved their names as far back as 1871. Twisting and marvelously narrow, the canyon continues to a section of slickrock requiring a scramble. The trail leads to a series of large water pockets. Ancient desert dwellers used these natural water tanks for drinking. If you continue just beyond the turn-off to The Tanks, you'll find beautiful Waterpocket Canyon opening to the south. From here, Capitol Wash continues for about 1.5 miles to the eastern boundary of the park. Beyond the boundary lies private land (requiring permission to access). From The Tanks most hikers retrace the one mile back to the start. Carry water.

User groups: Hikers only. No dogs, horses, or mountain bikes are allowed. No wheelchair access.

Permits: No day-use permit is required. A free backcountry permit is required for overnight camping. A $5 fee is charged to take the "Scenic Drive."

Maps: For a USGS topographic map, ask for Golden Throne. An excellent resource is the *Hiking Map & Guide to Capitol Reef National Park* from Earthwalk Press, available at the visitors center. Trails Illustrated's Fish Lake North & Central Capitol Reef covers the area.

Directions: From Torrey, take State Route 24 east 10.7 miles to the visitors center. Turn south on the "Scenic Drive" and continue for eight miles, then turn east on Capitol Gorge Road, which is rough and treacherous in rainy weather. The trailhead is two miles down this road.

Contact: Capitol Reef National Park, HC 70, Box 15, Torrey, UT 84775, 435/425-3791.

91 GOLDEN THRONE TRAIL
4.0 mi/2.0 hrs

southeast of Torrey in Capitol Reef National Park

Map 3.3, page 63

From near the trailhead that leads to The Tanks, you'll hike north on the Golden Throne

Trail, winding in and out of three side canyons, and gaining altitude to spots where views of Capitol Reef are utterly spectacular. After approximately one mile, you'll get your first look at Golden Throne, a gold-colored butte with vertical walls flying up 600 feet above the surrounding terrain. The trail ascends switchbacks before following the sweeping curve of the land up to finally reach an excellent viewing point with Golden Throne about a half mile to the north, Miners Mountain to the west, and the Henry Mountains far to the east. With a map and compass, and more time, you can continue north across slickrock country to reach Bear Canyon and then Grand Wash, a total distance of approximately five miles. From where the Golden Throne Trail ends, you'll have to retrace your steps two miles to the trailhead. Carry plenty of water.

User groups: Hikers only. No dogs, horses, or mountain bikes are allowed. No wheelchair access.

Permits: No day-use permit is required. A free backcountry permit is required for overnight camping. A $5 fee is charged to take the "Scenic Drive."

Maps: For a USGS topographic map, ask for Golden Throne. An excellent source of information is the *Hiking Map & Guide to Capitol Reef National Park* from Earthwalk Press, available at the visitors center. Trails Illustrated's Fish Lake North & Central Capitol Reef covers the area.

Directions: From Torrey, UT, take State Route 24 east 10.7 miles to the visitors center. Turn south on the "Scenic Drive" and continue for approximately eight miles. Then turn east on Capitol Gorge Road and drive two miles to the trailhead.

Contact: Capitol Reef National Park, HC 70, Box 15, Torrey, UT 84775, 435/425-3791.

92 LOWER PLEASANT CREEK TRAIL

4.5 mi one-way/8.0 hrs

southeast of Torrey in Capitol Reef National Park

Map 3.3, page 63

One of only a few streams that flows perennially in this region of Utah, Pleasant Creek runs from Boulder Mountain, through a lovely slickrock canyon in the Waterpocket Fold, and on to eventually enter the Fremont River east of the park. Cottonwoods, tamarisks and other plants that require constant water grow along the creek. About one mile in, the canyon narrows and begins a long series of irresistible twists. A short distance before the creek leaves the park, the canyon begins to open up. At the park boundary, most hikers turn around and return the 4.5 miles to the trailhead, gaining about 400 feet of elevation. You may choose to turn east and follow the boundary for about a quarter mile to where a four-wheel-drive road connects the park boundary to the Notom-Bullfrog Road, a total distance of approximately two additional miles. The water of Pleasant Creek should be disinfected before drinking.

User groups: Hikers only. No dogs, horses, or mountain bikes are allowed. No wheelchair access.

Permits: No day-use permit is required. A free backcountry permit is required for overnight camping. A $5 fee is charged to take the "Scenic Drive."

Maps: For a USGS topographic map, ask for Golden Throne. An excellent resource is the *Hiking Map & Guide to Capitol Reef National Park* from Earthwalk Press, available at the visitors center.

Directions: From Torrey, take State Route 24 east 10.7 miles to the visitors center. Turn south on the "Scenic Drive" and continue for 10.5 miles to the trailhead on the east side of the road.

Contact: Capitol Reef National Park, HC 70, Box 15, Torrey, UT 84775, 435/425-3791.

93 BURRO WASH TRAIL

11.0 mi/6.0–7.0 hrs

southeast of Torrey and partially in Capitol Reef National Park

Map 3.3, page 63

Walk west up Burro Wash to find one of the best slot canyons in Utah. You'll be on BLM land for the first couple of miles, and share the trail with four-wheel-drive vehicles. Shortly before it enters the park, however, the wash narrows, requiring vehicles to turn around. From here on of the trail continues into one the narrowest slot canyons you'll ever hike; at times it's no more than 18 inches wide. The canyon continues for more than 1.5 miles, twisting its way into the park. After heavy rains, you may find pockets of water and quicksand. Other obstacles include chockstones requiring scrambling to pass. You can turn back at any time, but those who persist through the narrows will find the wash grows in width before it reaches the crest of the Waterpocket Fold and wonderful views that few hikers see. The total elevation gain is about 1,300 feet. No practical campsites exist. Check the weather before entering. A sudden rain could mean a life-threatening flash flood. Carry plenty of water.

User groups: Hikers only. No dogs, horses, or mountain bikes are allowed. No wheelchair access.

Permits: No day-use permits are required. Parking and access are free.

Maps: For USGS topographic maps, ask for Golden Throne and Notom. An excellent source of information is the *Hiking Map & Guide to Capitol Reef National Park* from Earthwalk Press, available at the visitors center. Trails Illustrated's Fish Lake North & Central Capitol Reef covers the area.

Directions: From Torrey, take State Route 24 east 20 miles. Turn south on the Notom-Bullfrog Road for 7.5 miles to Burro Wash. There is no developed parking area here, but pulling off to the side of the road is allowed. A typical passenger vehicle should do fine on this rough dirt road, but it's usually impassable after heavy rains.

Contact: Capitol Reef National Park, HC 70, Box 15, Torrey, UT 84775, 435/425-3791.

94 RED CANYON TRAIL
5.4 mi/3.0 hrs

southeast of Torrey in Capitol Reef National Park

Map 3.3, page 63

From the end of the road to Cedar Mesa Campground, you'll see the majestic red cliffs standing above Red Canyon, your box-canyon destination. The trail follows an abandoned jeep route with fabulous views of rock towers dominating the ridge of the Waterpocket Fold. The trail ends approximately 1.5 miles into the hike when you walk onto the hard bottom of Red Canyon Wash. But then you'll turn up the wash. The wash narrows, and then explodes into a vast amphitheater where Red Canyon ends and sandstone walls rise silently all around. Pleasant campsites on benches shaded by piñon

and juniper will entice you to spend the night. The trail out retraces the 2.7 miles in. Carry plenty of water.

User groups: Hikers only. No dogs, horses, or mountain bikes are allowed. No wheelchair access.

Permits: No day-use permits are required. A free backcountry permit is required for overnight camping. Parking and access are free.

Maps: For USGS topographic maps, ask for Sandy Creek Benches and Bitter Creek Divide. An excellent source of information is the *Hiking Map & Guide to Capitol Reef National Park* from Earthwalk Press, available at the visitors center.

Directions: From Torrey, take State Route 24 east 20 miles. Turn south on the unpaved Notom-Bullfrog Road for 21 miles, and turn west into the Cedar Mesa Campground. Notom-Bullfrog Road may be impassable after a heavy rain.

Contact: Capitol Reef National Park, HC 70, Box 15, Torrey, UT 84775, 435/425-3791.

Chapter 4

COURTESY OF THE NATIONAL PARK SERVICE

Northeastern Utah

Northeastern Utah

Although northeastern Utah, with Wyoming to the north and Colorado to the east, offers all that is wondrous about the Rocky Mountain Province, diversity here is, once again, the name of the geological game. In this region, for instance, the immense and often desert-like Uinta Basin covers a huge section of the land, much of it a part of the Uintah and Ouray Indian Reservation. Northeast Utah was once the rich stomping ground for uncounted numbers of dinosaurs, and you can wander in sandstone canyons and among their bones. But more of that below. First, the mountains.

In the Uinta Mountains numerous peaks, 24 to be exact, punch skyward to elevations exceeding 13,000 feet. The core of these mountains is protected by the High Uintas Wilderness, and here you can stand at the highest point in the state, Kings Peak, at 13,528 feet. Ridges rise like shattered battlements embracing cirques surpassing common descriptive words. Rivers plunge from the high basins, rushing down U-shaped valleys whittled out of the stone by ancient glaciers. Hundreds of miles of maintained trails lead through thick forests, lush meadows, and along the tumbling, crystalline rivers and streams. You can hike across vast expanses of subalpine and alpine terrain, across high valleys and higher plateaus. You'll find some laborious trails in the Uintas, but, overall, the land is much less steep and far gentler on your legs than the Wasatch Range to the west. You can see just about all of it, with at least a bird's-eye view, from the Highline Trail's more than 60 miles of trans-Uintas hiking. For high-country hiking, the Highline Trail is undoubtedly one of the nation's best.

Out of an estimated 1,400 lakes, you'll find many to match any dream. Aerial stocking keeps many of the lakes productive, and anglers take cutthroat, rainbow, brown, brook, and golden trout, as well as arctic grayling.

These mountains, forested in lodgepole pine, spruce, aspen, and fir, are home to an abundance of wildlife: elk, deer, moose, and mountain goats, black bears and mountain lions, coyotes, raccoons, porcupines, martens, badgers, and bobcats. These animals have adjusted their lives to the fact that snow lingers long here, often through June on the highest terrain.

Northeast of the Uintas lies Flaming Gorge National Recreation Area. Much of the Flaming Gorge Reservoir, formed by a dam on the Green River, is in Wyoming, but the best of the scenery, by far, awaits in Utah. From the visitors center in Utah, sheer red cliffs fall almost 1,500 feet to the lake. You can hike above and below the towering red cliffs, past tortured rock formations, and along a waterway full of trout. Forested campgrounds are nestled near the clear blue lake from which bass and trout are routinely caught. With approximately 66 square miles of surface area, the lake attracts many boaters, some who fish, some who water-ski, and some who just soak up the sights.

East of the Uintas you'll find Dinosaur National Monument, the bulk of it lying in Colorado. A subtropical region about 145 million years ago, just the right combination of shifting sands and temperature have today left here one of the densest concentrations of dinosaur bones on earth. You must see the quarry, which is in Utah, but the monument has so much more to offer. Named for the bones, the monument also celebrates the union of the Green and Yampa Rivers, both of which travel through deep, majestic canyons. You can get an overview by taking the Harpers Corner Scenic Drive into Utah from the monument's headquarters in Colorado. But you need to hike the trails, some easily accessible from the visitors center in Utah, to truly get a feel for Dinosaur. And you definitely want to go home with a feel for Dinosaur, and for all of northeastern Utah.

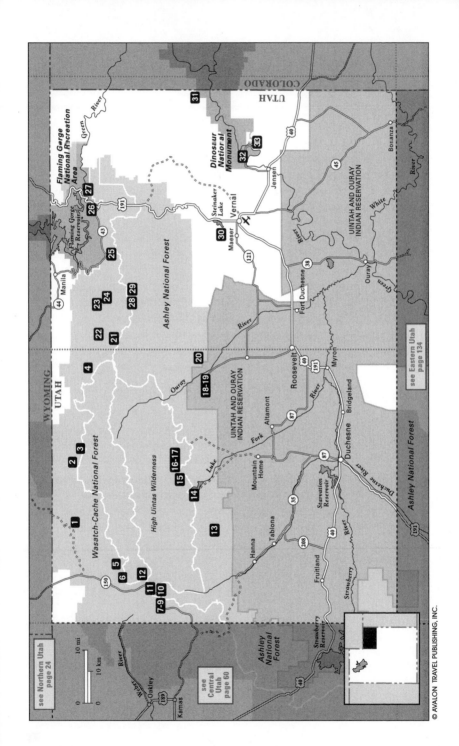

1 TOKEWANNA PEAK LOOP
25.0 mi/3–4 days

northeast of Kamas just south of the Wyoming border

Map 4, page 112

When summer days find crowds just south in the High Uintas Wilderness, this region of the Wasatch-Cache National Forest offers quiet and solitude in beautiful mountain terrain. After a wade through the west fork of Blacks Fork River, the trail runs south along the river, following an old dirt road for about a mile. At a trail junction turn east, away from the river. Now the route becomes steep with lots of switchbacks before the gentler descent to the middle fork of Blacks Fork. When you reach the river you're six miles into the hike. A congregation of old log cabins sits on the middle fork, and you'll find abundant campsites here and further up the waterway. The trail, however, sees very little use and grows more and more faint as you move south. Keep the water to the east all the way to Bob's Lake at the foot of the great treeless bulk of Tokewanna Peak. Bob's Lake has no acceptable campsites, but a grassy flat below the lake offers exceptional spots to set a tent, and you may catch dinner in the still waters of the lake. If you want to hang out and climb Tokewanna, the easiest route ascends to the saddle west of the peak from where a simple scramble takes you up. At 13,165 feet, the peak provides an awesome view of the long crest of the Uintas to the south. To continue the loop, climb the ridge west of Bob's Lake and descend to the west fork. An accurate topographical map is highly recommended, but this cross-country piece of the route, steep at times, gets an overall rating of not-too-bad. Hike down the west fork and back to the starting point.

User groups: Hikers, dogs, and horses. No wheelchair access.

Permits: No permits are required. Parking and access are free.

Maps: For USGS topographical maps, ask for Lyman Lake, Red Knob, and Mount Lovenia.

Trails Illustrated's High Uintas Wilderness covers the area.

Directions: From Kamas, take State Route 150 northeast for 48 miles. Turn east on Forest Service Road 058 for 17 miles. At the turnoff to Little Lyman Lake, turn sharply back west on Forest Service Road 063 and go six miles to the road's end at the west fork of Blacks Fork River, and park. Four-wheel-drive vehicles are recommended on 063.

Contact: Wasatch-Cache National Forest, Evanston Ranger District, 1565 Highway 150, Box 1880, Evanston, WY 82931, 307/789-3194.

2 CHINA MEADOWS TO RED CASTLE
22.0 mi/2–3 days

south of Evanston, WY

Map 4, page 112

Ⓕ In terms of trail maintenance and ease of travel, this path is probably the best on the north slopes of the Uinta Mountains. You'll hike south through heavily forested land, gaining altitude along a stream that usually offers excellent fishing. Downside: popularity. Red Castle, at the end of the journey, rises like a, well, red rock castle, its cracked walls reflected in the waters of Red Castle Lake. This lake is the largest of numerous bodies of water in this very popular area, an area that includes Lower Red Castle, Upper Red Castle, and East Red Castle Lakes. Total elevation gain to Red Castle Lake is about 1,800 feet. A veritable smorgasbord of fine campsites is offered, and the lake fishing typically ranks good to excellent. This area is definitely worth a few days of your life.

User groups: Hikers, dogs, and horses. No wheelchair access.

Permits: No permits are required. Parking is free. An access fee of $5 is collected in a trailhead box.

Maps: For USGS topographic maps, ask for Bridger Lake and Mount Powell. Trails Illustrated's High Uintas Wilderness covers the area.

Directions: From Mountain View, WY, take State Route 410 south toward Robertson. After six miles, where 410 makes a hard left (west), continue due south toward Bridger Lake Guard Station. After 12 miles, turn west on Forest Service Road 072 towards China Meadows and drive seven miles. Park on the south end of the meadows, past the campground, near the trailhead.

Contact: Wasatch-Cache National Forest, Mountain View Ranger District, 321 Highway 414, P.O. Box 129, Mountain View, WY 82939, 307/782-6555.

3 HENRYS FORK CAMPGROUND TO KINGS PEAK
32.0 mi/3–4 days

south of Evanston, WY

Map 4, page 112

Kings Peak (13,528 feet) stands taller than any other summit in Utah, and gets inundated with climbers during prime climbing season, which is usually July and August. Snow remains high in the Uintas well into summer most years, and is the cause of the late-summer human rush. Plan accordingly. Several approaches to Kings Peak are possible, including via Yellowstone Creek or from the Uinta River. The latter, being the shortest, is the most popular. From Henrys Fork Campground, the trail heads south, gaining altitude gracefully for 5.5 miles. At that point you can take a side trip west through a lovely and often-visited lake-filled basin. If you're keen on reaching the summit, continue due south, past Dollar Lake and up the switchbacks to Gunsight Pass. It is extremely difficult to miss this slim notch in the ridge. From the pass, the trail drops east into gorgeous Painter Basin and climbs west to Anderson Pass, from which you can scramble from boulder to boulder to reach the summit after gaining a little over 4,000 feet total in elevation. Whether you bag the peak or not, the route rates as a great backpacking trip with

numerous beautiful campsites, especially on the Henrys Fork side of the hike.

User groups: Hikers, dogs, and horses. No wheelchair access.

Permits: No permits are required. Parking and access are free.

Maps: For USGS topographic maps, ask for Gilbert Peak NE and Kings Peak. Trails Illustrated's High Uintas Wilderness covers the area.

Directions: From Mountain View, WY, take State Route 410 south towards Robertson. After six miles, where 410 makes a hard left (west), continue due south toward Bridger Lake Guard Station. After 12 miles, turn east on Forest Service Road 077 toward Henrys Fork. After 11.5 miles, turn west for the .75-mile drive to Henrys Fork Campground. Park near the trailhead.

Contact: Wasatch-Cache National Forest, Mountain View Ranger District, 321 Highway 414, P.O. Box 129, Mountain View, WY 82939, 307/782-6555.

4 KABELL LAKE TRAIL
10.0 mi/2 days

south of Evanston, WY

Map 4, page 112

Increasingly popular with backpackers, Kabell Lake, and its smaller sister lake, lie in forested terrain just inside the High Uintas Wilderness. The trail starts out on an old road that traverses the south end of Hoop Lake and requires you to get your feet wet in a stream. Then it runs south, gains elevation, and crosses a ridge on its way to Kabell Meadows. From the meadows, the trail continues south to lovely Island Lake. This is the shortest of several routes to Island Lake (other routes are discussed later in this chapter). After the meadows, watch for a side trail that runs west from the main trail. The side trail will take you to Kabell Lake in a half mile. At lakeside you'll have gained about 1,200 feet in elevation. The best campsites lie in the trees north of the lake. From Island Lake, the main trail goes on to the Highline Trail and virtually endless possibilities for extended backpacking trips. From Kabell Meadows, a trail runs west over Thompson Pass to a less-visited region of lakes and allows for a potential loop back to Hoop Lake.

User groups: Hikers, dogs, and horses. No wheelchair access.

Permits: No permits are required. Parking and access are free.

Maps: For USGS topographic maps, ask for Hoop Lake and Fox Lake. Trails Illustrated's High Uintas Wilderness covers the area.

Directions: From Mountain View, WY, take State Route 414 southeast 22 miles to Lonetree. Continue one mile east of Lonetree, turn south on the road to Hoop Lake, then drive 11 miles to the lake. The road continues to the south shore of the lake and the trailhead.

Contact: Wasatch-Cache National Forest, Mountain View Ranger District, 321 Highway 414, P.O. Box 129, Mountain View, WY 82939, 307/782-6555.

5 AMETHYST BASIN
12.0 mi/2 days

northeast of Kamas

Map 4, page 112

Amethyst Lake lies in a stunningly beautiful cirque and draws numerous hikers. The trail follows the Stillwater Fork. However, if you like to fish, consider leaving the trail near the water and fishing for trout in the deep pools. At 2.5 miles, not long after it enters the High Uintas Wilderness, the trail to Amethyst Basin leaves the main trail and heads southeast. Here the route climbs quickly, gaining more than 1,000 feet in elevation, before entering a string of attractive meadows and forested parks. You'll find Amethyst Lake nestled at the foot of bold cliffs that have crumbled into mighty talus slopes. You'll find numerous campsites (more than 200 feet from the water) in the area. If time allows, consider continuing the journey—after a good night's sleep—back to the main trail and south to West Basin or Middle Basin. Both options are lovely, lake-dotted, and less visited.

User groups: Hikers, dogs, and horses. No wheelchair access.

Permits: No permits are required. Parking and access are free.

Maps: For USGS topographical maps, ask for Christmas Meadows and Hayden Peak. Trails Illustrated's High Uintas Wilderness covers the area.

Directions: From Kamas, take State Route 150 east for 46 miles. Turn east on Forest Service Road 057 and drive 4.5 miles to Christmas Meadows where you can park near the trailhead.

Contact: Wasatch-Cache National Forest, Evanston Ranger District, 1565 Highway 150, Box 1880, Evanston, WY 82931, 307/789-3194.

6 HELL HOLE LAKE
8.0 mi/7.0 hrs

northeast of Kamas

Map 4, page 112

Although Hell Hole Lake lies just within the High Uintas Wilderness, most of the trail does not. The thing most appealing about Hell Hole is the fact that more dramatic scenery close by leaves this spot on the list of the seldom-seen. And, despite the name, the lake ranks high as a quiet and lovely destination. The trail ascends steadily up the waterway that drains Hell Hole Lake, with a total elevation gain of about 2,000 feet. Swampy meadows encompass the lake, providing an unobstructed view of the surrounding rocky ridges. Nearby stands of conifers offer splendid campsites, making Hell Hole a great overnight trip.

User groups: Hikers, dogs, and horses. No wheelchair access.

Permits: No permits are required. Parking and access are free.

Maps: For USGS topographical maps, ask for Christmas Meadows and Hayden Peak. Trails Illustrated's High Uintas Wilderness covers the area.

Directions: From Kamas, take State Route 150 east for 43.5 miles, and turn east on a four-wheel-drive track. The track leaves 150 about 2.5 miles before the turn to Christmas Meadows. The track may be followed for two miles to a second crossing of the stream where you can park. Some hikers park at the start of the track, adding four round-trip miles to the journey.

Contact: Wasatch-Cache National Forest, Evanston Ranger District, 1565 Highway 150, Box 1880, Evanston, WY 82931, 307/789-3194.

7 NOTCH MOUNTAIN LAKES LOOP
6.0 mi/8.0 hrs

east of Kamas

Map 4, page 112

This alpine hike is simply extraordinary. Numerous lake visits can be added to the basic loop, so if you have the time for at least an overnight here, take it. Amazingly, you can see most of this area with little more than 400 feet of elevation gain. The trail passes Lily Lakes right away, then continues north about a mile to Wall Lake. Skirting east around Wall Lake, the route continues north past Hope Lake to Twin Lakes. A quarter mile to the north stands the Notch in Notch Mountain; the trail passes through the Notch and on to more wild country and lakes. For now, however, you should head due west, cross country, to Three Divide Lakes, an excellent place to set up base camp and for fishing the lakes for trout. When you're ready to head back, hike south to Clyde Lake and pick up a trail on the west side that leads back past Watson, Linear, Ponds, and Cliff Lakes to Crystal Lake. This is a popular area, but it's wide enough for you to find a personal spot, especially if it's not a weekend.

User groups: Hikers, dogs, and horses. No wheelchair access.

Permits: No permits are required. Parking and access are free.

Maps: For a USGS topographical map, ask for Mirror Lake. Trails Illustrated's High Uintas Wilderness covers the area.

Directions: From Kamas, take State Route 150

east for 26 miles. Turn north on the road to Trial Lake and, after .75 mile, west on the road to Crystal Lake. This road ends in a half mile at a parking area.

Contact: Wasatch-Cache National Forest, Kamas Ranger District, 50 East Center Street, Kamas, UT 84036, 435/783-4338.

8 NORTH FORK OF THE PROVO RIVER LAKES SEMI-LOOP
5.0 mi/6.0 hrs

east of Kamas

Map 4, page 112

This area is comparable in quality to the Notch Mountain Lakes Loop. There's very little elevation gained and lost. Heading west from Crystal Lake, the trail begins as an old road then narrows to a well-used path. It crosses a footbridge and climbs gently to a saddle, then descends easily to Long Lake, the first destination. From Long Lake, hike southwest to Weir Lake and Pot Lake, then west to Duck Lake. From the south end of Duck Lake, you can take a short side trip south up the drainage to Beaver Lake. From the west side of Duck Lake, go north to beautiful Island Lake (with Ramona Lake lying just to the northeast). From Island Lake, take the trail back east to Long Lake, where you're only two miles from the start along the same track you came in on. Give yourself plenty of time. And carry fishing gear, as plenty of trout inhabit these waters.

User groups: Hikers, dogs, and horses. No wheelchair access.

Permits: No permits are required. Parking and access are free.

Maps: For USGS topographical maps, ask for Mirror Lake and Erickson Basin. Trails Illustrated's High Uintas Wilderness covers the area.

Directions: From Kamas, take State Route 150 east for 26 miles. Turn north on the road to Trial Lake and, after .75 mile, west on the road to Crystal Lake. This road ends after a half mile at a parking area.

Contact: Wasatch-Cache National Forest, Kamas Ranger District, 50 East Center Street, Kamas, UT 84036, 435/783-4338.

9 CRYSTAL LAKE LOOP
3.0 mi/2.5 hrs

east of Kamas

Map 4, page 112

Ⓕ A short, easy trail good for the whole family, this loop passes several attractive mountain lakes (with good fishing) before it crosses a footbridge. From there you'll hike past meadows bright with summer wildflowers, and end up at the Crystal Lake Road after a total of two miles. From there it's a one-mile walk back to your vehicle.

User groups: Hikers, dogs, and horses. No wheelchair access.

Permits: No permits are required. Parking and access are free.

Maps: For a USGS topographical map, ask for Mirror Lake. Trails Illustrated's High Uintas Wilderness covers the area.

Directions: From Kamas, take State Route 150 east for 26 miles. Turn north on the road to Trial Lake and, after .75 mile, west on the road to Crystal Lake. This road ends in a half mile at a parking area.

Contact: Wasatch-Cache National Forest, Kamas Ranger District, 50 East Center Street, Kamas, UT 84036, 435/783-4338.

10 BALD MOUNTAIN TRAIL
4.0 mi/4.0 hrs

northeast of Kamas

Map 4, page 112

Hike north from the trailhead to reach the top of Bald Mountain, the most accessible summit in this area. The whole family can do this one, and you'll all get an outstanding view of the western side of Uintas. The ascent of about 1,220 feet is gradual, and tree line comes quickly, so you don't have to wait for the great views. To stand on the highest point of broad, flat

Bald Mountain, you'll have to scramble over rocks after the trail disappears. Numerous lakes lie at your feet. The Wasatch Range stretches north-south to the west, while the east-west-running Uintas stand to the east.

User groups: Hikers and dogs. No wheelchair access.

Permits: No permits are required. Parking and access are free.

Maps: For a USGS topographical map, ask for Mirror Lake. Trails Illustrated's High Uintas Wilderness covers the area.

Directions: From Kamas, take State Route 150 east for 29 miles. At Bald Mountain Pass turn west into a parking lot near the trailhead.

Contact: Wasatch-Cache National Forest, Kamas Ranger District, 50 East Center Street, Kamas, UT 84036, 435/783-4338.

11 LOFTY LAKE LOOP
4.0 mi/5.0 hrs

northeast of Kamas

Map 4, page 112

Lofty Lake Loop offers excellent scenery and lovely backpacking not far from a major highway. You can hike it either way, but it may be easier to begin hiking northwest, since the elevation gain of about 800 feet is more gradual. About a mile from the trailhead, the trail to Meadow Lake and Holiday Park leaves to the northwest while the Lofty Lake Trail bends north. Spruce and fir shade the first mile or so, and you'll pass through a meadow. Then you'll reach Kamas Lake, where the best campsites are found. Continue the climb to Lofty Lake, crossing a pass on the way. If you're looking for a longer adventure, you can head north from the pass into a trailless area where more than a dozen small lakes sit close together. Back on the trail, continue on the loop to Scout Lake and Picturesque Lake, eventually ending up back at the trailhead.

User groups: Hikers, dogs, and horses. No wheelchair access.

Permits: No permits are required. Parking and access are free.

Maps: For a USGS topographical map, ask for Mirror Lake. Trails Illustrated's High Uintas Wilderness covers the area.

Directions: From Kamas, take State Route 150 east for 32 miles. The Pass Lake Trailhead is less than a mile past the Mirror Lake Campground on the west side of the road.

Contact: Wasatch-Cache National Forest, Kamas Ranger District, 50 East Center Street, Kamas, UT 84036, 435/783-4338.

12 HIGHLINE TRAIL TO FOUR LAKES BASIN
16.0 mi/2–3 days

northeast of Kamas

Map 4, page 112

Be warned: This section of the Highline Trail is probably the most popular. Still, after a day or two in here, you'll understand why. This is the eastern start of the High Uintas Wilderness Highline Trail. Day hikers and anglers often stop at Scudder Lake, or further along on a side trail to Wyman, Wilder, and Packard Lakes. Overnighters often head off on a branching trail north and uphill to outrageously beautiful Naturalist Basin. Any of these spots could be your destination, too. Or consider leaving the main trail 4.5 miles in to head south to the many lakes of Grandaddy Basin. If you stick to the main trail, you'll leave the Highline Trail just past Olga Lake to hike southeast into Four Lakes Basin with its swampy meadows, lakes, and ponds. The open banks are perfect for fly-fishing, and the human traffic runs lighter here. It's so beautiful, you may decide to stay.

User groups: Hikers, dogs, and horses. No wheelchair access.

Permits: No permits are required. Parking and access are free.

Maps: For a USGS topographical map, ask for Hayden Peak. Trails Illustrated's High Uintas Wilderness covers the area.

Directions: From Kamas, take State Route 150 east for 31.5 miles to Mirror Lake. Stay on 150 for another 2.5 miles past Mirror Lake. The trailhead and a large parking area stand on the east side of the road.

Contact: Wasatch-Cache National Forest, Kamas Ranger District, 50 East Center Street, Kamas, UT 84036, 435/783-4338; Ashley National Forest, Duchesne Ranger District, Box 981, Duchesne, UT 84021, 435/738-2482.

13 ROCK CREEK TRAIL TO SQUAW BASIN
14.0 mi/2–3 days

north of Duchesne

Map 4, page 112

Squaw Basin offers something other, more scenic Uinta basins do not: solitude. Rock Creek Trail follows the long, easy west shoreline of a reservoir, heading north from near a campground before entering the High Uintas Wilderness after three miles. It meets the junction with the trail to Squaw Basin after four miles. The trail to Squaw Basin climbs steeply for a couple of miles, and is wide open (that is, sunny) most of the way. Your reward is a less-visited mountain hideaway with several sparkling lakes including Squaw, Shamrock, and Rock. Total elevation gain is about 1,600 feet. From Squaw Basin, trails lead north to the heads of Rock and Fall Creeks or south to Brown Duck Basin. Back on the Rock Creek Trail, you can continue north, with the high peaks of the Uintas looming ahead, into a gorgeous lake-filled basin at the heads of Rock and Fall Creeks. Although this basin is the more spectacular of the two, it is also much more visited.

User groups: Hikers, dogs, and horses. No wheelchair access.

Permits: No permits are required. Parking and access are free.

Maps: For USGS topographic maps, ask for Tworoose Pass and Explorer Pass. Trails Illustrated's High Uintas Wilderness covers the area.

Directions: From Duchesne, take State Route 87 north for about 16 miles. Just after 87 turns sharply to the east, turn north on the Moon Lake Road (also called 21000 West) to Mountain Home for three more miles. Turn west and follow the signs 25 miles on pavement to Rock Creek/Upper Stillwater Reservoir. Park at the trailhead.

Contact: Ashley National Forest, Duchesne Ranger District, 85 West Main Street, Duchesne, UT 84021, 435/738-2482.

14 BROWN DUCK BASIN TRAIL
14.0 mi/2–3 days

north of Duchesne

Map 4, page 112

Lacking the splendor of some of the destinations of the Ashley National Forest, Brown Duck Basin still offers pleasant, sheltered campsites and a chance to catch dinner. During a week in early September, ignoring the chill, a group of us had the entire basin to ourselves. The trail moves steadily uphill from Moon Lake, gaining altitude without respite but also without steep grades, through deep forest, into the High Uintas Wilderness, all the way into the basin. Total elevation gain is about 1,500 feet. Brown Duck Lake, Island Lake, and Kidney Lake are clustered together in the southern half of the basin, surrounded by trees and offering sheltered campsites. The trail leads north for more than a mile to Atwine Lake, and about a mile more to Clements Lake, both in the northern half of the basin near numerous other smaller lakes. A trail also heads northwest into even more secluded Squaw Basin.

User groups: Hikers, dogs, and horses. No wheelchair access.

Permits: No permits are required. Parking and access are free.

Maps: For USGS topographic maps, ask for Kidney Lake and Oweep Creek. Trails Illustrated's High Uintas Wilderness covers the area.

Directions: From Duchesne, take State Route 87 north about 16 miles. Just after 87 turns sharply to the east, turn north on the Moon Lake Road to Mountain Home for three more

miles. Continue north approximately 20 miles from Mountain Home on the well-maintained Moon Lake Road (also called Forest Road 131) to Moon Lake and park near the trailhead on the west shore of Moon Lake. A campground lies near the trailhead.

Contact: Ashley National Forest, Roosevelt Ranger District, 650 West Highway 40, Roosevelt, UT 84066, 435/722-5018; Ashley National Forest, Duchesne Ranger District, 85 West Main Street, Duchesne, UT 84021, 435/738-2482.

15 CENTER PARK TRAIL
18.0 mi/2–3 days

north of Duchesne

Map 4, page 112

Because this trail starts high, you're feet stay dry. You also get good views right away. And there's another bonus: The elevation gain, only about 800 feet, is relatively easy. You'll cross into the High Uintas Wilderness after about two miles, climb briefly over a boulder field, and and then continue on to Garfield Basin. At a little over four miles, the trail passes Swasey Hole where almost a dozen small lakes lie hidden in the center and northern end of the hole. Scenic and offering forested campsites, Swasey Hole makes a great overnight spot. From there, the trail continues to Garfield Basin, which stands above the Yellowstone River and holds numerous lakes and beautiful campsites. Most of the lakes, some of which are quite small, can be found in the southern half of the basin. The trail meets the Highline Trail in the northern end of the basin. Many of the lakes of the Uintas were dammed prior to wilderness designation. You'll see these dams often hiking here. Near Superior Lake in Garfield Basin, an old stone building, once used by sheepherders, still stands near the trail.

User groups: Hikers, dogs, and horses. No wheelchair access.

Permits: No permits are required. Parking and access are free.

Maps: For USGS topographic maps, ask for Lake Fork Mountain and Garfield Basin. Trails Illustrated's High Uintas Wilderness covers the area.

Directions: From Duchesne, take State Route 87 north for about 16 miles, and turn north for three miles more to Mountain Home on the Moon Lake Road. Continue north from Mountain Home on a well-maintained road toward Moon Lake for 4.5 miles, then turn east on the road to Yellowstone, cross a bridge, and, in about a quarter mile, turn back north. Go four more miles to a fork in the road. Take the west fork (Forest Service Road 227) and continue for about eight miles to where it ends at the trailhead.

Contact: Ashley National Forest, Roosevelt Ranger District, 650 West Highway 40, Roosevelt, UT 84066, 435/722-5018.

■16 YELLOWSTONE CREEK TRAIL TO GARFIELD BASIN
14.0 mi one-way/2–3 days

north of Duchesne

Map 4, page 112

Unless you go after the temperature drops below freezing, get ready for a wet, muddy hike to an exceptionally lovely basin. One thing this trail does offer is more solitude than the more popular Swift Creek or Center Park Trails, both of which lead to the upper Yellowstone drainage. Another plus of the Yellowstone Creek Trail is the fact that it provides about 10 miles of relatively flat hiking. The route follows the creek, which often runs through wet meadows and requires periodic wading. At about 10 miles, the trail to Five Point Lake and the other lakes of Garfield Basin leaves the Yellowstone Trail and climbs quickly to the northwest with a total elevation gain of about 1,800 feet. The basin offers many campsites, fishing, and off-trail lakes to explore. The Highline Trail is accessible by continuing north either on the Yellowstone Trail or the trail through Garfield Basin.

User groups: Hikers, dogs, and horses. No wheelchair access.

Permits: No permits are required. Parking and access are free.

Maps: For USGS topographic maps, ask for Burnt Mill Spring, Lake Fork Mountain, Garfield Basin, and Mount Powell. Trails Illustrated's High Uintas Wilderness covers the area.

Directions: From Duchesne, take State Route 87 north about 16 miles. Just after 87 turns sharply to the east, turn north on the Moon Lake Road (also called 21000 West) to Mountain Home for three more miles. Continue north from Mountain Home on the well-maintained Moon Lake Road (here also called Forest Road 131) for 4.5 miles, then turn east on the road to Yellowstone, cross a bridge, and, in about a quarter mile, turn back north. Go about four miles, then turn east on Forest Service Road 119. When 119 branches east, continue north to the Swift Creek Campground and the trailhead. The trailhead is 7.5 miles from the turnoff onto 119.

Contact: Ashley National Forest, Duchesne Ranger District, 85 West Main Street, Duchesne, UT 84021, 435/738-2482.

■17 SWIFT CREEK TRAIL TO TIMOTHY LAKES
17.0 mi/2–3 days

north of Duchesne

Map 4, page 112

Following the same track as the Yellowstone Creek Trail for a short distance, the Swift Creek Trail leads off to the east, quickly turning back north and beginning a very long series of switchbacks up the ridge east of Yellowstone Creek. After it levels out somewhat, it reaches the shores of Deer Lake five miles from the start. At 5.5 miles the trail splits; the path to Timothy Lakes is to the east. The west fork of the trail goes to several lakes, including the popular Farmers Lake. Beyond Farmers Lake, the trail continues over Bluebell Pass to eventually meet the Yellowstone Trail in that drainage's upper basin. The trail to Timothy Lakes continues northeast, eases through some meadows, and arrives at the south end of East Timothy Lake after gaining a total of about 2,800 feet in elevation. To the north lie numerous lovely little lakes, including Center Timothy, West Timothy, and the three Carroll Lakes. You'll find good campsites up here, and plenty of solitude.

User groups: Hikers, dogs, and horses. No wheelchair access.

Permits: No permits are required. Parking and access are free.

Maps: For USGS topographic maps, ask for Burnt Mill Spring, Garfield Basin, and Mount Emmons. Trails Illustrated's High Uintas Wilderness covers the area.

Directions: From Duchesne, take State Route 87 north about 16 miles. Just after 87 turns sharply to the east, turn north on the Moon Lake Road (also called 21000 West) to Mountain Home for three more miles. Continue north from Mountain Home on the well-maintained Moon Lake Road (here also called Forest Road 131) for 4.5 miles, then turn east on the road to Yellowstone. You'll cross a bridge, and, in about a quarter mile, turn back north. Go four miles, then turn east on Forest Service Road 119. From the turnoff onto 119, it's about 7.5 miles to the trailhead at Swift Creek Campground (keep going north where 199 branches east).

Contact: Ashley National Forest, Roosevelt Ranger District, 650 West Highway 40, Roosevelt, UT 84066, 435/722-5018.

18 UINTA RIVER TRAIL TO HIGHLINE TRAIL
22.0 mi/2–3 days

north of Roosevelt

Map 4, page 112

This trail ascends the gorge of the Uinta River into splendid high basins below the crest of the Uinta Mountains, and provides relatively easy access to the Highline Trail. For about three miles the going gains little altitude, but the trail can be muddy around beaver ponds and across marshy land. Then you'll reach

Sheep Bridge where you leave the Uinta River Trail for the High Uintas Wilderness Loop. Continuing north along the river, the trail gains ground gradually, climbing higher above the waterway. There are several tributary creeks tumbling into the river, and small lakes lie at the heads of all of them (an invitation to do some bushwhacking). At about nine miles, at a major trail junction, the main Uinta River Trail turns west toward Painter Basin, and two miles of trail lead north to the Highline Trail. You'll have gained about 2,200 feet of elevation when you reach the Highline Trail. From the junction, you can turn back, hike east to Fox Lake, or continue on the Highline Trail.

User groups: Hikers, dogs, and horses. No wheelchair access.

Permits: No permits are required. Parking and access are free.

Maps: For USGS topographic maps, ask for Bollie Lake and Fox Lake. Trails Illustrated's High Uintas Wilderness covers the area.

Directions: From Duchesne, take State Route 121 north 10 miles to Neola. Continue due north on the paved road up Uinta Canyon to where the pavement ends at a junction at 7.5 miles. Turn (right), and continue for four miles. Take the east (right) fork before Big Springs and cross the Uinta River on a bridge. After crossing the bridge, turn northwest (left) on Forest Service Road 118 for 4.1 miles to trailhead parking on the west side of the road.

Contact: Ashley National Forest, Roosevelt Ranger District, 650 West Highway 40, Roosevelt, UT 84066, 435/722-5018.

19 HIGH UINTAS WILDERNESS LOOP
70.0 mi/1 week

north of Roosevelt

Map 4, page 112

This extended backpacking loop is arguably the best long mountain loop in Utah. The only unattractive aspect is its popularity. It starts, for about three miles, up the Uinta River Trail, leaving the river at Sheep Bridge to climb to the oft-visited Chain Lakes. You can stay here in lovely timbered campsites for the first night (the fishing here is excellent). The loop continues up to Lake Atwood, and the numerous smaller lakes that surround it. This, too, is a popular destination with abundant campsites in small stands of trees. From Atwood the route turns north into stunning Painter Basin below the high crest of the Uinta Mountains. Spend an extra night here and climb Kings Peak, the highest peak in Utah. Hike east (it's relatively easy going now) along the Highline Trail to Kidney Lakes, then Fox Lake. Finally, head down the Uinta River and back to the trailhead.

User groups: Hikers, dogs, and horses. No wheelchair access.

Permits: No permits are required. Parking and access are free.

Maps: For USGS topographic maps, ask for Bollie Lake, Mount Emmons, Kings Peak, and Fox Lake. Trails Illustrated's High Uintas Wilderness covers the area.

Directions: From Duchesne, take State Route 121 north 10 miles to Neola. Continue due north on the paved road up Uinta Canyon to where the pavement ends at a junction at 7.5 miles. Turn right and continue for four miles, then take the east (right) fork before Big Springs and cross the Uinta River on a bridge. After crossing the bridge, turn northwest (left) on Forest Service Road 118 for 4.1 miles to trailhead parking on the west side of the road.

Contact: Ashley National Forest, Duchesne Ranger District, 85 West Main Street, Duchesne, UT 84021, 435/738-2482.

20 WEST FORK OF WHITEROCKS TRAIL

14.0 mi/2 days

north of Roosevelt

Map 4, page 112

This access from the south slopes of the Uintas to the outstanding and very popular Fox Lake area offers lakes along the way,

beautiful scenery, and a stiff climb of approximately 1,400 feet. About four miles in and before much elevation gain, the trail passes between Cleveland Lake and Queant Lake where campsites abound. A trail heads from here northeast over a ridge to the Chepeta Lake area. The West Fork Trail continues northwest from Cleveland and climbs to Fox-Queant Pass, the high point of the hike. This climb is as rugged an ascent as any trailed ascent in the Uintas. At the pass you'll enter the High Uintas Wilderness, then drop to Fox Lake and the Highline Trail. If the possibility of crowds turns you off, camp near Cleveland or Queant and take a look at Fox the next day, returning to your camp for the next night.

User groups: Hikers, dogs, and horses. No wheelchair access.

Permits: No permits are required. Parking and access are free.

Maps: For USGS topographic maps, ask for Rasmussen Lakes, Chepeta Lake, and Fox Lake. Trails Illustrated's High Uintas Wilderness covers the area.

Directions: From Vernal, take State Route 121 west 24 miles. Turn north on a paved road for two miles to Whiterocks, and pass through town. Continue northeast eight miles to the Elkhorn Guard Station. Turn west on well-maintained Forest Service Road 117. At this writing, a sign reads "Elkhorn Loop." Take this road 18 miles to Forest Service Road 110. Turn northeast and drive for six miles. Turn northwest and into the West Fork of Whiterocks Trailhead.

Contact: Ashley National Forest, Vernal Ranger District, 355 North Vernal Avenue, Vernal, UT 84078, 435/789-1181.

21 ISLAND LAKE VIA SPIRIT LAKE

17.0 mi/2–3 days

west of Flaming Gorge National Recreational Area

Map 4, page 112

Many summer visitors enjoy Spirit Lake. Quite a few of those visitors hike west toward Island Lake along a relatively easy trail through beautiful high country with little overall elevation gain. After 1.5 miles of trail you'll reach the shores of Tamarack Lake, hiking into a region with a host of small lakes that supply water to the middle fork of Sheep Creek. If you've got time, spend it exploring this area. The trail continues west, entering the High Uintas Wilderness. At about four miles, a spur trail leads south one mile to Fish Lake, an excellent spot to camp and fish. You can continue on the main trail (with or without a visit to Fish Lake) to Island Lake or, more fun, strike out cross-country southwest from Fish Lake to Burnt Lakes, then west along a series of lakes and damp meadows to Island Lake. The cross-country trip offers a chance at splendid solitude and good fishing in addition to the same heart-stirring scenery and an ample supply of great campsites. Island Lake, sequestered beneath the crest of the Uintas, has lovely camping spots and sees fairly heavy use. A good trail from Island Lake heads south over a pass to Fox Lake and the Highline Trail and opportunities for exciting, extended backpacking trips.

User groups: Hikers, dogs, and horses. No wheelchair access.

Permits: No permits are required. Parking and access are free.

Maps: For USGS topographic maps, ask for Chepeta Lake and Fox Lake. Trails Illustrated's High Uintas Wilderness covers the area.

Directions: From State Route 414 about 2.5 miles east of Burntfork, WY, turn south on the graveled road to Spirit Lake. The road becomes Forest Service Road 221. Go 13.5 miles from 414 to Hickerson Park, and turn west on Forest Service Road 001 for 6.1 miles to Spirit Lake. There is a lodge and campground at the lake. The trailhead stands south of the lake, past the campground, before the turn west to the lodge.

Contact: Wasatch-Cache National Forest, Mountain View Ranger District, 321 Highway 414, P.O. Box 129, Mountain View, WY 82939, 307/782-6555.

22 NORTH FORK SHEEP CREEK TO SPIRIT LAKE

20 mi/2–3 days

west of Flaming Gorge Dam

Map 4, page 112

To pull this off you'll need a second car parked at the trailhead at Spirit Lake, unless you're up for a long hike on the Spirit Lake Road. The route up Sheep Creek is easy for a while, but the actual trail is often indistinct, making an accurate topographic map important. Look for blazes on trees in the forest (and look for moose in the meadows since they find this habitat appealing). A section of the trail loses its wildness, disappointingly following an old jeep double track. You'll cross the creek a few times, sometimes on log bridges. Abundant water and limitless pleasant campsites make most of this drainage a nice spot to settle down for the night. At about four miles, the route enters a large park. With about a mile to go before the trail meets the Tamarack Lake Trail, the climbing starts, and it doesn't end until you've gained almost 2,000 feet in elevation. It's almost seven miles total to the end of the Sheep Creek Trail, and there you should turn east, hiking past Tamarack Lake where you'll probably start seeing humans since it's not far now to the very popular Spirit Lake.

User groups: Hikers, dogs, and horses. No wheelchair access.

Permits: No permits are required. Parking and access are free.

Maps: For USGS topographic maps, ask for Phil Rico Mountain, Hoop Lake, and Chepeta Lake. Trails Illustrated's Flaming Gorge National Recreation Area covers the area.

Directions: From Flaming Gorge Dam, take US 191 south six miles. Turn west on State Route 44 and drive 14.5 miles, during which time 44 will turn to the north. Turn west on Forest Service Road 218 and drive about three miles. Forest Service Road 218 also turns to the north. Turn west on Forest Service Road 221 towards Spirit Lake and drive 10.5 miles.

Turn south on Forest Service Road 001 and drive about two miles to the trailhead on the west side of the road.

Contact: Ashley National Forest, Flaming Gorge Ranger District, P.O. Box 279, Manila, UT 84046, 435/784-3445.

23 RED LAKE TRAIL
14.0 mi/1–2 days

west of Flaming Gorge Dam

Map 4, page 112

Well marked and easy to follow, this trail climbs to several lovely lakes with ample campsites and an excellent chance to catch trout. Starting as an old jeep road across a meadow, the trail then grows rocky and heads uphill, climbing through pine and aspen forests. It crosses several meadows before reaching Tepee Lakes at about five miles. The lakes are cold and clear, and surrounded by possible tent sites. This is where the fishing is usually best. Two miles more brings you to the end of the trail at Red Lake, which is tucked into a tiny basin below the crest of the Uinta Mountains. The elevation gain for the hike is about 2,000 feet.

User groups: Hikers, dogs, horses, and mountain bikes. No wheelchair access.

Permits: No permits are required. Parking and access are free.

Maps: For a USGS topographic map, ask for Leidy Peak. Trails Illustrated's Flaming Gorge National Recreation Area covers the area.

Directions: From Flaming Gorge Dam, take US 191 south six miles. Turn west on State Route 44 and drive 14.5 miles, during which time 44 will turn to the north. Turn west on Forest Service Road 218 and drive about three miles. Forest Service Road 218 also turns to the north. Turn west on Forest Service Road 221 toward Spirit Lake and drive 4.7 miles. Turn south on Forest Service Road 096 for about two miles to the trailhead near the Browne Lake Campground.

Contact: Ashley National Forest, Flaming Gorge Ranger District, P.O. Box 279, Manila, UT 84046, 435/784-3445.

24 UTE MOUNTAIN TRAIL
4.0 mi/4.0 hrs

west of Flaming Gorge Dam

Map 4, page 112

After a peek at historic Ute Mountain Tower, built in the 1930s and the only fire-lookout tower still standing in the state, take the rocky Ute Mountain Trail downhill through a forest of pine, fir, and aspen. Expansive views of the Uinta Mountains to the south will delight anybody, and kids can negotiate this walk. Spruce trees appear more often as the short trail approaches the dam at Browne Lake. The lake has many campsites, but road access to the lake makes it a relatively popular site. Steps may be retraced back up Ute Mountain to the start, with an elevation gain of about 550 feet. Or someone can make the drive to Browne Lake while others do the hike. Browne Lake is home to several trailheads (including one for a trail to Red Lake) that serve as starting points for extensive hikes south into the Uinta Mountains.

User groups: Hikers, dogs, and mountain bikes. No wheelchair access.

Permits: No permits are required. Parking and access are free.

Maps: For USGS topographic maps, ask for Jensen Butte and Leidy Peak. Trails Illustrated's Flaming Gorge National Recreation Area covers the area.

Directions: From Manila, on the west side of Flaming Gorge Reservoir, take State Route 44 south. After about eight miles, turn west on Forest Service Road 218, which is the Sheep Creek Geologic Loop. After eight miles, you'll make a sharp turn west and travel 1.3 miles more to Forest Service Road 005, the road to Ute Mountain Tower. Turn south here and continue for one mile to the tower and a parking area.

Contact: Ashley National Forest, Flaming Gorge Ranger District, P.O. Box 279, Manila, UT 84046, 435/784-3445.

25 LEONA SPRINGS TRAIL
6.0 mi/6.5 hrs

west of Flaming Gorge Dam

Map 4, page 112

This trail is the easternmost access to the High-line Trail from the north slope of the Uinta Mountains, but it doesn't get an awful lot of use. The trail heads south, climbing moderately but steadily through the shadows of tall lodgepole pines and stands of aspens. At 1.3 miles in, Leona Springs lies about 600 feet off the trail to the east. If you're interested in an overnighter, this is a lovely spot. Plan on topping off your water bottles before continuing and, as always, disinfecting the water even though it might look safe to drink. From the springs, the trail grows more steep and rocky and, before it reaches Manila Park and the Highline Trail, it grows faint in places, virtually disappearing. You'll have gained about 2,000 feet in elevation. An accurate topographic map is recommended.

User groups: Hikers, dogs, and horses. No wheelchair access.

Permits: No permits are required. Parking and access are free.

Maps: For a USGS topographic map, ask for Elk Park. Trails Illustrated's Flaming Gorge National Recreation Area covers the area.

Directions: From Flaming Gorge Dam, take US 191 south six miles. Turn west on State Route 44 and drive 8.5 miles to the trailhead on the south side of the road.

Contact: Ashley National Forest, Flaming Gorge Ranger District, P.O. Box 279, Manila, UT 84046, 435/784-3445.

26 CANYON RIM TRAIL
5.0 mi one-way/3.0 hrs

in Flaming Gorge National Recreation Area

Map 4, page 112

Maintained for hikers and bicycles, this easy, almost flat trail connects the Greendale Overlook to the Red Canyon Visitors Center with parking areas at both ends. It's a fine opportunity for the whole family to take a hike. A loop in the middle of the trail offers an option of hiking away from the rim and along the picturesque eastern shore of Green Lake. Despite its proximity to Route 44, moose, elk, and deer have been sighted along the quieter portions of the trail. The overlook at the western end, down almost 1,500 feet into the Red Canyon of the Green River, ranks among the best easily accessible views in the state.

User groups: Hikers, dogs, and mountain bikes. No wheelchair access.

Permits: A self-service box in the parking area provides for the purchase of a $2-per-vehicle permit.

Maps: For USGS topographic maps, ask for Dutch John and Flaming Gorge. Trails Illustrated's Flaming Gorge National Recreation Area covers the area.

Directions: From Flaming Gorge Dam, take US 191 south for six miles. Turn west on State Route 44 for one mile to the rest area on the north side of the road, and park.

Contact: Ashley National Forest, Flaming Gorge Ranger District, P.O. Box 279, Manila, UT 84046, 435/784-3445.

27 LITTLE HOLE NATIONAL SCENIC TRAIL
7.0 mi one-way/6.0 hrs

in Flaming Gorge National Recreation Area

Map 4, page 112

From a boat launch, this gentle trail follows the Green River after it erupts from the dam and runs down the enormously scenic Red Canyon to another boat launch at Little Hole. Kids can enjoy this one. The massive red walls of Precambrian rock date back more than 600 million years. The river runs clear here, and large trout may be seen in the chilly water, a fact that attracts quite a few anglers. River otters have been reintroduced and may be seen playing along the riverbank. River-runners may also be seen on this stretch of water, which ranks as one of the most popular day floats in Utah. From a coniferous forest, the trail continues into drier country of pinyon and juniper, and finishes at a campground with public toilets. A shuttle service for vehicles is available in Dutch John. Contact the national forest office for details.

User groups: Hikers. No wheelchair access.

Permits: A self-service box in the parking area provides for the purchase of a $2-per-vehicle permit.

Maps: For USGS topographic maps, ask for Dutch John and Goslin Mountain. Trails Illustrated's Flaming Gorge National Recreation Area covers the area.

Directions: From Flaming Gorge Dam, 35 miles north of Vernal on US 191, take the access road east for a quarter mile to the boat launch. Park above the ramp.

Contact: Ashley National Forest, Flaming Gorge Ranger District, P.O. Box 279, Manila, UT 84046, 435/784-3445.

28 HIGHLINE TRAIL
60 mi one-way/1 week

in the Uinta Mountains

Map 4, page 112

Ⓕ Simply stated, this is not only the great mountain trail of Utah, it's one of the best in the nation. It can begin at Leidy Peak on the east end or near Mirror Lake on State Route 150 on the west end. It travels more than 60 miles, almost always above 10,000 feet, and almost always above timberline, along the crest of the High Uintas. It crosses the east-west extent of the High Uintas Wilderness, and gains and then loses a total of about two vertical miles of elevation. What hikers see is the very best of alpine and subalpine Utah. The Highline Trail can be taken in bite-size pieces by going up numerous drainages that contain side trails, hiking a portion of the Highline, and dropping down another drainage. But an end-to-end hike has massive appeal for someone willing to do the planning and preparation.

User Groups: Hikers, dogs, and horses. No wheelchair access.

Permits: No permits are required. Parking and access are free.

Maps: For USGS topographic maps, ask for (from east to west) Leidy Peak, Whiterocks Lake, Chepeta Lake, Fox Lake, Kings Peak, Mount Powell, Mount Lovenia, Red Knob, Explorer Peak, Hayden Peak, and Mirror Lake. Trails Illustrated's High Uintas Wilderness covers the area.

Directions: From Vernal, drive north on US 191 approximately 20 miles. Turn west on Forest Service Road 018, and follow this road for 13.5 miles. Turn north on Forest Service Road 043 for 10 miles to where it ends at the trailhead to Leady Peak.

Contact: Wasatch-Cache National Forest, Forest Supervisor, 8230 Federal Building, 125 South State Street, Salt Lake City, UT 84138, 801/524-3900; Ashley National Forest, Forest Supervisor, 355 North Vernal Avenue, Vernal, UT 84078, 435/789-1181.

29 HIGHLINE TRAIL: LEIDY PEAK TO CHEPETA LAKE
21.5 mi one-way/3 days

in the Uinta Mountains

Map 4, page 112

This end of the Highline Trail appeals to some more than others due to the fact that it receives less traffic (and less maintenance). On open ridges, the trail often disappears, but the route is cairned and the terrain is easy to follow. Also, the views are stunning. Leidy Peak (12,028 feet) stands visible ahead as the hike begins. The trail traverses the north side of the peak, staying above timberline and never dropping below 10,500 feet all the way to Chepeta Lake. You will gain about 1,600 feet of elevation overall. After passing several small lakes along the northern edge of Lakeshore Basin, the route crosses Gabbro Pass, just above Lake Wilde, after six miles, and then sinks down to Deadman Lake. Deadman Lake sits at the top of the Dry Fork Trail, which climbs directly up to the lake from Forest Service Road 104. The trail then crosses a pass to Whiterocks Lake, and continues with relative ease to Chepeta Lake. At Chepeta hikers can easily leave the Highline Trail via Forest Service Road 110, which pushes up from the south almost to the lake.

User Groups: Hikers, dogs, and horses. No wheelchair access.

Permits: No permits are required. Parking and access are free.

Maps: For USGS topographic maps, ask for Leidy Peak, Whiterocks Lake, Chepeta Lake. Trails Illustrated's High Uintas Wilderness covers the area.

Directions: From Vernal, drive north on US 191 for approximately 20 miles. Turn west on Forest Service Road 018 and follow it for 13.5 miles. Turn north on Forest Service Road 043 and continue 10 miles to the trailhead.

Contact: Ashley National Forest, Forest Supervisor, 355 North Vernal Avenue, Vernal, UT 84078, 435/789-1181.

30 McCONKIE RANCH PETROGLYPH TRAIL
4.0 mi/4.0 hrs

west of Vernal

Map 4, page 112

A sandstone wall above an old family homestead exhibits some of the finest rock art in the nation. Since the land is privately owned, great care should be taken to stay on the trail and to leave no trace of your passing. Within 50 feet of starting out, the first art appears. Boards have been placed here between boulders to grant better footing. By following the path along the wall for more than a mile, numerous petroglyphs can be seen. In several places, ladders must be climbed to discover some of the more memorable art. After a bare stretch of about a half mile, more petroglyphs appear. Look for "The Three Clowns," "The Three Kings," and a host of symbols and an-

imals, their true meaning lost to antiquity. This is a great hike for the whole family.

User groups: Hikers. No wheelchair access.

Permits: The trail is privately owned, and the owners request a small fee.

Maps: For a USGS topographic map, ask for Steinaker Reservoir.

Directions: From Vernal, take State Route 121 west for 3.5 miles. Turn north on 3500 West Street for 6.5 miles to the turnoff for the McConkie Ranch. Take this road about one mile to a parking area.

Contact: The McConkie Family, 10050 North Dry Fork, Vernal, UT 84078.

31 JONES HOLE TRAIL
8.0 mi/6.0 hrs

in Dinosaur National Monument

Map 4, page 112

Arguably the loveliest hike in the monument, this trail begins on the Jones Hole Creek's east side, and follows the waterway south to its confluence with the Green River. Born of springs above a fish hatchery, the creek has carved a rocky and narrow path for itself through buff-colored sandstone, providing something of an oasis in this arid country. Jones Hole Creek typically offers some fine fishing. A Utah fishing license is required. Box elders shade portions of the trail. About 1.5 miles into the hike, Ely Creek enters from the west, and here a footbridge crosses the water. Take the time to hike up Ely a short way to view the pictographs, credited to the Fremont peoples of a thousand years ago. Ely Creek is also a junction with the longer Sage Creek Trail that leads to Island Park on the river. Overnighters will have to camp here at Ely Creek and nowhere else on the trail. Campfires, too, are prohibited. At the Green River there's a lovely camping spot that may only be used by river rafters, but hikers are welcome to drop pack and enjoy lunch.

User groups: Hikers only. No dogs allowed. No wheelchair access.

Permits: A $10-per-vehicle entry fee is charged during the high visitation months of summer. No fee is charged during the winter (when the hiking may be more pleasant anyway). A free backcountry permit is required for overnight trail use and is available at the visitors center.

Maps: For a USGS topographic map, ask for Jones Hole. Trails Illustrated's Dinosaur National Monument covers the area.

Directions: From Vernal, on US 40, take US 191 north for five blocks. Turn east on 500 North and drive for 2.1 miles. Bear north past the county dump, and drive for approximately 40 miles on the Jones Hole Road to the Jones Hole Fish Hatchery. Park in the graveled area downstream of the tanks.

Contact: Dinosaur National Monument, 4545 Highway 40, Dinosaur, CO 81610, 970/374-3000.

32 SOUND OF SILENCE TRAIL
2.7 mi/2.5 hrs

in Dinosaur National Monument

Map 4, page 112

Crossing a wide sandy flat for about 220 yards, the trail enters Red Wash, a dry stream bed. Markers along the way help make this walk worth the effort of the whole family. The hike follows the wash for about a mile, narrowing in places where bold rocks protrude into the wash, and eventually entering a labyrinthine jumble of rock in which the route consistently bears right at junctions. Climbing onto a bench (elevation gain about 400 feet), the trail offers a view of Split Mountain (consisting of solidified sand dunes almost 300 million years old) to the north. Continuing along the bench, the trail loops back toward the starting point, and here the trail guidebook (available at trailhead) becomes an important part of route finding. The hike goes uphill, crosses a slope, descends a sandstone ledge, contours up another slope to a saddle, descends a gully, and finally reenters Red Wash not far from the trailhead. It is very important to watch where your feet

fall. The black crust on the dry surface of the ground is microbiotic soil, a community of algae, fungi, and moss, is and an important part of high desert ecology. The crust is a fragile, living thing, and one careless step may destroy a half-century of growth.

User groups: Hikers. No dogs allowed. No wheelchair access.

Permits: A $10-per-vehicle entry fee is charged during the high visitation months of summer. No fee is charged during the winter (when the hiking may be more pleasant anyway).

Maps: For a USGS topographic map, ask for Dinosaur Quarry. Guide books are available at the trailhead.

Directions: From Vernal, take US 40 east 13 miles to Jensen. Turn north on State Route 149 for seven miles to Dinosaur Quarry Visitors Center. The trailhead is approximately 2.5 miles past the visitors center on the north side of the road.

Contact: Dinosaur National Monument, 4545 Highway 40, Dinosaur, CO 81610, 970/374-3000.

33 DANIELS TRAIL (WITH HOG CANYON TRAIL SIDE TRIP)
11.5 mi/1–2 days

east of Vernal and starting in Dinosaur National Monument

Map 4, page 112

The trailhead lies within Dinosaur National Monument. In fact, before heading out, it's worth a visit to the Josie Morris ranch, preserved by the National Park Service. The trail passes the chicken coop of the ranch, and then the mouth of Hog Canyon opening from the north. The short trail up Hog Canyon, a striking box canyon, is worth the effort and is a great hike for kids. For Daniels Canyon, pass Hog Canyon, cross a fence, and head south toward Cub Creek. After crossing the creek, the path wanders along the south bank and ascends to a sagebrush-covered bench above the creek. Cattle have tromped out numerous tracks up to the bench. The trail passes through an open gate in an old fence and continues east, staying above the drainage and passing the boundary of the national monument to enter BLM land. The BLM land is under consideration for wilderness designation. The cliffs marking the edge of the Yampa Plateau stand to the north. At about five miles, the trail reaches a high ridgeline below the plateau after gaining about 1,800 feet in elevation. Here the view down the canyon just hiked, and on to the Tavaputs Plateau, is a great reward for the distance hiked. Although the trail continues, it enters private land, making this a good turn-around point.

User groups: Hikers. No wheelchair access.

Permits: A $10-per-vehicle entry fee is charged during the high visitation months of summer. No fee is charged during the winter (when the hiking may be more pleasant anyway).

Maps: For USGS topographic maps, ask for Split Mountain and Stuntz Reservoir. Trails Illustrated's Dinosaur National Monument covers the area.

Directions: From Vernal, take US 40 east 13 miles to Jensen. Turn north on State Route 149 for seven miles to Dinosaur Quarry Visitors Center. Continue for about seven miles more on 149 to the parking area for Josie Morris ranch.

Contact: Dinosaur National Monument, 4545 Highway 40, Dinosaur, CO 81610, 970/374-3000; BLM Vernal Field Office, 170 South 500 East, Vernal, UT 84078, 435/781-4400.

Chapter 5

COURTESY OF UTAH STATE PARKS AND RECREATION

Eastern Utah

E astern Utah, a large chunk of the great Colorado Plateau, remains pretty much as it has been for millions of years. You won't find many people, and you will find the most dramatic examples on earth of what erosion, given a free rein by time, can do.

Dominating the northern section of this region, the vast Tavaputs Plateau stands above the few roads and isolated small towns, cut in half by the Green River. At its edge, which falls off precipitously, the land has been sculpted into myriad grooves. From a distance this fluted edge may remind you of an immense line of books. The Book Cliffs demand your eyes when you drive I-70 from the Colorado-Utah border until you're over the San Rafael Swell about 20 miles west of the town of Green River. They are just about all you can see to the north. If you leave the interstate to drive north to Price, the Book Cliffs continue with you, rising above the highway to the east. A few hiking routes give access to the cliffs, the most attractive of which, I think, are along the Price River.

During the formation of the mountains of the western United States, about 65 million years ago, one great geologic uplift created the San Rafael Swell, south of the Book Cliffs and west of the town of Green River. The Swell, approximately 75 miles long and 30 miles wide, rises without much drama, except along its southeast face where the San Rafael Reef juts raggedly upward like the teeth of a monstrous saw blade. But within the Swell you'll find stunning buttes and canyons below rugged cliffs begging to be explored. If you want a canyoneering challenge, you won't find anything to match the Upper Black Box of the San Rafael River. And you'll find a lesser but tremendously satisfying challenge in the Lower Black Box. If you prefer beauty and wonder without the demands of the Boxes, the slots of Crack Canyon, Bell Canyon, Little Wild Horse Canyon, and The Chute should not be missed.

South of the Swell and south of Hanksville, the high desert bolts skyward in the arid Henry Mountains. This isolated range, reaching to more than 11,000 feet, was the last to be named and explored in America. From the peaks of the Henrys, this region of Utah stretches out in all directions. And several canyons formed by runoff from the Henrys provide superbly beautiful and seldom-trod routes down to Lake Powell.

East of the Swell and the Henry Mountains, one of the most popular national parks in the United States awaits: Arches. Here the vagaries of sedimentation and erosion have created, depending on how you define an arch and who did the counting, somewhere between 1,500 and 2,000 sandstone arches. Nothing symbolizes Utah more than the arches of Arches, including the one on the state's license plates. There are trails you can hike in minutes and trails you'll need at least an overnight to travel, and all of them lead to or by arches. And one trail, into the Fiery Furnace, requires a guide to assure you return from the mazelike complexity of the sandstone meanderings.

Through many of the arches you'll see the knife-edged ridges and sharp peaks of the La Sal Mountains, a backdrop to Moab. After chowing down on one of the world's best pizzas at Eddie McStiff's in Moab, you can drive the La Sal Mountains Loop Road for a peripheral look-see. But these mountains, Utah's second highest, provide views from the summits that overwhelm the senses. Along the trails you'll pass through forests and by an occasional lake, and you may see mountain lions and black bears, elk and deer, or the unusual ringtail cat and the slow-moving porcupine—all in a range that reaches only about 15 miles north to south and six miles east to west.

Nowhere does Utah display the splendor of its canyon country to a higher degree than in the more than 500 square miles of Canyonlands National Park, southwest of Arches National Park and the La Sals. Here the mightily eroded canyons of two rivers, the Colorado and the Green, divide the park naturally into three districts: Island in the Sky, the Needles, and the Maze. Many people take only short walks to the extravagant views of Island in the Sky, but this district offers excellent backpacking opportunities. The colorful sandstone formations of the Needles are accessible by short and long hiking trails. Less-visited, the tangle of canyons in the Maze are difficult to access (via long dirt roads) and challenging to hike. There is also a subunit of the park, Horseshoe Canyon, where you can hike beneath some of the most remarkable ancient rock art in existence.

Whatever hiking destination pleases you, you'll find it, and be deeply impressed by it, in Eastern Utah. But don't take my word for it. Get up and go.

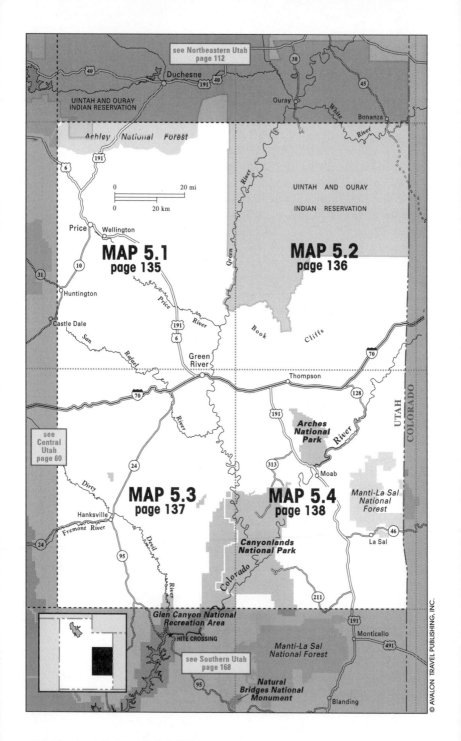

Map 5.1

Hikes 1–4
Pages 139–140

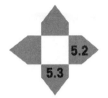

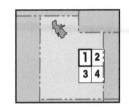

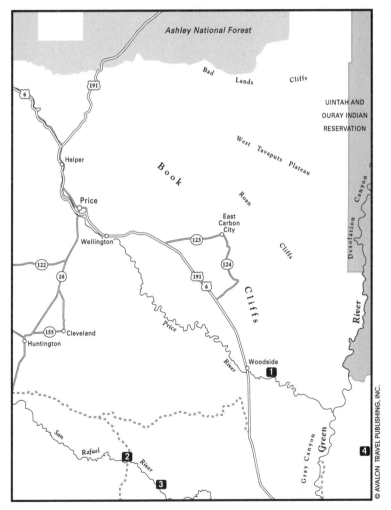

Map 5.2

Hike 5
Page 141

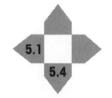

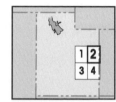

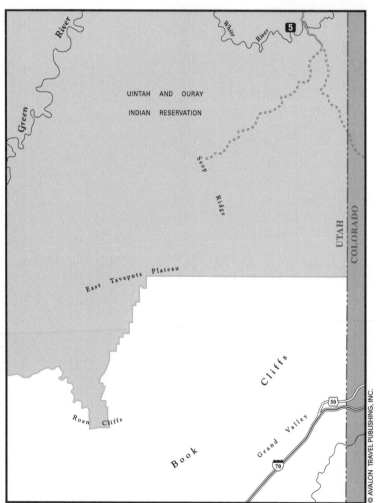

Map 5.3

Hikes 6–21
Pages 141–148

5.1
5.4

1 2
3 4

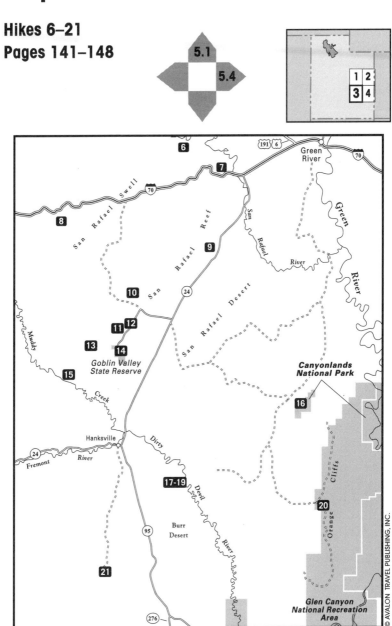

6

191 6

Green River

70

San Rafael Swell

70

San Rafael Reef

San Rafael River

Green River

8

9

River

10

San

24

San Rafael Desert

11 12

13

14

Muddy

Goblin Valley
State Reserve

15

Canyonlands
National Park

Creek

16

Hanksville

24

Fremont River

Dirty

17-19

Devil

River

Cliffs

20

95

Burr
Desert

Orange

21

© AVALON TRAVEL PUBLISHING, INC.

276

Glen Canyon
National Recreation
Area

Map 5.4

Hikes 22–53
Pages 149–163

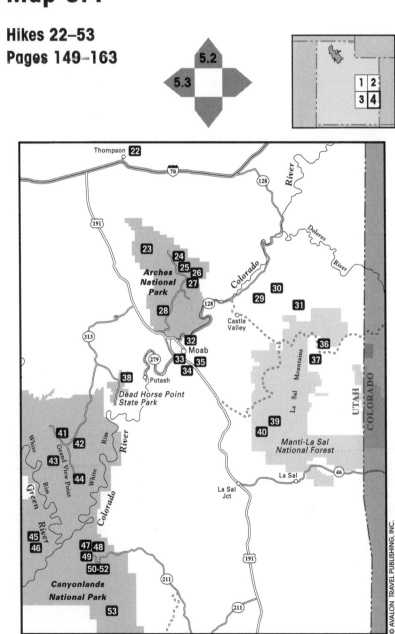

1 PRICE RIVER CANYON TO WATER CANYON

12.0 mi/1–2 days

southeast of Price

Map 5.1, page 135

The Price River, east of Woodside, pierces the great wall of the Book Cliffs on its way to join the Green River. The trail along the north side of the river follows a four-wheel-drive track for about two miles before reaching the mouth of Trail Canyon, which comes in from the north. Although it appears that some four-wheelers have ignored the sign forbidding motorized access to this canyon, it's still a lovely place to explore, and much of the area is under consideration for wilderness designation. The rugged trail follows the river along the north side of the canyon through an assortment of meadows, tamarisk stands, and rocky slopes. The Price River is a big meanderer, lined with tall cliffs colored in dark white, yellowish-orange, and red. Pictographs and petroglyphs adorn the naturally picturesque walls here and there, reminders of the ancient peoples who once wandered here. About three miles in, Water Canyon enters from the north. Although Water Canyon stops you a half mile up from the mouth, due to a sheer wall across the bottom, the sandy canyon floor provides pleasing campsites. Water, as the name implies, is in abundance. It's approximately six miles and 150 feet of elevation gain back to your vehicle. A much longer trip could be planned down the Price River Canyon into Gray Canyon and the Green River. If the Price River is low enough for fording, you can cross it to get to the shores of the Green River, which can then be hiked down to a trailhead just north of the town of Green River.

User groups: Hikers, dogs, and horses. No wheelchair access.

Permits: No permits are required. Parking and access are free.

Maps: For a USGS topographic map, ask for Jenny Canyon.

Directions: From Price, take US 6 south for about 36 miles. Turn east at Woodside on a dirt road that lies 175 yards north of the bridge over the Price River. After six miles, the road virtually disappears. Park where the road ends.

Contact: BLM Price Field Office, 125 South 600 West, Price, UT 84501, 435/636-3600.

2 SAN RAFAEL RIVER GORGE

15.0 mi one-way/1–2 days

southeast of Huntington

Map 5.1, page 135

This is a lovely and mostly easy canyon hike into the north end of San Rafael Swell. Along the way you'll spend a lot of time with wet feet and will get to see some exemplary pictographs. Following the river downstream, you may at first think you're in a valley. Later in the trip, deep in the gorge between Sids Mountain and a plateau called The Wedge, the walls stand gloriously more than 1,500 feet above the water. At four miles, North Salt Wash enters from the south and offers a nice side trip. Further along, at 6.5 miles, Virgin Spring Canyon also enters from the south. This canyon offers an interesting side trip, if time allows, and hides the first of the pictographs. At about 10 miles, Good Water Canyon enters from the north and, soon after, Cane Wash from the south. There are more pictographs in this area. An old road ascends Cane Wash. Numerous groves of cottonwoods offer very pleasant campsites all along the river. From Cane, the river meanders down to San Rafael Campground, and the end of the hike. The campground can be accessed by following Buckhorn Wash from Buckhorn Well. A little advance planning puts a vehicle at both ends and prevents the need for a long hike up the road and down Fuller Bottom Draw to back to the trailhead.

User groups: Hikers, dogs, and horses. No wheelchair access.

Permits: No permits are required. Parking and access are free.

Maps: For USGS topographic maps, ask for Sids Mountain and Bottleneck Peak.

Directions: Approximately two miles north of Castle Dale, on State Route 10, turn east on the Green River Cutoff, a dirt road. Drive 13 miles to Buckhorn Well, where you'll see a large metal tank, a pump house, and a watering trough. Turn south (right) at the junction, and then southwest (right) at the next junction, and drive 5.4 miles down Fuller Bottom Draw to the San Rafael River. You'll pass through two gates—be sure to leave them as you find them.

Contact: BLM Price Field Office, 125 South 600 West, Price, UT 84501, 435/636-3600.

3 UPPER BLACK BOX OF SAN RAFAEL RIVER
13.0 mi one-way/13.0 hrs

northwest of Green River

Map 5.1, page 135

The Upper Black Box, cut by the San Rafael River, may be the scariest and most adventurous hike in the state. If the river is running at anything less than 100 cubic feet per second (cfs), the Upper Box can be hiked with a lot of wading and some swimming. Anything between 100 and 400 cfs, and a lot of floating is required. At a cfs above 400, only those with a death wish enter the Upper Box. Flash floods can rage through the canyon at any time, so check the weather forecast for rain. River depth can be checked near the San Rafael Campground ($5 per night for camping; no water).

Starting from your vehicle, the hike/swim drops down a draw for about a half mile to the canyon's rim. An old trail descends to the river into a section known as Lockhart Box. Turn east and follow the river downstream into a sheer-walled, narrow, deep, dark canyon, an area sometimes referred to as the "Little Grand Canyon." Even if the water is low, wading and some swimming is required for about half the trip. A lifejacket or inner tube is necessary to safely cross the deep pools of the Upper Black Box. Although some small camping spots exist on ledges in the first section of this hike, few

people overnight. At about nine miles, a rock fall has blocked the canyon, requiring negotiation of a drop of 10 feet or so. Bring a short rope for this section. Just before the hike ends, a logjam has blocked the river. It is possible to work through the jam with some difficulty, but if you're not up to the task, an exit from the canyon exists. You can climb out to the north, near a second smaller rock fall before the jam. Below the jam, there's flat water down to Mexican Bend and the end of the Upper Black Box. Take the drainage north up to the road. A second vehicle parked here saves a five-mile walk back to the trailhead.

User groups: Hikers. No wheelchair access.

Permits: No permits are required. Parking and access are free.

Maps: For USGS maps, ask for Devils Hole, Drowned Hole Draw, and Mexican Bend.

Directions: From I-70, about 27 miles west of Green River, take Exit 129. Drive north 18 miles to the San Rafael Campground. Cross the bridge and turn east on the Mexican Mountain Road for 7.5 miles to where a small pond supports a few tamarisks on the south side of the road. Park here.

Contact: BLM Price Field Office, 125 South 600 West, Price, UT 84501, 435/636-3600.

4 TUSHER CANYON TRAIL
6.0 mi/4.0 hrs

north of Green River

Map 5.1, page 135

This area of the Book Cliffs, under consideration for wilderness designation, may require more walking to access in the future, which is great. For now, the hike from your vehicle is easy along the firm bottom of the wash, past stands of tamarisk lower down, juniper higher up. The walls rise dramatically on both sides. Water almost always runs in the canyon. For those wishing to camp, sites are abundant. For hikers with more time and interest, the left fork of Tusher Canyon can be hiked for many miles to the foot of the Tavaputs Plateau, called by some the "American Serengeti." Hiking onto the Tavaputs requires a permit from the Uintah and Ouray Indian Tribes, who own it.

User groups: Hikers, dogs, horses, and mountain bikes. No wheelchair access.

Permits: No permits are required. Parking and access are free.

Maps: For a USGS topographic map, ask for Tusher Canyon.

Directions: From Main Street in the town of Green River, take Hastings Road—the first road east of the river—north for about five miles. The asphalt ends, and a sign indicates the way to Swasey's Rapid Campground. Head toward the campground for about 500 yards, then take the second road that bears right. With a four-wheel-drive vehicle, this road can be taken for another six miles up Tusher Canyon. Where the road forks, bear left up the Left Fork of Tusher Canyon. It's possible to drive about two more miles before starting the hike.

Contact: BLM Price Field Office, 125 South 600 West, Price, UT 84501, 435/636-3600.

5 WHITE RIVER TRAIL
20.0 mi/2–3 days

south of Vernal

Map 5.2, page 136

The White River flows out of the Colorado Rockies and enters the Green River near Ouray, UT. It can be paddled all the way from Rangely, CO, to Ouray without difficulty, even by canoeists in the early stages of learning. For hikers, the banks of the White River can be walked downstream from your vehicle, through a wide canyon with beautiful scenery highlighted by the tall sandstone cliffs that line the canyon. The river can be easily hiked for about 10 miles along this serpentine section. Lovely campsites shaded by cottonwoods await. This area is under consideration for wilderness designation. Summer temperatures can be scorching. The best time to go is in spring, before the biting gnats and flies hatch and soon after the access road is passable.

User groups: Hikers. No wheelchair access.

Permits: No permits are required. Parking and access are free.

Maps: For a USGS topographic map, ask for Asphalt Wash.

Directions: From US 40 approximately 11 miles east of Jensen, turn south on the road to Bonanza. Drive 17 miles to this paved road's junction with State Route 45. Turn south and travel eight miles, through the oil storage site of Bonanza, past the BLM White River access site on the west side of the road. You'll come to a fork in the road. Bear west at the fork and drive about 10 miles to Asphalt Wash. Continue past Asphalt Wash, down to the White River, and park.

Contact: BLM Vernal Field Office, 170 South 500 East, Vernal, UT 84078, 435/781-4400.

6 LOWER BLACK BOX OF SAN RAFAEL RIVER
13.0 mi one-way/1–2 days

northwest of Green River

Map 5.3, page 137

The Lower Black Box, cut by the San Rafael River, may not be as scary or adventuresome as the Upper Black Box, but it's close. It's shorter, narrower, and not filled with as many obstacles. The hike, starting from your vehicle where the road turns really bad, heads east over a low pass and down to the river after about five miles. Cross the river, and head northwest cross-country (up the river), above the canyon, keeping the river on the left, for about three miles. About a half mile past Swazy's Leap, there's a route down to the river. Descend into the canyon, and follow the river downstream for the five miles of the Lower Black Box itself. You'll have to negotiate several rock fields and swim across several deep pools. Bring a lifejacket or inner tube for the water crossings. Check the weather forecast before you go (a flash flood could be fatal) and check in with the BLM to make sure the water level is not dangerously high. Not far into the Lower Box, an old bridge spans the gorge at its narrowest point. This is Swazy's Leap, and legend has it that a horse and rider have made the leap. Near the end of the hike lies warm Sulphur Spring. Although no campsites exist in the Lower Black Box, a pleasant camping place lies a half mile below Sulphur Spring, below where the river was crossed at the start of the hike. A fun trip involves setting camp at this campsite on the first day, hiking the Lower Box, and returning to camp for a second night.

User groups: Hikers. No wheelchair access.

Permits: No permits are required. Parking and access are free.

Maps: For a USGS topographic map, ask for Spotted Wolf Canyon.

Directions: From I-70, west of Green River, take Exit 129 and drive north 5.5 miles to Sinkhole Flat. From the north end of Sinkhole Flat, turn east at a junction. After two miles turn north at another junction, and drive three miles to Jackass Benches. Turn east (right) and drive 3.5 miles until the road gets very rough. It's about five miles from here to the river and the lower end of Lower Black Box, and a good four-wheel-drive vehicle can make it . . . maybe. My recommendation is to walk from where the road turns bad.

Contact: BLM Price Field Office, 125 South 600 West, Price, UT 84501, 435/636-3600.

7 BLACK DRAGON CANYON
6.0 mi/4.0 hrs

west of Green River

Map 5.3, page 137

This is an easy hike for all ages in a deep canyon decorated with pictographs. Near the mouth a large overhang, one you'll probably reach with your vehicle, offers a great campsite. An old jeep track provides a level walking surface for most of the hike. About 200 yards past the overhang, you'll find a panel of exceptional ancient drawings, including the "dragon" (which is red, not black). The pictographs

are the reason most hikers come here. Beyond the panel, after less than two miles of walking below tall, sculpted sandstone walls, the canyon forks. The south fork heads back toward I-70. The north fork offers more fascinating canyon walls. You can turn back at any time.

User groups: Hikers, dogs, and horses. No wheelchair access.

Permits: No permits are required. Parking and access are free.

Maps: For a USGS topographic map, ask for Spotted Wolf Canyon.

Directions: From Green River, take I-70 west approximately 15 miles. Turn north on a dirt road after mile marker 145, and go 1.1 mile. Turn west on another dirt road for a half mile to the mouth of Dragon Canyon.

Contact: BLM Price Field Office, 125 South 600 West, Price, UT 84501, 435/636-3600.

8 DEVILS CANYON
22.0 mi/2 days

west of Green River

Map 5.3, page 137

What you have here is a long, delightful canyon that sees little use or abuse from humans, even though a major highway passes less than a half mile away and provides easy access. Red and white sandstone walls tower above, and the canyon offers a section of fairly impressive narrows. Almost the entire hike follows a dry creek bed, but a spring runs year-round at about 11 miles from the start, pooling in a trough for cattle that graze here in winter. The route described here turns back at the spring, after an elevation gain of about 1,000 feet. If there's been a rain recently, you should be able to find water in potholes; otherwise it's the spring or nothing. Numerous short canyons open into Devils Canyon, and in any of those you can set a camp.

User groups: Hikers, dogs, and horses in the first section. No wheelchair access.

Permits: No permits are required. Parking and access are free.

Maps: For USGS topographic maps, ask for Copper Globe and Big Bend Draw.

Directions: From Green River, take I-70 west approximately 45 miles to Exit 114. Go southeast two miles to Justensen Flats, and turn south on a dirt road for a short distance to Devils Canyon. Without a four-wheel-drive, high-clearance vehicle, don't even try to reach the canyon bottom.

Contact: BLM Price Field Office, 125 South 600 West, Price, UT 84501, 435/636-3600.

9 STRAIGHT WASH
12.0 mi one-way/1–2 days

southwest of Green River

Map 5.3, page 137

A relatively well-kept secret, Straight Wash sees little human traffic and offers a couple of canyoneering challenges. Not far in from the mouth, and despite its name, the wash bends through the San Rafael Reef with its dramatic and beautiful sandstone walls. Beyond the reef, the big drops down the canyon's slopes are non-technical but not without risk. Be careful. Past the difficulties, you'll find a canyon virtually unvisited by humans. Toward the upper end, several draws branch off and invite exploration and, near Red Draw, the canyon enters a section of narrows thin enough to allow you to touch both sides at once. The northern end of Straight Wash may be accessed by a dirt road south from I-70 at Exit 129 if you'd like to see the narrows without having to climb around obstacles. In either case, you won't find water unless it's trapped in holes, so carry plenty.

User groups: Hikers and dogs. No wheelchair access.

Permits: No permits are required. Parking and access are free.

Maps: For USGS topographic maps, ask for Greasewood Draw and Arsons Garden.

Directions: From west of Green River, take State Route 24 (Exit 147) south for about 12 miles. Turn west up Iron Wash on a dirt road

at mile marker 148. The bottom of Iron Wash is usually deep sand; a four-wheel-drive, high-clearance vehicle is recommended. Get as close as possible to the mouth of Straight Wash before parking.

Contact: BLM Price Field Office, 125 South 600 West, Price, UT 84501, 435/636-3600.

10 TEMPLE MOUNTAIN LOOP
6.0 mi/4.5 hrs

north of Hanksville

Map 5.3, page 137

The picturesque and stately rise of Temple Mountain, just north of the ruins of an old mining town, has felt the digger's blade often. Miners came for uranium, and left numerous old cabins and rough roads, and hundreds of attempts to enter the earth via shafts and tunnels. Two old roads entirely encircle the mountain, offering loop routes. The lower route sees quite a bit of four-wheel-drive traffic, but the upper road, blocked by several rockslides but passable with easy scrambling, does not. Kids really enjoy this hike. There's a world of things to discover up here, especially if you're into history, and campsites near the old town aren't bad. Climbers can reach the top of Temple without too much difficulty from the north side. Be sure to check out the pictographs on the wall of South Temple Wash.

User groups: Hikers, dogs, horses, and mountain bikes. No wheelchair access.

Permits: No permits are required. Parking and access are free.

Maps: For a USGS topographic map, ask for Temple Mountain.

Directions: From Hanksville, take State Route 24 north 19.5 miles to the Temple Mountain junction. Turn west on a paved road for seven miles, parking just past where the pavement ends, near the ruins of the old mining town.

Contact: BLM Price Field Office, 125 South 600 West, Price, UT 84501, 435/636-3600.

11 CRACK CANYON
6.0 mi/4.0 hrs

north of Hanksville

Map 5.3, page 137

Crack Canyon hides some of the best narrows in the San Rafael Swell. It's not a long or difficult hike, though a few short drops must be negotiated. Crack Canyon narrows dramatically in three places where ancient water has eroded tortuous twistings, and where you'll have to twist a bit to get through. There are no good camping spots in the canyon, or water, but you can set a tent near your vehicle at the start.

User groups: Hikers and dogs. No wheelchair access.

Permits: No permits are required. Parking and access are free.

Maps: For USGS topographic maps, ask for Temple Mountain and Horse Valley.

Directions: From Hanksville, take State Route 24 north 19.5 miles to the Temple Mountain junction. Turn west on a paved road for seven miles to the ruins of an old mining town. About a quarter mile west of the ruins, turn southwest on Chute Canyon Road and drive 5.1 miles to the upper end of Crack Canyon.

Contact: BLM Price Field Office, 125 South 600 West, Price, UT 84501, 435/636-3600.

12 WILD HORSE CANYON
8.0 mi/6.0 hrs

north of Hanksville

Map 5.3, page 137

 This easy hike through Wild Horse Canyon runs beneath high sandstone walls that narrow to thin slots in a couple of places. Pictographs and petroglyphs are both found here, so keep your eyes peeled. There are a few nice camping spots, but one of the best is on the upper end after you've hiked about four miles and gained about 300 feet of elevation. Turn back whenever you wish, or hike out of Wild Horse Canyon into the drainage of Wild Horse Creek and back onto the road to the old min-

ing town. On the road you'll be about four miles from the trailhead. A vehicle on both ends eliminates the need for the road walk.

User groups: Hikers and dogs. No wheelchair access.

Permits: No permits are required. Parking and access are free.

Maps: For USGS topographic maps, ask for Temple Mountain and Horse Valley.

Directions: From Hanksville, take State Route 24 north 19.5 miles to the Temple Mountain junction. Turn west on a paved road for seven miles to the ruins of an old mining town. About a quarter mile west of the ruins, turn southwest on Chute Canyon Road and drive 1.9 miles to the upper drainage of Wild Horse Creek.

Contact: BLM Price Field Office, 125 South 600 West, Price, UT 84501, 435/636-3600.

13 BELL CANYON–LITTLE WILD HORSE CANYON LOOP
8.0 mi/7.0 hrs

north of Hanksville

Map 5.3, page 137

If you hiked and liked Crack Canyon, you'll love Little Wild Horse, home to some of the best narrows on the entire Colorado Plateau. Head north from your vehicle and up Bell Canyon to the northwest. At the top of Bell, you'll hit an old jeep road and turn northeast for a short walk to the top of Little Wild Horse Canyon. Little Wild Horse has more than 1.5 miles of continuous narrows, about half of which averages less than two yards in width, with places you'll have to turn sideways to negotiate. It's a fantasyland of slim sandstone meanderings. If you want to overnight, plan on setting a tent at the mouth of Little Wild Horse, but don't try to carry a full backpack through the narrows. And remember: Narrows this confining can be extremely dangerous in a flash flood, so check the weather forecast before entering.

User groups: Hikers and dogs. No wheelchair access.

Permits: No permits are required. Parking and access are free.

Maps: For a USGS topographic map, ask for Little Wild Horse Mesa.

Directions: From Hanksville, take State Route 24 north 19.5 miles to the Temple Mountain junction. Turn west on a paved road for five miles, then south on a gravel road for another six miles toward Goblin Valley State Park. The turns, at this writing, are marked with signs. About a mile before Goblin Valley, turn southwest on Wild Horse Road for about seven miles and park near the mouths of Little Wild Horse and Bell Canyons.

Contact: BLM Price Field Office, 125 South 600 West, Price, UT 84501, 435/636-3600.

14 GOBLIN VALLEY
1.0–5.0 mi/1.0–5.0 hrs

north of Hanksville

Map 5.3, page 137

One of the state's least-visited areas, Goblin Valley State Park is like nothing else in Utah. Once a seabed, the sea bottom hardened on exposure to the sun, but the layers below stayed softer. Erosion still eats away at the softer layers, leaving towers with caps, some of them very much like stone mushrooms, called "goblins." Some are stunted "dwarfs," rising up to 200 feet. The goblins, too numerous to count, are contained in a valley with a relatively flat floor. A covered observation deck, providing the only shade on this treeless terrain, overlooks the valley. From the deck, hikers can ramble at will. Kids are especially charmed by Goblin Valley, but anyone with an imagination can let it run wild here.

Goblin Valley State Park has two trails that cross higher ground above the valley. The Curtis Bench Trail (two miles long) rambles up and down across higher ground and offers views of distant peaks. The Carmel Canyon Loop leaves from near the observation deck and wanders for 1.5 miles through badlands toward a towering and picturesque butte called Molly's Cas-

tle. The trail then circles back to the road. Both are little used and obscure in places.

User groups: Hikers. Restrooms and the valley overlook are wheelchair accessible.

Permits: A fee of $5 per vehicle is charged to enter the park. For use of the park's campground, the fee is $14 per site. Reservations are available for any Utah state park by calling 800/322-3770.

Maps: For a USGS topographic map, ask for Goblin Valley.

Directions: From Hanksville, take State Route 24 north 19.5 miles to the Temple Mountain junction. Turn west on a paved road for five miles, then south on a gravel road for seven miles. The turns, at this writing, are marked with signs.

Contact: Goblin Valley State Park, P.O. Box 637, Green River, UT 84525, 435/564-3633.

15 MUDDY CREEK GORGE
15.0 mi one-way/1–2 days

north of Hanksville

Map 5.3, page 137

Muddy Creek has carved out an extravagantly deep canyon—the deepest canyon in the San Rafael Swell. It's a quiet route with miles of exceptionally pretty narrows known as The Chute. From near the old Hidden Splendor Mine, the route goes up Muddy Creek and into a land of steep walls and artistically carved stone. Although the route is not difficult, the gooey mud sticks to your feet, slowing progress, and there's no way to avoid it. The creek is seldom more than a few inches deep, unless it has rained recently. A hiking staff is helpful, allowing you to probe ahead for the occasional pool and balance in the mud. The water, as the name implies, runs thick with silt. Don't enter without an accurate weather forecast since a flash flood would be deadly. Slim tributaries to Muddy Creek are worth exploring. You can turn back at any time, or continue approximately 15 miles to where a road gives access to the gorge at Tomsich Butte. You may, of course, park a car at the upper end, or you can hike from the upper end down.

You can also hike downstream from the old mine, crossing back and forth through the shallow water, passing numerous old tunnels that remain from the mining era. There are camp sites on low sandy benches. Near the lower end of the gorge, after four miles of hiking, a large alcove sometimes has water seeping to the surface, and nearby an extremely tall drop throws a deluge into the gorge after rainstorms. Muddy Creek continues down to join the Fremont River near Hanksville and become the Dirty Devil River.

User groups: Hikers and dogs. Horses downstream. No wheelchair access.

Permits: No permits are required. Parking and access are free.

Maps: For USGS topographic maps, ask for Hunt Draw and Little Wild Horse Mesa.

Directions: From Hanksville, take State Route 24 north 19.5 miles to the Temple Mountain junction. Turn west on a paved road for five miles, then south on a gravel road for six miles toward Goblin Valley State Park. The turns, at this writing, are marked with signs. About a mile before Goblin Valley, turn southwest on Wild Horse Road (sometimes called Muddy River Road) for 14.1 miles to just past the old Delta/Hidden Splendor Mine.

Contact: BLM Price Field Office, 125 South 600 West, Price, UT 84501, 435/636-3600.

16 HORSESHOE CANYON TRAIL
7.0 mi/6.0 hrs

south of Green River

Map 5.3, page 137

Nowhere in America will you find anything comparable to the stunning and ancient Indian rock art of Horseshoe Canyon, a subunit of Canyonlands National Park. Some experts have declared that its equal does not exist on Earth, and it's all deep within one of the most beautiful canyons of the Colorado Plateau. Be sure to see the life-sized figures

and intricate artwork of The Great Gallery. Shortly after descending to the canyon's floor, the first artwork appears. The National Park Service offers guided tours of Horseshoe Canyon in spring and summer.

If you want to camp, pitch a tent near the parking area or hike up or down canyon until you're outside the park boundary. The sensitive nature of this area demands that no camping take place within the subunit boundaries. **User groups:** Hikers only. No dogs. No wheelchair access.

Permits: No permits are required. Parking and access are free.

Maps: For a USGS topographic map, ask for Sugarloaf Butte.

Directions: From west of Green River, take State Route 24 (Exit 147) south for approximately 24 miles. About a half mile south of the turnoff to Goblin Valley, turn east on a dirt road. Bear right at the first fork and left at the second fork, continuing to a junction at about 25 miles. Turn left here, and it's six miles more to the parking lot.

Contact: Canyonlands National Park, 2282 Southwest Resource Boulevard, Moab, UT 84532, 435/719-2313. For guided tours of Horse Canyon, contact the Maze District at 435/259-2652.

17 BEAVER WASH
6.0 mi/6.0 hrs

southeast of Hanksville

Map 5.3, page 137

In all the Dirty Devil River region, this is the only place you're likely to see beavers. Here their ceaseless activity has created a lush riparian habitat in an otherwise barren area. From the Angel Point Trailhead, hike southeast down a draw and a low ridge, then turn north across a bench and down to Angel Cove Spring. Here you'll be 1.5 miles from the trailhead, near where Beaver Creek joins the river. This is an ideal place to camp. The Angel Point Trail crosses the Dirty Devil River and climbs to Angel Point in four miles, but you should turn south and enter the solitude of Beaver Wash. The sandstone walls tower skyward, and water pools year-round, trapped by the beaver dams. The ponds make it somewhat difficult to walk here, but it's worth the effort.

User groups: Hikers. No wheelchair access.

Permits: No permits are required. Parking and access are free.

Maps: For USGS topographic maps, ask for Angel Cove, Angels Point, and Point of Rocks East.

Directions: From Hanksville, drive south for 10 miles on Highway 95. Turn east on Pool Springs Road. Drive 10 miles on Pool Springs Road. The road forks twice, and you take the left fork both times. After the 10 miles on Pool Springs Road, you turn east on the access road to Angel Point Trail.

Contact: BLM Henry Mountain Field Station, P.O. Box 99, Hanksville, UT 84734, 435/542-3461.

18 ROBBERS ROOST CANYON
60.0 mi/4–5 days

southeast of Hanksville

Map 5.3, page 137

A deep, gorgeous canyon with vast overhangs, alcoves, an arch, easy walking, sweet water, and immense solitude: There are few places like Robbers Roost Canyon, even here in canyon country. From the Angel Point Trailhead, hike southeast down a draw and a low ridge, then turn north across a bench and down to Angel Cove Spring. If the water is low enough, wade across the Dirty Devil River at the spring. Next, hike north a short distance to the mouth of Robbers Roost Canyon. Within the canyon, you'll soon reach a fork—the main canyon on the north. Both arms of Robbers Roost are stunning and include fascinating geology all the way to their ends. After about 60 miles of hiking, including the trip back to your vehicle, you've pretty much seen it all.

User groups: Hikers. No wheelchair access.

Permits: No permits are required. Parking and access are free.

Maps: For USGS topographic maps, ask for Angel Cove, Angels Point, and Point of Rocks East.

Directions: From Hanksville, take State Route 95 south for approximately 10 miles. Turn east on the road to Pool Spring. The road forks twice; take the left fork both times. When you are 10 miles from Route 95, turn east and drive another quarter mile to the Angel Point Trailhead.

Contact: BLM Henry Mountain Field Station, P.O. Box 99, Hanksville, UT 84734, 435/542-3461.

19 DIRTY DEVIL RIVER
36.0 mi one-way/3–4 days

starts southeast of Hanksville

Map 5.3, page 137

Many people know of the Dirty Devil River, but few walk its canyon. This section is a deep and lovely gorge, whittled out of the sandstone of the Colorado Plateau, overlooked by many travelers as it winds its serpentine way between the Henry Mountains and Canyonlands National Park. The Dirty Devil begins just north Hanksville at the confluence of Muddy Creek and the Fremont River. This route, from Angel Cove Spring to Poison Spring Canyon, keeps you wet as it goes back and forth across the river. The river crossings are usually no problem, but beware a short high-water period in spring. You can extend your trip by several days exploring numerous side canyons that offer striking scenery and, sometimes, cleaner water than runs in the silty Dirty Devil. Where Poison Spring Canyon opens on the river, a four-wheel-drive road ascends to State Route 95, and this is the only place a vehicle can reach the river.

User groups: Hikers. No wheelchair access.

Permits: No permits are required. Parking and access are free.

Maps: For USGS topographic maps, ask for

Angel Cove, Angels Point, Burr Point, and Stair Canyon. Trails Illustrated's Glen Canyon & Capitol Reef Areas covers the area.

Directions: From Hanksville, take State Route 95 south for approximately 10 miles. Turn east on the road to Pool Spring. The road forks twice; take the left fork both times. When you are 10 miles from Route 95, turn east and drive another quartermile to the Angel Point Trailhead.

Contact: BLM Henry Mountain Field Station, P.O. Box 99, Hanksville, UT 84734, 435/542-3461.

20 NORTH TRAIL TO THE MAZE
30.0 mi/2–3 days

east of Hanksville in the Maze District of Canyonlands National Park

Map 5.3, page 137

This route follows North Trail Canyon for about seven miles, then hits and follows a jeep track the rest of the way—another eight miles—to the Maze Overlook. The overlook is the best spot to get an overall peek at this district of the national park. The Maze is not only a riotous jumble of wandering canyons through utterly fascinating depths, it is also one of the most remote regions of Utah. This is an area that should only be entered by the most experienced and intrepid of canyon hikers. There are few marked trails, and getting lost forever is a distinct possibility once you're off established routes. Once at the overlook, the trail into the Maze descends into a world barely recognizable as of this planet. Go in only after the most careful of preparations. The jeep track, for those who don't want to hike North Trail Canyon, is accessible by following a four-wheel-drive road south from French Spring for about 11 miles, then turning east for a long, dusty, sandy, pitted, rocky drive to the overlook.

User groups: Hikers only. No dogs. No wheelchair access.

Permits: The park charges an entry fee of $10 per vehicle. Backcountry permits are required, reservations are strongly recommended, and a fee of $15 is charged for groups of up to five people.

Maps: For USGS topographic maps, ask for Elaterite Basin and Spanish Bottom. Trails Illustrated's Needles & Maze Canyonlands National Park covers the area.

Directions: From State Route 24 about 21 miles north of Hanksville and a half-mile south of the turnoff to Goblin Valley, turn east on a dirt road. Bear right, then bear left at forks in the road, passing the turnoff to Horseshoe Canyon and arriving, after approximately 45 miles, at the Hans Flat Ranger Station. Continue southeast another 2.5 miles, then turn east on the road at French Spring (a sign, at this writing, indicates "North Trail and Panorama Point") and drive a short distance to the trailhead on the south side of the road. A four-wheel-drive vehicle is highly recommended.

Contact: Canyonlands National Park, 2282 South West Resource Boulevard, Moab, UT 84532, 435/719-2313.

21 MOUNT ELLEN
3.0 mi/3.0 hrs

south of Hanksville in the Henry Mountains

Map 5.3, page 137

From Bull Creek Pass, this trail ascends the ridge of Mount Ellen north to two summits. The southern summit, at 11,615 feet, is the highest point in the Henry Mountains. The ridge walk is relatively easy, but there are some loose, slabby rocks to cross. From the top, the long crest of the Henrys runs south toward Lake Powell, the pastel sandstone of Capitol Reef sweeps along to the west, and the mysterious depths of Canyonlands National Park's Maze District lie due east.

User groups: Hikers and dogs. No wheelchair access.

Permits: No permits are required. Parking and access are free.

Maps: For a USGS topographic map, ask for Mount Ellen. Trails Illustrated's Glen Canyon & Capitol Reef Area covers the area.

Directions: From just west of Hanksville on State Route 24, drive south for approximately 33 miles on the Sawmill Basin Road to Lonesome Beaver Campground. From the campground, a rough road climbs for a couple of miles to Bull Creek Pass, which is south of Mount Ellen. Park at the pass.

Contact: BLM Henry Mountain Field Station, P.O. Box 99, Hanksville, UT 84734, 435/542-3461.

22 THOMPSON CANYON TRAIL
13.0 mi/1–2 days

east of Green River

Map 5.4, page 138

The Book Cliffs, the longest escarpment in the world, extend a deeply fluted wall, which resembles a shelf of giant books, for more than 250 miles. A huge wild and beautiful area expands behind the wall and is seldom traveled by humans. One of the easiest places to access the area lies up Thompson Canyon. Beyond a fence, the trail follows a creek upstream through sagebrush and scattered piñon pines and into a coniferous forest. Several large pictographs enhance the canyon's walls, and ample campsites lie along the canyon bottom. The upper canyon, where it crawls out onto a ridge via two ravines, is steep and rocky. On the ridge, however, camping is possible. If you're interested in a loop, hike east from the top of Thompson to meet the old jeep track that lines Sego Canyon. Follow this track back downhill.

User groups: Hikers, dogs, and horses to the upper canyon. No wheelchair access.

Permits: No permits are required. Parking and access are free.

Maps: For USGS topographic maps, ask for Sego Canyon and Bogart Canyon.

Directions: From Green River, take I-70 east for about 25 miles. Exit at Thompson Springs and drive north through the tiny town and up into Thompson Canyon. After four miles, the road forks. The west fork goes up Thompson Canyon, the east fork up Sego Canyon. Con-

tinue up Thompson Canyon for about three miles and park down canyon from a fence.

Contact: BLM Moab Field Office, 82 East Dogwood, Moab, UT 84532, 435/259-2100.

23 TOWER ARCH TRAIL
2.5 mi/2.0 hrs

north of Moab in Arches National Park

Map 5.4, page 138

If an arch is defined as anything big enough for you to crawl through, Arches National Park has more than 900. On the upper end of the scale, Tower Arch, named for a pinkish sandstone tower with a white cap standing just above the arch, spans a spectacular space in the Klondike Bluffs. The trail leads up a steep rocky ridge to a viewpoint, then continues up past a collection of towers called the Marching Men. Descending into a wash, the trail reaches a low point in about one mile and, from there, climbs up another ridge where cairns mark the trail. The overall elevation gain, however, is little more than 100 feet. After a quarter mile, Tower Arch looms above you. Time in the Klondike Bluffs, where walls rise as high as 400 feet above the ground, should not be hurried. Here erosion has whittled out an intricate maze of fins and pinnacles that invite hours of fascinating rambles.

User groups: Hikers only. No dogs or mountain bikes are allowed. No wheelchair access.

Permits: The park charges a $10-per-vehicle entry fee.

Maps: For a USGS topographic maps, ask for Klondike Bluffs. A park brochure, available from the visitors center, describes the trail. Trails Illustrated's Arches National Park covers the area.

Directions: From Moab, take US 191 north five miles to the park entrance on the north side of the road. Follow the park road north for 17 miles. Turn west on the Salt Valley Road—impassable in wet weather—and drive another eight miles. Turn west where a sign indicates

Tower Arch, and drive for a half mile to the parking area.

Contact: Arches National Park, P.O. Box 907, Moab, UT 84532, 435/719-2299.

24 DEVILS GARDEN TRAIL
7.5 mi/5.0 hrs

north of Moab in Arches National Park

Map 5.4, page 138

This popular trail easily places either first or second on everybody's list of best Arches National Park hikes. If you hike the entire 7.5 miles of this semi-loop, you'll see seven well-known arches, including one of the world's largest, as well as other arches and fascinating geologic formations. Devils Garden, where the hike starts, is a sandstone menagerie of unnumbered shapes and sizes with bushes and trees growing in every available spot. After .25 mile, short side trails lead to Pine Tree Arch and Tunnel Arch. At less than a mile, Landscape Arch rises to the west, an arch whose span looks fragile enough to collapse at any moment. Landscape Arch spans 102 yards and is almost unparalleled on earth. After Navajo, Partition, and Double O Arches, a side trail leads northwest to Dark Angel, a black-streaked desert spire. Many hikers backtrack from Dark Angel, but a scenic trail called the Devils Garden Primitive Loop circles north to more arches before joining the main trail after approximately two miles. From the end of the trail at Dark Angel, backpackers may keep going into a world of hidden rock art, secluded flats with scattered trees, and isolated arches. All water should be carried.

User groups: Hikers. No dogs or mountain bikes are allowed. No wheelchair access.

Permits: The park charges a $10-per-vehicle entry fee. A free backcountry permit is required for overnight trips.

Maps: For USGS topographic maps, ask for Mollie Hogans and Klondike Bluffs. A park brochure, available from the visitors center, describes the trail. Trails Illustrated's Arches National Park covers the area.

Directions: From Moab, take US 191 north five miles to the park entrance on the north side of the road. Follow the park road north for about 18 miles to where it ends at a parking area.

Contact: Arches National Park, P.O. Box 907, Moab, UT 84532, 435/719-2299.

25 LOST SPRING CANYON LOOP
12.0 mi/1-2 days

north of Moab starting in Arches National Park

Map 5.4, page 138

Arches National Park, with more arches than any other spot on earth, attracts, understandably, a large number of visitors. Lost Spring Canyon, on BLM land just east of the park, offers much of the same with far less traffic. From a parking area in the park, take the Sand Dune Arch Trail to its junction with the Broken Arch Trail and continue left for a couple of hundred yards to where a jeep track is visible. Take the jeep track east for about a half mile, where a view of the land to the east opens up. At about two miles the track nears the rim of Clover Canyon, a box canyon whose sheer walls allow no entry except at the canyon's mouth to the east. In another half mile or so, the track leaves the national park, dropping into Salt Wash where you'll be three miles total from the start. The track crosses Salt Wash, climbs out, crosses a flat mesa, and eventually drops into Lost Spring Canyon. By hiking down canyon, past the mouth of Fish Seep Draw (a picturesque side trip), which enters from the northeast, you'll reach the wide flat where Lost Spring Canyon meets Salt Wash. Staying near the west side of the flat, re-enter upper Salt Wash, following it back to the jeep track and from there back to the trailhead.

User groups: Hikers. No mountain bikes are allowed on the trail. No wheelchair access.

Permits: The park charges a $10-per-vehicle entry fee. A free backcountry permit is required for overnight trips within the park.

Maps: For a USGS topographic map, ask for

Mollie Hogans. Trails Illustrated's Arches National Park covers the area.

Directions: From Moab, take US 191 north five miles to the park entrance on the north side of the road. Follow the park road north 16 miles. Park on the east side of the road at the trailhead to Sand Dune Arch and Broken Arch.

Contact: Arches National Park, P.O. Box 907, Moab, UT 84532, 435/719-2299. BLM Moab Field Office, 82 East Dogwood, Moab, UT 84532, 435/259-2100.

26 FIERY FURNACE
2.0 mi/2.0 hrs

north of Moab in Arches National Park

Map 5.4, page 138

This is the park's most unusual hike: a wandering walk through a beautiful and utterly complex maze of rusty red sandstone fins (fins that "burn" with the sun's light). So difficult is route-finding that the park asks that no one enter the area without a guide. Getting lost is a very real possibility. You can sign up in advance at the visitors center for guided tours. The tours take you through deep crevices where the sky is a thin ribbon of blue hundreds of feet overhead, across dark grottoes, along narrow ledges, down narrow washes, and into, it seems, the very heart of the earth.

User groups: Hikers. No dogs. No mountain bikes allowed. No wheelchair access.

Permits: The park charges a $10-per-vehicle entry fee. Guided tours of the Fiery Furnace are $8 for adults, $4 for children 6–12 years of age.

Maps: For a USGS topographic map, ask for The Windows Section. A park brochure, available from the visitors center, describes the trail. Trails Illustrated's Arches National Park covers the area.

Directions: From Moab, take US 191 north five miles to the park entrance on the north side of the road. Follow the park road north 14 miles to the Fiery Furnace turnoff. Park here.

Contact: Arches National Park, P.O. Box 907, Moab, UT 84532, 435/719-2299.

27 DELICATE ARCH TRAIL
3.0 mi/2.0 hrs

north of Moab in Arches National Park

Map 5.4, page 138

For park visitors with time for only one hike, this is the one: a highly scenic and very popular trail to what is arguably the most photographed arch in the world. This is the park's most famous arch, one delicately sculpted, framing distant peaks. From the preserved ruins of an old homestead, the trail crosses a swinging bridge. Just before the trail enters a switchback, check out the old Indian pictograph on a short side trail, one of the few examples of rock art in the park. Soon the view opens up to the south. The trail dips and climbs through red and yellow sandstone, across slickrock, and past small hidden overhangs draped in garden green. It clings briefly to a vertical wall where a misstep could be hazardous. It gains about 500 feet in elevation. After 1.5 miles, Delicate Arch suddenly comes into view, standing alone, utterly beautiful. At 45 feet high and 33 feet across, it's not the largest arch in Utah, but the setting is unparalleled: the stark fins of the Fiery Furnace to the west, the Book Cliffs lined up to the north, the La Sal Mountains to the southeast. It's like an arch at the top of the world.

User groups: Hikers. No dogs or mountain bikes allowed on trail. No wheelchair access.

Permits: The park charges a $10-per-vehicle entry fee.

Maps: For USGS topographic maps, ask for The Windows Section and Mollie Hogans. A park brochure, available at the visitors center, describes the trail.

Directions: From Moab, take US 191 north five miles to the park entrance on the north side of the road. Follow the park road north approximately 12 miles to the Delicate Arch turnoff. Follow this road two miles to a parking area.

Contact: Arches National Park, P.O. Box 907, Moab, UT 84532, 435/719-2299.

28 LOWER COURTHOUSE WASH
12.0 mi/8.0 hrs

north of Moab in Arches National Park

Map 5.4, page 138

Without the dramatic arches of the rest of the park, Courthouse Wash is still a lovely canyon, lined with willows and cottonwoods, and an easy place to walk. You'll still see sculpted sandstone towers and walls. Perennial water keeps the vegetation relatively lush, and thus the hiking is easiest in the bed of a creek, which means you'll have wet feet for a lot of the time. This fact keeps numerous summer hikers barefoot. The route ends at US 191 about seven road miles from the trailhead, so leave a vehicle at both ends for convenience. The upper eight miles can also be hiked from where Courthouse Wash meets US 191, but the lower wash has the best scenery.

User groups: Hikers. No dogs or mountain bikes are allowed. No wheelchair access.

Permits: The park charges a $10-per-vehicle entry fee. A free backcountry permit is required for overnight trips.

Maps: For USGS topographic maps, ask for The Windows Section and Moab. Trails Illustrated's Arches National Park covers the area.

Directions: From Moab, take US 191 north five miles to the park entrance on the north side of the road. Follow the park road north 4.6 miles to a parking area on the west side of the road.

Contact: Arches National Park, P.O. Box 907, Moab, UT 84532, 435/719-2299.

29 MARY JANE CANYON
5.0 mi/4.0 hrs

northeast of Moab

Map 5.4, page 138

Long and lovely Mary Jane offers easy access to a bright red canyon watered by a year-round stream. Those facts combine to make this canyon hike a popular one. From the canyon mouth, head south toward the inspirational rock formations of Priest and Nuns, then turn southeast up Mary Jane Canyon, easily following the stream. You'll find plenty of campsites in the first two miles or so, but after that the canyon narrows too much for camping. At about 2.5 miles a slide of large boulders blocks the canyon, and most hikers turn back here. You'll have gained about 700 feet in elevation. If you want to climb out of the canyon for a peek at the gorgeous sculpted terrain in which the canyon lies, you'll have to backtrack out of the narrows and ascend the gentler slopes lower down. Despite its perennial run, the stream in Mary Jane is heavily alkaline and therefore not potable.

User groups: Hikers and dogs. No wheelchair access.

Permits: No permits are required. Parking and access are free.

Maps: For a USGS topographic map, ask for Fisher Towers.

Directions: From Moab, take US 191 north three miles. Turn west onto State Route 128 and drive 17.9 miles. Turn east on a good dirt road (Professor Creek Road, just before mile marker 18), and drive another two miles, parking near an irrigation tank.

Contact: BLM Moab Field Office, 82 East Dogwood, Moab, UT 84532, 435/259-2100.

30 FISHER TOWERS TRAIL
4.5 mi/5.0 hrs

northeast of Moab

Map 5.4, page 138

For sheer natural sandstone wonder, this hike ranks very high. The trail itself is an artful piece of work that follows contours wrapping around a mesa and to the top of a slim canyon falling away from the towers. You then pass along the foot of the towers to an aerie of a viewpoint with deep, eroded canyons, the La Sal Mountains to the south, the canyon of the Colorado River winding along to the west. The Fisher Towers are raw, red, and delightfully sculpted, broad from the approach, amazingly narrow from the viewpoint. The tallest, Titan, soars more than 900 feet up. This area is a rock climber's paradise, and an entertaining spectacle if you can see them working their way up.

User groups: Hikers and dogs. No wheelchair access.

Permits: No permits are required. Parking and access are free.

Maps: For a USGS topographic map, ask for Fisher Towers.

Directions: From Moab, take US 191 north three miles. Turn west onto State Route 128 and drive 21 miles. Go east on a dirt road where a sign, at this writing, indicates the turn to Fisher Towers. It's 3.1 miles more to the trailhead and a BLM picnic/camping area.

Contact: BLM Moab Field Office, 82 East Dogwood, Moab, UT 84532, 435/259-2100.

31 COTTONWOOD CANYON
14.0 mi/2–3 days

northeast of Moab

Map 5.4, page 138

Cottonwood Canyon ranks among the genuinely rugged canyoneering experiences. From Fisher Valley, the shallow mouth of the canyon opens to the northeast. For about half its journey, this deep, dark, narrow canyon plunges down a rough track. Ropes and climbing skills add greatly to your chance of making the entire trip to the gorge of the Dolores River. Side canyons worthy of exploration and usually supplying enough water to keep bottles full add to the adventure. There are spots wide and flat enough to set comfortable camps. The lower half of the canyon drops more gently than the upper half, but it keeps twisting and turning, remaining unusually narrow. You can turn back at any time, and you'll find climbing up easier than climbing down. From the lower end on the Dolores, you can hike west along the waterway, finally reaching State Route 128. Four-wheel-drive vehicles can make it up the Dolores for quite

a long way. Returning the seven miles up Cottonwood is far more fun, although you'll climb about 1,500 feet.

User groups: Hikers. No wheelchair access.

Permits: No permits are required. Parking and access are free.

Maps: For USGS topographic maps, ask for Fisher Valley and Blue Chief Mesa.

Directions: From Moab, take US 191 north approximately three miles. Turn west onto State Route 128 and drive about 21 miles. Turn east on the road to Fisher Towers, drive eight miles into Fisher Valley, and park.

Contact: BLM Moab Field Office, 82 East Dogwood, Moab, UT 84532, 435/259-2100.

32 NEGRO BILL CANYON
4.0 mi/4.0 hrs

north of Moab

Map 5.4, page 138

Four-wheel-drive tracks lead up this canyon for about a mile. After a short walk from the parking area, the trail drops into the canyon and follows a creek for easy hiking. At times the canyon is narrow, and the creek must be waded in several places, so plan on wet feet. At .75 mile a pleasant camping spot sits near a couple of pools in the creek. Along the way deep alcoves support green gardens of growth. About a mile in, the trail climbs up to a desert flat, crosses it,, and enters a side canyon (the second side canyon coming in from the south). Up this canyon a half mile stands Morning Glory Natural Bridge with its 243-foot span. The bridge suddenly appears as you walk under it. With the pool beneath it, Morning Glory lies hidden like an oasis in the desert. Much more of the main canyon can be explored, and water is almost always found along the way.

Negro Bill Canyon was once considered for wilderness designation, stimulating a heated battle over its use by four-wheelers. Those wishing to drive up the canyon won the battle.

User groups: Hikers, dogs, and horses. No wheelchair access.

Permits: No permits are required. Parking and access are free.

Maps: For USGS topographic maps, ask for Moab and Rill Creek. Trails Illustrated's Arches National Park covers the area.

Directions: From Moab, take US 191 north three miles. Turn east on State Route 128 for another 3.1 miles and park at the mouth of Negro Bill Canyon on the east side of the road.

Contact: BLM Moab Field Office, 82 East Dogwood, Moab, UT 84532, 435/259-2100.

33 BEHIND-THE-ROCKS
1.0–5.0 mi/1.0–8.0 hrs

southwest of Moab

Map 5.4, page 138

From your vehicle, head east up an old jeep track. The track breaks out on top of the Moab Rim with commanding views of the surrounding area. What lies ahead is an astounding maze of huge fins of Navajo sandstone, some more than a quarter mile long, some several hundred feet thick and high. It's like a vast rock was sliced up by an even vaster knife. To the east the fins run toward Spanish Valley (and Moab), to the west the Colorado River. There are no maintained trails in Behind-the-Rocks. You are on your own to wander aimlessly and endlessly. If you feel lost, remember the fins runs east-west. Follow them west and you'll reach an overlook of the Colorado River. Some of the little valleys in here suddenly end in steep pour-offs that defy climbing, so care is recommended while exploring. Even though it's so close to Moab, this area's solitude and uniqueness has led to it being put under consideration for wilderness designation.

User groups: Hikers and dogs. No wheelchair access.

Permits: No permits are required. Parking and access are free.

Maps: For a USGS topographic map, ask for Moab.

Directions: From US 191 in Moab, turn west on Kane Creek Boulevard near the south end

of town. Take this road three miles to just past the first cattle guard. Park at a small pullout on the east side of the road.

Contact: BLM Moab Field Office, 82 East Dogwood, Moab, UT 84532, 435/259-2100.

34 HIDDEN VALLEY TRAIL
4.0 mi/3.0 hrs

south of Moab

Map 5.4, page 138

Hidden from Moab by a huge wall of sandstone lies a valley with great views. The trail climbs to the base of the Moab Rim and then ascends a series of steep switchbacks to the rim. Heading northwest, the trail enters Hidden Valley, a wide plain secreted behind the rim. Rising to a low ridge separating the southern half of the valley from the northern half, the trail crosses the northern half and bears west toward a low pass. The top of this pass is about two miles from the starting point, and about 700 feet higher in elevation. Moab lies to the north; beyond that is Arches National Park. To the southwest the land drops into the maze-like intricacy of Behind-the-Rocks. Although day-hikers often turn back from the pass, the trail continues down for about 600 yards to join the jeep track that leads into Behind-the-Rocks, making a long Hidden Valley/Behind-the-Rocks trip possible. Overnight camping is possible if plenty of water is carried.

User groups: Hikers and dogs. No wheelchair access.

Permits: No permits are required. Parking and access are free.

Maps: For a USGS topographic map, ask for Moab.

Directions: From Moab, take US 191 south approximately three miles and turn west onto Angel Rock Road. After two blocks, turn north onto Rimrock Road for a short drive to a parking area.

Contact: BLM Moab Field Office, 82 East Dogwood, Moab, UT 84532, 435/259-2100.

35 MILL CREEK CANYON TRAIL
1.6 mi/2.0 hrs

southeast of Moab

Map 5.4, page 138

A short and wet walk to a natural swimming pool describes this hike. The trail crosses a grassy flat and enters a narrow canyon to follow a creek for a brief while before crossing it. Where the North and South Forks of Mill Creek meet, stay left up the North Fork, walking sometimes in willows, sometimes in the water. Keep an eye open for a panel of rock art less than 10 feet up on the wall to the right. Follow the sound of the waterfall up .75 mile to where a natural pool offers shallows for wading and a deep spot for jumping.

User groups: Hikers. No wheelchair access.

Permits: No permits are required. Parking and access are free.

Maps: For USGS topographic maps, ask for Moab and Rill Creek.

Directions: From Moab, take 300 South east for four blocks. Turn south onto 400 East and go about 200 yards, then turn east on Mill Creek Drive. Drive one mile, then turn onto Power House Lane for .9 mile to the trailhead and a parking area at the end of the road.

Contact: BLM Moab Field Office, 82 East Dogwood, Moab, UT 84532, 435/259-2100.

36 LOWER BEAVER CREEK
24.0 mi/2–3 days

east of Moab in the La Sal Mountains

Map 5.4, page 138

This striking backpacking route follows the tumbling path of Beaver Creek through a very remote and picturesque canyon. Flowing out of lovely Beaver Basin in the La Sal Mountains, creek water is available year-round and shaded campsites are plentiful along the wooded banks of the creek. Increasingly tall slickrock walls rise in convolutions above the creek. Isolation and solitude are your constant companions before the hike ends in the gorge of the Dolores River. The mouth of Beaver Creek is accessible by a track following the gorge about 10 miles down from Gateway, CO.

User groups: Hikers and dogs. No wheelchair access.

Permits: No permits are required. Parking and access are free.

Maps: For USGS topographic maps, ask for Mount Waas and Dolores Point North.

Directions: From Moab, take US 191 north three miles. Turn west onto State Route 128 and drive 16 miles. Turn east on the road up Castle Valley for 11 miles to where the route keeps left on the Castleton-Gateway Road. At 21.5 miles from 128 on the Castleton-Gateway Road, the Beaver Basin Road leaves to the south. Continue another mile to where the road crosses Beaver Creek, and park.

Contact: Manti–La Sal National Forest, Moab Ranger District, 62 East 100 North, Moab, UT 84532, 435/259-7155. BLM Moab Field Office, 82 East Dogwood, Moab, UT 84532, 435/259-2100.

37 BEAVER BASIN TRAIL
8.0 mi/8.0 hrs

east of Moab in the La Sal Mountains

Map 5.4, page 138

This route follows an old jeep track for much of the way toward the open sprawl and beauty of Beaver Basin and the head of Beaver Creek. From Dons Lake, hike south up the relatively open, forested terrain of La Sal Mountain State Forest, using the double track as a guide. Soaring skyward to the north is Mount Waas, rising to more than 12,000 feet. The old road ends at the abandoned McCoy Mine after four miles and almost 3,000 feet of elevation gain, but you can keep ascending on a path partially scarred by four-wheelers. The trail continues to the west and south enroute to Jackass Pass. From the pass, connecting trails offer a longer trip into the La Sal Mountains.

User groups: Hikers, dogs, and mountain bikes. No wheelchair access.

Permits: No permits are required. Parking and access are free.

Maps: For a USGS topographic map, ask for Mount Waas.

Directions: From Moab, take US 191 north three miles. Turn west onto State Route 128 and drive 16 miles. Turn east on the road up Castle Valley for 11 miles to where the route keeps left on the Castleton-Gateway Road. At 21.5 miles from 128 on the Castleton-Gateway Road, the Beaver Basin Road leaves to the south. Park here or, with a four-wheel-drive, continue up the Beaver Basin Road and park just past Dons Lake, about 1.5 miles in. Keep in mind that four-wheel-drive vehicles can ascend all the way into the basin, a fact that keeps some hikers out.

Contact: Manti–La Sal National Forest, Moab Ranger District, 62 East 100 North, Moab, UT 84532, 435/259-7155.

38 DEAD HORSE POINT
4.0 mi/2.5 hrs

southwest of Moab near Canyonlands
National Park

Map 5.4, page 138

The overlook from Dead Horse Point down 2,000 feet to the Colorado River and across the rust, white, and buff sandstone of Canyonlands National Park defies description and certainly ranks among the best overlooks in the entire world. It's an easy trail—one the whole family can enjoy. The Point can be accessed by car, but take the easy main trail from the visitors center along the rim, watching the view grow more and more dramatic to the east and south, feeling the sense of wonder deepen. More trail miles can extend your hike all the way around the top of the magnificent jut of the point, providing more overlooks west and north.

User groups: Hikers. No wheelchair access.

Permits: The park charges an entry fee of $7 per vehicle. The campground charges a fee of $14 per site. Reservations for any Utah state park are available at 800/322-3770.

Maps: For a USGS topographic map, ask for Shafer Basin. A park brochure describes the trail. Trails Illustrated's Needles & Island in the Sky Canyonlands National Park covers the area.

Directions: From nine miles northwest of Moab on US 191, turn southwest on State Route 313. Drive 15.1 miles to the turnoff to Dead Horse Point State Park. Drive another eight miles to road's end at the park.

Contact: Dead Horse Point State Park, P.O. Box 609, Moab, UT 84532, 435/259-2614.

39 MOUNT TUKUHNIKIVATZ TRAIL
5.0 mi/6.0 hrs

southeast of Moab in the La Sal Mountains

Map 5.4, page 138

Seen from the Moab area, the oft-snow-capped Mount Tukuhnikivatz is one of a trio of central peaks that rise higher than any other points in the La Sal Mountains. Its summit offers the best overall view of the region. From La Sal Pass, the trail begins by following an old double track, now closed to motorized vehicles, north to cross a meadow and enter a thick stand of spruce. At a second clearing, the route leaves the track and heads (trailless) west up a ridge toward Old Tuk. At the top of the ridge the terrain turns to alpine tundra. At the crest, with Mount Peale to the east, turn west and scramble the last half-mile to Old Tuk's summit at 12,482 feet. Loose rock makes the last bit of going somewhat difficult. From this chilly vantage point, after gaining about 2,300 feet in elevation, vast desert and canyon country stretches out west and south. Mount Peale, at 12,721 feet, rises higher, but the traverse over to its summit is extremely hazardous, with sheer drops, and shouldn't be taken lightly.

User groups: Hikers. No wheelchair access.

Permits: No permits are required. Parking and access are free.

Maps: For USGS topographic maps, ask for Mount Tukuhnikivatz and Mount Peale.

2,000 feet down from Dead Horse Point

Directions: From Moab, take US 191 south 22.5 miles. Turn east on State Route 46 and continue for approximately 15 miles, passing through the little town of La Sal and bearing left on Canopy Gap Road. Turn north on the La Sal Creek Road and proceed eight miles to La Sal Pass. Park at the pass.

Contact: Manti–La Sal National Forest, Moab Ranger District, 62 East 100 North, Moab, UT 84532, 435/259-7155.

40 DARK CANYON BASIN TRAIL
3.0 mi/4.0 hrs

southeast of Moab in the La Sal Mountains

Map 5.4, page 138

Dark Canyon's upper basin is simply the most scenic in all the La Sal Mountains. The trail follows an old jeep track west from a switchback at the mouth of the canyon for about a half-mile to a ruined corral. Dark Canyon Basin, a huge cirque eroded between Mount Peale and Mount Mellenthin, lies ahead. From the corral, hike south through tall trees, cross a stream, and turn west to follow the stream uphill. Since there is no maintained trail, look for game trails that contour westward and then southward up a steep forested slope toward the basin. Higher up, a steep boulder field can be seen tumbling

out of the upper basin. Stay on the west side of the boulders, where the footing is more secure, and climb up toward the basin. As the terrain levels out, you'll enter an alpine wonderland dotted with krummholz, the vast slopes of Peale to the south, the immense wall of the ridge that connects Peale and Mellenthin to the west. A small tarn lies like a jewel in a rock setting. It is possible to follow the outflow of the upper basin down into a lower basin and then cut across above timberline to meet the route of ascent. Or you can retrace the route taken up.

User groups: Hikers and dogs. No wheelchair access.

Permits: No permits are required. Parking and access are free.

Maps: For a USGS topographic maps, ask for Mount Peale.

Directions: From Moab, take US 191 south for 7.9 miles. Turn east on a connecting road, then, after a half mile, back south on Valley Drive. After 11.5 miles, turn east on Geyser Pass Road. After eight miles more, turn south onto Dark Canyon Road and continue for 4.5 miles. Park off the road at a switchback at the mouth of Dark Canyon.

Contact: Manti–La Sal National Forest, Moab Ranger District, 62 East 100 North, Moab, UT 84532, 435/259-7155.

41 SYNCLINE LOOP TRAIL
8.3 mi/1–2 days 🥾4 🥾8

southwest of Moab in the Island in the Sky District of Canyonlands National Park

Map 5.4, page 138

It's hard to beat this trail in the Island in the Sky District. It takes you completely around Upheaval Dome and into one of the strangest places on Earth. Proceeding west from the Crater View Trailhead, the rough trail descends broken rock slopes for 3.4 miles to the floor of Upheaval Canyon. If you're prepared for a couple of days of backpacking, consider hiking down the canyon to the Green River, located deep in Labyrinth Canyon. It's a beautiful walk of seven round-trip miles. Back at the head of Upheaval Canyon, the loop trail climbs steeply out of the canyon and passes an access trail of 1.5 miles in length, one-way, to the crater of the dome. Ponder this: Despite the wealth of knowledge amassed by geologists, nothing yet explains the existence of Upheaval Dome. The main trail continues into Syncline Valley with its cottonwoods, pinyons, junipers, and campsites. Eventually the trail ascends slickrock ledges on its way back to the trailhead. Overall elevation gain for the entire trip is about 1,300 feet. With so much to see, you really should try to spend at least a couple of days in here.

Before leaving to circle Upheaval Dome, take the short Crater View Trail from the same trailhead and look more than 1,000 feet down into the moon-like interior of the dome. With only 200 feet of elevation gain, this worthwhile hike is especially good for kids.

User groups: Hikers only. No dogs. No wheelchair access.

Permits: The park charges an entry fee of $10 per vehicle. Backcountry permits are required for overnight trips (reservations are strongly recommended; a fee of $15 is charged and the groups are limited to seven people).

Maps: For a USGS topographic map, ask for Upheaval Dome. Trails Illustrated's Needles & Island in the Sky Canyonlands National Park covers the area.

Directions: From nine miles northwest of Moab on US 191, turn southwest on State Route 313. You'll enter Canyonlands National Park after 18 miles. Continue south on the park road, turning west at a major intersection nine miles into the park. This roads ends in five miles at a parking lot and trailhead at the foot of Upheaval Dome.

Contact: Canyonlands National Park, 2282 South West Resource Boulevard, Moab, UT 84532, 435/719-2313.

42 MESA ARCH LOOP TRAIL
0.5 mi/0.5 hr 🥾1 🥾7

southwest of Moab in the Island in the Sky District of Canyonlands National Park

Map 5.4, page 138

This short hike, great for the whole family, goes to a low arch of Navajo Sandstone that frames a seemingly limitless expanse of red rock country. Little signs along the way identify high-desert plants. The top of the arch is easily accessible but strongly advised against since a slip off the backside means a 500-foot fall. The nice vista from the rim near the arch includes the La Sal Mountains to the east, the White Rim 1,200 feet below, and the Colorado River.

User groups: Hikers. No dogs or bikes. No wheelchair access.

Permits: The park charges an entry fee of $10 per vehicle.

Maps: For a USGS topographic map, ask for Musselman Arch. A park brochure, available at the trailhead, describes the trail. Trails Illustrated's Needles & Island in the Sky Canyonlands National Park covers the area.

Directions: From northwest of Moab on US 191, turn southwest on State Route 313. Take 313 to the visitors center, a distance of 32 miles from Moab. Continue south on the park road to the trailhead on the east side of the road, six miles past the visitors center.

Contact: Canyonlands National Park, 2282 South West Resource Boulevard, Moab, UT 84532, 435/719-2313.

43 MURPHY BASIN SEMI-LOOP TRAIL
9.8 mi/8.0 hrs

southwest of Moab in the Island in the Sky District of Canyonlands National Park

Map 5.4, page 138

A rough-and-tumble path, Murphy Trail literally drops off the side of the Island in the Sky mesa. Tricky switchbacks descend from the trailhead, then, at 1.5 miles, the main trail splits. Take the left fork down into the basin and across its sandy bottom, eventually hitting the White Rim Jeep Trail. Turn north and take the road somewhat steeply up to where a sign indicates the Murphy Trail heading northeast. Campsites along the jeep road only allow vehicle-based camps, so look for a quieter spot if you're backpacking. Once on the trail again, you'll continue along the gentle rise of Murphy Hogback, which offers stunning views of the colors and sculpted sandstone of Canyonlands. It's 2.8 miles to where the trail forks, and another 1.5-mile grunt back up the switchbacks with about 1,400 feet of elevation gain to the trailhead.

User groups: Hikers only. No dogs. No wheelchair access.

Permits: The park charges an entry fee of $10 per vehicle. Backcountry permits are required for overnight trips, reservations are strongly recommended, and a fee of $15 is charged for groups as large as seven.

Maps: For USGS topographic maps, ask for Monument Basin and Turks Head. Trails Illustrated's Needles & Island in the Sky Canyonlands National Park covers the area.

Directions: From nine miles northwest of Moab on US 191, turn southwest on State Route 313, entering Canyonlands National Park after 18 miles. Continue south on the park road 12 miles to the trailhead on the west side of the road.

Contact: Canyonlands National Park, 2282 South West Resource Boulevard, Moab, UT 84532, 435/719-2313.

44 GRAND VIEW TRAIL
2.0 mi/1.5 hrs

southwest of Moab in the Island in the Sky District of Canyonlands National Park

Map 5.4, page 138

This short, easy walk is good for all ages. You'll proceed from Grand View Overlook, indisputably the most popular overlook in the entire park, out to the southernmost tip of the vast Island in the Sky mesa. The depth and extent of the canyons, their bottoms far below, is breathtaking. The Henry Mountains rise to the west, the Abajos to the south, the La Sals to the east. Nearer at hand to the west, the even waters of the Green River flow through outstanding Stillwater Canyon. Away in all directions are the tan, buff, white, red, and orange walls of Canyonlands.

User groups: Hikers only. No dogs. No wheelchair access.

Permits: The park charges an entry fee of $10 per vehicle.

Maps: For a USGS topographic map, ask for Monument Basin. A park brochure describes the trail. Trails Illustrated's Needles & Island in the Sky Canyonlands National Park covers the area.

Directions: From nine miles northwest of Moab on US 191, turn southwest on State Route 313, entering Canyonlands National Park after 18 miles. Continue south on this road to where it ends in a parking lot 15 miles from the park entrance. The trail begins near the parking lot.

Contact: Canyonlands National Park, 2282 South West Resource Boulevard, Moab, UT 84532, 435/719-2313.

45 THE MAZE LOOP FROM CHIMNEY ROCK
10.0 mi/8.0 hrs

east of Hanksville in the Maze District of Canyonlands National Park

Map 5.4, page 138

This loop spends part of its time on the plateau above the Maze and part of its time down in a stunning canyon, where it passes one of the best ancient pictograph panels in the world. It's an excellent introduction to this district of the park. Take the second (on the left) of the four trails from Chimney Rock, and head north across the plateau. After three miles of easy walking, the route bends west and then descends to the floor of one of the canyons of the Maze. Soon the route reaches the mouth of Pictograph Fork Canyon and some fine campsites. You'll see the Maze Overlook far ahead (a good side trip adding about four miles to the loop). Turn up Pictograph Fork and find the Indian panel in .75 mile. About 1.5 miles past the panel, a large side canyon branches to the southeast and leads back to the trailhead.

User groups: Hikers only. No dogs. No wheelchair access.

Permits: The park charges an entry fee of $10 per vehicle. Backcountry permits are required for overnight trips, reservations are strongly recommended, and a fee of $15 is charged (group size limited to five people in the Maze).

Maps: For USGS topographic maps, ask for Elaterite Basin and Spanish Bottom. Trails Illustrated's Needles & Maze Canyonlands National Park covers the area.

Directions: From Hanksville, take State Route 95 south approximately 45 miles to where the road crosses the Dirty Devil River on a bridge near the north end of Lake Powell. Take the dirt road that heads north 1.2 miles south of the bridge. At every junction, stay on the main dirt road. At about 30 miles, at a main junction in Waterhole Flat, turn east and follow the signs toward the Dollhouse. At about 18 miles from the junction in Waterhole Flat, look for the signed Chimney Rock Trailhead. Access to this trailhead is not possible without a high-clearance, four-wheel-drive vehicle.

Contact: Canyonlands National Park, 2282 South West Resource Boulevard, Moab, UT 84532, 435/719-2313.

46 CHOCOLATE DROPS TRAIL
9.0 mi/8.0 hrs

east of Hanksville in the Maze District of Canyonlands National Park

Map 5.4, page 138

Part of an area of the Maze known as the Land of Standing Rocks, the Chocolate Drops, visible for miles around, are four rectangular towers of stone rising from the ridge separating Pictograph Fork and South Fork Horse Canyons. It's an easy 4.5-mile walk north along the ridge to Chocolate Drops, with great views of the canyons on either side. There's only one obstacle: a steep section of slickrock. But it shouldn't be a problem if you take your time. Where the route grows somewhat vague, cairns mark the path. Return by retracing your steps, gaining about 550 feet of elevation.

User groups: Hikers only. No dogs. No wheelchair access.

Permits: The park charges an entry fee of $10 per vehicle. Backcountry permits are required for overnight trips, and reservations are strongly recommended. A fee of $15 is charged, with group size limited to five people in the Maze.

Maps: For USGS topographic maps, ask for Elaterite Basin and Spanish Bottom. Trails Illustrated's Needles & Maze Canyonlands National Park covers the area.

Directions: From Hanksville, take State Route 95 south approximately 45 miles to where the road crosses the Dirty Devil River on a bridge near the north end of Lake Powell. Take the dirt road north after driving 1.2 miles south of the bridge. At every junction, keep to the main dirt road. At about 30 miles in on this road, at a main junction in Waterhole Flat, turn east and follow signs to the Dollhouse. At about 15 miles from the junction in Waterhole Flat, look for the Chocolate Drops Trailhead on the north side of the road. Access to this trailhead is not possible without a high-clearance, four-wheel-drive vehicle.

Contact: Canyonlands National Park, 2282 South West Resource Boulevard, Moab, UT 84532, 435/719-2313.

47 CONFLUENCE OVERLOOK TRAIL

10.0 mi/1–2 days

northwest of Monticello in the Needles District of Canyonlands National Park

Map 5.4, page 138

The Green River ends its long journey from Wyoming by pouring placidly out of Stillwater Canyon to meet the mighty Colorado River in a gorge that lies more than 1,000 feet below the overlook at the end of this trail. The route easily wanders over brushy flats and along sandy washes with rounded knobs of sandstone dotting the terrain, gaining about 300 feet of elevation overall. From high points along the way, the sandstone of Canyonlands spreads out around you, mountains rising in the distance in all directions. No fence guards the rim of the gorge, so walk carefully. Overnighters should camp well off the trail.

User groups: Hikers and mountain bikes. No dogs. No wheelchair access.

Permits: The park charges an entry fee of $10 per vehicle. Backcountry permits are required for overnight trips, and reservations are strongly recommended. A fee of $15 is charged, with groups limited to seven.

Maps: For USGS topographic maps, ask for The Loop and Spanish Bottom. Trails Illustrated's Needles & Island in the Sky Canyonlands National Park covers the area.

Directions: From US 191 about 14 miles north of Monticello, take State Route 211 west 29 miles to the national park. It's three miles more to the visitors center, and nine miles total across Squaw Flat to the trailhead at the end of the road.

Contact: Canyonlands National Park, 2282 South West Resource Boulevard, Moab, UT 84532, 435/719-2313.

48 SLICKROCK LOOP TRAIL

3.0 mi/3.0 hrs

northwest of Monticello in the Needles District of Canyonlands National Park

Map 5.4, page 138

This relatively short walk gives a great overview

of the elements of Canyonlands: the plants, the rocks, the vistas of sandstone mesas, buttes, canyons, and cliffs. Like almost all the routes in southeastern Utah, you won't find real trails on this three-mile hike. Instead, cairns lead the way over slickrock and along sandy washes. A couple of short spur trails lead to worthwhile overlooks, but the entire hike has great views.

User groups: Hikers. No wheelchair access.

Permits: The park entrance fee is $10 per vehicle.

Maps: For a USGS topographic map, ask for The Loop. Trails Illustrated's Needles & Island in the Sky Canyonlands National Park covers the area.

Directions: From US 191 about 14 miles north of Monticello, take State Route 211 west 29 miles to the national park. It's three miles more to the visitors center, and nine miles total across Squaw Flat to the trailhead on the north side of the road.

Contact: Canyonlands National Park, 2282 South West Resource Boulevard, Moab, UT 84532, 435/719-2313.

49 PINHOLE POINT LOOP

0.6 mi/1.0 hr

northwest of Monticello in the Needles District of Canyonlands National Park

Map 5.4, page 138

This very easy walk offers an introduction to pothole ecology. You'll find abundant life in these small, natural sandstone holes that fill with water in the early spring. You may see tiny shrimp, worms, snails, perhaps a toad or two. When you tire of looking down, just look around: High points along the trail offer splendid views across the Needles District.

User groups: Hikers only. No dogs. No wheelchair access.

Permits: The park entrance fee is $10 per vehicle.

Maps: For a USGS topographic map, ask for The Loop. A park brochure, available at the visitors center, describes the trail. Trails

Illustrated's Needles & Island in the Sky Canyonlands National Park covers the area.

Directions: From US 191 about 14 miles north of Monticello, take State Route 211 west 29 miles to the national park. It's three miles more to the visitors center, and seven miles total across Squaw Flat to the trailhead on the south side of the road.

Contact: Canyonlands National Park, 2282 South West Resource Boulevard, Moab, UT 84532, 435/719-2313.

50 DRUID ARCH TRAIL
10.5 mi/1–2 days

northwest of Monticello in the Needles
District of Canyonlands National Park

Map 5.4, page 138

Here you can hike into the heart of the Needles District and up to one of the largest and most lovely arches in all of Canyonlands. There's some steeper terrain near the start of the hike, but the going is generally not too rough. The route rambles among the tall spires and ragged red fins of the Needles, and spends a lot of time ascending the sandy bottom of Elephant Canyon to the arch in the amphitheater at the head of the canyon. Campsites are abundant here. At a trail junction at 1.5 miles, go west. At three more trail junctions, keep heading south. Deciding which way to go is not difficult, but the Trails Illustrated map makes the choices even easier. The route ends after 5.2 miles in the amphitheater below sculpted walls that rise as much as 600 feet. To actually reach the foot of this somewhat elephant-shaped (use your imagination) arch requires scrambling over rock. This may be dangerous, however, and is unnecessary to appreciate this natural wonder.

User groups: Hikers only. No dogs. No wheelchair access.

Permits: The park charges an entry fee of $10 per vehicle. Backcountry permits are required for overnight trips, and reservations are strongly recommended. A fee of $15 is charged for groups of up to seven people.

Maps: For USGS topographic maps, ask for

The Loop and Druid Arch. Trails Illustrated's "Needles & Island in the Sky Canyonlands National Park" covers the area.

Directions: From US 191 about 14 miles north of Monticello, take State Route 211 west 29 miles to the national park. It's three miles more to the visitors center, and 5.5 miles total to where the road to Squaw Flat bears south. Drive past the entrance to Campground B and onto the dirt road heading west. At three miles past the turnoff from the main road, park at the Elephant Hill Trailhead on the south side of the road.

Contact: Canyonlands National Park, 2282 South West Resource Boulevard, Moab, UT 84532, 435/719-2313.

51 CHESLER PARK SEMI-LOOP
10.5 mi/1–2 days

northwest of Monticello in the Needles
District of Canyonlands National Park

Map 5.4, page 138

Following the same first two miles as the Druid Arch Trail, the Chesler Park Trail then heads west to Chesler Park, an open grassland towered over by sandstone spires and probably the most popular backpacking destination in the Needles. Popularity has demanded a restriction on where and when camps can be set. The route circles entirely around Chesler Park and enters, on the south end, a section of trail called the Joint—a joint being, in this case, a very narrow slice out of the sandstone. Down within the confines of the Joint Trail, one of the most fascinating in Canyonlands, you may find your shoulders brushing the opposing walls. The east side of Chesler offers a chance to add about five miles to the trip by paying your respects to Druid Arch. Otherwise, complete the circle around Chesler and retrace your steps to the trailhead.

User groups: Hikers only. No dogs. No wheelchair access.

Permits: The park charges an entry fee of $10 per vehicle. Backcountry permits are required for overnight trips, and reservations are strongly recommended. A fee of $15 is charged for groups of up to seven people.

Maps: For USGS topographic maps, ask for The Loop, Druid Arch, and Spanish Bottom. Trails Illustrated's "Needles & Island in the Sky Canyonlands National Park" covers the area.

Directions: From US 191 about 14 miles north of Monticello, take State Route 211 west 29 miles to the national park. It's three miles more to the visitors center, and 5.5 miles total to where the road to Squaw Flat bears south.Drive past the entrance to Campground B and onto the dirt road heading west. At three miles past the turnoff from the main road, park at the Elephant Hill Trailhead on the south side of the road.

Contact: Canyonlands National Park, 2282 South West Resource Boulevard, Moab, UT 84532, 435/719-2313.

52 DEVILS POCKET SEMI-LOOP
11.0 mi/1–2 days

northwest of Monticello in the Needles District of Canyonlands National Park

Map 5.4, page 138

This lesser-known route skirts Chesler Park and passes beneath what are arguably the most dramatic spires in the Needles. Following the same first four miles as the Chesler Park Trail, the hike into Devils Pocket then turns north at a trail junction. The terrain from here sees very little traffic. One reason, perhaps, is the fact that you must, at times, crawl through such narrow slots that you'll need to drag your pack behind you. About 1.5 miles from the Chesler Park Trail, at a junction, head east past the Devils Kitchen Four-Wheel-Drive Camp. A long loop leads south and back to the Chesler Park Trail, where you can turn east again and retrace your steps to the trailhead. The total elevation gain is about 700 feet.

User groups: Hikers only. No dogs. No wheelchair access.

Permits: The park charges an entry fee of $10 per vehicle. Backcountry permits are required for overnight trips, and reservations are strong-

ly recommended. A fee of $15 is charged for groups of up to seven people.

Maps: For USGS topographic maps, ask for The Loop, Druid Arch, and Spanish Bottom. Trails Illustrated's "Needles & Island in the Sky Canyonlands National Park" covers the area.

Directions: From US 191 about 14 miles north of Monticello, take State Route 211 west 29 miles to the national park. It's three miles more to the visitors center, and 5.5 miles total to where the road to Squaw Flat bears south. Drive past the entrance to Campground B and onto the dirt road heading west. At three miles past the turnoff from the main road, park at the Elephant Hill Trailhead on the south side of the road.

Contact: Canyonlands National Park, 2282 South West Resource Boulevard, Moab, UT 84532, 435/719-2313.

53 ANGEL ARCH TRAIL
1.0 mi/2.0 hrs

northwest of Monticello in the Needles District of Canyonlands National Park

Map 5.4, page 138

Angel Arch sweeps across the sky, larger and more picturesque than any other arch in Canyonlands. But there's much more to see on the way. First, just past the visitors center, hike the .25-mile loop to Roadside Ruin, the most easily accessible Anasazi granary in the park. Next, drive the Salt Creek Jeep Road, which offers splendid scenery on the eastern side of the Needles. Numerous drainages open onto the jeep road, inviting exploration. If you enjoy map reading, find a drainage about three miles up the road which leads west to a junction of five canyons. I call this area "Five Fingers." It has lovely campsites, spring water, hidden evidence of the Anasazi, and solitude. During a week one spring, a small group of us saw or heard nothing but the raucous cry of ravens and the rustle of wind in the junipers. Angel Arch, if you're still interested, stands at the end of a one-mile-long, well-marked spur road, and a well-tromped .5-mile walk that gains about 450 feet of elevation. From the road you can see the arch carved out of a black-streaked fin. It's topped with a balanced rock resembling an angel with folded wings.

User groups: Hikers only. No dogs. No wheelchair access.

Permits: The park charges an entry fee of $10 per vehicle. Backcountry permits are required for overnight trips, and reservations are strongly recommended. A fee of $15 is charged for groups of up to seven people.

Maps: For USGS topographic maps, ask for The Loop and Druid Arch. Trails Illustrated's "Needles & Island in the Sky Canyonlands National Park" covers the area.

Directions: From US 191 about 14 miles north of Monticello, take State Route 211 west 29 miles to the national park boundary and another three miles to the visitors center. At a junction of roads about one mile past the visitors center, turn south toward Salt Creek. About a half mile down this road, turn east on a dirt road, again following signs to Salt Creek. After one mile, the Salt Creek Jeep Trail heads south for another 10 miles to the trailhead.

Contact: Canyonlands National Park, 2282 South West Resource Boulevard, Moab, UT 84532, 435/719-2313.

Chapter 6

© FRANK JENSEN/UTAH TRAVEL COUNCIL

Southern Utah

Southern Utah

J ust about anyone who has heard of Utah, even those with only the faintest of knowledge, can speak of the sandstone magnificence of the southern region of the state. If they haven't seen it in person, they've seen pictures. You should see it in person, though, stretched out before or towering mightily above your booted feet, sometimes colored (and even at times shaped) like a rainbow. There is, as so many have noted, nothing like it anywhere else on Earth.

The Colorado Plateau that covers nearly half of Utah covers nearly all of southern Utah, and at the heart of the southern region lies the Grand Staircase–Escalante National Monument. At almost 1.9 million acres, there is no larger monument in the lower 48 states. You can hike along the silty flow of the Escalante River for approximately 90 miles, spending weeks or even months exploring side canyons that lead to more side canyons that lead to nowhere and everywhere. There are passages in which you'll have to turn sideways to squeeze through. There are secret campsites tucked into the bases of cliffs, beneath overhangs eroded from canyon walls. At the end of the river, you can soak your feet in Lake Powell. But the Grand Staircase–Escalante is so much more than the river canyon and its tributaries. You'll find, for instance, some of the best canyon hikes in the world at the bottom of Hackberry and Kitchen Canyons, and along the Paria River.

Not far north of the Escalante River, you can choose to accept what truly ranks as one of the most challenging canyon hikes on Earth: Death Hollow in the Box–Death Hollow Wilderness. Although not as challenging as Death Hollow, The Box, too, is worthy of several days of your life. Further north of the river a small and far less-visited piece of Capitol Reef National Park hides two utterly splendid hikes: Upper and Lower Muley Twist Canyons.

West of Grand Staircase–Escalante you can, and really should, hike the trails of Bryce Canyon and Zion National Parks. The core of

Bryce Canyon is really not a canyon but several natural amphitheaters carved from an enormous pink cliff. Easily accessed overlooks give you the expansive views. Hikes into the fairyland of hoodoos, spires, and other magical rock formations on the trails give you the intimacy with Bryce Canyon that you want. The famous Narrows of Zion attracts many hikers, and deservedly so, and some of the park's most stunning scenery can be seen from your vehicle if you drive the highway through Zion Canyon. But get out and walk the rugged terrain of the northwest section of the park, where the fewest feet fall. You can see Kolob Arch, and go farther into the wildest portion of Zion.

East of Grand Staircase–Escalante, and east of Glen Canyon National Recreation Area, lie numerous hikes that provide more than the grandeur of canyon country. Here in the Grand Gulch Primitive Area and the Dark Canyon Wilderness, for example, you'll hike around bend after bend to find Anasazi ruins dating back to pre-Columbian days and unparalleled in the excellence of their preservation. There are so many more places to see ruins, in canyons such as Road, Arch, Owl Creek, Fish Creek, and Slickhorn, and this chapter will take you there. In southeast Utah you can swim the Black Hole of White Canyon, hike beneath the massive natural bridges in their national monument, and walk the trails into Anasazi history at Hovenweep.

Tired of the canyons? It's difficult to imagine. Even if you aren't, you should consider the isolated Henry Mountains, the last range in America to be explored.

Southern Utah offers Snow Canyon State Park, Kodachrome Basin State Park, Coral Pink Sand Dunes State Park, the Pine Valley Mountain Wilderness, the Paria Canyon–Vermilion Cliffs Wilderness, the Ashdown Gorge Wilderness, Cedar Breaks National Monument, the Valley of the Gods, and, well, the list eventually comes to an end, but the wonder never ceases.

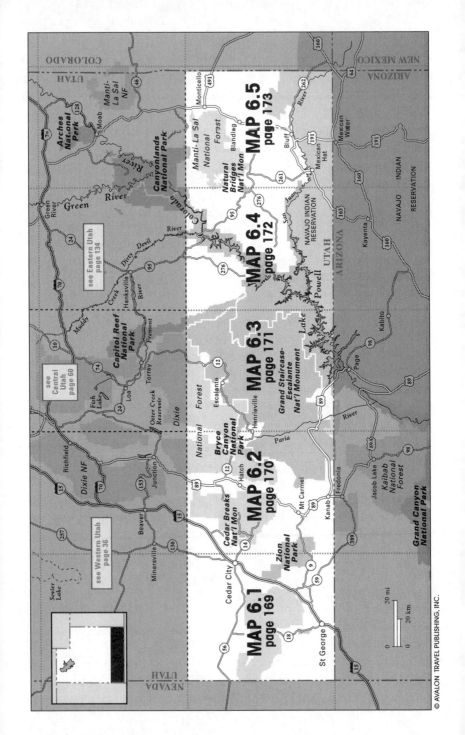

Map 6.1

Hikes 1–14
Pages 174–180

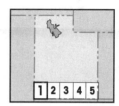

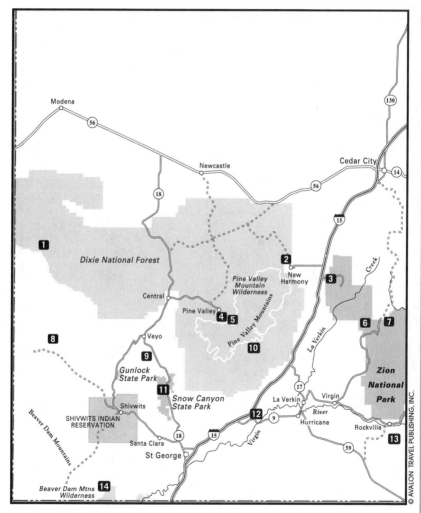

Map 6.2

Hikes 15–33
Pages 181–190

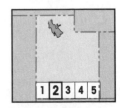

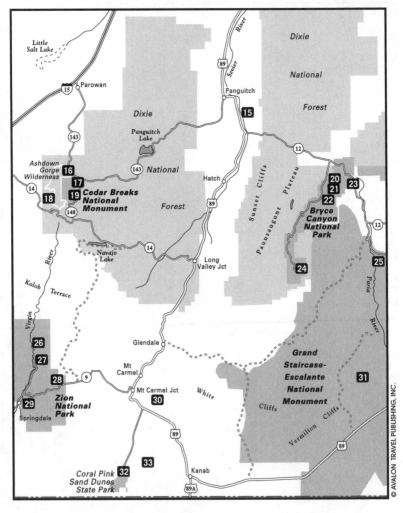

Map 6.3

Hikes 34–59
Pages 190–202

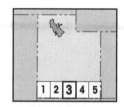

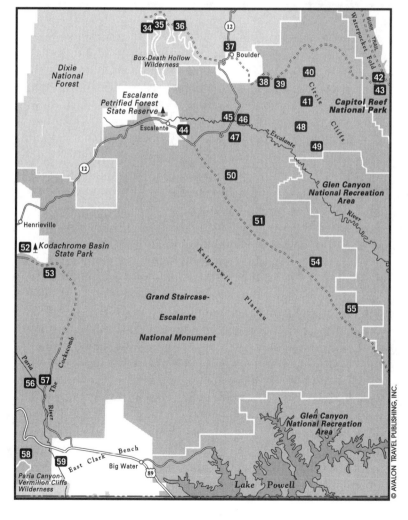

Map 6.4

Hikes 60–71
Pages 203–208

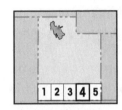

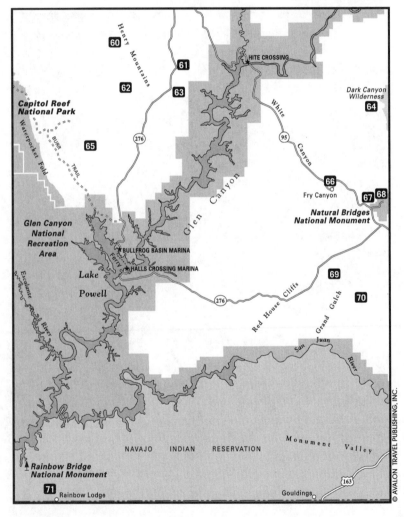

Map 6.5

Hikes 72–83
Pages 209–215

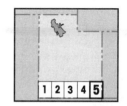

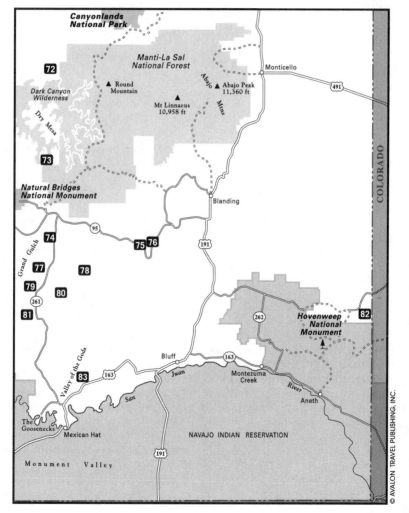

1 SOUTH BOUNDARY TRAIL
10.0 mi/8.0 hrs 🥾 ⚑

northwest of St. George in the Dixie National Forest

Map 6.1, page 169

Pine Park Campground, where the trail starts, sees little use. There are no fees, sites are available on a first-come, first-served basis, and there is no drinking water. The South Boundary Trail heads east into a hectic array of BLM ravines, ridges, and canyons. There is, at this writing, a sign indicating the trail, but without the sign it may be hard to find it. Hike up the hill just beyond the sign for a few hundred yards to find a faint path near the base of a ridge. Turn right, and soon the trail becomes more visible as it runs through a forest of piñon and juniper. At .75 mile into the hike, the trail eases into a meadow with a spring supplying water. Cross the stream, and climb the north side of Pine Canyon with its fine views of a forest highlighted with ragged volcanic jumbles of rock. Continuing to rise, the trail crawls out of the trees and up a ridge, and virtually disappears. Watch for cairns indicating the route. After some up and down hiking, about four miles from the campground, the trail arrives at Mud Flat. Total elevation gain: about 1,000 feet. The trail here, sometimes used by horses, is much easier to follow, and enters Colie Flat at five miles from the trailhead. Colie Flat hosts a junction with the White Hollow Trail, which could allow a loop back (about four miles) to Forest Service Road 001 and then a long walk back to Pine Park Campground. If camping is an option, Colie Flat does just fine, and provides an opportunity to climb Water Canyon Peak, whose summit stands just one mile to the north. The peak, at 7,380 feet, gives an excellent look over this forested area.

User groups: Hikers, dogs, and horses. No wheelchair access.

Permits: No permits are required. Parking and access are free.

Maps: For USGS topographic maps, ask for Pine Park and Water Canyon Peak.

Directions: From Enterprise, take State Route 120 west 15 miles. (The pavement turns to dirt eight miles out along Shoal Creek, and the dirt road becomes known as Forest Service Road 300.) Turn southwest onto twisty Forest Service Road 001, and follow it seven miles to Pine Park Campground.

Contact: Dixie National Forest, Pine Valley Ranger District, 196 East Tabernacle Street, St. George, UT 84770, 435/652-3100; BLM Cedar City Field Office, 176 East D. L. Sargent Drive, Cedar City, UT 84720, 435/586-2401. There is a very helpful Interagency Information Office at 435/688-3246.

2 ASPEN SPRING TRAIL
11.0 mi/1–2 days 🥾 ⚑

north of St. George just north of the Pine Valley Mountain Wilderness

Map 6.1, page 169

Climbing all the way, with relative ease until it gets very steep in the last section, this trail gives access to lovely pools and quiet forested land north of the Pine Valley Mountain Wilderness. You'll follow Comanche Canyon and have to wade its creek several times, as task that may be difficult in spring's high water. The creek pools in places large enough to invite a dip in hot weather. Above Comanche Spring, a thick stand of maples offers shade and what looks like a good camping spot. Toward the end of the canyon, the trail begins to switchback and crosses sections of slickrock before breaking out on top near the serene setting of Aspen Spring. A fine camping spot lies near the spring. Your total elevation gain will be about 2,200 feet.

User groups: Hikers, dogs, and horses. No wheelchair access.

Permits: No permits are required. Parking and access are free.

Maps: For USGS topographic maps, ask for New Harmony, Stoddard Mountain, and Page Ranch.

Directions: From St. George, take I-15 north approximately 35 miles. Take the exit to New

Harmony, and drive the five miles west of the interstate to the town. Follow Main Street to a T junction and turn north down a dirt road one mile to the trailhead.

Contact: Dixie National Forest, Pine Valley Ranger District, 196 East Tabernacle Street, St. George, UT 84770, 435/652-3100.

3 KOLOB ARCH TRAIL
14.4 mi/2 days

in the northwest section of Zion National Park

Map 6.1, page 169

Kolob Arch is one of the largest and most spectacular arches in the world, spanning approximately 300 feet, and this trail passes through some of the most outstanding scenery in Zion National Park. You'll head south from Lee Pass, dropping into the drainage of Timber Creek and reaching the creek in about a mile. Here you'll find stately cottonwoods shading pleasant campsites. The trail then turns west to climb a ridge before dropping down to La Verkin Creek and its lovely canyon. It's easy going along La Verkin Creek for about two miles to a side trail to Kolob Arch. The Kolob Arch Trail is well marked and very well used despite the fact that it's rough at times. It climbs up and down a canyon, leading for a half mile north to a viewpoint of the arch, high on the rust and pale red sandstone of the canyon's wall. You can return the 7.2 miles to the start or, once back on the La Verkin Creek Trail, continue east to the junction of the Willis Creek and Hop Valley Trails. What lies ahead are excellent backpacking opportunities along perennial waterways through forests of evergreens with tremendous cliffs towering near and far.

User groups: Hikers. No wheelchair access.

Permits: The park charges a $20-per-vehicle entry fee, which is good for seven days. No permits are required for day use. Overnight camping requires a backcountry-use permit available at the visitors centers at Zion and Kolob Canyons. The cost is $10 for 1–2 people, $15 for 3–7 people, and $20 for 8–12 people.

Maps: For a USGS topographic map, ask for Kolob Arch. Trails Illustrated's Zion National Park covers the area.

Directions: From Cedar City, take I-15 south 18 miles to the Kolob Canyons exit (Exit 40). Drive east about four miles to Lee Pass, and park at the trailhead.

Contact: Zion National Park, SR 9, Springdale, UT 84767, 435/772-3256.

4 SUMMIT TRAIL
45.0 mi one-way/1 week

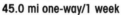

north of St. George in the Pine Valley Mountain Wilderness

Map 6.1, page 169

Pine Valley Mountain stands like a vast tree-clad island in the southeastern Utah desert. The Summit Trail leads along the crest of the Pine Valley Mountain Wilderness, through spectacular scenery. Along this often strenuous track, with about 3,300 feet of overall elevation gain, you'll drop in and climb out of picturesque and hidden valleys. The trail can be started at either end, south or north. From the south end, you'll climb quickly into the most scenic section of the wilderness, and then the hike grows easier toward the north. From the north, you gain more altitude overall, and you have to conclude the hike with miles of hard climbing. South-to-north appeals most to me. From the south (from the Equestrian Campground), the trail ascends Forsythe Creek. There's usually plenty of water low in Forsythe Creek, but not again until Further Water Canyon. Whipple Valley and Mill Flat usually have water, especially in early season. Campsites are fine in the valleys. The trail ends at Pinto Spring with road access. Several loops are available if the entire Summit Trail cannot be hiked. It's possible, for instance, to return to the starting point from Further Water Canyon, Whipple Valley, and Mill Flat. Check in before your trip to learn the availability of water.

User groups: Hikers, dogs, and horses. No wheelchair access.

Permits: No permits are required. Parking and access are free.

Maps: For USGS topographic maps, ask for Central East, Signal Peak, Saddle Mountain, Grass Valley, Page Ranch, and Pinto.

Directions: From St. George, take State Route 18 north 24 miles to Central. Turn east for six miles to Pine Valley. Park in the Equestrian Campground just past the town on the east side.

Contact: Dixie National Forest, Pine Valley Ranger District, 196 East Tabernacle Street, St. George, UT 84770, 435/652-3100.

5 WHIPPLE VALLEY TRAIL
12.0 mi/1–2 days

north of St. George in the Pine Valley Mountain Wilderness

Map 6.1, page 169

This trail climbs steeply, with about 2,000 feet of elevation gain, into the heart of the Pine Valley Mountain Wilderness. From the trailhead, 2.5 miles of hiking take you up to a saddle for the descent into Hop Canyon. The first two of these miles offer very little shade, but then the trees begin. There is a path down Hop Canyon, if you wish to explore, but the Whipple Valley Trail climbs out of Hop Canyon heading north. The trail really gets steep, switchbacking up vigorously, providing great looks at some of Pine Valley Mountain's spires, pinnacles, and hoodoos. Then you drop into the beauty of Whipple Valley, the area's largest meadow, with its spring and two creeks. Snug camping spots can be found among the rocks. With time, make your way a bit west into West Valley (an accurate topographic map will guide you), one of the loveliest little places in this wilderness.

User groups: Hikers, dogs, and horses. No wheelchair access.

Permits: No permits are required. Parking and access are free.

Maps: For USGS topographic maps, ask for Central East and Grass Valley.

Directions: From St. George, take State Route 18 north 24 miles to Central. Turn east for

eight miles to Pine Valley. Turn left at the Pine Valley Church and drive four miles. Park at the far end of the Pine Valley Campground and Recreation Area.

Contact: Dixie National Forest, Pine Valley Ranger District, 196 East Tabernacle Street, St. George, UT 84770, 435/652-3100.

6 HOP VALLEY TRAIL TO KOLOB ARCH
14.0 mi/2–3 days

in the northwest section of Zion National Park

Map 6.1, page 169

To begin with, the drive to the trailhead alone ranks among the most scenic in Utah. What lies ahead is one of Zion's loveliest and least-used trails. From the trailhead, the hike heads north, dropping a bit in elevation, then rising slowly along the foot of the brush-laden slopes of Firepit Knoll, a large cinder cone just to the east. Meandering through oaks and sagebrush, the sandy trail crosses a wide valley. At 1.5 miles, the trail passes through a fence and enters private property for the next 2.5 miles. Cattle may be encountered and, of course, the rights of the property owner to have things left alone must be respected. Beyond the fence, the track rambles among pines and oaks, crosses a dry wash, and ascends to a fork in the track. Stay to the right, and climb into the shadow of cracked cliffs, and down a ridge where the drop turns into a series of steep switchbacks ending on the floor of the amazing Hop Valley. What's so amazing? How about a remarkably flat and grassy floor, narrow, and bounded by walls of sandstone rising to more than 600 feet? It is something otherworldly that just doesn't belong here. Cross the valley, passing a couple of side canyons, and then a thick stand of trees at the wide mouth of Langston Canyon that runs away to the northeast. Then through a second gate, beyond which camping is allowed. There should be water flowing in the stream near the trail. Pleasant campsites await on a long bench east of the trail. Leaving Hop Valley, the trail ascends somewhat steeply to the top of a rise, then descends another bench, and finally down a second series of switchbacks to La Verkin Creek and the trail that follows it. After seeing few, or no, people in Hop Valley, the more popular La Verkin Creek Trail might seem crowded. The trip can turn around here, or continue west approximately one mile to the favored destination of Kolob Arch. Your elevation gain on this hike will be about 1,100 feet.

User groups: Hikers. No wheelchair access.

Permits: The park charges a $20-per-vehicle entry fee, which is good for seven days. No permits are required for day use. Overnight camping requires a backcountry-use permit available at the visitors centers at Zion and Kolob Canyons. The cost is $10 for 1–2 people, $15 for 3–7 people, and $20 for 8–12 people.

Maps: Trails Illustrated's Zion National Park covers the area. For a USGS topographic map, ask for Smith Mesa.

Directions: From the east end of Virgin, on State Route 9, drive north on the Kolob Reservoir Road for 12.5 miles. Turn north at a sign for the Hop Valley Trailhead.

Contact: Zion National Park, SR 9, Springdale, UT 84767, 435/772-3256.

❼ WEST RIM TRAIL
14.5 mi one-way/2 days

in Zion National Park

Map 6.1, page 169

Zion National Park is one of Utah's favorite backpacking destinations, and this popular trail is one of the most used with good reason: It's a pleasant walk through extremely scenic terrain. From the northern end, it wanders gently south along Horse Pasture Plateau, descending easily into Potato Hollow where there are great campsites. Greatheart Mesa, one of the best known landmarks of the park, stands to the west. At the start of Telephone Canyon, you'll have to make a choice because two options exist: east through Telephone or west along the rim. Although the trail along the rim is longer by 1.5

miles, it is far more scenic, and I suggest that option. Not too far beyond where the trails reunite, a spring issues from the earth, and descent gets more serious. At three miles from the spring, a side trail offers a climb to Angels Landing and a must-see view of the park. Be careful, however: This side trail runs steep and narrow, so much so that the park has provided handrails in places. Back on the main trail, a series of 21 switchbacks, called Walter's Wiggles, have been literally cut from the cliff. The trail ends on the North Fork of the Virgin River after losing about 3,000 feet of elevation. Zion Lodge, near the south end of the West Rim Trail, offers a shuttle service to the northern trailhead for a fee, and a free ride (at this writing) from the southern end of the trail.

User groups: Hikers. No wheelchair access.

Permits: The park charges a $20-per-vehicle entry fee, which is good for seven days. Overnight camping requires a backcountry-use permit available at the visitors centers at Zion and Kolob Canyons. The cost is $10 for 1–2 people, $15 for 3–7 people, and $20 for 8–12 people.

Maps: For USGS topographic maps, ask for Kolob Reservoir, The Guardian Angels, and Temple of Sinawava. Trails Illustrated's Zion National Park covers the area.

Directions: From the east end of Virgin on State Route 9, go north on Kolob Reservoir Road for 21 miles. Turn east on Lava Point Road (the turn is marked at this writing). Drive about one mile toward Lava Point, then, at a junction, continue east another 1.3 miles down to the trailhead. Wet conditions can make the last stretch treacherous.

Contact: Zion National Park, SR 9, Springdale, UT 84767, 435/772-3256.

❽ LONE PINE ARCH TRAIL
3.0 mi/2.0 hrs

northwest of St. George

Map 6.1, page 169

This desert walk can be pleasant, and it can be hot. It takes you into a lonely and seldom seen section of Utah for a peek at an isolated arch. From a gate, you'll hike east along an old jeep track, with very little elevation gain, heading toward a high and pale red Navajo sandstone wall. Not easily seen, the arch stands about mid-slope on the wall with a large ponderosa pine growing about 50 feet above it. It's a nice place to settle down with a picnic lunch and forget the frantic pace of modern life.

User groups: Hikers and dogs. No wheelchair access.

Permits: No permits are required. Parking and access are free.

Maps: For a USGS topographic map, ask for Motoqua.

Directions: From old US 91 about three miles north of Shivwits, take the Motoqua Road west for 17 miles. Turn north on a road just past Red Hollow where a sign (at this writing) reads "USMX Gold Strike Mine." Drive 1.7 miles and turn east just before a cattle guard. Drive a half mile to a fence with a gate, and park.

Contact: BLM St. George Field Office, 345 East Riverside Drive, St. George, UT 84720, 435/688-3200.

9 RED MOUNTAIN TRAIL

10.0 mi/6.0 hrs

northwest of St. George

Map 6.1, page 169

The Red Mountain Trail is actually a very old jeep double track, sandy at first, leading southwest from a parking spot. It passes through piñon and juniper before climbing onto rocky ground. Then it crosses an undulating plateau and tops out, after 1.5 miles, with a stunning view northeast over the Pine Valley Mountains. Another mile, and the trail provides an excellent look down lovely Snow Canyon to the south with its colorful cliffs of red and white. The overlook of Snow Canyon is the geographic high point of the trail, but a short distance further and the city of St. George comes into view. Tracing the canyon rim, the trail turns south, then back to the west, and crosses a rock gardenlike area before ending just over five miles from the trailhead on the extensive rocky plateau that is the summit of Red Mountain. Pinnacles of Zion National Park are visible to the east, the rich Red Mountains to the west. Total elevation gain for the hike is only about 400 feet.

User groups: Hikers, dogs, and horses. No wheelchair access.

Permits: No permits are required. Parking and access are free.

Maps: For USGS topographic maps, ask for Santa Clara and Veyo.

Directions: From St. George, take State Route 18 north. About 500 yards past mile marker 15, turn west onto the Red Mountain Road. Travel another 500 yards on this road to a junction of several roads. Keep going due west for a short distance to a place to park where the dirt road narrows to more of a trail.

Contact: BLM St. George Field Office, 345 East Riverside Drive, St. George, UT 84720, 435/688-3200. There is a very helpful Interagency Information Office at 435/688-3246.

10 OAK GROVE TRAIL TO SIGNAL PEAK

8.0 mi/9.0 hrs

northeast of St. George in the Pine Valley Mountain Wilderness

Map 6.1, page 169

Oak Grove Campground lies, indeed, in a lovely stand of oaks. A fee of $5 is charged for camping (first-come, first-served), and water is available. This trail is a steep one, struggling up from the campground three miles to the ridgeline of the Pine Valley Mountains. Well-defined, the trail descends for a quarter mile more to a junction of trails. Head west on the Further Water (sometimes called Summit) Trail. The forest is thick and carpeted in a dense mat of organic material, almost unbelievable so near the Utah desert. The trail wanders west past the head of Further Water Canyon, across an alpine meadow, and begins to traverse Signal Peak. The peak stands south of the trail. From here a short bushwhack is required to reach the summit. The density of the forest makes Signal Peak difficult, if not impossible, to see from the trail. An accurate map and compass are necessities. Signal Peak, at 10,365 feet, rises higher than any other point in the county, and gives a sensational and commanding view of the deep and green forest of the Pine Valley Mountain Wilderness and east to the sandstone towers of Zion National Park.

User groups: Hikers, dogs, and horses. No wheelchair access.

Permits: No permits are required. Parking and access are free.

Maps: For a USGS topographic map, ask for Signal Peak.

Directions: From St. George, take I-15 north 11 miles to Leeds. Take the Leeds exit and drive to the north end of town. Take Forest Service Road 32 northwest for nine miles to the Oak Grove Campground, and park near the trailhead.

Contact: Dixie National Forest, Pine Valley Ranger District, 196 East Tabernacle Street, St. George, UT 84770, 435/652-3100.

11 WEST CANYON TRAIL
7.0 mi/6.0 hrs

north of St. George in Snow Canyon State Park

Map 6.1, page 169

Despite the name, Utah's most-visited state park has nothing to do with snow. Instead, the name comes from a couple of early pioneers named Snow. The trail leads from the park up the west fork of Snow Canyon. Desert vegetation (creosote, cactus, hackberry, yucca) dots the floor of the canyon, whose orange and yellowish sandstone walls rise like natural sculptures. Jagged hunks of black lava lie scattered among the vegetation, reminders of the lava flows that scoured this area probably less than 10,000 years ago. This is an easily accessible trail through some the state's lowest elevations. Snow Canyon State Park offers several short, scenic trails, including a .75-mile hike to the West Canyon Overlook past several lava caves.

User groups: Hikers, dogs, horses, and mountain bikes. No wheelchair access except to the restrooms and showers.

Permits: The park charges an entry fee of $5 per vehicle. Campsites are available for $14 per night, and advance reservations are recommended. Call 800/322-3770 to make a reservation in any Utah state park.

Maps: For a USGS topographic map, ask for Santa Clara.

Directions: From St. George, UT, take State Route 18 north 11 miles to the turnoff for the park.

Contact: Snow Canyon State Park, 1002 Snow Canyon Drive, Ivins, UT 84738, 435/628-2255.

12 QUAIL CREEK TRAIL
2.0 mi/1.5 hrs

northeast of St. George

Map 6.1, page 169

Short and sweet describes this trail. It starts on the west side of the parking area, and meanders through cottonwoods and willows in the bottom of the Quail Creek drainage. Despite the trees, this trail is firmly rooted in the Red Cliffs Desert. The trail reaches a lovely waterfall and pool after .6 mile. Above the falls, the trail continues at a steeper angle, arriving at a second pool after an elevation gain of only about 200 feet. The slope high above the pool, beneath an overhang, was once home for an ancient. Vandals have destroyed much of the site, but pictographs remain. If time allows you to extend the one-mile hike to the second pool, ease around the pool and continue up the slot canyon that enters the Quail Creek drainage. Extremely old steps in the stone must be climbed on the right side of the stream, and a fall could be hazardous. A short way above the steps, the canyon splits, the main canyon bearing right. Exploration from this point is pleasant and easy. Virtually unknown and, thankfully, untouched sites of prehistoric people may be discovered by the curious and determined.

User groups: Hikers and dogs. No wheelchair access.

Permits: No permits are required. Parking and access are free.

Maps: For a USGS topographic map, ask for Harrisburg Junction.

Directions: Northeast of St. George on I-15, take the Harrisburg exit (Exit 16). Go east .75 mile, then turn north on old US 91 for 4.3 miles. Turn west on the paved Red Cliffs Campground Road. Go two miles to the campground, where you'll find the trailhead.

Contact: Dixie National Forest, Pine Valley Ranger District, 196 East Tabernacle Street, St. George, UT 84770, 435/652-3100; BLM St. George Field Office, 345 East Riverside Drive, St. George, UT 84720, 435/688-3200. There is a very helpful Interagency Information Office at 435/688-3246.

13 CANAAN MOUNTAIN RAMBLE
15.0 mi one-way/2–3 days

east of St. George

Map 6.1, page 169

Here, above the Vermilion Cliffs, you'll find some of the best scenery in southern Utah, certainly comparable to the sandstone splendor of Zion National Park just to the north, and seen by far fewer people. You'll need accurate topographical maps and a compass, and skills with both. The route is obscure at times, marked with cairns at others. Canaan Mountain rises above the surrounding terrain to form a long, wide ridge falling away an average of 2,000 feet on three sides. Although the route can be followed from either end—from Eagle Crags on the north or from Short Canyon and Squirrel Canyon on the south (just northeast of Hildale)—north-to-south seems a bit easier to follow to me. From the north, the trail passes the majestic towers of Eagle Crags, and climbs through a series of crevices to the rim of the mountain. From there, ramble south along the ridge. Your total elevation gain will

be just shy of 3,000 feet. Groves of pine and aspen provide shady campsites, but water may be hard to find, especially on the north end. Toward the south end you'll have the choice of descending Water Canyon or Squirrel Canyon to Short Canyon and the end of the route. There's a small lake about 1.5 miles south of the head of Water Canyon (check your map) with very nice campsites. The route down Squirrel is easier and more popular, but both end up at the same place.

User groups: Hikers. No wheelchair access.

Permits: No permits are required. Parking and access are free.

Maps: For USGS topographic maps, ask for Smithsonian Butte, Hildale, Springdale West, and Springdale East.

Directions: From Rockville on State Route 9, head south from the east side of town on the paved road that crosses the Virgin River. After 200 yards, where the pavement turns west, keeping going south on a dirt road for 1.5 miles to a small parking area at the Eagle Crags Trailhead.

Contact: BLM St. George Field Office, 345 East Riverside Drive, St. George, UT 84720, 435/688-3200. There is a very helpful Interagency Information Office at 435/688-3246.

14 BULLDOG KNOLLS
8.0 mi/6.0 hrs

southwest of St. George

Map 6.1, page 169

From the trailhead, this hike goes up a dark canyon carved into the Bulldog Knolls. It's prime habitat for the Mojave rattlesnake, a dangerous reptile when harassed. After a half mile, the canyon opens up, and the Joshua trees and cacti that have dotted the landscape all along now grow larger. Continue north from the canyon, gaining altitude toward a ridge, and enter a large wash paved in small rocks and pebbles. The wash bends to the east and goes on for two miles. Where it begins to grow seriously steep is a good place to end the hike. If you're an ambitious pedestrian, however, scramble up the loose rock to attain the summit of Scrub Point (6,786 feet) in about two miles. In early spring, when the "ouchie" plants (cholla, barrel cactus, prickly pear, hedgehog cactus) are in bloom in purple, red, and yellow, these mountains are most inviting. Otherwise, here lies the hottest, driest, lowest, and, anthropomorphically speaking, meanest portion of Utah.

User groups: Hikers, dogs, and horses. No wheelchair access.

Permits: No permits are required. Parking and access are free.

Maps: For a USGS topographic map, ask for Jarvis Peak.

Directions: From Shivwits, take old US 91 south 15 miles. Turn east on Bulldog Canyon Road. A sign (at this writing) indicates the turn. Drive 2.5 miles, through the Woodbury Desert Study Area, keeping to the right and on the main road, until you pass a cattle guard. Turn north on a rugged old jeep track for a half mile, and park where the track ends.

Contact: BLM St. George Field Office, 345 East Riverside Drive, St. George, UT 84720, 435/688-3200. There is a very helpful Interagency Information Office at 435/688-3246.

Casto Canyon

⓯ CASTO CANYON TO LOSEE CANYON LOOP
13.0 mi/10.0 hrs

southeast of Panguitch

Map 6.2, page 170

Four-wheel-drive access to part of this route will disturb the wilderness purist, but it remains an excellent loop through very scenic red-rock canyon bottom and forested rim country. If you only have time to hike in and out of Casto Canyon, at least do that. It's a smaller, much quieter version of Bryce Canyon to the south. The visually inspiring geological formations—the spires, towers, pinnacles, and hoodoos—extend all the way up Casto. At four miles up Casto, at a trail junction, turn south to head for Losee Canyon. You'll find yourself facing

five miles of highlands. About four-fifths of the way across the highlands, the route crosses the Little Desert, a region of badlands, then descends into Losee Canyon, whose upper region of rock formations, caves, and alcoves compares with Casto Canyon. Before descending, you'll have gained about 950 feet in elevation. At the mouth of Losee, there's one mile of dirt road to walk to complete the loop. If you want to do an overnighter, either carry plenty of water or go in early spring when you'll probably find water in a spring or two.

User groups: Hikers, dogs, horses, and mountain bikes. No wheelchair access.

Permits: No permits are required. Parking and access are free.

Maps: For a USGS topographic map, ask for Casto Canyon. Trails Illustrated's Paunsaugunt Plateau, Mount Dutton, Bryce Canyon covers the area.

Directions: From Panguitch, take US 89 south four miles. Turn east on Forest Service Road 118, and drive over the Sevier River (on a bridge) four miles more to the trailhead.

Contact: Dixie National Forest, Powell Ranger District, P.O. Box 80, Panguitch, UT 84759, 435/676-9300.

16 TWISTED FOREST TRAIL
2.0 mi/2.0 hrs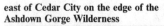

east of Cedar City on the edge of the Ashdown Gorge Wilderness

Map 6.2, page 170

Few, if any, living things in America reach the age of bristlecone pines. The gray, gnarled bristlecones of the Twisted Forest, their bark thick and wrinkled, average over 1,000 years in age. Marked by rock cairns, the trail winds through the forest, the trees well-spaced in the red soil by nature so they each get a share of the sparse nutrients. The overall elevation gain is only about 100 feet, but the trail ends at a breathtaking overlook of the Ashdown Gorge Wilderness and on to the red fins and 2,500-foot-deep amphitheater of Cedar Breaks National Monument. Winter snows may close the access road and other roads in this area. Call ahead in winter for information.

User groups: Hikers, dogs, and kids. No wheelchair access.

Permits: No permits are required. Parking and access are free.

Maps: For a USGS topographic map, ask for Flanigan Arch. Trails Illustrated's Dixie National Forest covers the area.

Directions: From Parowan, take State Route 143 south for approximately eight miles. Turn west on the Dry Lakes Road, bearing left when it forks. Follow this road 9.9 miles to the trailhead where parking is available.

Contact: Dixie National Forest, Cedar City Ranger District, 82 North 100 East, Cedar City, UT 84721, 435/865-3200.

17 RATTLESNAKE TRAIL
10.0 mi/1–2 days

east of Cedar City in the Ashdown Gorge Wilderness

Map 6.2, page 170

This route is difficult to follow. You'll need an accurate topographic map and some map-reading skills. The scenery is awesome, the hike exciting and demanding. From your vehicle, hike along the fence that marks the boundary of Cedar Breaks National Monument. You'll cross a small meadow, pass through some trees, and head southwest toward the edge of the ridge. The trail then descends steep switchbacks, and your first view of the geological fantasy land of Cedar Breaks opens up. When the trail comes to a junction in a grove of aspens, go left. From here the unmaintained trail grows faint, but blazes on trees are sometimes helpful. When the trees give way to meadows, rock cairns mark the route, which eventually enters a flat before descending more switchbacks to Rattlesnake Creek. The route follows the creek down to Ashdown Gorge. You've now lost 3,400 feet of elevation in five miles, and you'll probably enjoy camping before trekking up and out. There's some private land in here, so check with a ranger if you plan to stay overnight. It is also possible to hike down Ashdown Gorge to State Route 14, about four miles more, if you planned ahead and have a vehicle waiting.

User groups: Hikers and dogs. No wheelchair access.

Permits: No permits are required. Parking and access are free.

Maps: For a USGS topographic map, ask for Flanigan Arch. Trails Illustrated's Dixie National Forest covers the area.

Directions: From Parowan, take State Route 143 south approximately 16 miles. Just north of the boundary of Cedar Breaks National Monument, turn west on a dirt road. At this writing, a sign for Rattlesnake Creek indicates the turn. Drive about a mile and park just off the road.

Contact: Dixie National Forest, Cedar City Ranger District, 82 North 100 East, Cedar City, UT 84721, 435/865-3200.

18 POTATO HOLLOW TRAIL
10.0 mi/1–2 days

southeast of Cedar City in the Ashdown Gorge Wilderness

Map 6.2, page 170

The Ashdown Gorge Wilderness, small yet accessible, may well rank as Utah's least-known designated wildland. The Potato Hollow Trail gives you a great look at the winding, ragged, beautiful Ashdown Gorge. From the trailhead, the path falls quickly through a forest dominated by fir and aspen all the way down to Ashdown Creek in about 2.5 miles. Before reaching the creek, it enters a large piece of private land that is surrounded by designated wilderness. It's OK to walk the land, but not OK to camp there. Ashdown Gorge (the gorge itself) lies within the piece of private land, down canyon from where the trail hits the creek. The two-mile length of the gorge, often narrow, is infinitely worthy of quiet exploration. Up canyon the going gets rougher, and staying in or near the bed of the creek eases the journey a bit. In two miles you'll cross the Cedar Breaks National Monument Boundary to find a breathless view of a dramatic amphitheater. The hike back to the parking area is a grunt of an elevation gain: about 1,600 feet. Checking with the Forest Service concerning water levels in the gorge should be high on the list of things to do first.

User groups: Hikers and dogs. No wheelchair access.

Permits: No permits are required. Parking and access are free.

Maps: For USGS topographic maps, ask for Flanigan Arch, Brian Head, and Webster Flat. Trails Illustrated's Dixie National Forest covers the area.

Directions: From Cedar City, take State Route 14 southeast for approximately 13 miles and about a half mile past the Cedar Canyon Campground. Turn north on the Crystal Spring Road for 1.1 mile to where the road ends at the Potato Hollow Trailhead.

Contact: Dixie National Forest, Cedar City Ranger District, 82 North 100 East, Cedar City, UT 84721, 435/865-3200.

19 ALPINE POND LOOP TRAIL
2.0 mi/1.5 hrs

east of Cedar City in Cedar Breaks National Monument

Map 6.2, page 170

A fine hike with kids, this relatively gentle trail rambles through an old-growth forest with ancient bristlecone pines. It passes a delightful pond and reaches a midpoint at Chessman Ridge Overlook. From here you can look down 2,000 feet into the vast amphitheater of Cedar Breaks National Monument, filled with fins, spires, columns, and delightful colors. If you want the overlook without the hike, you can stop your vehicle there on the way to the trailhead. The other half of the loop wanders on a parallel course, along the opposite side of the pond, to the starting point. Here, at 10,000 feet, winter snows typically close the monument from mid-October to mid-May.

User groups: Hikers. No wheelchair access except at the overlook and restrooms.

Permits: The monument charges an entry fee of $3 per person for ages 17 and up.

Maps: For a USGS topographic map, ask for Brian Head. A national monument brochure, available at the trailhead, describes the trail.

Directions: From Cedar City, take State Route 14 east 19 miles. Turn north on State Route 148 for seven miles to the trailhead on the west side of the road.

Contact: Cedar Breaks National Monument, 2390 West Highway 56, Suite #11, Cedar City, UT 84720, 435/586-9451.

20 NAVAJO LOOP– QUEEN'S GARDEN LOOP
3.0 mi/2.5 hrs

east of Cedar City in Bryce Canyon National Park

Map 6.2, page 170

Sunset Point is the trailhead for some of the best easy hiking that Bryce Canyon has to offer.

The trails, therefore, are quite popular. Drop down from the Navajo Loop Trail sign via switchbacks. At the end of the switchbacks, the trail passes through a narrow channel in the orange rock. Wall Street appears on the right, and the trail begins to weave up and down for about a mile across the floor of the astounding amphitheater of Bryce Canyon. Pink and gold spires, columns, and pinnacles stand like silent sentinels guarding the approach to the Queen. At signed trail intersections, choose the route to the Queen's Garden, where a formation known as Queen Victoria reigns over a huddle of grotesquely beautiful smaller formations called hoodoos. From the Queen, you'll have to retrace a few steps to the main trail and the return to the parking area.

User groups: Hikers. No wheelchair access.

Permits: The park entrance fee, good for seven days, is $20 per vehicle.

Maps: Trails Illustrated's Bryce Canyon National Park covers the area. A park brochure describes the trail.

Directions: From State Route 12, drive south into the national park on State Route 63. After a stop at the visitors center, drive one mile south on the park road to Sunset Point.

Contact: Bryce Canyon National Park, P.O. Box 170001, Bryce Canyon, UT 84717, 435/834-5322.

21 FAIRYLAND LOOP TRAIL
8.0 mi/5.0 hrs

east of Cedar City in Bryce Canyon National Park

Map 6.2, page 170

This popular trail leads past some of the most fascinating geological formations in the park and through a section of badlands with about 1,000 feet of elevation loss and gain. To borrow a phrase: The wonders never cease. After soaking up the awe-inspiring view of Fairyland Canyon's hoodoo-filled amphitheater from Fairyland Point at the trailhead, descend the wide trail along a ridge on the east side of the canyon. Vistas down lower Fairyland Canyon

are followed by ascents and descents that lead across the ridge into Campbell Canyon. Here a very short spur trail leads to Tower Arch. Back on the main trail, you'll head up Campbell Canyon, past remarkable hoodoos and the deeply-cut white Chinese Wall. From below Sunrise Point, the trail turns north on the Rim Trail for an easy 2.5 miles back to Fairyland Point. It is also possible to shuttle a vehicle around to Sunrise Point and end the hike here.

User groups: Hikers only. No wheelchair access.

Permits: The park entrance fee, good for seven days, is $20 per vehicle.

Maps: Trails Illustrated's Bryce Canyon National Park covers the area. A park brochure, available at the visitors center, describes the trail.

Directions: From State Route 12, drive south into the national park on State Route 63. After a stop at the visitors center, drive three miles on the park road to the Fairyland Road. Turn east and drive a half mile to a parking area.

Contact: Bryce Canyon National Park, P.O. Box 170001, Bryce Canyon, UT 84717, 435/834-5322.

22 UNDER-THE-RIM TRAIL
22.5 mi one-way/2 days

east of Cedar City in Bryce Canyon National Park

Map 6.2, page 170

This is the longest backpacking trail in the park. It stays, as the name suggests, just below the rim of the extensive Paunsaugunt Plateau, so the most unique geological features of the park can only be seen from a distance. Still, you get to make intimate contact with a lovely section of the park. From the trailhead, the route rolls up and down as it descends into the canyon. The descent covers three miles, but stop 1.5 miles down to check out the unusual rock formations known as The Hat Shop. You'll reach a creek, and after five more miles under the rim, you'll enter the Sheep Creek–Swamp Canyon section, the most spectacular part of the trail. This section can also be seen from connecting trails between the Under-the-Rim Trail and the highway, if you don't wish to hike the entire 22.5 miles. Sheep Creek makes an excellent choice for camping. After leaving Swamp Canyon, the trail sees far less traffic; the second half of the hike, however, is steep, with nearly 2,000 feet of elevation gain. On the plus side, the distant views are much better as elevation is gained. As you plan your hike, be sure to check which springs are running, and pick your campsites accordingly.

User groups: Hikers only. No wheelchair access.

Permits: The park entrance fee, good for seven days, is $20 per vehicle. A backcountry camping permit is required, and the cost is $5 per group regardless of the size of the group or the length of the trip.

Maps: For USGS topographic maps, ask for Bryce Point, Tropic Reservoir, and Rainbow Point. Trails Illustrated's Bryce Canyon National Park covers the area.

Directions: From State Route 12, drive south into the national park on State Route 63. After a stop at the visitors center, drive 1.5 miles south on the park road, turn east, drive two miles more, and park at the Bryce Point Trailhead. The end of the trail is at Rainbow Point, 15.5 miles further south at the end of the park road.

Contact: Bryce Canyon National Park, P.O. Box 170001, Bryce Canyon, UT 84717, 435/834-5322.

23 GOLDEN WALL TO CASTLE BRIDGE LOOP
2.5 mi/2.0 hrs

just northwest of Bryce Canyon National Park

Map 6.2, page 170

This hike offers splendid views of the geological wonders of Red Canyon, which is sometimes referred to as Bryce Canyon's "little sister." It's not difficult, and kids can enjoy it. The trail starts west of the visitors center and ascends gradually for one mile to a panoram-

ic viewpoint after passing a junction with the Castle Bridge Trail. From the viewpoint, descend via the Castle Bridge Trail, switchbacking down through weird rock formations and past what may be the most unusual balanced rock in the state. This trail rejoins the Golden Wall .7 miles from the parking area.

User groups: Hikers and dogs. No wheelchair access except to the visitors center.

Permits: No permits are required. Parking and access are free.

Maps: For a USGS topographic map, ask for Wilson Peak. Trails Illustrated's Paunsaugunt Plateau, Mount Dutton, Bryce Canyon covers the area.

Directions: From the junction of State Routes 12 and 63 at the northwest corner of Bryce Canyon National Park, take 12 west approximately 13 miles and park at the Red Canyon Visitor Center.

Contact: Dixie National Forest, Cedar City Ranger District, 1789 Wedgewood Lane, Cedar City, UT 84720, 435/865-3200.

24 BRISTLECONE LOOP
1.0 mi/1.0 hr

east of Cedar City in Bryce Canyon National Park

Map 6.2, page 170

This trail crosses the highest terrain in the national park, with accompanying views, and provides a peek at what is considered the oldest living thing in the park. The elevation gain is only about 200 feet, and the whole family will have a great time. From the first overlook along the trail, you'll get a close-up view of the reddish-orange rock of the Paunsaugunt Plateau with the dark cliffs of the Kaiparowits Plateau in the distance. At the second overlook, check out the Pink Cliffs, the last step of the "Grand Staircase" that starts on the Grand Canyon's north rim and "steps up" as it moves north. Here stands a bristlecone pine estimated to be 1,600 years old. From there the trail loops around—with views north across the park—and back to the starting point.

User groups: Hikers. No wheelchair access.
Permits: The park entrance fee, good for seven days, is $20 per vehicle.
Maps: Trails Illustrated's Bryce Canyon National Park covers the area. A park brochure, available at the visitors center, describes the trail.
Directions: From State Route 12, drive south into the national park on State Route 63. After a stop at the visitors center, take the park road south 17 miles to the end of the road and a parking area.
Contact: Bryce Canyon National Park, P.O. Box 170001, Bryce Canyon, UT 84717, 435/834-5322.

25 UPPER PARIA RIVER GORGE
24.0 mi/2–3 days

south of Cannonville

Map 6.2, page 170

Although Buckskin Gulch and the Lower Paria River Gorge rank among the best canyon hikes in the world, the less dramatic Upper Paria River Gorge should not be ignored, especially if you enjoy solitude. The scenery isn't that bad either, and a scenic trip can be augmented greatly by adding a couple of days and hiking up side canyons such as Willis Creek, Bull Valley Gorge, and Deer Creek. Heck, take a week. It's worth it. The Upper Paria once provided a "road" connecting the towns of Cannonville and Pahreah, and you'll pass by the ruins of at least five long-abandoned ranches. You can still hike right out of Cannonville, but the first five or six miles offer little to see. The access via Little Dry Valley is very easy, but the gorge may also be accessed via Willis Creek or Bull Valley Gorge, both of which provide fascinating narrows and more difficult going. Water is always available in springs, seeps, and perennial streams flowing in from side canyons. Some truly awesome petroglyphs and pictographs are found up Deer Creek.

Plan on wading through the Paria a few times—an easy but wet job. A through-hike requires a vehicle at both ends, but you can hike up or down the canyon half way, returning to your starting point, without too much difficulty. The south end of the Upper Paria can be easily accessed by traveling US 89, the highway from Kanab, UT, to Page, AZ, and turning north between mile markers 30 and 31 on a good dirt road for about six miles.

User groups: Hikers and dogs. No wheelchair access.
Permits: No permits are required. Parking and access are free.
Maps: For USGS topographic maps, ask for Cannonville, Bull Valley Gorge, Deer Range Point, Calico Peak, and Fivemile Valley.
Directions: From Cannonville on State Route 12, take Cottonwood Canyon Road southeast approximately five miles toward Kodachrome Basin State Park. About a mile after crossing the Paria River (really just a creek here), park off the road at the head of Little Dry Valley.
Contact: BLM Kanab Field Office, 318 North First East, Kanab, UT 84741, 435/644-4600; Grand Staircase–Escalante National Monument, 190 East Center, Kanab, UT 84741, 435/644-4300.

26 THE NARROWS
17.5 mi one-way/1–2 days

in Zion National Park

Map 6.2, page 170

Not only does this hike qualify as the most famous in Zion National Park, it certainly ranks among the best canyon hikes in Utah. From the trailhead, the route heads down the North Fork of the Virgin River. After an easy mile with tree-clad slopes rolling away from the river (more a stream here), you might be lulled into a false sense of security. Sandstone cliffs soon work their way down toward the banks, and the water must be waded several times. The cliffs continue to rise, and the canyon continues to narrow. Fir and maple shadow the trail. Camping is possible along this section, and allowed all the way down to

Big Springs, but there is no camping below Big Springs. After six miles of hiking, the first really narrow section is entered. The top of the cliffs now stand about 500 feet above. At about seven miles a waterfall, passable by a gap on the river's left, almost stops progress. Soon the trail reaches the confluence of the North Fork with Deep Creek, and the waterway more than doubles in size. Campsites appear on benches above the river after Deep Creek adds its water to the flow. Springs and seeps attract birds and support green growth, adding a lovely touch to the trip. At about 10 miles, Kolob Creek runs into the river from the northwest and, about a half mile later, the hike enters The Grotto, a deep alcove (and a spectacular place to set a camp). About 12 miles into the hike, Big Springs, the largest spring on the river, rushes out of the rocks, and provides the last opportunity to camp. The next two miles never see the sun. The walls tower 2,000 feet above, and barely 20 feet apart. Deep pools must be waded . . . or swum. At about 14 miles, large-mouthed Orderville Canyon enters from the east, and the final three-plus miles pass quickly (although some wading in the water is still required). The first half of summer offers the prime hiking season for The Narrows—after spring runoff and before the rainy season.

User groups: Hikers only. No wheelchair access.

Permits: The park charges a $20-per-vehicle entry fee good for seven days. A permit is required, even for day use, and will be issued no more than 24 hours prior to the hike, depending on the weather forecast. Overnight camping requires a backcountry-use permit—$10 for 1–2 people, $15 for 3–7 people, $20 for 8–12 people—available at the visitors centers at Zion and Kolob Canyons.

Maps: For USGS topographic maps, ask for Temple of Sinawava, Clear Creek Mountain, and Straight Canyon. Trails Illustrated's Zion National Park covers the area.

Directions: From Mount Carmel Junction, take State Route 9 west approximately 13 miles.

Turn north on a paved road that becomes a good dirt road after a few miles. This roads winds north, with lots of side roads that should be avoided, eventually crossing the North Fork of the Virgin River and reaching Chamberlain's Ranch after 17 miles. Another half mile remains to the trailhead along a rough, rutty road, and a high-clearance vehicle is recommended.

Contact: Zion National Park, SR 9, Springdale, UT 84767, 435/772-3256.

27 EMERALD POOLS TRAIL
2.0 mi/2.0 hrs

in Zion National Park

Map 6.2, page 170

One of the park's most walked trails, this little hike, good for the whole family, eases up a side canyon of Zion Canyon to a series of quiet pools that reflect the soaring sandstone walls. A stream from the springs typically supports lush vegetation. The elevation gain is a bit over 300 feet.

User groups: Hikers. There's an optional wheelchair-accessible trail to the lower pool.

Permits: The park charges a $20-per-vehicle entry fee.

Maps: For a USGS topographic map, ask for Temple of Sinawava. Trails Illustrated's Zion National Park covers the area.

Directions: From just north of Springdale, enter the national park. Take the park road north 2.5 miles to the trailhead on the west side of the road.

Contact: Zion National Park, SR9, Springdale, UT 84767, 435/772-3256.

28 EAST RIM TRAIL
16.5 mi one-way/2 days

in Zion National Park

Map 6.2, page 170

The East Rim Trail rates as an excellent backpacking trip with exemplary views of the geologic splendor of Zion, especially in the last five miles. Keep in mind that this trail, too, is very popular. The path heads north along Clear Creek, then climbs slowly to the vast mesa that stands over Zion Canyon. It then wanders along the top of the mesa to Stave Spring, near which you'll find campsites and water. Camping near Stave Spring offers the possibility of a couple of side trails. The Cable Mountain and Deer-trap Mountain Trails both end at overlooks that are simply spectacular. Cable Mountain provides the better view, but either viewpoint can be reached in an hour or so of walking from Stave Spring. Back on the main trail, however, you'll turn north into Echo Canyon, and descend southwest into ever more narrower and shadowy depths to Weeping Rock. Zion Lodge offers a shuttle service to the East Rim Trailhead for a fee, and a free ride (at this writing) back to the lodge from trail's end near Weeping Rock.

User groups: Hikers. No wheelchair access.

Permits: The park charges a $20-per-vehicle entry fee good for seven days. Overnight camping requires a backcountry use permit—$10 for 1–2 people, $15 for 3–7 people, $20 for 8–12 people—available at the visitors centers at Zion and Kolob Canyons.

Maps: For USGS topographic maps, ask for Temple of Sinawava, Springdale East, The Barracks, and Clear Creek Mountain. Trails Illustrated's Zion National Park covers the area.

Directions: From the south entrance to Zion National Park, just north of Springdale, take State Route 9 east approximately 11 miles to the east entrance. Just to the west of the entrance station, turn north on a dirt road and proceed a quarter mile to the trailhead.

Contact: Zion National Park, SR 9, Springdale, UT 84767, 435/772-3256.

29 WATCHMAN TRAIL
3.0 mi/2.0 hrs

near the south entrance in Zion National Park

Map 6.2, page 170

This relatively short trail is richly scenic, offering a view of the southern end of Zion

Canyon that you can't get anywhere else. The trail from South Campground heads up a small canyon and climbs a short series of switchbacks, with about 400 feet of elevation gain, to a bench where a loop walk opens vistas: the massive Towers of the Virgin to the north, Zion Canyon stretching away north, splendid cliffs and crags, the towering red Watchman to the south. If you're here with little ones, beware the drastic drop-offs from the rim.

User groups: Hikers. No wheelchair access.

Permits: The park charges a $20-per-vehicle entry fee.

Maps: For a USGS topographic map, ask for Springdale East. Trails Illustrated's Zion National Park covers the area.

Directions: From just north of Springdale, enter the national park. In .3 mile, turn east to South Campground and follow the signs about one mile to the amphitheater and parking at the trailhead.

Contact: Zion National Park, SR 9, Springdale, UT 84767, 435/772-3256.

30 DIANA'S THRONE
0.8 mi/1.0 hr

north of Kanab

Map 6.2, page 170

A short ascent brings you to a peak with impressive views of the surrounding terrain in an area being considered for wilderness designation. From your vehicle, hike toward the hill below the Throne's saddle (it stands right ahead). Contour along the rough surface of the white sandstone into the gap between the Throne and the white cliffs that stand behind. It's an easy scramble from there to the saddle. It's an easy, if a bit tricky, scramble to the summit. The rim of the White Cliffs still rise 250 feet above you. The valley of Kanab Creek winds below. To the west is Zion National Park, and beyond that the Pine Valley Mountains. The legend about a woman named Diana who threw herself off this peak, dying from a broken heart, is doubtful. This view makes you feel like living forever.

User groups: Hikers. No wheelchair access.

Permits: No permits are required. Parking and access are free.

Maps: For a USGS topographic map, ask for Mount Carmel.

Directions: From Kanab, take US 89 north about 10 miles. Turn north on a dirt road, just south of mile marker 77, heading toward the White Cliffs, and crossing old Highway 89. In .6 mile, turn north (right) and drive another .25 mile to where the road ends.

Contact: BLM Kanab Field Office, 318 North First East, Kanab, UT 84741, 435/644-4600.

31 MOLLIES NIPPLE
10.0 mi/8.0 hrs

northeast of Kanab

Map 6.2, page 170

The most scenic peak in this area, Mollies Nipple got its name from the wife of John Kitchen, who homesteaded this region. What an interesting way to be remembered! Hike east from your vehicle, up to a ridge, and you'll see your pointed destination. You can't miss it. Hike down into and across a valley, and up the peak from the southwest. A bit of scrambling—hand and foot work with exposure to steep drops—is required to reach the top, with about 1,600 feet of elevation gain overall if you make the summit. If you have time, before leaving the area, hike north along the road from the pass for about a half mile. But beware: Driving this stretch can be hazardous due to deep sand. Turn east and almost immediately north up a tributary canyon to Swag Canyon. Soon you'll see cliff dwellings tucked into an overhang. Not only are these ancient homes the only ones nearby, they are also built facing north, something the Anasazi only rarely did. You can also access Mollies Nipple via Kitchen Canyon and Starlight Canyon.

User groups: Hikers and dogs. No wheelchair access.

Permits: No permits are required. Parking and access are free.

Maps: For USGS topographic maps, ask for Deer Range Point.

Directions: From Kanab, take US 89 east approximately 26 miles. Turn north at mile marker 37, drive to a pass, and park.

Contact: Grand Staircase–Escalante National Monument, 190 East Center, Kanab, UT 84741, 435/644-4300.

32 SAND DUNES BOUNDARY TRAIL
5.5 mi/5.0 hrs

west of Kanab in Coral Pink Sand Dunes State Park

Map 6.2, page 170

The vast Colorado Plateau was once loose sand, now revealed as slickrock, hardened by pressure over eons. Here the red rock country of Utah is still pink sand, shifted by wind into colorful dunes. The Boundary Trail skirts the southern end of the 2,000 acres of dunes within Coral Pink Sand Dunes State Park, and much of the hiking is tough, as it's slow going through the loose sand. Don't expect a rippled desert barren of life. Piñon and juniper, yucca and sunflowers, and other vegetation survive in this harsh environ. Two other short trails offer a look at this area: a signed half-mile-long nature trail, and a 1.5-mile romp to the top of a dune that rises 200 vertical feet.

User groups: Hikers only. No wheelchair access to the trail.

Permits: The park charges an entry fee of $5 per vehicle. Campsites are available at $14 per night, and advance reservations are recommended. Call 800/322-3770 to make a reservation in any Utah state park.

Maps: For a USGS topographic map, ask for Yellow Jacket Canyon. A park brochure, available at the visitors center, describes the trail.

Directions: From Kanab, take US 89 north 7.1 miles. Turn southwest on Hancock Road for nine miles to the park.

Contact: Coral Pink Sand Dunes State Park, P.O. Box 95, Kanab, UT 84741, 435/648-2800.

33 SOUTH FORK INDIAN CREEK TRAIL
1.0 mi/1.0 hr

west of Kanab

Map 6.2, page 170

This short series of switchbacks descends for a half mile into the South Fork of Indian Creek Canyon to a panel of Indian pictographs (strange animal shapes, odd faces) dating back approximately 800 years. The hiking is easy, and the whole family can enjoy it. Senseless acts of vandalism have forced the BLM to fence off the panel, but the trail comes close enough for a good look. If time allows, plan a more extended trip into this little used area, which is under consideration for wilderness designation, and explore the rims and forested canyons of this compact region.

User groups: Hikers and dogs. No wheelchair access.

Permits: No permits are required. Parking and access are free.

Maps: For a USGS topographic map, ask for Yellow Jacket Canyon.

Directions: From Kanab, take US 89 north 7.1 miles. Turn southwest on Hancock Road for six miles. Turn south onto Sand Spring Road and drive 2.1 miles to the trailhead.

Contact: BLM Kanab Field Office, 318 North First East, Kanab, UT 84741, 435/644-4600.

34 THE BOX
9.0 mi one-way/5.0 hrs

north of Escalante in the Box–Death Hollow Wilderness

Map 6.3, page 171

Unlike the dramatic challenge of Death Hollow, The Box is a pleasant walk through a particularly scenic and narrow canyon cut by the perennial flow of Pine Creek. Trees often shade the route. As you hike south, losing elevation, the canyon walls rise higher and higher until they tower more than 1,000 above. As so often is true in canyon country, no real trail exists. Just follow the stream south, crossing it often to find the best path. There's no way to come out of The Box with dry feet, but the water seldom rises up your legs more than a foot or so. The canyon widens toward the lower end, but suddenly narrows again before joining Hells Backbone Road about 11 road miles from the starting point.

User groups: Hikers only. No wheelchair access.

Permits: No permits are required. Parking and access are free.

Maps: For USGS topographic maps, ask for Posy Lake and Wide Hollow Reservoir. Trails Illustrated's Canyons of the Escalante covers the area.

Directions: From Escalante, take Hells Backbone Road north approximately 19 miles to the trailhead on the south side of the road.

Contact: Dixie National Forest, Escalante Ranger District, P.O. Box 246, Escalante, UT 84726, 435/826-5400.

35 DEATH HOLLOW
30.0 mi one-way/3–4 days

north of Escalante starting in the Box–Death Hollow Wilderness

Map 6.3, page 171

Most agree: Death Hollow offers one of the most exciting and challenging canyon hikes in the world. But it's also an utterly beautiful journey. Only the best prepared, however, should go. The route drops about 1,000 feet in the first mile, then eases up for another 10 waterless miles. Finally, as you reach the Upper Narrows, you'll find water—muddy, stagnant pools that require swimming. Depending on water level, some pools may extend to 50 yards. Between the pools, the canyon is often blocked with fallen rocks that require slow climbing up and down. Water should be flowing by the time you reach the end of the Upper Narrows, and the walking, though wet, is much easier. The Lower Narrows, an astoundingly beautiful section, requires more swimming, but the water is typically clear. Bring a small inflatable air

36 SAND CREEK
20.0 mi one-way/3 days

**northeast of Escalante and crossing the
Box–Death Hollow Wilderness**

Map 6.3, page 171

From its start near the northern boundary of the Box–Death Hollow Wilderness to its end on the Upper Escalante River, Sand Creek offers a challenging route. It passes through a slim canyon choked, at times, by boulders, long dead and fallen trees, and thick stands of willows and brush. What you get for your effort is a chance at blissful solitude in richly scenic terrain . . . and lots of scratches on exposed skin. The canyon drops steeply and narrowly for the first few miles, and it takes more than a half-day of walking to get to the first camping spot. From here, campsites are relatively abundant between narrow sections. Sandstone walls rise higher and higher as you travel south. You'll lose a total of about 3,000 feet in elevation as you go. Although the hiking grows easier in places, there is always some obstacle ahead until the last couple of miles. When Sand Creek joins the Escalante River, turn east for a little over three miles to State Route 12.

User groups: Hikers and dogs. No wheelchair access.

Permits: No permits are required. Parking and access are free.

Maps: For USGS topographic maps, ask for Roger Peak, Escalante, and Calf Creek. Trails Illustrated's Canyons of the Escalante covers the area.

Directions: From Escalante, take Hells Backbone Road north about 28 miles to the trailhead near the head of Sand Creek.

Contact: Dixie National Forest, Escalante Ranger District, P.O. Box 246, Escalante, UT 84726, 435/826-5400; Grand Staircase-Escalante National Monument, 190 East Center, Kanab, UT 84741, 435/644-4300.

© JANET REFFERT/GARFIELD COUNTY TOURISM

Be prepared for Death Hollow.

mattress or a life jacket to assist in crossing the pools. Also bring a short rope to assist in negotiating some of the drops. From below the Lower Narrows, it's easy walking down to the Escalante River and along the river west to the town of Escalante.

User groups: Hikers only. No wheelchair access.

Permits: No permits are required. Parking and access are free.

Maps: For USGS topographic maps, ask for Roger Peak and Escalante. Trails Illustrated's Canyons of the Escalante covers the area.

Directions: From Escalante, take Hells Backbone Road north approximately 20 miles to the trailhead on the south side of the road. The trailhead is two miles west of Hells Backbone Bridge.

Contact: Dixie National Forest, Escalante Ranger District, P.O. Box 246, Escalante, UT 84726, 435/826-5400. Grand Staircase-Escalante National Monument, 190 East Center, Kanab, UT 84741, 435/644-4300.

37 BOULDER MAIL TRAIL
16.0 mi one-way/2–3 days

west of Boulder

Map 6.3, page 171

Long ago, horses and mules were used to pack mail and other supplies along this route between the towns of Boulder and Escalante. Now it is a challenging hike, largely cross-country, demanding map and compass skills, although you will on occasion find rock cairns marking the way. Although the overall climb is slight, do not be deceived: The route climbs in and out of Sand Creek, Death Hollow, Mamie Creek, and a few other unnamed drainages. Out of the canyons, you'll be treated to expansive and spectacular views across the slickrock. Down in Mamie Creek take the time to follow the drainage south about a mile to Mamie Creek Natural Bridge, which stands about 30 feet above the dry creek bed. The hike finishes at the same trailhead that begins the Upper Escalante River hike.

User groups: Hikers, dogs, and horses. No wheelchair access.

Permits: No permits are required. Parking and access are free.

Maps: For USGS topographic maps, ask for Boulder Town, Calf Creek, and Escalante. Trails Illustrated's Canyons of the Escalante covers the area.

Directions: From Escalante, take State Route 12 east approximately 25 miles to Hells Backbone Road. Turn west .25 mile to the start of the Boulder Mail Trail. Parking is available here, or drive another two miles south on the dirt road that leads past the Boulder Landing Strip.

Contact: Grand Staircase–Escalante National Monument, 190 East Center, Kanab, UT 84741, 435/644-4300.

38 DEER CREEK TO HIGHWAY 12
17.0 mi one-way/2–3 days

southeast of Boulder

Map 6.3, page 171

Hiking south from the trailhead along the flow of Deer Creek, you'll sink into a green world hidden below colorful and barren slickrock benches. After a couple of miles (it's easier on the west side of the creek) the canyon deepens and narrows, and soon the easiest walking is often in the water, which slows progress. Numerous plants find suitable habitat down here in the shade—a stark contrast to the dry world above. There may be pools of water to negotiate, depending on the time of year. Some functional campsites exist along the creek, but you'll find no great camping spots until you reach the confluence with Boulder Creek. The route continues down to the Escalante River, a distance of about 7.5 miles from the trailhead, and up the river to State Highway 12, gaining about 800 feet of elevation in the process. You can, as an alternative, hike up Boulder Creek to the town of Boulder.

User groups: Hikers. No wheelchair access.

Permits: No permits are required. Parking and access are free.

Maps: For a USGS topographic map, ask for King Bench. Trails Illustrated's Canyons of the Escalante covers the area.

Directions: From just south of the town of Boulder, take the Burr Trail Road east approximately 6.5 miles to the trailhead.

Contact: Grand Staircase–Escalante National Monument, 190 East Center, Kanab, UT 84741, 435/644-4300.

39 THE GULCH TO HIGHWAY 12
27.0 mi one-way/3–4 days

southeast of Boulder

Map 6.3, page 171

If you've hiked around the Escalante River much, you'll find this route filled with the usual stunning array of sandstone formations. In other words, this is an outstanding natural area. The entire hike ranks as relatively easy, with the usual wetness from water crossings (always along the river) and minor scratches from willows. There are short sections in the Lower Gulch, where the water has carved its way through narrow openings, requiring a challenging bit of climbing, crawling, and good luck. About 30 feet of rope is very useful here. You can also give up, backtrack, and climb up out of the Gulch to hike along the west rim. You'll find ample campsites, but keep in mind that the Gulch can be dry during summer months. Once at the Escalante River, you can hike approximately 14.5 miles to Highway 12 or continue down the river for more adventure. With time on your hands, consider a hike north up the Gulch from the same trailhead. It's an easy walk that opens up more and more onto wide sandstone benches. Turn around and retrace your steps whenever you choose.

User groups: Hikers. No wheelchair access.

Permits: No permits are required. Parking and access are free.

Maps: For USGS topographic maps, ask for King Bench and Red Breaks. Trails Illustrated's Canyons of the Escalante covers the area.

Directions: From just south of the town of Boulder, take the Burr Trail Road east approximately 11 miles to the trailhead. Hike south.

Contact: Grand Staircase–Escalante National Monument, 190 East Center, Kanab, UT 84741, 435/644-4300.

40 HORSE CANYON
26.0 mi/2–3 days

southeast of Boulder

Map 6.3, page 171

As you hike south, Horse Canyon lies wide and open at first, but then narrows and begins to meander beneath high, desert-varnished walls on its scenic journey down to the Escalante River. You'll pass small arches and overhangs, and interesting little semi-caves scooped out of the walls with signs that cattle relax in these shady spots. About half way to the river, Wolverine Creek enters from the east, and then Little Death Hollow, also from the east. Both of these side trips are extremely worthy and discussed later in this chapter. You'll likely be quite a ways down Horse Canyon before you encounter

water. From the mouth of Little Death Hollow, it's not far to the wide mouth where Horse Canyon meets the Escalante, and the end of the 13-mile one-way journey.

User groups: Hikers. No wheelchair access.

Permits: No permits are required. Parking and access are free.

Maps: For USGS topographic maps, ask for Pioneer Mesa, King Bench, and Red Breaks. Trails Illustrated's Canyons of the Escalante covers the area.

Directions: From just south of the town of Boulder, take the Burr Trail Road east approximately 19 miles. Turn south on the road to Wolverine Petrified Wood Area, and drive 5.75 miles to where the road turns west and starts to climb. Park here.

Contact: Grand Staircase–Escalante National Monument, 190 East Center, Kanab, UT 84741, 435/644-4300.

41 WOLVERINE CREEK
5.0 mi one-way/4.0 hrs

southeast of Boulder

Map 6.3, page 171

The primary attraction of this route is the black petrified wood that litters the ground, a reminder of the ancient forest that once stood here. The hike heads southwest along an obvious drainage for about 1.5 very easy miles, then continues southwest after joining the main drainage of Wolverine Creek. The canyon now begins to meander and grow more and more narrow. Despite the name, you'll probably see little or no water along the five miles to Horse Canyon. This route makes an excellent return from a trip down Little Death Hollow, allowing you to hike a loop of approximately 17 miles.

User groups: Hikers, dogs. No wheelchair access.

Permits: No permits are required. Parking and access are free.

Maps: For USGS topographic maps, ask for Pioneer Mesa and King Bench. Trails Illustrated's Canyons of the Escalante covers the area.

Directions: From just south of the town of Boulder, take the Burr Trail Road east approximately 19 miles. Turn south on the road to Wolverine Petrified Wood Area, and drive 10.2 miles to where a sign relates facts about the area. Park here. A four-wheel-drive vehicle is recommended.

Contact: Grand Staircase–Escalante National Monument, 190 East Center, Kanab, UT 84741, 435/644-4300.

42 UPPER MULEY TWIST CANYON SEMI-LOOP

10.0 mi/1–2 days

southeast of Torrey in Capitol Reef National Park

Map 6.3, page 171

There just isn't another hike in this national park offering a greater variety of fascinating geological formations. You'll see five arches along the way as you walk deep in a defile within the Waterpocket Fold and take a beautiful rim trek. From the same trailhead, you may have time for the Strike Valley Overlook Trail, a round-trip of about one mile to the top of the Waterpocket Fold and a view up and down the dramatic valley that parallels the strike, or long axis, of the Fold. The Muley Twist route heads north along the sandy bottom of Muley Twist Canyon, following the bottom for five miles and past the five arches. Just past the fifth arch, the trail climbs up and around a pour-off that blocks passage along the canyon bottom, and soon ascends to the canyon's rim and the top of the Waterpocket Fold, a 100-mile-long slickrock bulge in the earth. At this point, you've gained a total of about 800 feet in elevation. This rim trail turns back south along the rim for about two miles, with extravagant views reaching southeast toward Lake Powell, north to the Henry Mountains, and along the Fold. Then the trail descends into the canyon near the first arch. From there, you'll retrace your steps to the trailhead. Numerous campsites exist along the way, but be sure to carry enough water for the entire trip.

User groups: Hikers. Mountain bikes are allowed on the first 2.5 miles. No wheelchair access.

Permits: No day-use permits are required. A free overnight permit is required and available at the visitors center. Parking and access are free.

Maps: For USGS topographic maps, ask for Bitter Creek Divide and Wagon Box Mesa. An excellent source of information is the *Hiking Map & Guide to Capitol Reef National Park* from Earthwalk Press, available at the visitors center.

Directions: From Torrey, take State Route 24 east nine miles past the visitors center. Turn south on the Notom-Bullfrog Road for about 35 miles. After several miles this road turns into a well-maintained gravel road. Turn west on the Burr Trail Road for 3.25 miles, and then north on another dirt road. The trailhead is 3.1 miles down this road. If you start the hike at the trail register, about a half mile in from the last road junction, you'll add about five miles to your journey.

Contact: Capitol Reef National Park, HC 70, Box 15, Torrey, UT 84775, 435/425-3791.

43 LOWER MULEY TWIST CANYON SEMI-LOOP

18.0 mi/2 days

southeast of Torrey in Capitol Reef National Park

Map 6.3, page 171

This canyon is so narrow in places that mules once had to twist to get through—at least that's the legend. Though fascinating, this canyon is less dramatic than Upper Muley Twist. Lower Muley Twist was, in fact, a wagon route for a while. After about four miles in the ever-twisting canyon, the Cut-Off Trail heads east to The Post on Notom-Bullfrog Road, allowing a much shorter hike if time is a limiting factor. The best of Lower Muley Twist, however, lies below the Cut-Off. Deep alcoves and huge overhangs have been whittled from the canyon walls by eons of moving water—water that no longer flows here. Several side canyons open to the south. At 10.5 miles, an especially large and sandy-bottomed alcove, sometimes called Cowboy Camp, offers a great campsite near the midpoint of the route. However, like the many other campsites in the area, this one is dry. In fact, you probably won't find water on this entire hike. Not far below Cowboy Camp, Muley Twist bends east, the canyon narrows, the walls grow shorter and shorter, and the trail becomes a sandy gully. Watch for a trail heading east, and take it two miles to the Brimhall Arch Trail, which heads north for about 5.5 miles to The Post. From there, it's five miles more, by road, to the starting point. You can park a second car here if you want to avoid the five-mile road walk.

User groups: Hikers. Mountain bikes are allowed on the first 2.5 miles. No wheelchair access.

Permits: No day-use permits are required. A free overnight permit is required and available at the visitors center. Parking and access are free.

Maps: For USGS topographic maps, ask for The Post and Wagon Box Mesa. An excellent source of information is the *Hiking Map & Guide to Capitol Reef National Park* from Earthwalk Press, available at the visitors center.

Directions: From Torrey, take State Route 24 east nine miles past the visitors center. Turn south on the Notom-Bullfrog Road for about 35 miles. After several miles this road turns into a well-maintained gravel road. Turn west on the Burr Trail Road for two miles to the trailhead on the south side of the road.

Contact: Capitol Reef National Park, HC 70, Box 15, Torrey, UT 84775, 435/425-3791.

44 UPPER ESCALANTE RIVER
15.0 mi one-way/2 days

just east of Escalante

Map 6.3, page 171

The upper section of the Escalante River, from the town of Escalante to State Route 12 at Calf

Creek, is the easiest section of the river to hike. It's also a highly scenic route that includes colorful sandstone walls and overhangs, Anasazi ruins, petroglyphs, an arch, and a natural bridge. This route also provides access to the lower end of Death Hollow, which joins the river from the north at roughly the half-way point, and the lower end of Sand Creek, which enters from the north near the end of the route. Not far below the entry of Sand Creek, you'll see the arch, framed where it stands by darkly stained walls. Below the arch, look for Escalante Natural Bridge. The route ends two miles past the natural bridge at a manmade bridge on Route 12 (15 miles from the town of Escalante). The hiking is easy, but because of the river, you'll have wet feet for much of the trip. Campsites are abundant, and water is always available.

User groups: Hikers and dogs. No wheelchair access.

Permits: No permits are required. Parking and access are free.

Maps: For USGS topographic maps, ask for Escalante and Calf Creek. Trails Illustrated's Canyons of the Escalante covers the area.

Directions: From Escalante, take State Route 12 east approximately one mile. At a small cemetery, turn north and drive another mile, bearing left at a fork in the road. Park at a small but obvious parking area.

Contact: Grand Staircase–Escalante National Monument, 190 East Center, Kanab, UT 84741, 435/644-4300.

45 LOWER CALF CREEK FALLS TRAIL
5.5 mi/3.0 hrs

east of Escalante

Map 6.3, page 171

This trail, which follows Calf Creek, is a pleasant, sandy, and easy route for the whole family. Signs along the way provide information about the area. The route comes to a dead-end at a veritable desert oasis: a 126-foot waterfall plunging into a delightful pool—a great spot for a summer swim. You'll gain about 200 feet of elevation, and pass beneath buff and pink sandstone walls. Keep your eyes peeled for Anasazi pictographs and ruins.

User groups: Hikers and dogs. No wheelchair access.

Permits: No permits are required. Parking and access are free.

Maps: For a USGS topographic map, ask for Calf Creek. A trail guide is available at the trailhead. Trails Illustrated's Canyons of the Escalante covers the area.

Directions: From Escalante, take State Route 12 east approximately 16 miles to the Calf Creek Campground on the northwest side of the road. The trail starts near the north end of the campground.

Contact: Grand Staircase–Escalante National Monument, 190 East Center, Kanab, UT 84741, 435/644-4300.

46 LOWER ESCALANTE RIVER
70.0 mi one-way/7–10 days

east of Escalante

Map 6.3, page 171

Hiking along the Escalante River ranks as one of the best extended backpacking trips in canyon country. Campsites are abundant and pleasant, and water is always available, although you might need to let it settle before filtering. The sandstone wonders are endless, and numerous side trips beg to be taken. A group of us spent more than a month exploring the entire Escalante River, and then came back for two more weeks to see some of the things we missed on the first trip. We could easily have stayed longer to see more. If you lack the desire or time to do the entire route, several side canyons offer "escape routes," including Horse Canyon, Silver Falls Creek, Phipps Wash, Harris Wash, and Twenty-five Mile Wash. It would be a shame to fail to climb onto King Bench for the view, or up Little Death Hollow for the adventure. You'll walk

in the river many times, bully your way through stands of willows, and risk getting stuck temporarily (but not dying) in quicksand here and there. The canyon of the Escalante once extended 30 miles more, but those last 30 miles are now beneath the placid waters of Lake Powell. Hiking all the way down to the lake is worth the effort, just to see what it looks like when a canyon is drowned by a lake. You can leave the Escalante by hiking up and out of Coyote Gulch via Hurricane Wash. Keep in mind that the hike out Coyote Gulch adds about 14 miles to the 70 of the lower Escalante. Beware that the mouth of Coyote Gulch often lies underwater, requiring you to backtrack almost to the mouth of Stevens Canyon and ascend to the west rim before dropping into Coyote Gulch. After all is said and done, be sure you've done the Lower Escalante.

User groups: Hikers and dogs. No wheelchair access.

Permits: No permits are required. Parking and access are free.

Maps: For USGS topographic maps, ask for Calf Creek, King Bench, Red Breaks, Silver Falls Bench, Egypt, Scorpion Gulch, King Mesa, and Stevens Canyon South. Trails Illustrated's Canyons of the Escalante covers the area.

Directions: From Escalante, take State Route 12 east approximately 15 miles to where the road crosses the river on a bridge, and park.

Contact: Grand Staircase–Escalante National Monument, 190 East Center, Kanab, UT 84741, 435/644-4300.

47 PHIPPS WASH TO HIGHWAY 12
6.5 mi one-way/5.0 hrs

east of Escalante

Map 6.3, page 171

If you only have a day to walk in the Escalante area, this is not a bad way to spend it: route finding on slickrock, a scenic canyon, an arch, a natural bridge, and a short walk along the Escalante River. Head east from your vehicle, toward an obvious V in the slickrock, through the V, and down, carefully, over a slickrock slope to the sandy bottom. Wander north and east, among domes of slickrock, and eventually you'll hit the main Phipps Wash. If you end up walking south, you'll have to climb out of this side wash to gain Phipps. Hike generally north in Phipps Wash. Toward the mouth of the wash on the Escalante River, Phipps Arch stands at the end of a scramble from a short box canyon opening to the east, and Maverick Natural Bridge up a side canyon opening to the west. Once on the river, it's less than a mile up to Highway 12.

User groups: Hikers. No wheelchair access.

Permits: No permits are required. Parking and access are free.

Maps: For USGS topographic maps, ask for Tenmile Flat and Calf Creek. Trails Illustrated's Canyons of the Escalante covers the area.

Directions: From Escalante, take State Route 12 east approximately 11 miles. The road turns sharply south, then north. Where it turns north, take the dirt road—Sheffield Road—east for a quarter mile. Find a place to pull off and park.

Contact: Grand Staircase–Escalante National Monument, 190 East Center, Kanab, UT 84741, 435/644-4300.

48 LITTLE DEATH HOLLOW
7.5 mi one-way/6.0 hrs

southeast of Boulder

Map 6.3, page 171

Before it joins Horse Canyon, Little Death Hollow involves crawling, climbing, and, at times, stuffing yourself through about 1.5 miles of extreme slots. Walk southwest at first, staying north of the wash for the easiest hiking, along a wash that provides little of unusual interest. Then the canyon begins to narrow and twist. Convoluted walls are often easily touched on both sides by extending your arms. The sky is reduced to a thin ribbon of faded blue. Logjams stand up to 25 feet above, indicating the depth and power of flash floods. Boulders

sometimes block the passage, requiring scrambling over and, at least once, crawling under. With a backpack, you'll be shoving or dragging the load for part of the journey. Start early because the first safe camping spot lies where Little Death Hollow widens at Horse Canyon. From there, you can hike up and out Horse Canyon, up and out Wolverine Creek, or down to the Escalante River. You can also park a vehicle at both ends.

User groups: Hikers. No wheelchair access.

Permits: No permits are required. Parking and access are free.

Maps: For USGS topographic maps, ask for Wagon Box Mesa, Pioneer Mesa, and Red Breaks. Trails Illustrated's Canyons of the Escalante covers the area.

Directions: From just south of the town of Boulder, take the Burr Trail Road east approximately 19 miles. Turn south on the road to Wolverine Petrified Wood Area, and drive 13 miles, or about three miles past the area of petrified wood, and park near a corral southwest of the road. A four-wheel-drive vehicle is recommended.

Contact: Grand Staircase–Escalante National Monument, 190 East Center, Kanab, UT 84741, 435/644-4300.

49 SILVER FALLS CREEK
18.5 mi one-way/2 days

southeast of Boulder

Map 6.3, page 171

Here is a lovely canyon hike—an easy walk along an often-sandy bottom. This route was once used as a wagon road that went down Silver Falls Creek and up Harris Wash. Along the 8.5 miles to the Escalante River, the canyon narrows and widens again, providing numerous campsites in the last two miles. The sandstone walls that bound the canyon are often streaked with silvery-black desert varnish. About halfway to the river, topographic maps show a spring that seldom offers more than a trickle of water. Below this point, however, you can usually find water. About a mile below the seep, look for a deep overhang in which a man named Hobbs, one of the first to walk this route, scratched his name. Not far below where Silver Falls Creek enters the Escalante River, Harris Wash leaves to the west. The 10 miles up Harris complete this one-way hike.

User groups: Hikers. No wheelchair access.

Permits: No permits are required. Parking and access are free.

Maps: For USGS topographic maps, ask for Wagon Box Mesa and Silver Falls Bench. Trails Illustrated's Canyons of the Escalante covers the area.

Directions: From just south of the town of Boulder, take the Burr Trail Road east approximately 19 miles. Turn south on the road to Wolverine Petrified Wood Area, and drive another 19 miles. Turn south where the Moody Road joins this road, and travel another 2.7 miles to a parking spot.

Contact: Grand Staircase–Escalante National Monument, 190 East Center, Kanab, UT 84741, 435/644-4300.

50 HARRIS WASH
20.0 mi/2 days

southeast of Escalante

> Map 6.3, page 171

This is a very easy walk in a highly scenic canyon that ends on the Escalante River, and a popular route to reach the Escalante for longer backpacking trips. Wide open at first, the wash suddenly narrows, entering the confines of a sandstone canyon, the walls decoratively streaked with desert varnish. Watch for unusually deep and shadowy overhangs carved out of the walls. Water can almost always be found running down the wash not far from the trailhead. Harris Wash runs generally east, and side canyons sometimes provide additional water from the south. If you find water running in from the south, hike up these side canyons and you might find pools deep enough for a dip. Campsites are abundant.

Once at the Escalante River, 10 miles into the hike, you can turn back, hike up or down the river, or continue across the river and up Silver Falls Creek. Just so you know: It's about 43 miles from the mouth of Harris Wash down the Escalante River to Lake Powell.

User groups: Hikers. No wheelchair access.

Permits: No permits are required. Parking and access are free.

Maps: For USGS topographic maps, ask for Red Breaks and Silver Falls Bench. Trails Illustrated's Canyons of the Escalante covers the area.

Directions: From Escalante, take State Route 12 east for five miles. Turn south on the Hole-in-the-Rock Road for 11 miles. Turn north up Harris Wash Road, and drive another 6.1 miles to the trailhead.

Contact: Grand Staircase–Escalante National Monument, 190 East Center, Kanab, UT 84741, 435/644-4300.

51 TWENTY-FIVE MILE WASH– EGYPT TRAIL LOOP
25.0 mi/2–3 days

southeast of Escalante

> Map 6.3, page 171

Two of the best uses of the lower 13 miles of Twenty-five Mile Wash is as an escape from the Escalante after a long hike along that river or as an easy access to the Escalante in order to explore its lower section. This wash, although attractive in its lower reaches, offers little in terms of the extraordinary. Very wide at the start, it narrows, the sandstone boundaries growing higher and higher, as it nears the mouth. Consider, however, hiking from the mouth of Twenty-five Mile up the Escalante River, and west up Fence Canyon, and up a long slickrock slope to the Egypt Trailhead. It's a grunt of an elevation gain of about 1,200 feet with increasingly splendid views over this slickrock heaven. At the Egypt Trailhead, you'll be six road miles from the starting point. With two vehicles you can, of course, avoid the road walk, but it's an easy hike with plenty of expansive views. On the other hand, you can avoid the long grunt by starting at the Egypt Trailhead and hiking this loop route in reverse.

User groups: Hikers. No wheelchair access.

Permits: No permits are required. Parking and access are free.

Maps: For USGS topographic maps, ask for Sunset Flat and Egypt. Trails Illustrated's Canyons of the Escalante covers the area.

Directions: From Escalante, take State Route 12 east five miles. Turn south on Hole-in-the-Rock Road for 20 miles. Turn north on Egypt Road, and drive 3.5 miles to where the road crosses Twenty-five Mile Wash. Park here.

Contact: Grand Staircase–Escalante National Monument, 190 East Center, Kanab, UT 84741, 435/644-4300.

52 PANORAMA LOOP TRAIL
3.0 mi/2.0 hrs
southeast of Cannonville in Kodachrome Basin State Park

Map 6.3, page 171

As the name of this very popular state park implies, Utah doesn't get more colorful: red, white, orange, yellow, green, pink, even purple. From south of the park's campground, the trail, suitable for all ages, bends north to pass the first short spur trail to The Hat Shop. This spur passes Ballerina Spire, a formation seldom found outside this area—a monolithic chimney or "sand pipe." The park has at least 67 sand pipes. A second spur trail leads to Secret Pass, a thin path through a narrow rock channel. A third spur trail, more than a mile long, takes you to several geysers and Cool Cave. Looping back toward the start, you'll be treated to views of all the colors of the park. Other short trails lead to the awesome Shakespeare Arch and to Chimney Rock, the largest of the sand pipes.

User groups: Hikers, dogs, and mountain bikes. No wheelchair access.

Permits: The park charges a $5-per-vehicle entry fee. If you want to camp in the park's campground, the fee is $14. Reservations for any Utah state park are available by calling 800/322-3770.

Maps: For USGS topographic maps, ask for Henrieville and Slickrock Bench. A park brochure, available at the visitors center, describes the trail.

Directions: From Cannonville on State Route 12, take Cottonwood Canyon Road southeast seven miles to Kodachrome Basin State Park.

Contact: Kodachrome Basin State Park, P.O. Box 238, Cannonville, UT 84718, 435/679-8562.

53 HACKBERRY CANYON
18.0 mi one-way/2–3 days

southeast of Cannonville

Map 6.3, page 171

Here is a strikingly beautiful canyon with very little human use in an area under consideration for wilderness designation. Soon after you head out on the trail, the canyon narrows as it drops through and across Navajo sandstone. After about two miles, the floor of the canyon turns sandy at Round Valley Draw. At about 2.5 miles, a side canyon enters from the northeast. Up this side canyon, the terrain opens into a large and very scenic basin—well worth the walk if you have the time. It's not until almost nine miles down the canyon before you find water, so carry plenty from the start. About 12 miles into the hike, a huge piece of canyon wall collapsed in 1987, blocking the canyon and the creek and backing up the water into a small lake. The lake water eventually created a path through the rock wall, and now a scramble takes you over the rocks. As Hackberry Canyon widens, about 1.5 miles below the rockfall, look for a side canyon entering from the west. This leads about 1.5 miles to Sam Pollock Arch. This is a spectacular arch, and an adventuresome side trip requiring a climb past a 20-foot waterfall. About two miles more down the main canyon and it bends east, entering a gorge for its last two miles before hitting Cottonwood Canyon Road. The mouth of Hackberry Canyon on Cottonwood Canyon Road is 12.5 miles north of US 89. Park a vehicle at both ends for a quick return to the starting point.

User groups: Hikers, dogs, and horses. No wheelchair access.

Permits: No permits are required. Parking and access are free.

Maps: For USGS topographic maps, ask for Slickrock Bench and Calico Peak.

Directions: From Cannonville on State Route 12, take Cottonwood Canyon Road southeast approximately 12 miles, or 4.9 miles past Kodachrome Basin State Park. Turn south on a dirt road for 2.2 miles to a wooden corral. Park here.

Contact: Grand Staircase–Escalante National Monument, 190 East Center, Kanab, UT 84741, 435/644-4300.

54 PEEK-A-BOO AND SPOOKY GULCHES
8.0 mi/7.0 hrs

southeast of Escalante

Map 6.3, page 171

(F) Hiking north from your vehicle, you'll soon descend a crack into the Dry Fork of Coyote Gulch. Turn east to discover two of the narrowest and most fascinating slot canyons on the Colorado Plateau, and a fun way to spend a day. Peek-a-boo Gulch, opening on the Dry Fork first and from the north, requires a bit of climbing in order to get in. From there the slot runs from somewhat wide and sandy to seriously narrow. The next slot, also opening from the north, is Spooky Gulch. In Spooky it's almost like crawling through the belly of a sandstone snake; it's not for the claustrophobic. A bit further down Dry Fork, Brimstone Gulch opens to the north. You'll have to walk up Brimstone a ways to find narrows, but they're worth the trek. Beware: Recent rain make the slots discouragingly wet.

User groups: Hikers. No wheelchair access.

Permits: No permits are required. Parking and access are free.

Maps: For a USGS topographic map, ask for Big Hollow Wash. Trails Illustrated's Canyons of the Escalante covers the area.

Directions: From Escalante, take State Route 12 east five miles. Turn south on Hole-in-the-Rock Road for 26 miles. Turn north on Dry Fork Road, and drive 1.5 miles to a parking area.

Contact: Grand Staircase–Escalante National Monument, 190 East Center, Kanab, UT 84741, 435/644-4300.

55 HURRICANE WASH TO COYOTE GULCH
28.0 mi/2–3 days

southeast of Escalante

Map 6.3, page 171

Hurricane Wash runs long but easily into lower Coyote Gulch, providing easy access to a world of natural wonder: two arches, a bridge, cascading waterfalls, impressive overhangs, and the sculpted splendor of sandstone. This could be a backpacking trip for a family of strong hikers, and Coyote Gulch offers an escape from the Lower Escalante River after an extended backpacking trip. After about eight miles of hiking northeast down open Hurricane Wash, you'll turn east down Coyote Gulch, passing massive Jacob Hamblin Arch, Coyote Natural Bridge, and Cliff Arch along the way to the river. You'll find water and plentiful pleasant campsites. The return trip of 14 miles gains a gradual 1,100 feet of elevation.

User groups: Hikers. No wheelchair access.

Permits: No permits are required. Parking and access are free.

Maps: For USGS topographic maps, ask for Big Hollow Wash, King Mesa, and Stevens Canyon South. Trails Illustrated's Canyons of the Escalante covers the area.

Directions: From Escalante, take State Route 12 east five miles. Turn south on Hole-in-the-Rock Road for 33.5 miles to the Hurricane Wash Trailhead on the east side of the road.

Contact: Grand Staircase–Escalante National Monument, 190 East Center, Kanab, UT 84741, 435/644-4300.

56 KITCHEN CANYON
16.0 mi/2 days

northeast of Kanab

Map 6.3, page 171

Although Kitchen Canyon can be a part of an Upper Paria River Gorge journey, it is worthy of a special trip if you only have time for an overnighter, or even a long day hike. This trip has a little bit of just about everything canyon country offers: towering sandstone walls, Anasazi ruins, petroglyphs, historic ruins of old ranches, a waterfall, a small lake, even the remains of an old movie set. From your vehicle, hike about five miles up the Paria River, past several old ranch sites, and plan on getting your feet wet during crossings. Turn west up Kitchen Canyon, and look for evidence of the Anasazi. In about a mile, Starlight Canyon opens to the south, offering excellent campsites and clear water before it narrows dramatically. Just above Starlight Canyon, Kitchen Falls blocks Kitchen Canyon, but a steep trail allows you to keep going around the falls. You'll soon see the ruins of several cabins. Turn around for hike back at small Nipple Lake. Although the lake is accessible via four-wheel-drive vehicle, and permission to access it may be granted by the owners, hiking up from the Paria River is far more interesting. Contact the BLM for information on how to access the owners.

User groups: Hikers and dogs. No wheelchair access.

Permits: No permits are required. Parking and access are free.

Maps: For USGS topographic maps, ask for Deer Range Point, Calico Peak, and Fivemile Valley.

Directions: From Kanab, take US 89 east approximately 35 miles. Turn north between mile markers 30 and 31 on a good dirt road. A sign to Old Pahreah marks the turn. Drive six miles and park near the Paria River.

Contact: BLM Kanab Field Office, 318 North First East, Kanab, UT 84741, 435/644-4600.

Grand Staircase–Escalante National Monument, 190 East Center, Kanab, UT 84741, 435/644-4300.

57 PARIA-HOGEYE-HACKBERRY LOOP
25.0 mi/2–3 days

northeast of Kanab

Map 6.3, page 171

This exciting loop takes you through some of Utah's most remote and wild canyon country. The route starts north up the Upper Paria River Gorge for about five miles, then turns northeast up Hogeye Canyon. Hogeye is the fourth big side canyon on the east side of the river after the start. Several springs supply water here. About four miles up Hogeye, the main canyon turns sharply southeast. After another quarter mile, the canyon forks. Take the left fork, and ascend to the rim of the canyon. From there, head southeast across a mesa called Lower Death Valley, and enter a tributary of Hackberry Canyon after 1.5 miles. You should soon see the impressive span of Sam Pollock Arch. Follow the creek in Hackberry down to Cottonwood Creek, and follow Cottonwood Creek down to the Paria River. Turn up the river, passing through the Paria Box. The Paria Box, narrow and full of shadows, may be the most memorable part of this journey.

User groups: Hikers and dogs. Horses along the Paria River. No wheelchair access.

Permits: No permits are required. Parking and access are free.

Maps: For USGS topographic maps, ask for Calico Peak and Fivemile Valley.

Directions: From Kanab, take US 89 east approximately 35 miles. Turn north between mile markers 30 and 31 on a good dirt road. A sign to Old Pahreah, at this writing, marks the turn. Drive six miles and park near the Paria River.

Contact: Grand Staircase–Escalante National Monument, 190 East Center, Kanab, UT 84741, 435/644-4300.

58 BUCKSKIN GULCH
23.0 mi one-way/2–3 days

east of Kanab in the Paria Canyon–Vermilion Cliffs Wilderness

Map 6.3, page 171

This trip justifiably ranks among the best canyon hikes on Earth. You'll travel through approximately 12 miles of narrows before the gulch opens onto the Lower Paria River Gorge. After about 4.5 miles of hiking east down Buckskin Gulch, Wire Pass enters from the west. You can leave Buckskin here to make it a short day hike. You can also enter Buckskin via Wire Pass by driving another four miles from the Buckskin Gulch Trailhead and hiking down from the Wire Pass Trailhead. The 1.5-mile journey down Wire Pass is a beautiful trip all on its own, and there are petroglyphs near where Wire Pass meets Buckskin. From the mouth of Wire Pass, you'll spend less time in the narrows of Buckskin (a worthwhile consideration since the first campsite lies about 11 miles in from the Buckskin Gulch Trailhead). Despite the narrowness, the hiking is easy most of the way. After about eight miles of down Buckskin Gulch, you'll enter the first of numerous pools of water that must be crossed. These pools are typically stagnant and rather disgusting to wade through, but the water seldom rises higher than about mid-thigh. At about 11 miles, or 6.5 miles from the mouth of Wire Pass, the Middle Trail climbs out of the gulch to the north, allowing you to ascend to camping spots. Down in the canyon, you'll have to continue to near the end of Buckskin to camp. About four miles below Middle Trail, deep down in the dark narrows, a rock jam blocks easy progress. A 50-foot rope is helpful here. There are campsites about a mile below the rock jam, and shortly thereafter is the Paria River. The hike up the Paria River Gorge to White House Campground and the end of this trip is about seven miles. About 11.5 miles of road separate the start from the finish. About 44 miles from Kanab on US 89, and south of the highway, lies the Paria Ranger Station, a place you should stop at first to make a final check on the weather forecast. A flash flood in Buckskin is a death sentence to hikers caught on the bottom.

User groups: Hikers only. No wheelchair access.

Permits: Advance reservations are required for use and limited in number for overnighters. A fee of $5 per person per day in charged to all hikers. Day hikers may pay the use fee at the trailhead without a reservation.

Maps: For USGS topographic maps, ask for Pine Hollow Canyon, West Clark Bench, and Bridger Point.

Directions: From Kanab, take US 89 east approximately 35 miles. Turn south from the top of a ridge called The Cockscomb and follow the dirt road 4.5 miles to the trailhead.

Contact: BLM Kanab Field Office, 318 North First East, Kanab, UT 84741, 435/644-4600.

59 LOWER PARIA RIVER GORGE
37.0 mi one-way/4–5 days

east of Kanab in the Paria Canyon–Vermilion Cliffs Wilderness

Map 6.3, page 171

This beautiful canyon hike ends at Lee's Ferry on the Colorado River. Many hikers start by descending Buckskin Gulch, and then head down the Lower Paria River Gorge to Lee's Ferry, a distance of about 38 miles. From White House Campground, where this description starts, the first seven miles takes you through an utterly beautiful canyon bounded by slickrock walls to the confluence of Buckskin Gulch and the Paria River. You can turn back here, but you'd miss out. Not far below the confluence, the canyon enters Arizona, where it winds its serpentine way past arches and overhangs, splendid benches, and intriguing side canyons. Campsites are abundant for at least half the distance from the confluence to Lee's Ferry, but this hike is extremely popular and the sites are often full, especially in summer.

User groups: Hikers and dogs. No wheelchair access.

Permits: Advance reservations are required for overnight use. A fee of $5 per person per day is charged. Day hikers may pay the use fee at the trailhead.

Maps: For USGS topographic maps, ask for West Clark Bench and Bridger Point for the Utah portion. Wrather Arch, Water Pockets, Ferry Swale, and Lees Ferry cover the Arizona portion.

Directions: From Kanab, take US 89 east approximately 44 miles. Turn south on the road to White House Campground, and drive two miles to the campground and the trailhead.

Contact: BLM Kanab Field Office, 318 North First East, Kanab, UT 84741, 435/644-4600.

60 MOUNT PENNELL
9.0 mi/8.0 hrs

south of Hanksville in the Henry Mountains

Map 6.4, page 172

At 11,371 feet, Mount Pennell is the second-highest point in the Henry Mountains. You'll find a pleasantly rounded peak splattered with evergreens right to the top, a cooling respite from the typical heat below. Despite the elevation gain of about 3,000 feet, the route up Mount Pennell, devoid of really steep stuff, is relatively easy going. You can follow the dirt road north from Straight Creek, and then west, parallel to the creek. It's far more interesting, however, to ascend a faint path along the perennial flow of the creek west past the abandoned Wolverton Mill site where stone was pulverized in hopes of extracting gold. From the mill site, ascend due north to the old road, then head up the road to its end. From there, follow the ridge north to the summit. The best views run south along the Waterpocket Fold to Lake Powell.

User groups: Hikers and dogs. No wheelchair access.

Permits: No permits are required. Parking and access are free.

Maps: For a USGS topographic map, ask for Mount Pennell. Trails Illustrated's Glen Canyon & Capitol Reef Area covers the area.

Directions: From the junction of State Route 95 and State Route 276, south of Hanksville, take Route 276 south 4.5 miles. Turn west on a dirt road and drive 2.5 miles. Turn southwest and pass the Trachyte Ranch, staying to the north at intersections, passing Coyote Benches, and driving another eight miles from the ranch to an intersection. Turn south, drive a half mile to Straight Creek, and park.

Contact: BLM Henry Mountain Field Station, P.O. Box 99, Hanksville, UT 84734, 435/542-3461.

61 MAIDENWATER CREEK–TRAIL CANYON LOOP
12.0 mi/1–2 days

south of Hanksville

Map 6.4, page 172

Stunningly beautiful, the canyon Maidenwater Creek has cut from Mount Hillers to Trachyte Creek is a hidden jewel, virtually invisible to vehicles driving the highway. Hiking east, down the canyon, this journey offers deep swimming holes that you simply have to swim in. Negotiating the drops into these pools is a canyoneering challenge; a short length of rope is helps. If you plan to camp, bring a small inflatable air mattress to float your gear across. Near the mouth of Maidenwater, you can camp in heartbreakingly lovely surroundings near Trachyte Creek. Travel south along Trachyte Creek for a half mile, then head westward up the easy bottom of Trail Canyon, gaining about 450 feet of elevation. You'll reach State Route 276 a half mile south of the starting point.

User groups: Hikers. No wheelchair access.

Permits: No permits are required. Parking and access are free.

Maps: For a USGS topographic map, ask for Black Table. Trails Illustrated's Glen Canyon & Capitol Reef Areas covers the area.

Directions: From Hanksville, take State Route 95 south for approximately 25 miles. Turn south on State Route 276 and drive 9.5 miles (between mile markers 9 and 10) to a parking spot on the east side of the road.

Contact: BLM Henry Mountain Field Station, P.O. Box 99, Hanksville, UT 84734, 435/542-3461.

62 MOUNT HILLERS
9.0 mi/8.0 hrs

south of Hanksville in the Henry Mountains

Map 6.4, page 172

Mount Hillers, at 10,722 feet, is the third highest of all the Henry Mountains behind Mounts Ellen and Pennell. From Starr Spring Campground, the ascent is directly up the ridge to the northwest. This is a somewhat challenging and always interesting route that demands constant altitude gain as well as scrambling around stark sandstone fins that erupt from the ridge. The elevation gain is a rugged 4,500 feet. You'll be passing through stands of bristlecone pines with views toward Lake Powell opening to the south. If you want to bag the summit with far less energy output, drive west from the campground, around the base of the mountain to Cass Creek, and up Cass Creek to the northwest shoulder of the mountain. From there it's less than two miles (steep miles) past the ruins of the old Starr Mine to the summit.

User groups: Hikers and dogs. No wheelchair access.

Permits: No permits are required. Parking and access are free.

Maps: For USGS topographic maps, ask for Mount Pennell and Cass Creek Peak. Trails Illustrated's Glen Canyon & Capitol Reef Area covers the area.

Directions: From the junction of State Route 95 and State Route 276, south of Hanksville, take Route 276 south 17 miles. Turn west on a dirt road and drive 4.2 miles to Starr Spring Campground.

Contact: BLM Henry Mountain Field Station, P.O. Box 99, Hanksville, UT 84734, 435/542-3461.

63 SWETT CANYON
15.0 mi/2 days

south of Hanksville

Map 6.4, page 172

Flowing below the north slopes of the "Little Rockies," Swett Creek has carved out a narrow canyon with high, steep walls all the way to Lake Powell. Heading east, down the canyon, the hiking is gentle and usually easy, with some rocks to scramble over in a few places. Only rarely will you see other people. You probably won't find water in the canyon, unless it's trapped in holes beneath low, shaded overhangs on the canyon floor. About two-thirds of the way to the lake you'll enter Glen Canyon National Recreation Area, and at about seven miles you'll pass a towering spire called Hoskinnini Monument. No really good campsites exist in the canyon, although you can throw down a bag here and there, but there's fine camping at the mouth of the canyon on the shore of Lake Powell after 7.5 miles of walking. The hike back up gains about 500 feet in elevation. As with all of Utah's narrow canyons, a flash flood could be fatal. Checking on the weather with land managers is strongly recommended before heading out.

User groups: Hikers. No wheelchair access.

Permits: No permits are required. Parking and access are free.

Maps: For a USGS topographic map, ask for Mount Holmes. Trails Illustrated's Glen Canyon & Capitol Reef Areas covers the area.

Directions: From Hanksville, take State Route 95 south for approximately 25 miles. Turn south on State Route 276 and drive 14.1 miles to where Swett Creek crosses in a large culvert beneath the road. Park on the east side of the road.

Contact: BLM Henry Mountain Field Station, P.O. Box 99, Hanksville, UT 84734, 435/542-3461.

64 SUNDANCE TRAIL–DARK CANYON TRAIL

5.0–20.0 mi/1–5 days

west of Monticello

Map 6.4, page 172

The Sundance Trail descends gradually for about two miles to the rim of Dark Canyon and an extravagant view into its shadowed depths. From the rim, the trail, less easy to follow now, goes down a ridge to the east and drops into Dark Canyon. "Drops" is the correct word choice: more than 1,100 feet of elevation loss in less than a mile. Lean-To Canyon comes in from the north, then Lost Canyon from the south. Camping spots are plentiful after first reaching Dark Canyon; however, after Lost Canyon, they virtually disappear for several miles. With time on your hands, days of glorious exploration await in Dark Canyon, and up Lost and Lean-To Canyons. Your time will be spent beneath massively high and beautifully eroded sandstone walls that block the sun for the greater part of each day.

User groups: Hikers and dogs. No wheelchair access.

Permits: No permits are required. Parking and access are free.

Maps: For USGS topographic maps, ask for Indian Head Pass and Black Steer Canyon. Trails Illustrated's Manti–La Sal National Forest covers the area.

Directions: From Blanding, take US 191 south three miles. Turn west on State Route 95 for 54.1 miles. Just north of mile marker 54, turn onto County Road 208A and drive five miles to a junction. Turn east, still on 208A, and drive four miles more. Turn north on County Road 209 A for three miles to the trailhead.

Contact: BLM Monticello Field Office, 435 North Main, Monticello, UT 84535, 435/587-1500.

65 BULLFROG CANYON

15.0 mi one-way/2 days

south of Hanksville at the southern end of the Henry Mountains

Map 6.4, page 172

Flowing off of Mount Pennell and into Lake Powell, Bullfrog Creek has, over the centuries, carved an exquisitely lovely canyon through the badlands south of the Henry Mountains. You'll start south down the east rim of Fourmile Canyon, keeping an eye peeled for an easy slope to hike down into the canyon. The route covers about three miles of Fourmile, despite its name, passing through several narrow sections and with a steep pour-off blocking the route about halfway down. You can negotiate the pour-off easily on the west side. You should find water within a couple of miles of the start, and you will probably have this quiet place to yourself. Once on the bottom of Bullfrog Canyon, the going runs along easily to the south, with Clay Canyon opening from the west at about five miles from the start. Clay reveals distinctively different terrain along its three-mile length. It's a wide canyon with a bottom often covered in a thick layer of colorful clay. You can turn back at any time, but it's worth continuing down Bullfrog for about 10 miles to the Middle Point Road just above Lake Powell.

User groups: Hikers and dogs. No wheelchair access.

Permits: No permits are required. Parking and access are free.

Maps: For USGS topographic maps, ask for Clay Point and Hall Mesa.

Directions: From the junction of State Routes 95 and 276, south of Hanksville, take Route 276 south 17 miles. Turn west on a dirt road and drive 4.2 miles to Starr Spring Campground. Drive past the campground, headed southwest, for approximately 15 miles to the head of Fourmile Canyon, and park.

Contact: BLM Henry Mountain Field Station, P.O. Box 99, Hanksville, UT 84734, 435/542-3461.

66 LOWER WHITE CANYON– THE BLACK HOLE

13.0 mi one-way/2 days

west of Blanding starting in Fry Canyon

Map 6.4, page 172

The lower section of White Canyon extends the pleasant and scenic hiking of the upper section, but it includes the extraordinary Black Hole, one of the most intense hiking challenges in the world. Increasingly popular, the Black Hole can be experienced as a day hike by entering White Canyon near mile marker 57 and exiting just west of mile marker 55. You might consider the shorter hike since getting a full backpack through the Black Hole can be extremely difficult. In addition to some truly narrow narrows, and a few potholes that may require swimming, the Black Hole itself requires about 500 feet of nonstop swimming through cold water, even in the high heat of summer. Bring something inflatable to float your pack and, perhaps, yourself. Short lengths of rope are also helpful Check with the ranger in Monticello before you go. Flash floods can surge through the narrows with enough force to create Class 4 rapids.

User groups: Hikers. No wheelchair access.

Permits: No permits are required. Parking and access are free.

Maps: For USGS topographic maps, ask for Jacobs Chair, Mancos Mesa NE, and Copper Point.

Directions: From Blanding, take US 191 south for three miles. Turn west on State Route 95 for 45 miles to the Fry Canyon Lodge.

Contact: BLM Monticello Field Office, 435 North Main, Monticello, UT 84535, 435/587-1500.

67 NATURAL BRIDGES LOOP

8.5 mi/6.0 hrs

west of Blanding in Natural Bridges National Monument

Map 6.4, page 172

Nowhere are natural bridges found as close together as in Natural Bridges National Monument, and the three here are exemplary. You can look at bridges from the road, but it's just not the same as walking beneath them. This hike starts from the parking area above Sipapu Bridge. The trail descends a stone stairway, then hugs the canyon wall, traveling .7 mile to the floor of White Canyon. To the east rises Sipapu Bridge—at 220 feet tall and 268 feet in width the world's second-largest natural bridge. The route follows the canyon downstream (west) about two miles, past a well-preserved Anasazi ruin, to Kachina Bridge. From there you can ascend a trail back to the rim of the canyon, gaining about 500 feet in elevation, and cross a flat covered in piñon and juniper for about two miles back to the start. This route cuts short the loop to all three bridges. The third and smallest bridge, Owachomo, lies three miles up Armstrong Canyon, which opens onto White Canyon not far from Kachina Bridge. From Owachomo Bridge (106 feet high with a 180-foot span), the entire loop can be completed by climbing up the trail to the mesa above, and crossing the mesa for 2.5 miles on a trail back to the starting point. You can also leave a vehicle on the rim above Owachomo to avoid the last 2.5 miles.

User groups: Hikers. No wheelchair access except to the visitor center.

Permits: The monument entry fee is $6 per vehicle. Camping is allowed only in the monument's campground at $10 per site. No reservations are accepted.

Maps: For a USGS topographic map, ask for Moss Back Butte. A monument brochure, available at the visitors center, describes the trail. Trails Illustrated's Manti-La Sal National Forest covers the area.

Directions: From Blanding, take US 191 south three miles. Turn west on State Route 95 for 31 miles. Turn north on State Route 275 and drive five miles to the visitors center. Continue on the monument road for a quarter mile, then turn north on Bridge View Drive (one-way) and continue three miles to the Sipapu Bridge Trailhead.

Contact: Natural Bridges National Monument, HC 60 Box 1, Lake Powell, UT 84533, 435/692-1234.

68 UPPER WHITE CANYON
16.0 mi one-way/1–2 days

west of Blanding starting in Natural Bridges National Monument

Map 6.4, page 172

White Canyon runs east to west, paralleling State Route 95. It is one of the major drainages cutting through Cedar Mesa and running into what used to be Glen Canyon, now Lake Powell. This upper section of White Canyon starts in Natural Bridges National Monument, allowing you a peek at the bridges, and ends at Fry Canyon. You can also start by descending into the canyon west of the monument near mile marker 81, missing the bridges and the monument's entry fee. Upper White is a beautiful canyon, meandering beneath soaring white sandstone walls with easy hiking along the bottom. This route passes fascinating side-trip possibilities up K&L Canyon, Hideout Canyon, and Cheesebox Canyon, if you don't mind having to swim and do some serious climbing. You can also enter White Canyon via a rough trail descending from near mile marker 75 near the mouth of Cheesebox. Upper Cheesebox Canyon, with some great and challenging narrows, can be reached by taking the Cheesebox Road north from mile marker 67 on State Route 95. Hike up Fry Canyon to end this journey in Upper White Canyon, keeping an eye open for Anasazi ruins. You can leave a second vehicle at Fry Lodge at the head of Fry Canyon.

User groups: Hikers. No wheelchair access.

Permits: The monument entry fee is $6 per vehicle or $3 per person. No permits are required for White Canyon.

Maps: For USGS topographic maps, ask for Moss Back Butte, The Cheesebox, and Jacobs Chair.

Directions: From Blanding, take US 191 south for three miles. Turn west on State Route 95 for 31 miles. Turn north on State Route 275 and drive five miles to the visitors center. Continue on the monument road for a quarter mile, then turn north on Bridge View Drive (one-way) and continue three miles to the Sipapu Bridge Trailhead.

Contact: Natural Bridges National Monument, HC 60 Box 1, Lake Powell, UT 84533, 435/692-1234; BLM Monticello Field Office, 435 North Main, Monticello, UT 84535, 435/587-1500.

69 COLLINS SPRING TO GRAND GULCH
4.0 mi/3.0 hrs

west of Blanding in Grand Gulch Primitive Area

Map 6.4, page 172

An old cowboy camp near the start of Collins Canyon adds a touch of history to this short and pleasant hike two miles down Grand Gulch. Collins Spring makes the best access point for hikers who wish to see the lower section of Grand Gulch, including its mouth on the San Juan River. The scenery is not especially great until you reach the lower canyon, but the hiking is easy, losing only about 200 feet of elevation, and campsites are plentiful. This is your best chance for solitude in the popular Grand Gulch Primitive Area, but the ruins, if that's what you want to see, are congregated in the upper part of the gulch.

User groups: Hikers only. No wheelchair access.

Permits: Advance permits are required, and a fee of $8 per person is charged for overnight trips regardless of the length of your stay. Day hikers pay a fee of $2 per person.

Maps: For a USGS topographic map, ask for

Pollys Pasture. Trails Illustrated's Grand Gulch Plateau covers the area.

Directions: From Blanding, take US 163 south for three miles. Turn west on State Route 95 and drive 32 miles. Turn south on State Route 276, the road to Hall's Crossing, and drive about seven miles. Turn south on a dirt road (Gulch Creek Road) and drive 6.5 miles to a parking area. Deep sand in spots may necessitate four-wheel drive.

Contact: BLM Monticello Field Office, 435 North Main, Monticello, UT 84535, 435/587-1500.

70 GOVERNMENT TRAIL TO GRAND GULCH
8.0 mi/6.0 hrs

west of Blanding in Grand Gulch Primitive Area

Map 6.4, page 172

From the parking area, hike north almost three miles along a closed jeep road to reach the actual trailhead. Grand Gulch is less than a mile down the trail, and it's only four miles to the bottom of the gulch. You'll pass two Anasazi ruins before reaching, in 1.5 miles, the Big Man Pictograph Panel on the canyon's east wall. The panel, an exemplary expression of ancient art, lies 200 feet or so above the canyon's floor. This section of the Grand Gulch is very beautiful, and campsites abound.

User groups: Hikers only. No wheelchair access.

Permits: Advance permits are required, and a fee of $8 per person is charged for overnight trips regardless of the length of your stay. Day hikers pay a fee of $2 per person.

Maps: For a USGS topographic map, ask for Pollys Pasture. Trails Illustrated's Grand Gulch Plateau covers the area.

Directions: From Blanding, take US 163 south for three miles. Turn west on State Route 95 for 30 miles. Turn south on State Route 261 and drive 13.5 miles. Turn west on a dirt road and drive 7.5 miles, bearing right at all forks, to a parking area beside a small pond.

Contact: BLM Monticello Field Office, 435 North Main, Monticello, UT 84535, 435/587-1500.

71 TRAIL TO RAINBOW BRIDGE
26.0 mi/2–3 days

on the shore of Lake Powell in Rainbow Bridge National Monument

Map 6.4, page 172

 A trail as desolately beautiful as it gets leads to the world's largest natural bridge: Rainbow Bridge, spanning about 275 feet and reaching a height of 309 feet. You'll cross territory owned and held sacred by the Navajo Nation, and your trip must respect those values. Leaving abandoned Rainbow Lodge, the trail starts west of the ruins and skirts the bottom of revered Navajo Mountain before dropping down a series of steep switchbacks into Cliff Canyon. Several miles into Cliff Canyon, the trail traverses out of the canyon and into the drainage of Redbud Creek. Following this drainage to its confluence with Bridge Creek in Rainbow Bridge Canyon, the trail eases down into Rainbow Bridge National Monument. Accurate topographic maps and a check on the availability of water prior to heading out is highly recommended. The 13 miles back to the starting point gains about 2,000 feet of elevation. Most visitors to Rainbow Bridge come by boat from Wahweap Marina near Glen Canyon Dam, and hike a moderately difficult half-mile trail to see the site.

User groups: Hikers. No wheelchair access.

Permits: A permit from the Navajo Nation is required. Contact The Navajo Nation, Recreational Resource Department, Box 308, Window Rock, AZ 86515, 602/871-6647.

Maps: For USGS topographic maps, ask for Navajo Begay and Rainbow Bridge. Trails Illustrated's Glen Canyon & Capitol Reef Area covers the area.

Directions: From Page, AZ, take State Highway 98 south approximately 53 miles. Turn north on the rough Navajo Mountain Road

(Route 16) for 35.1 miles to abandoned Rainbow Lodge.

Contact: Glen Canyon National Recreation Area, P.O. Box 1507, Page, AZ 86040, 928/608-6404.

72 FABLE VALLEY
18.0 mi/2 days

west of Monticello

Map 6.5, page 173

Here is a less-visited (and far less geologically fascinating) alternative to the shadowed depths of Dark Canyon, which lies lying nearby to the south. Fable Valley lies open, with low and gently sloping sandstone walls, spotted with sagebrush and often grassy on the floor. From the trailhead, the route travels about two miles to the canyon's rim, and drops into the canyon via an old cattle track. You'll then wander north, down the canyon, often on sandy benches above a creek, without a trail to follow. At about three miles, Fable Spring pours its waters into the creek from the east. This is a nice camping spot, and a good place to turn around for a day hike. But Fable Valley runs north for another six miles before turning east and climbing past a waterfall to a road. Put a vehicle at each end for a one-way hike of nine miles.

User groups: Hikers and dogs. No wheelchair access.

Permits: No permits are required. Parking and access are free.

Maps: For USGS topographic maps, ask for Bowdie Canyon East and Fable Valley. Trails Illustrated's Manti–La Sal National Forest covers the area.

Directions: From Blanding, take US 191 south three miles. Turn west on State Route 95 for 31 miles. Turn north on State Route 275 for one mile. Turn east on a dirt road headed toward Maverick Point and drive eight miles (about two miles past Bears Ears Pass) to a T junction. Turn east for four miles, then turn north of Forest Service Road 88 for 18 miles. Turn west on Forest Service Road 091 for 12 miles. Turn north on an old track headed into Fable Valley, and park almost immediately.

Contact: BLM Monticello Field Office, 435 North Main, Monticello, UT 84535, 435/587-1500.

73 WOODENSHOE–DARK CANYON–PEAVINE LOOP
40.0 mi/4–5 days

west of Monticello in the Dark Canyon Wilderness

Map 6.5, page 173

This hike takes you into one of the most fascinating areas of Utah's canyon country, the Dark Canyon Wilderness. It is an area of beauty and solitude filled with ancient Indian ruins, artifacts, and pictographs. This is a splendid backpacking trip. From the trailhead, work your way west down into Woodenshoe Canyon. No real trail exists, and the going is a bit rocky for the first couple of miles, but then the hiking eases up along the bottom of Woodenshoe. Cherry Canyon enters from the east after about four miles, and the first of numerous Anasazi cliff dwellings appears below Cherry. When Woodenshoe enters Dark Canyon, turn east and work your way up canyon. Two thousand vertical feet of towering sandstone walls make the bottom of the canyon "dark." The route continues up Dark Canyon for about one mile, then turns south up Peavine Canyon as an old jeep track. Where Kigalia Canyon bears east, stay to the west in Peavine for about five miles to the road. You now have a four-mile walk along the road to the starting point (leave a second vehicle at the head of Peavine Canyon if you prefer to drive). Water is typically plentiful in spring.

User groups: Hikers and dogs. No wheelchair access.

Permits: No permits are required. Parking and access are free.

Maps: For USGS topographic maps, ask for Poison Canyon, Warren Canyon, and Black Steer Canyon. Trails Illustrated's Manti–La Sal National Forest covers the area.

Directions: From Blanding, take US 191 south three miles. Turn west on State Route 95 for 31 miles. Turn north on State Route 275 for one mile. Turn east on a dirt road headed toward Maverick Point and drive eight miles (about two miles past Bears Ears Pass) to a T junction. Turn west for four miles to the head of Woodenshoe Canyon. Turn north along the east side of Woodenshoe a short distance until the road ends, and park.

Contact: Manti–La Sal National Forest, Monticello Ranger District, P.O. Box 820, Monticello, UT 84535, 435/587-2041; BLM Monticello Field Office, 435 North Main, Monticello, UT 84535, 435/587-1500.

◼74◼ GRAND GULCH
108.0 mi/10 days

southwest of Blanding in Grand Gulch Primitive Area

Map 6.5, page 173

The very popular hike into Grand Gulch is far more than a walk through an outstanding and vast sandstone canyon. This is an unforgettable journey into Anasazi history. Nowhere in Utah are the ruins and art of the Anasazi more concentrated and in such well-preserved condition. The four miles of Kane Gulch from the ranger station provide the most-used access to Grand Gulch. At about 4.5 miles, only a half-mile into Grand Gulch, you'll see Junction Ruins, the largest in the Gulch, and worthy of a day trip if that's all the time you have. All the ruins—dozens of them—are concentrated in the upper gulch, and many hikers leave Grand Gulch by walking out Bullet Canyon. You can also enter via Bullet and exit via Kane, seeing a lot of what the Anasazi left along the way. Another access is via Collins Spring, much further south. Still another lies along the Government Trail. A less-used entry lies down rough and rugged Todie Canyon. Few backpackers actually hike Grand Gulch all the way down to the San Juan River, but I found great satisfaction in making the entire journey. As a bonus, I had the lower Grand Gulch all to myself until I reached the

river to find boaters. The walking is not difficult, with few obstacles other than some stands of willows. Water should be available, but check with the ranger prior to your trip to be sure.

User groups: Hikers only. No wheelchair access.

Permits: Advance permits are required, and a fee of $8 per person is charged for overnight trips regardless of the length of your stay. Day hikers pay a fee of $2 per person.

Maps: For USGS topographic maps, ask for Kane Gulch, Cedar Mesa North, Pollys Pasture, Red House Spring, and Slickhorn Canyon West. Trails Illustrated's Grand Gulch Plateau covers the area.

Directions: From Blanding, take US 163 south for three miles. Turn west on State Route 95 for 30 miles. Turn south on State Route 261 and drive four miles to the Kane Gulch Ranger Station.

Contact: BLM Monticello Field Office, 435 North Main, Monticello, UT 84535, 435/587-1500.

◼75◼ MULE CANYON
14.0 mi/1–2 days

southwest of Blanding

Map 6.5, page 173

Starting along an easy-to-walk bottom, Mule Canyon winds up and northwest gently into Cedar Mesa sandstone, a faint pink and white rock, for about seven miles before the going gets rough. Water seeps through cracks in the canyon wall here and there, giving life to wildflowers and greenery. Campsites are plentiful and pleasant. Cliff dwellings, ruins of the ancient Anasazi, cling to the sides of the canyon in several locations, protected, sometimes, by walls that seem to have no other purpose other than defense. You'll see petroglyphs, and may discover pottery shards, chipped flint, or other artifacts, all of which are protected by law (a fact that has failed to keep hikers from illegally carrying off tons of relics of this vanished culture). With simple road access, Mule Canyon offers a relatively popular and excellent chance to step back in time, visiting some of the best-preserved ruins in the region. Mule Canyon extends south of State Route 95, and shelters several well-preserved ruins, but access is more difficult, requiring negotiation of several drops. And, if you have time and interest, about .75 mile further up the same dirt road, the North Fork of Mule Canyon offers an almost equally memorable hike.

User groups: Hikers, dogs, and mountain bikes. No wheelchair access.

Permits: No permits are required. Parking and access are free.

Maps: For USGS topographic maps, ask for South Long Point and Hotel Rock. Trails Illustrated's Grand Gulch Plateau covers the area.

Directions: From Blanding, take US 163 south for three miles. Turn west on State Route 95 for 23 miles, passing through the great wall of the Comb Ridge. Turn north on a dirt road for a half mile, until the road crosses Mule Canyon, and park. If you reach Mule Canyon Ruin on 95, you've gone too far.

Contact: BLM Monticello Field Office, 435 North Main, Monticello, UT 84535, 435/587-1500.

76 ARCH CANYON
26.0 mi/1–4 days

southwest of Blanding

Map 6.5, page 173

About 100 yards north of a parking spot, Arch Canyon Creek runs out of an opening in the sandstone to the west. Immediately inside the canyon, the first of numerous Anasazi ruins appears, fenced off in an attempt to protect it from cattle. Four-wheel-drivers have pushed up the canyon for several miles, and the hiking is easy on reddish sandy soil. Piñon pine, juniper, cacti, spiky clumps of yucca, and other common desert vegetation are ubiquitous. After about 2.5 miles, the first of several side canyons enters from the north. With time and interest, these side canyons are definitely worth exploring. Both the first and second side canyons, for

instance, end in a spring and a ruin. It should go without saying, but here it is anyway: Do not touch, tromp over, or otherwise harm the ruins. These ruins are a treasure of great value. At a large junction, about 1.5 miles past the second side canyon, Texas Canyon joins Arch Canyon from the west. The hike now enters the Manti–La Sal National Forest. You'll find excellent campsites in a pine grove, and an impressive circular arch. Texas Canyon runs almost due west for more than two miles, forking north and south and inviting lengthy exploration. Arch Canyon heads north before bending back to the west, with a major side canyon called Butts Canyon. If you hike to the end of Arch, you'll walk about 13 miles and gain a total of about 3,000 feet of elevation. Unlike some nearby and more popular hikes, upper Arch Canyon receives relatively light human traffic. Water is almost always available. As with so many hikes in canyon country, you can turn back whenever you wish, missing only the wonder that lies around the next bend. All things considered, this is a jewel of an opportunity for a quiet journey.

User groups: Hikers, dogs, and mountain bikes. No wheelchair access.

Permits: No permits are required. Parking and access are free.

Maps: For USGS topographic maps, ask for South Long Point and Hotel Rock. Trails Illustrated's map Manti–La Sal National Forest covers the area.

Directions: From Blanding, take US 163 south for three miles. Turn west on State Route 95 for 14 miles, passing through the great wall of Comb Ridge. At the bottom of the wide wash at the foot of Comb Ridge, the highway crosses a bridge. After crossing the bridge, turn north on the dirt road up the wash for 2.5 miles and for about 200 yards past a small but still-active ranch. Park in a grove of towering cottonwoods.

Contact: BLM Monticello Field Office, 435 North Main, Monticello, UT 84535, 435/587-1500; Manti–La Sal National Forest, Monticello Ranger District, P.O. Box 820, Monticello, UT 84535, 435/587-2041.

77 TODIE CANYON TO GRAND GULCH

2.5 mi one-way/3.0 hrs

southwest of Blanding in Grand Gulch Primitive Area

Map 6.5, page 173

Probably the most interesting thing about entering Grand Gulch via Todie Canyon is that few hikers do it. On my trip down Todie I missed the cairn marking the entry point, attempted a descent at a point that proved hazardous, and backtracked along the rim to find the cairn. It's a rough-and-tumble canyon with sections of slickrock to slide down and boulders to climb over. One Anasazi ruin sits high on the north wall near the start. No good campsites exist before Grand Gulch. Almost all hikers continue up or down Grand Gulch; few attempt to regain the rim by hiking up Todie.

User groups: Hikers only. No wheelchair access.

Permits: Advance permits are required, and a fee of $8 per person is charged for overnight trips, regardless of the length of your stay. Day hikers pay a fee of $2 per person.

Maps: For a USGS topographic map, ask for Kane Gulch. Trails Illustrated's Grand Gulch Plateau covers the area.

Directions: From Blanding, take US 163 south for three miles. Turn west on State Route 95 for 30 miles. Turn south on State Route 261 and drive 8.1 miles. Turn west on Todie Flat Road and drive one mile to the head of the canyon.

Contact: BLM Monticello Field Office, 435 North Main, Monticello, UT 84535, 435/587-1500.

78 FISH CREEK–OWL CREEK CANYONS LOOP

15.5 mi/2–3 days

southwest of Blanding

Map 6.5, page 173

Fish Creek Canyon and Owl Creek Canyon offer excellent hiking, although the going is rugged at times, through highly scenic canyons rich in Anasazi ruins. Although many of the ruins are in better condition than even those in nearby Grand Gulch, quite a few of them lie inaccessible in high alcoves, the steps to them long gone. Still, there's plenty to see. The loop can be hiked in either direction, but this route heads down Owl and up Fish. Start south from the trailhead, and hike for a quarter mile before dropping steeply into Owl Creek Canyon. The first ruin stands not far from the trailhead, and several ruins can be seen up the south fork of Owl Creek. You should see several more ruins along the six or so miles of the main canyon before it meets with Fish Creek, and you'll pass huge and picturesque Nevills Arch. At the confluence with Fish Creek, 6.5 miles from the trailhead, turn north up Fish Creek. If you have time, however, you'll find more ruins lower in Fish Creek Canyon and up its tributary, McCloyd Canyon. This loop goes up Fish Creek about six miles, past many Anasazi sites, to a major junction. Turn west at the junction, and continue about .5 mile to a spring. Here's a fine place to set a camp and explore further up both of the forks of Fish Creek. When you're ready to leave Fish Creek, there's a steep trail up the south wall from the spring that gains more than 600 feet of elevation. Back on the rim you'll find a trail that crosses the mesa 1.5 miles back to the starting point.

User groups: Hikers. No wheelchair access.

Permits: Advance permits are required, and a fee of $8 per person is charged for overnight trips regardless of the length of your stay. Day hikers pay a fee of $2 per person.

Maps: For USGS topographic maps, ask for Snow Flat Spring Cave and Bluff NW. Trails Illustrated's Grand Gulch Plateau covers the area.

Directions: From Blanding, take US 163 south for three miles. Turn west on State Route 95 for 30 miles. Turn south on State Route 261 and drive 5.5 miles, or 1.5 miles past the Kane Gulch Ranger Station. Turn east on a dirt road (Long Spike Road) for 5.5 miles to a parking area.

Contact: BLM Monticello Field Office, 435 North Main, Monticello, UT 84535, 435/587-1500.

79 BULLET CANYON TO GRAND GULCH

7.0 mi one-way/1–2 days

southwest of Blanding in Grand Gulch Primitive Area

Map 6.5, page 173

Ⓕ Unlike nearby Todie Canyon, Bullet Canyon offers a relatively easy and popular hike down into Grand Gulch. Near the start there are some slickrock slopes to descend, and a couple of steps down with enough drop to where you'll want to ease your backpack over first. Along the way at least five Anasazi ruins will be passed, including the impressive Jailhouse Ruin and, nearby, the Perfect Kiva Ruin. Grand Gulch lies a little over seven miles from the trailhead, and from here you can hike up or down the Gulch, or retrace your steps to the start gaining about 1,000 feet in elevation.

User groups: Hikers only. No wheelchair access.

Permits: Advance permits are required, and a fee of $8 per person is charged for overnight trips regardless of the length of your stay. Day hikers pay a fee of $2 per person.

Maps: For USGS topographic maps, ask for Cedar Mesa North and Pollys Pasture. Trails Illustrated's Grand Gulch Plateau covers the area.

Directions: From Blanding, take US 163 south for three miles. Turn west on State Route 95 for 30 miles. Turn south on State Route 261 and drive 11 miles. Turn west on a dirt road where a sign, at this writing, indicates Bullet Canyon, and drive one mile to the trailhead.

Contact: BLM Monticello Field Office, 435 North Main, Monticello, UT 84535, 435/587-1500.

80 ROAD CANYON

14.0 mi/1–2 days

southwest of Blanding

Map 6.5, page 173

Ⓕ Hike northeast on a "trail" created by the tread of other people's feet, and ease down into upper Road Canyon. An easy walk down the canyon will reveal numerous Anasazi ruins—

some of the best you'll find in Utah. As always, the ruins are built on the north wall, facing the sun. A little over halfway to where the North Fork of Road Canyon joins the main canyon, Seven Kivas Ruins, probably a ceremonial center, contains what may be the best-preserved kivas remaining today. Remember to leave them be. From the mouth of North Fork you are approximately seven miles and 1,000 feet of climbing back to your vehicle. Your hike, however, can extend up the North Fork for more ruins and more sandstone wonder. There is often surface water in Road Canyon, but carry plenty.

User groups: Hikers, dogs, and mountain bikes. No wheelchair access.

Permits: No permits are required. Parking and access are free.

Maps: For a USGS topographic map, ask for Snow Flat Spring Cave.

Directions: From Blanding, take US 163 south for three miles. Turn west on State Route 95 for 30 miles. Turn south on State Route 261 and drive 13.5 miles. Near mile marker 19 turn east on a dirt road. You'll see a sign for "Cigarette Spring," and a trail register about a mile in from the pavement. Two more miles of driving ends at a parking spot near the head of Road Canyon.

Contact: BLM Monticello Field Office, 435 North Main, Monticello, UT 84535, 435/587-1500.

81 SLICKHORN CANYON LOOP

14.5 mi/1–3 days

southwest of Blanding

Map 6.5, page 173

Ⓕ Slickhorn Canyon, one of several major (and beautiful) drainages that empty into the San Juan River, offers somewhat rugged hiking to numerous Anasazi ruins. It doesn't match the splendor of Grand Gulch, but it does offer at least 11 ruins in scenic settings, if you hike up side canyons. It also offers something else you may cherish: solitude.

There are no maintained trails, but hiker usage has created a path down First Fork Canyon into Slickhorn Canyon. At least one pour-off will requires hiking back and up onto benches to pass. Along the main canyon floor, the hiking gets easier in several open, sandy areas. Some of the ruins are not easily seen from the canyon floor, so take some time to explore alcoves and overhangs. Remember the Anasazi liked to place their homes for maximum sun exposure. You'll find plenty of campsites, if you choose an overnighter. Along this route, after you enter Slickrock Canyon, four side canyons open from the east. A ruin stands high up in the first side canyon, and at least four ruins stand in the second side canyon. The third side canyon seems to have no ruins. The fourth side canyon is Trail Fork Canyon; go up this canyon, past a couple of ruins and east back to the mesa top. The last couple of miles require some scrambling over steep sections. After gaining about 1,000 feet in elevation and the dirt road on the mesa, you'll have 4.5 road miles back to the starting point. If you leave a vehicle at both ends, your "loop" will be only about 10 miles long (without the side canyons).

User groups: Hikers. No wheelchair access.

Permits: No permits are required. Parking and access are free.

Maps: For USGS topographic maps, ask for Pollys Pasture and Slickhorn Canyon East. Trails Illustrated's Grand Gulch Plateau covers the area.

Directions: From Blanding, take US 163 south for three miles. Turn west on State Route 95 for 30 miles. Turn south on State Route 261 and drive 13.5 miles. Turn west on Slickhorn Road and drive about 2.5 miles to for a fork. Take the left fork and drive 1.5 miles. Turn west and continue for a half mile to the First Fork Trailhead.

Contact: BLM Monticello Field Office, 435 North Main, Monticello, UT 84535, 435/587-1500.

82 SQUARE TOWER TRAIL
2.5 mi/2.0 hrs

in Hovenweep National Monument near the Colorado border

Map 6.5, page 173

The Ute Indians call this area "deserted valley" or *hovenweep*, but this region has been used by humans for over 10,000 years, and 700 years ago the Anasazi reached their cultural peak here in the Four Corners area. They left behind six well-developed housing complexes that exist today as ruins in Hovenweep National Monument. A visitors center is open year-round from 8 A.M. to 4.30 P.M., and trail use is limited to daylight hours. The Square Tower Trail is a self-guided hike actually composed of two loops: one is two miles, the other just a half mile. This trail takes you to the best preserved of all the sites: Square Tower, Hovenweep Castle, Twin Towers, Hovenweep House, Stronghold House, and others. Something mysterious, almost eerie, surrounds the ruins, raising questions: Why build here in this barren region? Why build such defensible oval, circular, square, and D-shaped towers? Why leave, and where to? It is impossible to walk away unimpressed. Other sites, such as Holly, Hackberry, Goodman Point, and Cutthroat Castle, are accessible by hiking a nine-mile, round-trip trail across the Colorado border.

User groups: Hikers. Wheelchair access only to the visitors center and picnic area.

Permits: There is a $6 per vehicle entrance fee. Camping is allowed only in the monument's campground for $10 per site. No reservations are accepted.

Maps: For a USGS topographic map, ask for Ruin Point. A trail guide is available at the visitors center.

Directions: From Blanding, take US 191 south for 14.8 miles. Turn east on State Route 262 for 8.7 miles to Hovenweep Road. Continue east on Hovenweep Road for 16 miles to the national monument. All but the final two miles are paved, and the dirt road is typically easy to negotiate unless a heavy rain has fallen recently.

Contact: Hovenweep National Monument, McElmo Route, Cortez, CO 81321, 970/562-4282.

83 VALLEY OF THE GODS
1.0–10.0 mi/1–2 days

west of Bluff

Map 6.5, page 173

Not far south of Valley of the Gods, across the San Juan River, Monument Valley attracts many travelers, and deservedly so. It is a stunning area. It also lies on the Navajo Reservation, and all backcountry travel is heavily restricted and prohibited entirely without a Navajo guide. Not so in the BLM's Valley of the Gods, a piece of earth smaller in size but almost as stunning. From the 17-mile-long dirt road that encircles the valley, you'll see monuments, towers, spires, buttes, peaks, and balanced rocks. You'll find no developed campsites, no toilets, no water, no noise, and, very often, no other people. There are no trails, but you can follow the tracks left in the earth by earlier hikers. Camping is allowed anywhere space allows, and there's lots of space. Day hikes are sufficient to see the red-rock magnificence of this place, but don't count on a few hours being enough to satisfy a hunger for natural sandstone beauty.

User groups: Hikers, dogs, and mountain bikes. No wheelchair access.

Permits: No permits are required. Parking and access are free.

Maps: For USGS topographic maps, ask for Mexican Hat and Cigarette Spring Cave. Trails Illustrated's Grand Gulch Plateau covers the area.

Directions: From Bluff, take US 163 west for 16.5 miles, and turn north on the Valley of the Gods Road.

Contact: BLM Monticello Field Office, 435 North Main, Monticello, UT 84535, 435/587-1500.

© FRANK JENSEN/UTAH TRAVEL COUNCIL

Resource Guide

National Forests

Ashley National Forest
Duchesne Ranger District
Box 981
Duchesne, UT 84021
435/738-2482

Ashley National Forest
Flaming Gorge Ranger District
P.O. Box 279
Manila, UT 84046
435/784-3445

Ashley National Forest
Forest Supervisor
355 North Vernal Avenue
Vernal, UT 84078
435/789-1181

Ashley National Forest
Roosevelt Ranger District
650 West Highway 40
Roosevelt, UT 84066
435/722-5018

Ashley National Forest
Vernal Ranger District
355 North Vernal Avenue
Vernal, UT 84078
435/789-1181

Dixie National Forest
Cedar City Ranger District
82 North 100 East
Cedar City, UT 84721
435/865-3200

Dixie National Forest
Escalante Ranger District
P.O. Box 246
Escalante, UT 84726
435/826-5400

Dixie National Forest
Pine Valley Ranger District
196 East Tabernacle Street
St. George, UT 84770
435/652-3100

Dixie National Forest
Powell Ranger District
P.O. Box 80
Panguitch, UT 84759
435/676-9300

Dixie National Forest
Teasdale Ranger District
P.O. Box 90
Teasdale, UT 84773
435/425-9500

Fishlake National Forest
Beaver Ranger District
575 South Main Street
Beaver, UT 84713
435/438-2436

Fishlake National Forest
Fillmore Ranger District
390 South Main Street
Fillmore, UT 84631
435/743-5721

Fishlake National Forest
Loa Ranger District
138 South Main Street
Loa, UT 84747
435/836-2811

Fishlake National Forest
Richfield Ranger District
115 East 900 North
Richfield, UT 84701
435/896-9233

Manti–La Sal National Forest
Moab Ranger District
62 East 100 North
Moab, UT 84532
435/259-7155

Manti–La Sal National Forest
Monticello Ranger District
P.O. Box 820
Monticello, UT 84535
435/587-2041

Manti–La Sal National Forest
Price Ranger District
599 West Price River Drive
Price, UT 84501
435/637-2817

Sawtooth National Forest
Minidoka Ranger District
3650 South Overland Avenue
Burley, ID 83318
208/678-0430

Uinta National Forest
Forest Supervisor
88 West 100 North
Provo, UT 84601
801/342-5100

Uinta National Forest
Heber Ranger District
125 East 100 North
Heber City, UT 84032
435/342-5200

Uinta National Forest
Pleasant Grove Ranger District
390 North 100 East
Pleasant Grove, UT 84062
801/342-5240

Uinta National Forest
Spanish Fork Ranger District
44 West 400 North
Spanish Fork, UT 84660
801/342-5260

Wasatch-Cache National Forest
Evanston Ranger District
1565 Highway 150, Box 1880
Evanston, WY 82931
307/789-3194

Wasatch-Cache National Forest
Forest Supervisor
8230 Federal Building
125 South State Street
Salt Lake City, UT 84138
801/524-3900

Wasatch-Cache National Forest
Kamas Ranger District
50 East Center Street, P.O. Box 68
Kamas, UT 84036
435/783-4338

Wasatch-Cache National Forest
Logan Ranger District
1500 East Highway 89
Logan, UT 84327
435/755-3620

Wasatch-Cache National Forest
Mountain View Ranger District
321 Highway 414, P.O. Box 129
Mountain View, WY 82939
307/782-6555

Wasatch-Cache National Forest
Ogden Ranger District
507 25th Street
Ogden, UT 84403
801/625-5112

Wasatch-Cache National Forest
Salt Lake Ranger District
6944 South 3000 East
Salt Lake City, UT 84121
801/733-2660

Bureau of Land Management

BLM Cedar City Field Office
176 East D. L. Sargent Drive
Cedar City, UT 84720
435/586 2401

BLM Fillmore Field Office
35 East 500 North
Fillmore, UT 84631
435/743-3100

BLM Henry Mountain Field Station
P.O. Box 99
Hanksville, UT 84734
435/542-3461

BLM Kanab Field Office
318 North First East
Kanab, UT 84741
435/644-4600

BLM Moab Field Office
82 East Dogwood
Moab, UT 84532
435/259-2100

BLM Monticello Field Office
435 North Main
Monticello, UT 84535
435/587-1500

BLM Price Field Office
125 South 600 West
Price, UT 84501
435/636-3600

BLM Salt Lake Field Office
2370 South 2300 West
Salt Lake City, UT 84119
801/977-4300

BLM St. George Field Office
345 East Riverside Drive
St. George, UT 84720
435/688-3200

BLM Vernal Field Office
170 South 500 East
Vernal, UT 84078
435/781-4400

National Parks, Monuments, and Recreation Areas

Arches National Park
P.O. Box 907
Moab, UT 84532
435/719-2299

Bryce Canyon National Park
P.O. 170001
Bryce Canyon, UT 84717
435/834-5322

Canyonlands National Park
2282 Southwest Resource Boulevard
Moab, UT 84532
435/719-2313

Capitol Reef National Park
HC 70, Box 15
Torrey, UT 84775
435/425-3791

Cedar Breaks National Monument
2390 West Highway 56, Suite #11
Cedar City, UT 84720
435/586-9451

Dinosaur National Monument
4545 Highway 40
Dinosaur, CO 81610
970/374-3000

Glen Canyon National Recreation Area
P.O. Box 1507
Page, AZ 86040
928/608-6404

**Grand Staircase–Escalante
National Monument**
190 East Center
Kanab, UT 84741
435/644-4300

Hovenweep National Monument
McElmo Route
Cortez, CO 81321
970/562-4282

Natural Bridges National Monument
HC 60 Box 1
Lake Powell, UT 84533
435/692-1234

Timpanogos Cave National Monument
RR3 Box 200
American Fork, UT 84003
801/756-5239

Zion National Park
SR 9
Springdale, UT 84767
435/772-3256

State Parks

Antelope Island State Park
4528 West 1700 South
Syracuse, UT 84075
801/773-2941

Coral Pink Sand Dunes State Park
P.O. Box 95
Kanab, UT 84741
435/648-2800

Dead Horse Point State Park
P.O. Box 609
Moab, UT 84532
435/259-2614

Fremont Indian State Park
11550 West Clear Creek Canyon Road
Sevier, UT 84766
435/527-4631

Goblin Valley State Park
P.O. Box 637
Green River, UT 84525
435/564-3633

Kodachrome Basin State Park
P.O. Box 238
Cannonville, UT 84718
435/679-8562

Snow Canyon State Park
1002 Snow Canyon Drive
Ivins, UT 84738
435/628-2255

Other Resources

Mountain Trails Foundation
P.O. Box 754
Park City, UT 84060
435/649-6839

Maps

National Geographic Maps (Trails Illustrated)
P.O. Box 4357
Evergreen, CO 80437
800/962-1643

U.S. Geological Survey (USGS)
2329 Orton Circle
West Valley City, UT 84119-2047
801/908-5000

Index

Notes

Notes

Notes

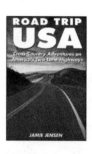